Early Modern Literature in History

Within the period 1520–1740, this large, very well-established series with notable international representation discusses many kinds of writing, both within and outside the established canon. The volumes may employ different theoretical perspectives, but they share an historical awareness and an interest in seeing their texts in lively negotiation with their own and successive cultures. This series is approaching a hundred titles on a variety of subjects including early modern women's writing; domestic politics; drama, performance and playhouses; rhetoric; religious conversion; translation; travel and colonial writing; popular culture; the law; authorship; diplomacy; the court; material culture; childhood; piracy; and the environment.

Emma Rhatigan • Jackie Watson
Editors

Mapping the Early Modern Inns of Court

Writing Communities

palgrave
macmillan

Editors
Emma Rhatigan
English
University of Sheffield
Sheffield, UK

Jackie Watson
Independent Scholar
Oxford, UK

ISSN 2634-5919 ISSN 2634-5927 (electronic)
Early Modern Literature in History
ISBN 978-3-031-77444-7 ISBN 978-3-031-77445-4 (eBook)
https://doi.org/10.1007/978-3-031-77445-4

This Palgrave Macmillan imprint is published by the registered company Springer Nature Switzerland AG.
The registered company address is: Gewerbestrasse 11, 6330 Cham, Switzerland

Acknowledgements

We are grateful to all the contributors to this volume for their hard work, enthusiasm, and patience.

We would also like to thank the participants in the Mapping the Early Modern Inns of Court seminars and the 2023 'Shakespeare Association of America seminar "Performance Cultures in and around the Inns at Court".'.

Particular thanks to the general editors of the *Early Modern Literature in History* Series, Andrew Hadfield and Michelle O'Callaghan, for their invaluable help in shaping the volume and to Jessica Winston, who provided last-minute help sourcing images.

At the University of Sheffield, Emma Rhatigan would like to thank Marcus Nevitt, Anna Reynolds, Tom Rutter, and Cathy Shrank for helpful and supportive conversations. She is also grateful to Alan, Harriet, Fraser, and Lewis for their patience when work on the volume intruded on family life.

Jackie Watson would like to thank Sue Wiseman, Birkbeck College, London, for her support during doctoral research on the Inns of Court.

Contents

Notes on Contributors

Blessin Adams traded a career as a police officer in the Norfolk Constabulary for academia, where she received her PhD from the University of East Anglia for her research into law and literature in the notebooks of law students at the early modern inns of court. She has a particular interest in the cultural and legal history of murder and violent death, and is the author of *Great and Horrible News: Murder and Mayhem in Early Modern Britain*, published by William Collins. She is currently working on her next book, which is focused on women and violent crime in the early modern period.

Jessica Apolloni is an associate professor of English at Christopher Newport University, where she developed the Global Conference on Women and Gender. She specialises in comparative law and literature in the early modern period. Her scholarship and reviews have most recently appeared in or are forthcoming from *Law, Culture and the Humanities*, *Renaissance Quarterly*, *Shakespeare Studies*, *Shakespeare Bulletin*, *Studies in Philology*, *Forum Italicum*, and the *Journal of British Studies.*

Felicity Brown is a lecturer in English Literature, 1550–1760, at Christ Church, Oxford. Her research centres on constructions of (and crises in) authority in early modern literature. She is currently completing a monograph on dramatic adaptations of the Arthurian legend and beginning a project on the life and work of John Dryden.

Joshua Eckhardt is a professor of English at Virginia Commonwealth University. He traced a few books to John Selden's library in *Religion Around John Donne* (Pennsylvania State University Press, 2019). He surveyed other books of Selden's at the conference on the inns of court organized by Romola Nuttall and Julian Neuhauser at King's College London. With Jason P. Rosenblatt, he is editing the Oxford edition of *The Discourse of John Selden, Esq. (Table Talk)*, forthcoming in 2025.

Penelope Geng is an associate professor of English at Macalester College, where she teaches courses on early modern literature, Shakespeare, law and literature, and disability. She is the author of *Communal Justice in Shakespeare's England: Drama, Law, and Emotion* (University of Toronto Press, 2021). Her articles and essays have appeared in *Studies in Philology*, *The Sixteenth Century Journal*, *The Ben Jonson Journal*, *Law, Culture and the Humanities*, *Situating Shakespeare Pedagogy in US Higher Education*, and *The Shakespearean International Yearbook: Disability Performance and Global Shakespeare*. She is working on her second monograph, provisionally titled 'Disabled by Law', which uncovers the deep influence of feudalism on early modern notions of disability, racial purity, and able-bodied citizenship. With Jennifer E. Row (French, UMN), she is the co-convener of Uncommon Bodies, a workshop devoted to the study of early modern disability, embodiment, race, and performance.

Sharon J. Harris is assistant professor of English at Brigham Young University where she teaches courses in Shakespeare, seventeenth-century English literature, and literary theory. She studies the intersections of literature and music in the early modern period and holds degrees in music, humanities, and literature. The recipient of fellowships from the Newberry and Huntington libraries, her current research examines the uses and reappropriations of English masques and their music across the seventeenth century.

Arthur F. Marotti is distinguished professor of English Emeritus at Wayne State University in Detroit where he serves as a Director of its Emeritus Academy. He is the author of *John Donne, Coterie Poet* (University of Wisconsin Press, 1986; reissued 2008); *Manuscript, Print and the English Renaissance Lyric* (Cornell University Press, 1995); *Religious Ideology and Cultural Fantasy: Catholic and Anti-Catholic Discourses in Early Modern England* (University of Notre Dame Press, 2005); (with Steven W. May); *Ink, Stink Bait, Revenge and Queen Elizabeth: A Yorkshire*

Yeoman's Household Book (Cornell University Press, 2014); and *The Circulation of Poetry in Manuscript in Early Modern England* (Routledge, 2021). In addition, he has edited or co-edited nine collections of scholarly essays and has written numerous book chapters and articles. He is currently, with Steven W. May, working on an edition of the poems of Dr Richard Andrews and, with a team of five other scholars, a database of rare or unique poems found in sixteenth- and seventeenth-century English manuscripts.

Julian T. S. Neuhauser received their PhD from King's College London in 2022, for a thesis on Thomas Coryate's London-based socio-literary life. They were (along with Dr Romola Nuttall) a co-organiser of the 2019 'The Early Modern Inns of Court and the Circulation of Text' conference. Their work on the social form taken by Thomas Coryate's literary network has appeared in *The Review of English Studies*. Additionally, they are an expert in early modern literary technologies and use practice-based methods (writing with quills and ink and handpress printing) to teach and research early modern literature.

Emma Rhatigan is senior lecturer in English in the School of English at the University of Sheffield. Her research and publications focus on early modern texts in performance (both drama and preaching), and their audiences. She is co-editor of *The Oxford Handbook of the Early Modern Sermon* (Oxford University Press, 2011) and is editing a volume of John Donne's Inns of Court sermons for *The Oxford Edition of the Sermons of John Donne*.

Renae Satterley has been a librarian at Middle Temple since 2006 and has been researching Robert Ashley and his library for 18 years. She completed her MLIS at McGill University in Montreal and has recently submitted her PhD thesis on Ashley's library and translations at Queen Mary University of London. She has published extensively on Ashley's library, but also on law librarianship, pre-1800 women stationers connected to the inns of court, and the library at Doctors' Commons. Her current interests include the second-hand book trade as evidenced by booksellers' codes, and subject-specific marginalia, in particular early modern legal marginalia.

Emily Stevenson is a lecturer in Renaissance and Early Modern Literature at the University of York. Between 2018 and 2022, she was a doctoral and then postdoctoral researcher on the TIDE (Travel, Transculturality and Identity in England *c.* 1550–1700) project at the University of Oxford.

Her doctoral research examined the communities and networks which surrounded Richard Hakluyt and *The Principal Navigations of the English Nation*, using a combination of literary, historical, and social network analysis. She has published articles in *Renaissance Studies*, *Cultural and Social History*, and *Parergon*, and is currently working on a monograph based on her doctoral research.

Jackie Watson is an independent scholar whose work covers law and literature, epistolarity and the senses. Her first monograph, *Epistolary Courtiership and Dramatic Letters: Thomas Overbury and the Jacobean Playhouse* was published by Edinburgh University Press in 2024. She co-edited *The Senses in Early Modern England* (Manchester University Press, 2015) and has chapters on inns drama and audiences in *Players and Playgoing in Early Modern England* (Cambridge University Press, 2022) and *Shakespeare/Sense* (Bloomsbury, 2020).

Jessica Winston is professor of English at Idaho State University. She is co-editor with James Ker of *Elizabethan Seneca: Three Tragedies* (Modern Humanities Research Association, 2012) and the author of *Lawyers at Play: Literature, Law, and Politics at the Early Modern Inns of Court, 1558–1572* (Oxford University Press, 2016). Her research now emphasises two areas: Tudor drama in performance and Shakespeare pedagogy.

Lauren Working is lecturer in Early Modern Studies at the University of York. Her publications include *The Making of an Imperial Polity: Civility and America in the Jacobean Metropolis*, which jointly won the Royal Historical Society's 2021 Whitfield Prize, and an introduction to Shakespeare's *The Tempest* for Oxford World's Classics (2024). Her public engagement work on material culture and Anglo-Indigenous relations has led to collaborations with museums and heritage sites including the National Portrait Gallery, National Trust, and Bodleian Library, Oxford.

List of Figures

CHAPTER 1

Introduction: Mapping the Early Modern Inns of Court

Emma Rhatigan and Jackie Watson

Mapping the Early Modern Inns of Court

Mapping the Early Modern Inns of Court is a volume structured around our understanding of the literary communities which developed both within and without these legal institutions. Recognised for some time by scholars as influential centres of creative and intellectual activity, the inns are now thought to have played a key part in the development of ideas, literary endeavour, and wider action in the sixteenth and seventeenth centuries. This volume brings together some of the new directions being taken in current scholarship on the inns in order to illuminate their status as important physical, intellectual, and international spaces and to offer fresh insights into their literary and cultural investments and interactions.

E. Rhatigan (✉)
English, University of Sheffield, Sheffield, UK
e-mail: e.k.rhatigan@shef.ac.uk

J. Watson
Independent Scholar, Oxford, UK
e-mail: jacqueline.watson@some.ox.ac.uk

E. Rhatigan, J. Watson (eds.), *Mapping the Early Modern Inns of Court*, Early Modern Literature in History,
https://doi.org/10.1007/978-3-031-77445-4_1

We take as our structural principle the theoretical concept of mapping. As Andrew Gordon and Bernhard Klein have explained, this term has been used to describe 'a particular cognitive mode of gaining control over the world, of synthesising cultural and geographical information, and of successfully navigating both physical and mental space' (Gordon and Klein 2001: 3). 'Mapping' is thus a framework which allows us to interrogate not only the physical and imaginative spaces of individual inns and innsmen's movements between and beyond these spaces, but also how the spaces of the inns were socially produced and were themselves shaping influences on the innsmen who inhabited them. The volume is structured in three sections. The first focuses attention on the institutions of the inns of court, and what that meant in terms of day-to-day life, learning, and recreation. The middle section goes on to look at the inns as part of early modern London, with illustrations of their embedded connection to, and interaction with, the cultural life of the city and the court. The final section looks more widely at the innsmen's links to cultures and ideas beyond early modern London. Together these sections attend to the innsmen not only as writing communities in themselves, but as participants in a complex of intersecting networks reaching out into London and beyond.

New Approaches to the Inns of Court

Early studies of the inns of court were vital in establishing the foundations: what early modern legal learning looked like; who attended the inns and why; reasons for the rise in the numbers of innsmen in the latter part of the sixteenth century. Work across the last 50 years has relied upon seminal texts such as Wilfrid Prest's *The Inns of Court under Elizabeth I and the Early Stuarts, 1590–1640* (1972) and Philip J. Finkelpearl's *John Marston of the Middle Temple: An Elizabethan Dramatist in His Social Setting* (1969), as well as John Baker's *Introduction to English Legal History* (1971). Indeed it is a sign of the importance of these texts, and the growing interest in legal history and culture, that both Prest's and Baker's works have been recently revised and republished.[1] Joined to this body of early work, researchers have also benefited from access to primary material through the work of Alan Nelson and John R. Elliott in their inns of court volume for *Records of Early English Drama* (2010).

[1] Baker's has seen five editions, most recently by Oxford University Press in 2019, and Prest's a second edition from Cambridge University Press in 2023.

This body of scholarship now constitutes part of a wider law and literature field. Building on studies such as James Boyd White's *The Legal Imagination* (1973), the range of this field is illustrated by the contributions to the *Oxford Handbook of English Law and Literature: 1500–1700* (Hutson 2017). Stimulated by key works such as Lorna Hutson's *The Invention of Suspicion: Law and Mimesis in Shakespeare and Renaissance Drama* (2007) and Bradin Cormack's *A Power to Do Justice: Jurisdiction, English Literature, and the Rise of Common Law, 1509–1625* (2007), and influential collections such as *Rhetoric and Law in Early Modern Europe* (Hutson and Kahn 2001), recent developments in thinking about the legal imaginary are demonstrated in monographs such as Judith Hudson's *Crime and Consequence in Early Modern Literature and Law* (2022) and Penelope Geng's *Communal Justice in Shakespeare's England: Drama, Law, and Emotion* (2021).

Of special importance to this volume's focus on the inns of court and literary production is a collection now just over a decade old, *The Intellectual and Cultural History of the Early Modern Inns of Court* (Archer, Goldring, and Knight 2011), illustrating the wide range of innsmen's influence on early modern thought and culture. Michelle O'Callaghan's *The English Wits: Literature and Sociability in Early Modern England* (2007) profoundly affected thinking on the interactions between innsmen, and Will Tosh's *Male Friendship and Testimonies of Love in Shakespeare's England* (2016) illuminated further the homosociality of the inns. These works predominantly focused on the late sixteenth and early seventeenth centuries, but Jessica Winston's influential *Lawyers at Play: Literature, Law, and Politics at the Early Modern Inns of Court, 1558–1581* (2016) drew us back to the 1560s and the developing literary culture that influenced more familiar later figures. More recently, the nature of legal performance, and the connections between verbal production in the courtroom and on stage, was the topic of Julie Stone Peters's wide-ranging book, *Law as Performance: Theatricality, Spectatorship, and the Making of Law in Ancient, Medieval, and Early Modern Europe* (2022), where the final chapter focused on the interaction between legal performativity and the institutional practice of the early modern inns of court. Interest in critical race theory has attended to the inns too, with Lauren Working's *The Making of an Imperial Polity: Civility and America in the Jacobean Metropolis* (2020) exploring the early modern inns of court context of early American colonisation. Working's attention to New World travel, enabled by the interest and investment of innsmen, complements Nandini

Das's recent study *Courting India: England, Mughal India and the Origins of Empire* (2023) in which she analyses England's early diplomatic relationship with India 'led by Middle Templar Thomas Roe'.

The Inns and Innsmen

Contributors throughout the collection base their work in a common understanding of what an innsman in the early modern period was, and this, as Winston has argued, can be helpfully understood through Pierre Bourdieu's concept of 'habitus': 'a subjective but not individual system of internalised structures, schemes of perception, conception, and action common to all members of the same group' (1977: 86; Winston 2016: 32). The early chapters of the collection start by establishing the common understanding and the institutionality of the inns, and the impact habitus had on the thinking, the shared experience, and the activities of men who were members of them. These first four chapters illustrate the effect of that institutional context in different areas of innsmen's literary, intellectual, and professional lives: from the writing of legal notebooks, explored by Blessin Adams, to the importance of communal worship, underlying the work of Emma Rhatigan, to the significance of the revels in Jackie Watson's chapter. These 'internalised structures, schemes of perception, conception, and action' also underpin the importance of music and dance that is Sharon Harris's focus, and Jessica Apolloni and Renae Satterley's exploration of innsmen's participation in textual translation. In the final chapter of the volume Lauren Working and Emily Stevenson argue that a combination of sociability, literary play, and interest in travel was part of the Middle Templar's habitus and that this shaped their participation in colonisation.

How we read the inns relies in part on our perception of the institutions' specific physical spaces and their affordances. Early chapters look at the importance of halls, chapels, and chambers. The shared experience of innsmen is sited in such spaces, and many of the contributors in the volume explore their specific qualities. Of particular importance to all four inns was the hall: a multivalent space, connected with quotidian eating and sociability, as well as regular and special performance. In her chapter on revelry and the production of *Twelfth Night* in Middle Temple hall, Watson uses details of the hall to explore its significance as a performance space, while Apolloni takes us to Inner Temple hall and the performance of law and revenge in *Gismond of Salerne* (1566). The meaning and significance

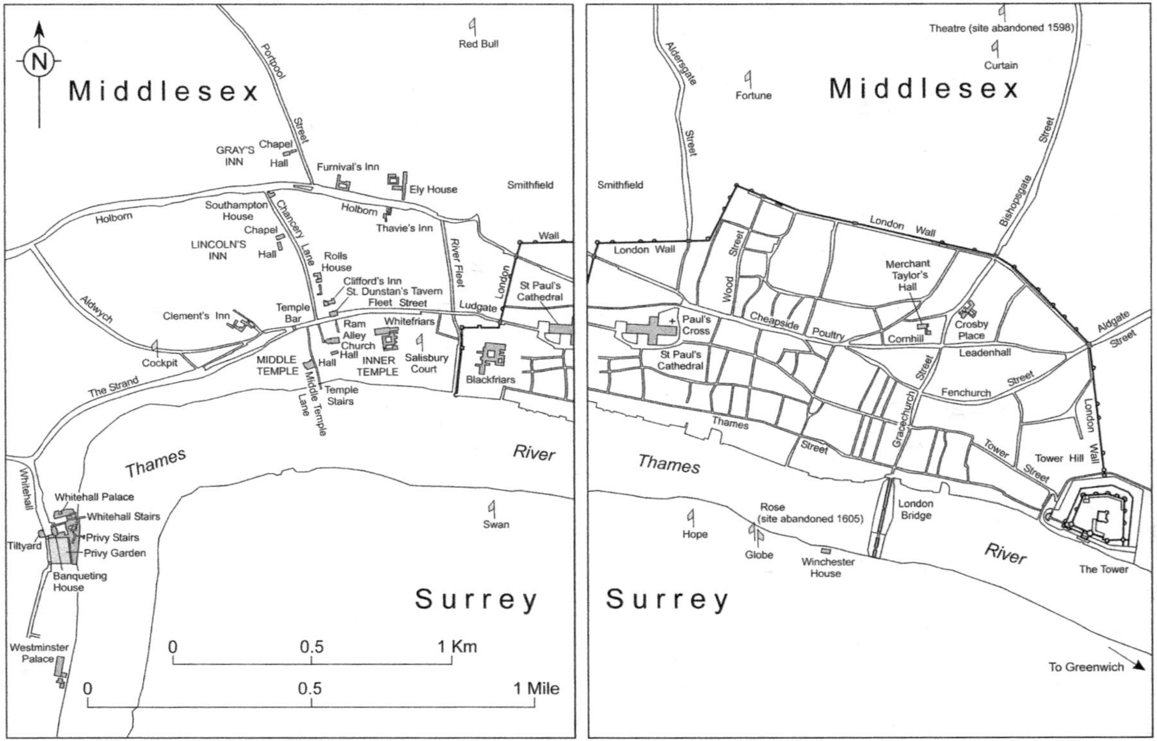

Fig. 1.1 Map of London and area, *c.* 1620, prepared by Subhash Shanbhag. Originally published in Alan Nelson and John R. Elliott, eds. 2010. *Records of Early English Drama: Inns of Court*. Cambridge: Brewer. vol. 1, pp. xcviii–xcix

of the space of the hall, like that of chapels or chambers, relies upon the interactions between those in it: collusion between actors and audience members, for instance, or a rupture of the in-group with violent consequences. We will return below to these interactions, as well as to the more regular performativity and communality of being 'in commons': eating and conversing together.

Later chapters develop this physical institutionality with a focus on libraries such as Robert Ashley's, the basis for Satterley's exploration of translation culture, and John Selden's, explored by Joshua Eckhardt and Julian Neuhauser. Libraries provided a reflective space for reading and thought, but also a place to share intellectual interests with other men. Hence Eckhardt's and Neuhauser's chapter explores the physical layout of Selden's private library at nearby Whitefriars, clearly accessed by many innsmen, in order to draw conclusions about his intellectual world. Their method is similar to that of Working and Stevenson, who investigate the chamber of Richard Hakluyt the elder, where his Ortelius map was consulted by other innsmen and a wider circle, to draw out these men's fascination with travel.

The spaces enabling these interactions are also spaces of learning of course and, from the enactment of legal process to the performance of social status, different things would have been learnt within them. As Prest demonstrated 50 years ago, if we consider the purpose of men's residence at the inns, we will see that only a proportion attended for training that led to a professional legal career; a key element in the men's habitus, learning about the law, was generally agreed to be more broadly helpful in the period. Thus, although not all innsmen were called to the bar, or even began their time at the inns intending to do that, they would have expected to learn something about the law while they were there, and therefore had familiarity with key texts and ideas. Using the term, 'non-learners' to refer to those innsmen not entering the law professionally, Baker reminds us that 'It would certainly have made sense for all of them at least to buy a *Littleton*, a statute-book, and a book on justices, to acquaint them with the minimal knowledge necessary to run their estates and their counties' (2011: 10). This common knowledge of legal texts, however much or little they were read, would have combined with some participation in structured learning such as disputations, mooting, and readings, in the shared space of the inns' halls. Thus, the rhetorical skill that was such a key part of humanist learning also became a part of an innsman's habitus.

More independently of this institutional learning, perhaps within a group of fellow students, many would have engaged too in the production of legal notebooks and Adams examines the interface between the law and creativity in one of these texts from Middle Temple. As she reminds us, in his 1605 'Grammar Lecture' Francis Beaumont characterised innsmen as 'plodders' and 'revellers' (the latter being the men Baker terms the 'non-learners'), but through Adams's chapter we can see that the overlap between the qualities of these two kinds of student often blurs that binary distinction. Maintaining a steady and single-minded course towards legal success must have been relatively rare and the notebooks illustrate how legal learning was combined with wider interests.

Communality at the Inns

Communality, what John Donne terms 'conversation', in the sense of 'consorting or having dealings with others . . . society, intimacy', is a recurring theme throughout the collection.[2] The innsmen and their servants lived, worked, and socialised in close proximity and, as scholars have emphasised, the fact that the inns were not incorporated, but maintained by voluntary association, only strengthened the importance of the social practices which gave expression to their status as a community (Baker 1986: 45–74; Winston 2016: 40). The inns were, as Watson reminds us in this volume, homosocial environments in which an individual's success relied on male friendship and patronage. Moreover, as Adams's chapter explains, living in community brought not only opportunities for social and professional advancement, but also emotional benefits. Innsmen were keenly aware of the mental and physical dangers of overwork and isolation, and appreciated the importance of friendship and communal play in order to ward off melancholy.

The chapters in this volume shed new light on both the constitution and the expression of community at the inns. Penelope Geng's work draws attention to the servants and labourers whose work underpinned day-to-day life in the societies. Her chapter not only reminds us that these servants facilitated the innsmen's performances of community—they, for example, sourced, cooked, and served the food which was consumed 'in commons'—but that providing care for these servants could be one way in

[2] *Oxford English Dictionary*, s.v. "conversation (n.)," July 2023, https://doi.org/10.1093/OED/1997277413.

which the benchers sought to enact their collective identity as Christian magistrates. By tracing the institutional care offered to John Somerscales, butler at Gray's Inn, when he became mentally ill and unable to work, Geng analyses the expression, but also the limits, of the inn's paternalism.

One of the key forms through which the innsmen gave expression to their communality was 'conference'; discussion, conversation, and debate were central to the inns' creation and perpetuation of community. Thus, as Satterley observes, Robert Ashley claimed he gained the requisite knowledge for his translations not only from travel and books, but also from conference, including, no doubt, the intellectual networks which he enjoyed at the Middle Temple (Ashley 1627: Long S2^{v}). The chapters in this volume testify to the range this conference could take, including the legal exercises (such as readings and moots); sermons in the Gray's Inn and Lincoln's Inn chapels, as well as the Temple Church; the *joco seria* and literary extracts copied into legal notebooks; plays; poetry; and informal lectures, such as that discussed by Working and Stevenson when Richard Hakluyt the Elder instructed his younger cousin on the Ortelius map in his chamber at the Middle Temple. Though vastly different in content and tone all these texts and performances enabled the intellectual exchange through which the innsmen maintained their fellowship.

Together, the chapters in this collection illustrate the extent to which the production and consumption of texts were central to communal life at the inns. This is exemplified in the multiple hands in the legal notebook analysed by Adams, and it also underpins the work of Arthur Marotti and Eckhardt and Neuhauser whose chapters illustrate how professional and social bonds were expressed in the circulation of both manuscripts and printed texts. Marotti's chapter demonstrates not only how poetry in manuscripts of inns' provenance often shows itself attuned to the concerns of innsmen, but that the profoundly social practices of sharing, lending, and copying texts reinforced friendships within and between the inns. Eckhardt and Neuhauser's analysis of the handwritten catalogue to John Selden's library shows how in among Selden's vast and diverse collection were books which bore testimony to the community and literary heritage of the inns: John Donne's *Six Sermons* (1634), containing two sermons preached at Lincoln's Inn in 1620, and *Coryates Crudites* (1611), a number of whose mock commendatory verses were contributed by innsmen. Conference at the inns also, however, transcended apparently clear boundaries between textual and oral culture. The vibrant culture of plays brought debate to the stage, the sermons collected by John Selden were first delivered in the Lincoln's Inn pulpit, and not only would much of the poetry discussed by Marotti have been read and enjoyed out loud, but this verse also includes songs potentially both written and performed at the inns. Community at the inns was rooted in the sound, no less than the texts, of conference.

Communality, however, brought its own ethical challenges and the Lincoln's Inn sermons by John Donne which form the focus of Rhatigan's chapter offer a far from sanguine analysis of the inns' fellowships. Donne shows himself keenly aware of the moral dangers as well as the potential benefits of corporate living and he urges his congregation to consider how the competing loyalties of professional bonds, friendship, and patronage ties might draw an individual away from their religious duty. Watson's chapter illustrates how community at the inns was inextricably bound up with social and professional competition, drawing our attention to the ritualised violence of mockery and verbal shaming at Middle Temple. Such 'in-group language' could play an important role in shaping collective homosocial identities, but it was also testimony to a culture of sublimated violence, which frequently erupted into actualised violence. Hence both Rhatigan and Watson reference the attack when John Davies entered the hall of the Middle Temple on 9 February 1598 and struck Richard Martin over the head with a bastinado.

Learning and Creativity

Communal learning, based on interactions between members in the shared spaces of the inns, led to a common value placed on specific skills and ideas that formed part of the early modern innsman's habitus. Many of the skills were performative, based on the need to demonstrate articulacy and knowledge within a community. Winston's chapter, examining the mechanisms of legal learning in mooting and revelling, makes a connection between this legal training and the performance of institutional drama, demonstrating how important the latter was for the development of legal identity. She connects perceptively innsmen's playful performance of legal exercises in the inn's hall with the importance of calm and control evinced in Gray's Inn's 1587 performance of *The Misfortunes of Arthur* before the royal court.

Building on Winston's work on translation culture at the inns (2016: 99–124), the focus on institutional drama continues in Felicity Brown's chapter, where George Gascoigne's style takes centre stage. Through her examination of his contribution to the jointly written *Jocasta*, again at Gray's Inn, Brown illustrates the importance of classical learning to inns' writers, and the ways in which they adapt that learning to their own creative output. The inns' importance to the extensive field of classical reception documented in Patrick Cheney and Philip Hardie's second volume of the *Oxford History of Classical Reception in English Literature* (2015) is also clear in Winston's work on *Misfortunes*, as well as Apolloni's analysis of the Inner Temple's *Gismond of Salerne*. Both these latter chapters explore the influence of Senecan drama, key translations of which were emerging from the inns in the 1560s and 1570s. This is a cultural milieu where the innsmen's place in translation culture contributed directly to the production of original work, which in turn played an active role in the development of drama in English. As Brown reminds us, citing the work of Richard Helgerson, 'The value of creative English literature was still being established' in this period (1976); the role innsmen played in this process is illustrated in these chapters.

The creativity that led Gascoigne to show what one recent scholar describes as 'a commitment to resisting prescriptive protocols of compositional decorum' (Desai 2023: 34) exemplifies innsmen's regular combination of traditional learning with generic playfulness. Marotti's exploration of 'stray' poets sharing work across the inns is a clear demonstration of this tendency which, beyond drama and poetry, can also be seen in Adams's work on legal notebooks. Here the combination of legal reports and notes on meetings where men told *joco seria* provide evidence for her argument that the inns offered 'opportunities for serious-minded law students to practise skills of argument, memory, invention, oratory, rhetoric and wit'. Their interest in the expression of ideas is clear, whether the ideas were legal ones or not, and whether the expression was verbal or written.

Within and Without the Inns

Together the chapters in the volume shed new light on how even those students who were dedicated to legal study, the 'plodders', explored diversions beyond the law. The legal notebooks analysed by Adams contain materials which testify to their owners' interests in literature, music, religion, history, and philosophy and, more broadly, the contributors in the volume think about the innsmen's participation in dance, drama, poetry, and translation. For all their concern with their own institutional identity, the inns were culturally porous, drawing on and contributing to the intellectual worlds of early modern London.

Innsmen's involvement in drama and contemporary cultures of performance gains particular attention in the volume. For example, Apolloni responds to recent work in the area of legal and performance studies in her close reading of *Gismond of Salerne*, performed for Queen Elizabeth by members of the Inner Temple in 1566. Apolloni asks how inns drama explored ethical issues surrounding law, violence, and revenge, arguing that the play's inns of court authors used their female protagonist to question who has authority to 'perform' the law.

The inns engaged culturally with the page, no less than the stage, and Eckhardt and Neuhauser's work on John Selden's library points to the close relationship between innsmen and the London book trade. This relationship is further illustrated in Harris's study of John Playford's *The English Dancing Master* (1651) which draws attention to the location of the music printer's shop in the heart of the inns, in or near the porch of the Temple Church, which adjoined the Inner Temple and was across the street from the Middle Temple. As Harris explains, this meant one of the major centres of music printing in Interregnum and Restoration London was centred on the inns, a location Playford capitalised on as he cultivated an inns of court market for his books. Similarly, Satterley notes that Robert Ashley's *Of the interchangeable course, or variety of things in the whole world* (1594) was printed and sold by Charles Yetsweirt, whose printshop was on Fleetstreet near the Middle Temple Gate, once again illustrating the close relationships between innsmen, printers, and stationers.

The cultural promiscuity of the innsmen has, of course, been long appreciated, if not fully documented; however, a new emerging emphasis in the chapters in this volume is of the inns as socially, as well as culturally, porous. Just as architecturally their buildings were integrated with and encroached on by the wider urban environment, so too did innsmen move between and without the inns. For the contributors of this collection, the inns emerge less as closed societies, and more as nodes in a complex network of intersecting communities. Those innsmen who had attended one of the universities brought the social connections they had formed as students with them. This is vividly illustrated in the manuscript miscellanies examined by Marotti, a number of which originated at the universities and then travelled with their owners to the inns of court. Within the urban location of London innsmen were then ideally placed to expand their social networks. For example, several of the men who penned the commendatory verses which prefaced *Coryates Crudites* also socialised at the Mermaid and Mitre taverns and were members of parliament. Thus, the copy of the work in Selden's library discussed by Eckhardt and Neuhauser would have been associated with a social network which took in, but also reached beyond, the inns. Similarly, the poets studied by Marotti moved between the inns, taverns, parliament, and the court. John Vaughan, for example, was a member of parliament and also held a post at court as comptroller of the household to Charles, prince of Wales. For all their institutional loyalty to their inn, innsmen juggled multiple identities and allegiances.

Perhaps the innsmen were most ambidextrous in this period in their relation to the royal court. Lawyers, like other professionals, required patronage. Meanwhile, many of the so-termed revellers at the inns, students who did not intend to practise the law, aspired to a role at court or were seeking to become administrators or diplomats. For example, as Satterley's analysis of the paratexts to Ashley's translations illustrates, Ashley was using his scholarship to demonstrate his erudition, learning, and suitability to serve the commonweal with an eye to attracting patronage. The innsmen's relationship with court culture comes under particular scrutiny in both Harris's and Watson's chapters. Harris attends to the inns' appropriation of that most courtly of genres, the masque, while Watson considers how the inns' revels provided the participants with an opportunity to refine the skills required for success in a courtly career. Such abilities ranged from rhetorical dexterity to the ability to perform on the dancefloor, but underpinning them all was a deep-seated concern with self-presentation. Tellingly, a not dissimilar concern with self-fashioning is discussed by Brown in her exploration of the innsman George Gascoigne's performance of the 'prodigal-turned-moralist'. As Watson observes, innsmen were highly attuned to the need to perform, socially, no less than professionally. However, Harris and Marotti also draw out ambivalences in the inns' attitudes to court culture. Harris argues that the inns brought a more popular dimension to the genre of the masque, adapting courtly dancing into the country dancing included in their revels, and in the inns of court poetry studied by Marotti, the innsmen's fear of social exclusion runs alongside their socially aspirational experiments in courtly lyric. As Marotti argues, the misogynistic rant of a poem such as 'An Elegy on an invitation to a wedding', in which the speaker berates his mistress for marrying a man of higher status, expresses 'social as well as amorous frustration'.

For all their attention to the political and social world of the court, the innsmen's interests reached far beyond Whitehall and, indeed, beyond national borders. Thus, one of the important collective contributions the chapters in this volume make is to open up new avenues of research which place the inns in an international context. Apolloni's reading of *Gismond* illustrates how the innsmen's reading included not only classical texts and translations, but also more recent Italian adaptations, showing how inns drama grew out of a literary culture which was both intertextual and international. Satterley's chapter demonstrates how innsmen's translations were central to the thriving book trade between England and Europe, while Eckhardt's and Neuhauser's study of John Selden's library draws attention to his investment in foreign authors (an investment far greater than that he makes in contemporary English ones). As they observe, although Selden did not travel beyond England, he was surrounded by 'one of the most linguistically and geographically diverse collections of books' located in a single location in England. Indeed, innsmen were keen consumers of works of travel and exploration. Satterley shows how Robert Ashley collected cosmographies and treaties about travel, including works by Richard Hakluyt and Samuel Purchas, and used the paratextual spaces in his translation *Cochin-China* (1633) to promote trade in the area now known as Vietnam. Stevenson and Working demonstrate that he was not alone in such global interests. Their chapter illustrates the different ways in which Middle Templers engaged with exploration and conquest, ranging from the reading material in their libraries and their collections of maps and globes, to the sugars, spices, and tobacco consumed in the hall and the silver plate used at banquets. Together the chapters in this volume warn against allowing the inns' preoccupations with their own institutional affairs to blind us to their members' active involvement with national and international concerns. Indeed, as Working and Stevenson stress, the very 'conference and sociability which fostered the inns' communality, also fuelled the societies' global interests.

Mapping the Early Modern Inn/Inns

There is, however, a difficulty in editing a collection of essays on any aspect of 'the inns of court'. Early modern scholars, whether they be legal historians, literary scholars, or those exploring the interaction between the two, usually refer to the inns as if they are a single unit. Whether it be 'innsmen', or 'writing at the inns', 'inns culture' or 'an inns of court training', the expression is a shorthand suggesting some level of homogeneity between Middle and Inner Temple, Lincoln's Inn, and Gray's Inn. It is a similar usage as referring to Oxford or Cambridge University when both are composed of self-governing individual institutions, with important areas of distinctness. In many ways, of course, these are useful and acceptable shorthand terms, and perhaps impossible to avoid. The permeability between the inns, with men from one inn sharing ideas and projects with those from another; the joint enterprises between inns and between groups of men living there; and the clear areas of common ground in terms of training and activities, all seem to excuse the use of the hypernym. Yet, when we look below the surface, questions emerge. Can we generalise about factors in inns of court men's mental make-up, and propose a joint habitus, or should we more precisely point out areas in common amongst men from a particular inn? Are even those qualities that we consider typical really traits of 'the inns of court'? Were particular legal or cultural interests shared across the four, or were they the product of particular combinations of individuals, within one of the institutions or perhaps in a friendship group across inn-borders? How and why did the characteristics of a particular inn and its membership change over time?

This volume is not going to solve the big question here; indeed, that is more than an edited collection can do. But in mapping the inns we do aim to work with precision where we can and consider whether we are trying to generalise beyond the evidence. The equivocation in our title, 'Writing Communities', is thus intentional. Innsmen wrote in communities with shared ideas and experiences, and some shared attitudes to text and style; but also, their writing focuses on the communities in which they live and enables a modern reader to reconstruct some of the key facets of these groups. However, even as we analyse these literary communities in which innsmen participate, we wish to remain attentive to the ways in which communities can be retrospectively imposed on groupings which were far more fractured or multifarious. The chapters in this volume should thus be read as speaking to the shared experience of innsmen, while also drawing attention to the distinct qualities of individual inns at specific moments in time.

Works Cited

Archer, Jayne Elisabeth, Elizabeth Goldring, and Sarah Knight, eds. 2011. *The Intellectual and Cultural History of the Early Modern Inns of Court*. Manchester: Manchester University Press.

Ashley, Robert. 1627. *Almansor*. London.

Baker, John H. 1971. *An Introduction to English Legal History*. London: Butterworths.

———. 1986. "The Inns of Court and Chancery as Voluntary Associations." 45–74 in *The Legal Profession and the Common Law: Historical Essays*. London: Hambledon Press.

———. 2011. "The Third University 1450–1550: Law School or Finishing School?" in *The Intellectual and Cultural History of the Early Modern Inns of Court*, edited by Jayne Elisabeth Archer, Elizabeth Goldring, and Sarah Knight, 8–24. Manchester: Manchester University Press.

Bourdieu, Pierre. 1977. *Outline of a Theory of Practice*. Cambridge: Cambridge University Press.

Cheney, Patrick, and Philip Hardie, eds. 2015. *Oxford History of Classical Reception in English Literature, Volume 2: 1558–1660*. Oxford: Oxford University Press.

Cormack, Bradin. 2007. *A Power to Do Justice: Jurisdiction, English Literature, and the Rise of Common Law, 1509–1625*. Chicago: Chicago University Press.

Das, Nandini. 2023. *Courting India: England, Mughal India and the Origins of Empire*. London: Bloomsbury.

Desai, Adhaar Noor. 2023. *Blotted Lines: Early Modern English Literature and the Poetics of Discomposition*. Ithaca, NY: Cornell University Press.

Finkelpearl, Philip J. 1969. *John Marston of the Middle Temple: An Elizabethan Dramatist in His Social Setting*. Cambridge, MA: Harvard University Press.

Geng, Penelope. 2021. *Communal Justice in Shakespeare's England: Drama, Law and Emotion*. Toronto: Toronto University Press.

Gordon, Andrew, and Bernhard Klein, eds. 2001. *Literature, Mapping, and the Politics of Space in Early Modern Britain*. Cambridge: Cambridge University Press.

Helgerson, Richard. 1976. *The Elizabethan Prodigals*. Berkley: University of California Press.

Hudson, Judith. 2022. *Crime and Consequence in Early Modern Literature and Law*. Edinburgh: Edinburgh University Press.

Hutson, Lorna, and Victoria Kahn, eds. 2001. *Rhetoric and Law in Early Modern Europe*. New Haven: Yale University Press.

Hutson, Lorna. 2007. *The Invention of Suspicion: Law and Mimesis in Shakespeare and Renaissance Drama*. Oxford: Oxford University Press.

———, ed. 2017. *Oxford Handbook of English Law and Literature: 1500–1700*. Oxford: Oxford University Press.

Nelson, Alan, and John R. Elliott, eds. 2010. *Records of Early English Drama: Inns of Court*. Cambridge: Brewer.

O'Callaghan, Michelle. 2007. *The English Wits: Literature and Sociability in Early Modern England*. Cambridge: Cambridge University Press.

Peters, Julie Stone. 2022. *Law as Performance: Theatricality, Spectatorship, and the Making of Law in Ancient, Medieval, and Early Modern Europe*. Oxford: Oxford University Press.

Prest, Wilfrid R. 1972. *The Inns of Court under Elizabeth I and the Early Stuarts 1590–1640*. London: Longman.

Tosh, Will. 2016. *Male Friendship and Testimonies of Love in Shakespeare's England*. London: Palgrave Macmillan.

White, James Boyd. 1973. *The Legal Imagination: Studies in the Nature of Legal Thought and Expression*. Boston, MA: Little, Brown.

Winston, Jessica. 2016. *Lawyers at Play: Literature, Law, and Politics at the Early Modern Inns of Court, 1558–1581*. Oxford: Oxford University Press.

Working, Lauren. 2020. *The Making of an Imperial Polity: Civility and America in the Jacobean Metropolis*. Cambridge: Cambridge University Press.

PART I

Within the Inns

CHAPTER 2

Acting Like a Lawyer: Mooting, *The Misfortunes of Arthur*, and Legal Professional Identity

Jessica Winston

In an early scene in *The Misfortunes of Arthur* (1587), a play about the death of the legendary British king, Queen Guenevora dwells on the return of Arthur after his absence of nearly a decade. Although worrying about the imminent discovery of her adulterous affair with Arthur's son, Mordred, the queen positions herself as a wronged spouse, insisting that she wants revenge equal to another aggrieved wife, Medea. She hopes to '[f]rame out some trap beyond all vulgar guile, / Beyond Medea's wiles'. She will '[s]pare no revenge, b'it poison, knife, or fire' (Hughes 1587: A2^{v}). Guenevora's unbridled vengefulness, along with the reference to Medea, aligns her with the impassioned revengers in the tragedies of the ancient Roman playwright, Seneca—revengers who, like Medea, pursue extreme means to punish those who have wronged them. These similarities point to Seneca's shaping influence on *Misfortunes.* While the plot comes from British chronicle and legend, the play uses a form closely modelled on Senecan tragedy, with lengthy

J. Winston (✉)
English, Idaho State University, Pocatello, ID, USA
e-mail: jessicawinston@isu.edu

E. Rhatigan, J. Watson (eds.), *Mapping the Early Modern Inns of Court*, Early Modern Literature in History,
https://doi.org/10.1007/978-3-031-77445-4_2

speeches, biting dialogue, and impassioned, vengeful characters. Indeed, one index of this influence is that one third of the lines are close translations from Seneca's drama (Nuttall *et al.* 2021: 124). Yet, having positioned herself as a Senecan revenger in a neo-Senecan play, shortly after these lines, Guenevora's character makes a startling about face. While Senecan characters seek retribution even at the risk of their own lives, Guenevora renounces her plan, resolving to go to a convent, 'Where daily penance done for each offense, / May render due revenge for every wrong' (A4[v]). If Guenevora is a Senecan revenger in a Senecan-style play, why does she abruptly abandon her Senecan drive for revenge?

Critics have long recognised that *Misfortunes of Arthur* is deeply engaged with Senecan form and style. Writing well over a century ago, J. W. Cunliffe influentially described the play as 'entirely after Seneca's manner' (1893: 52). Writing more recently, Felicity Brown showed that *Misfortunes*'s engagement with Seneca reveals its 'central preoccupation: its own imaginative, imitative process', particularly the process of translation (2021: 158). Yet critics have not commented on those moments where the play seems to reverse or turn away from some characteristic features in Seneca. Guenevora's change of heart is one example. Yet, as I will describe in more detail below, similar anti-Senecan moves occur elsewhere. The ghost of Gorlois, who opens the play cursing the house of Arthur, ultimately sees the realisation of his hoped-for punishments. Unlike the revengers of Senecan drama, whose dissatisfaction leaves room for a continued cycle of violence, Gorlois returns to hell content, saying, in essence, everything is better now and will remain so. What are we to make of these anti-Senecan movements?

This chapter argues that a key to understanding the anti-Senecan elements of *Misfortunes* lies in exploring the contexts and social function of its original performance. The play was written in 1587 by Thomas Hughes, and other law students at Gray's Inn, for performance before the queen at Greenwich. In that venue, the innsmen presented a prologue calling attention to their background and identity as law students, and thereby constructing for the queen an image of themselves as legal professionals: they are men whose legal training and serious dispositions make them central to the governance of the country. This prologue, with its emphasis on legal professional identity, provides a framework for understanding the play and those curiously anti-Senecan turns. For, like the prologue, but in more subtle ways, the play constructs an idea of the law students creating the drama. Through the drama, the players fashion themselves as calm, restrained men, who (through their performance of impassioned characters) occupy the heights of emotion but still—like Guenevora does within the play—rein in that emotion, modulating high passion into even-keeled dispassion. In other words, the play uses and resists Senecan motifs to promote an idea (perhaps an ideal) of the players as committed, serious legal professionals whose calm, controlled behaviour helps to maintain the stability of the commonweal.

This chapter presents this argument about legal identity in both the prologue and the play. But to develop this point, I shall first consider the construction and performance of legal identity in the medieval and early modern legal exercises, the moots. By understanding the moots, it becomes easier to recognise the construction of legal identity in both the prologue to and play of *Misfortunes*. So, it is to the moots that we first turn.

Mooting and Legal Identity

In an important book on *Law as Performance*, Julie Stone Peters has shown that legal education at the inns, especially mooting, trained aspiring lawyers 'not just in how to be a lawyer but how to look like one' (2022: 25). In the moots, members of the inns took on roles as advocates, clients, and judges, and, in this way, the legal exercises fostered practices of 'impersonation, dissimulation, and make believe', all of which helped to shape 'their identity as lawyers' as well as their sense of 'the profession of law' (25). Through mooting, students learned that being a lawyer involved a type of 'ironical dissimulation' (296), whereby they adopted the persona of the lawyer even as they learned to assume an ironised distance from that persona. To understand how moots construct legal identity, it will be useful to lay out what moots are and how they worked.

The early modern inns of court had an established system of oral exercises for learning the law. These exercises involved readings, or lectures on statutes by senior members of the inns; moots, or 'formal disputations . . . in which the learner played a more active role' (Baker and Thorne 1990, xvi); and boltings, a somewhat opaque practice that involved discussing questions arising from the moots but without pleadings (Prest 2023: 156; Baker and Thorne 1990: lxxv). Yet moots were the most common, and arguably most important, legal exercise, since they were crucial for students (inner barristers) to be called to the bar, and thereby to attain the minimum credential needed to plead cases in the higher courts at Westminster, such as the court of the king's bench. Those called to the bar, utter barristers, continued to participate in the moots. Eventually, they could give a reading, lectures on a legal statute, thus becoming a reader. Readers could in time become leaders of their inn, called benchers (or pensioners at Gray's Inn). Yet, as Baker observes, the progression through the ranks was 'inseparable from the performance of moots' (1990: lvii).

There were many kinds of moots, 'petty and grand, chapel, house, term, hall, fire and library' (Prest 2023: 154). Regardless of type, or the inn in which they occurred, the basic approach was the same. Each moot focused on a hypothetical case, often an outlandish situation involving property and inheritance. These cases were collected by law students and now survive in notebooks, such as those Blessin Adams discusses in Chap. 5. In general, notes do not record specific disputations on a case (Baker and Thorne 1990: xxxiii), but they must have generated lively avenues of thought, since many were recycled through the centuries, appearing in multiple moot books over time. Some cases were popular enough to earn special names, such as 'Fitzjohn', 'Kyppok', and 'Wyleby' (Baker and Thorne 1990: xliii).

While moots taught the technicalities of law, they also existed as 'an evening's entertainment' (Aikenhead 1977: 248). Part of this entertainment came from the cases themselves: a blend of legal technicality and bizarre, implausible situations—or, at least, ideally implausible ones. An example is the case of 'Isaac and Jacob', a title alluding to the biblical story of Jacob and Esau, though the moot case bears little resemblance to that. It involves two brothers, but also adultery, a series of secret pregnancies, and (for good measure) an abbot, an outlaw, and a single woman. The original case, as in all moot cases, would have been presented in Law-French, a mixture of French, English, and Latin. Here it is in J. H. Baker's translation:

> Two brothers, who are villeins [tenants] purchase a carucate of partible land to which an advowson [clergyman] is appendant; the lord ousts them and leases a half to one of them to hold in villeinage, and leases the other half [to the other] in the same way. The elder brother marries; the husband dies, his wife being secretly pregnant; the lord marries her; she is delivered of a son and dies; the lord takes another wife and [he] dies, his wife being secretly pregnant; the younger villein marries her; she is previously lain, so that she is pregnant by him; the husband dies; she is delivered of two twin sons; the woman dies; the two twins and the third son begotten by the lord enter and

> partition among themselves; the elder twin brings a writ of right of advowson against an abbot, who joins the mise, and then the twin is nonsuited, so that final judgement is awarded; then he enfeoffs the abbot of his share with the king's license; the abbot disseizes the other twin of his share; the elder twin enters the same abbey and is professed, and the elected abbot, and brings a *quare impedit* against the younger twin and against the son begotten of the lord and again the son begotten by the first vein; and the son begotten by the first villein brings a writ of neifty against the younger twin and against the son begotten by the lord; and brings two men in proof, one of them an outlaw, the other an excommunicate, and a single woman. *Ceux que droit.* (Baker and Thorne 1990: 18)

The case involves numerous legal technicalities, and it is designed to be difficult, even impossible, to discern who might have an obvious claim to this land. Faced with this tangled story, members of the inns would not have resolved the issue of who should get what. Rather, the aim was to 'find the correct procedure to adopt in court' (Baker and Thorne 1990: xlvi). Put another way, the point was 'not to settle an abstract point of law but to frame an issue in a legally acceptable form' (xlix). Thus, the closing phrase, '*Ceux que droit*' is a formulaic expression, likely asking in a shortened form, 'The parties with the right wish to be advised how to go about their recovery' (xlvi). The emphasis was on the *how* (the procedure or type of writ involved in bringing the case) rather than the outcome (who precisely should inherit this land).

While moots were complex and technical, scholars have speculated that they were unlikely to have been dull affairs. Karen Cunningham suggests that the moots' constructed fictions were (and are) surprisingly interesting, even alarming. Analysing the 'Isaac and Jacob' moot above, she describes its 'particularly competitive vision', where 'alliances shift swiftly, even among brothers, and devotions dissolved one into another' (2002: 27). Anyone, regardless of gender, rank, or relationship (wives, bastards, abbots, strangers) can potentially 'initiate action'; all have 'disruptive agency' (28). While the fictions must have been intriguing, even unsettling, they were (and are) also amusing. This makes sense, since, as Adams shows in Chap. 5, 'modes of play were not wholly distinctive, nor mutually exclusive' and 'Serious-minded law students were not so puritanical as to wholly reject rebellious or disruptive play'. Furthermore, the cases must have prompted baffled appreciation, even enjoyment, of the fictionalised complexity. How could one possibly untangle the property rights of all those secret children, or keep straight which brother, twin, or secret child they were discussing? In Baker's words, the point of the moot was 'to raise knotty points in some profusion' (1990: xlvi). Improbability was not an issue. Baker explains, 'It does not seem to have mattered too much whether they were examples ever likely to be met with in the real world' (2000: 39). The point was to 'exercise the mind' by posing a 'mind-stretching remote contingency' (Baker 2000: 39, 45).

While moots exercised the legal mind, they also entertained. They can be helpfully understood, along the lines that Julie Stone Peters has laid out, as partially scripted theatre. The theatrical aspect of the moots is evident in their logistics. A moot court was modelled on the actual courts of justice (Bellot 1922: 171), which helped students to rehearse for roles in a real court. The moots also involved complex cues and blocking. William Dugdale's mid-seventeenth-century description conveys this complexity, which can seem almost as outlandish as the cases being discussed.

> Immediately after supper the benchers assemble themselves in the bay window at the upper end of the hall; where standing in order according to their antiquity, there repair unto them two gentlemen under the bar [i.e. inner barristers] whose turn it is to recite the pleadings. Who, after a low obeisance, demand whether it be their pleasure to hear a moot, and depart with an affirmative answer. Then the benchers appoint who amongst themselves to argue the case . . . When it is agreed on who are to argue, all the benchers depart out of the hall, leaving the rest of the company there. The two arguers walk a turn in the court or garden until the hall be prepared and made ready for them; which being done, they return into the hall and stay at the cupboard, demanding if the mootmen be ready . . . [A]ll parties being ready, the two benchers appointed to argue, together with the reader elect, take their places at the bench table, the ancient bencher sitting in the midst, the second on his right hand, and the reader-elect on his left. Then the mootmen also take their place, sitting on a form close to the cupboard and opposite the benchers. On the one side of them sits one of the students that recites the pleading, and the other on the other side. The pleadings are first recited by the students, then the case put and argued by the barristers, and lastly by the reader-elect and benchers, in manner and form aforesaid . . . The moot being ended, all parties return to the cupboard, where the mootmen present the benchers with a cup of beer and a slice of bread; and so the exercise for that night is ended. (Dugdale 1666: 208–209)

Here, Dugdale describes a complex practice. Reports going back to the early sixteenth century capture many of the same details (Baker and Thorne 1990: lx), with a considerable amount of to-ing and fro-ing (Peters 2022: 274–75). Moots had a formulaic structure with clearly delineated roles and expectations.

At the same time, this formal structure allowed for, even invited, improvisation and breaks in the plan. For instance, noting that a single student would play *both* the client and the client's attorney, Peters details the comedy of the moot's roll call when a judge would first ask whether the attorney was there (yes) and then ask the same for the client. The client's formal answer, which would have been made in an actual court, was 'yes, here by his attorney', even though, in the moots, the client and attorney were played by the same person (2022: 277). Looking back to Dugdale, a similar point can be made about the formulaic question, would senior members like to hear a moot? The mootmen would 'depart with an affirmative answer'; it seems unlikely that the answer was ever negative. But if the answer was rarely, even never, 'no', the question itself is a humorous absurdity. We also know that breaks in formality occurred for less humorous reasons. For instance, in the *Black Books* of Lincoln's Inn, there is an episode in which a student was expelled after having pulled a barrister's hair and ears when the barrister rendered a decision that he felt was not in his favour (Aikenhead 1977: 247).

Thus, as Peters says, even as moots taught the technicalities of law, they also inculcated a formal as well as semi-improvisational style of being, moving, and thinking as a lawyer. At least some were consciously aware of this function. Thomas Elyot, for one, felt strongly that the moots taught eloquent speaking, seeing them as an extension of traditions of ancient rhetoric, stating that 'in the learning of the laws of this realm, there is at this day an exercise wherein is a manner, a shadow, or figure of the ancient rhetoric. I mean the pleading used in court and chancery called moots' (1962: 53). Numerous scholars have articulated this connection. Margaret McGlynn has written of the oral learning exercises at the inns, 'the system was focused on developing habits of mind rather than imparting a set body of information' (2003: 57). For Cunningham, mooting encouraged 'continuous improvisations', 'speculative play', and the 'multiplication of possibilities and positions' (2002: 32). They were 'ritual performance', but were also 'continuously eroded by the acts of improvisation demanded by that performance' (32). Indeed, the moots were quotidian, esoteric productions in which members gave memorised speeches and improvised their parts, repeatedly practising the art of legal oratory while circling a Möbius strip of ritual and mock ritual, formality, and spontaneity (whether in the form of hilarity or violence). In this way, moots functioned both as formal legal exercises and a kind of improvisational theatre. And it is this structure that is generative of legal identity. For the moots were 'halfway between solemn ritual and farce' (Peters 2022: 297), a format that educated legal men to be lawyers even as they developed the understanding that they were not to take themselves too seriously—at least when they were in front of others with similar training.

Yet if, in the moots, future lawyers learned to be—and to present themselves—as serious, but without taking themselves too seriously, at least initially, this identity does not seem to translate into the *Misfortunes of Arthur*. Here the performers announce that they are legal men, and they perform a version of legal identity, but in a style that is so serious, earnest, and sincere that it hardly seems to be a performance.

Constructing Law in the Prologue to *Misfortunes*

We can discern differences between the legal identities presented in moots and *Misfortunes* in the prologue to the play, written by Gray's Inn student Nicholas Trotte. Here, three muses drag five prisoners, students of Gray's Inn, onto the stage. One Muse explains that the men are servants of Astraea, goddess of justice, or law. But, she contends, Astraea trains her servants in law and in so doing teaches them to 'forget and scorn / the noble skills of language and of arts, / the wisdom that discourse of stories teach', and all other 'ornaments' of 'knowledge' (Hughes 1587: 1).[1] Astraea especially 'doth distain' poetry, scorning it as folly. Thus, the Muse protests, Astraea erases arts from the minds of her servants. On this *tabula rasa*, she 'supplie[s] instead':

> Forsooth some old reports of altered laws,
> Clamors of courts and cavils upon words.
> Grounds without ground, supported by conceit
> And reasons of more subtlety than sense. (1)

[1] The prologue is a handwritten text in the opening leaves of the printed edition of *Misfortunes*. It lacks page signatures, so the citations refer to the individual pages.

The Muse singles out the moots: 'What shall I say of moot points strange and doubts / Still arguéd but never yet agreed?' (2). For this Muse, law, perhaps most especially mooting, is the opposite of 'the noble skills of language and of arts', a futile exercise in nonsense, characterised as 'clamors', 'grounds without ground', and 'points strange'.

The captured men offer a defence. Their first loyalty is indeed to Astraea: 'Unto Astraea's name we honor bear / Whose sound perfections we do more admire / Than all the vaunted store of Muses gifts', such as 'poetry', 'history', and 'eloquence' (2–3). The arts are distractions, for such pleasures cannot 'win Astraea's servants to remove / Their service once devote to better things' (3). They defend mooting, in particular, asserting that the practice is productive: 'One doubt in moots by argument increased / Clears many doubts' (3). Conceding the Muse's individual points, they then correct the starting assumption, saying that law and arts are not mutually exclusive. For, they claim, they never did 'banish nor reject' any 'ornaments of knowledge nor of tongues'. Rather, they insist 'With Muses still we intercourse allow' (3), a point reinforced by the fact that they are about to perform a play.

In the prologue, the Innsmen demonstrate their ability in poetry. They show that the arts can survive even in the minds of legal men. But it is worth noting what they do not do, which is to suggest that their literary abilities might be an extension of their training in law, or vice versa. It is possible to discern this rhetorical road not taken in those references to the moots, where the point-counterpoint focuses narrowly on the question of whether moots are useful within the field of law. Their idea that moots might be unhelpful, even as a form of legal training, has some merit, since the exercises were presented in Law French and, as we have seen, concerned elaborate, implausibly tangled issues related to property ownership. Even Francis Bacon, a member of Gray's Inn who was close to *Misfortunes*, having contributed to its dumb shows, is known to have complained that the learning exercises (specifically readings), served only to 'stir concise and subtle doubts' (1642: A4^{r}), a point that echoes the criticism of moots. In his book *Lawiers Logike*, another member of Gray's Inn, Abraham Fraunce, contended that moots do not always teach the substance of law, but instead allow men to 'jangle of moot conceits' and to 'climb to the bar, and bar [themselves] utterly from the substance of the common law' (1588: R1^{v}). The prologue participates in a larger question about the value of the legal exercises, but to the question of whether mooting itself is a linguistic art or performance, the prologue is clear that mooting lies within a legal domain, a discursive arena that is distinct from poetry, eloquence, history, and the arts generally. In the prologue, mooting is the opposite of a 'noble skill of language and of arts'.

This positioning is odd, since (as we have seen), there was a tradition of linking mooting with those noble skills. As we have heard, Elyot felt that moots were a 'shadow' of 'ancient rhetoric'. Bacon complained about readings precisely because of their connection to the arts: he felt that 'Readings of ancient time' were more useful and bore 'more fruit'—and could do again (1642: A3[r]). Fraunce explicitly connected law, rhetoric, and poetry, and in *Lawiers Logike*, drew 97 direct quotations from Spenser's *The Shepheardes Calendar* to illustrate rhetorical and logical principles (Koller 1940: 110). In Chap. 5 Blessin Adams shows parallels between the rhetorical moves involved in mooting and other kinds of communal literary play and Julie Stone Peters demonstrates that mooting taught lawyerly decorum and developed professional identities through performance: 'These exercises not only taught legal substance but offered essential practice in courtroom performance' (2022: 255). In light of the tradition connecting mooting, rhetoric, and performance, it seems very possible that Trotte's assessment of the moots is more deliberate than offhand—that is, he may purposefully position moots solely as legal exercises, and not as rhetorical shows, amusing fictions, or improvisational performance. According to the prologue, law students maintain some artistic skill (*viz.* the actual play), but the connection between law and the arts stops there. There are no 'noble skills of language and of art' in the law—or at least not in the learning of it.

Admittedly, the prologue's *primary* aim is not to explore interconnections of art and law. It serves as an apology by dramatic amateurs who are about to perform for the queen. 'Look', they seem to say, 'It's a play by law students. Although we think we have some ability in poetry, mainly we have our desire to do well. Please don't judge us too harshly'. Even if Trotte thought that law (or mooting) was a rhetorical art, in this context, it makes sense to downplay that connection. For if the performers are so practised in the arts, maybe the audience would have greater hopes for their play. Still, it would be possible to calibrate the audience's hopes without structuring the prologue around an absolute division between law and arts, such that one of the most common rhetorical and performative things that the law students did (mooting) is positioned as an activity that has nothing to do with rhetoric, performance, or the arts in general.

The prologue's separation of law and art makes more sense if we consider its additional aim, to construct and perform a public version of legal professional identity. As the men conclude their defence, they make the remarkable claim that the work of common law lawyers maintains monarchic power and general order in the commonwealth, supporting 'prerogative of prince' and 'respect of peers' (3). According to Curtis Perry, the prologue presents 'the gentlemen of Gray's Inn as sophisticated citizen-subjects offering service and admonitory advice to the queen' (2011: 535–56). In his discussion of the play itself, Perry persuasively demonstrates that the admonitory message comes out in the drama's 'concern with empire and domestic instability' (510), a critique of a type of imperial and expansionist ambition that leaves the nation open to internal strife. In this sense, while the men downplay expectations about their poetic abilities, they also enlist poetry to defend the common law and their profession. It is their poetry that earns an audience before the queen, which they use to describe and defend their role in protecting the realm. Furthermore, even as the prologue raises and asserts the social importance of the legal profession, it also constructs an image of legal professional identity. For the prologue goes on to describe the men of Gray's Inn as a serious bunch. They have 'attentive minds and serious wits', which they use to 'revolve records of deep judicial acts' (3). They take their time 'to weigh with steady and indifferent hand / Each word of law' (3). They are a committed, even-handed, solemn group, and this seriousness is an essential part of their legal identity.

Yet, by contrast with the moots, in the prologue to *Misfortunes*, the performance of legal identity comes with none of the ironical distancing that, as we have discussed, is a characteristic of mooting. This observation provides another way to understand why the prologue positions law and arts as compatible, but entirely different, activities, forestalling ideas about deeper similarities. The prologue perhaps avoids (even implicitly resists) drawing this connection because to do so would emphasise the rhetorical and performative connections between law and drama, between moots and *Misfortunes*. And such a connection would potentially call attention to the fact that the Innsmen's serious legal demeanour is learned and performed, not innate, thereby undercutting their efforts at presenting themselves as essentially sober characters. In other words, as Peters observes, the moots are performances of legal identity. So is the prologue to *Misfortunes*. Yet, unlike the moots, the prologue downplays that the legal men are, in fact, performing.

To be sure, this point may seem counterintuitive, since the prologue is itself a mini-play and it introduces a play, where men enact a variety of characters and roles. The Innsmen are obviously performing, but the performance differs crucially from the moots. In the moots one performs the part of a lawyer with an ironical distance; in the prologue to *Misfortunes*, the lawyers present themselves as approaching their drama and their dramatic roles with the thoughtful conviction and gravity of purpose that is innate to their legal selves. At least in this prologue, what it means to act like a lawyer is to suppress the extent to which one might be understood to be acting. To act like a lawyer is to convey that being a lawyer is not an act.

Distancing the Passions in *Misfortunes*

The prologue to *Misfortunes* then is concerned with the performance of legal identity. This concern provides insight into the social function and structure of the play itself. To return to ideas about Seneca that began this chapter, as I hope to show, the play uses and resists Senecan motifs to build on and reinforce the image of legal professionals begun in the prologue. *Misfortunes of Arthur* is a serious work dealing with an important, high-minded topic in British legend, the death of King Arthur, a subject that bolsters the association of the legal men with weighty topics and a general concern for the history and welfare of the country. At the same time, the play presents this tale in Senecan tragic form, but contrary to the usual association of Senecan tragedy with high emotion, this play deploys the Senecan tragic conventions in order to show performers restraining, even neutralising or eliminating, disruptive passions within several of the characters. In this way, the play bolsters the vision of legal men presented in the prologue: these are men who, while inhabiting characters who exhibit the high, overweening emotion typical of Senecan characters, demonstrate an ability to restrain, curb, and ultimately subdue their characters' emotion. In this way, they imply that they—the group performing the play—have an innate temperament and sobriety to maintain stability of the state.

On the face of it, *Misfortunes* is hardly a story of personal composure or national stability. It focuses on less savoury elements of King Arthur's origins and the ignominious events leading to his death. The play's backstory involves Arthur's father, Uther Pendragon, who hosted a feast to celebrate his defeat of the Saxons. At the banquet, enamoured of the wife of Gorlois, Duke of Cornwall, he seduced her, leading to the birth of twins, Arthur and Anne. He later killed Gorlois in battle. Many years after, Uther Pendragon died, poisoned by the Saxons, and Arthur comes to the throne. After an affair with his twin sister, resulting in the birth of Mordred, Arthur marries Guenevora. The king departs to make a war against Rome, leaving Mordred in charge, at which point Guenevora and Mordred have a lengthy affair.

The play begins on the eve of Arthur's triumphant return. In the opening scene, the ghost of Duke Gorlois rises from the dead to curse Arthur for the actions of his father. For notwithstanding 'Pendragon's poisoned end', Gorlois feels that 'mischief's measure' has not yet been 'all fulfilled' ($A1^r$), and he curses the house of Arthur. As the play opens, Guenevora professes continued love for Mordred. Mordred seeks to protect his rule, declaring war on Arthur, who is reluctant to enter a battle where he will kill his own son. In the end, Mordred dies in a gruesome scene in which he deliberately runs on Arthur's sword, a move that allows him to get close enough to his father to slay him. As the play closes, Arthur lies on his deathbed. In the closing scene, Gorlois gloats over his successful revenge and returns to the underworld. Mischief managed.

In her discussion in Chap. 10 of an early Gray's Inn play, George Gascoigne's *Jocasta* (*c.* 1566–1567), Brown states that Innsmen engaged with the classics in ways that were both playful and professionally important. That point also applies here. In *Misfortunes*, the engagement with Senecan conventions is integral to the construction and presentation of legal identity.

In terms of the play's adaptation of this form, it is useful to review briefly some salient features of Senecan drama, particularly its focus on the passions. Seneca presents characters in the throes of the highest emotions, anger and jealousy, pursuing alarming and extreme acts of revenge. Rage is the 'all-consuming subject of Senecan tragedy' (Braden 1985: 2), often embodied in a common character-type, the vengeful ghost, who initiates the downfall of those who have wronged them, or their offspring. The spectres represent an unrelenting and uncontrolled desire for revenge. For instance, Seneca's *Thyestes* begins with the ghost of Tantalus being dragged by a Fury from Hades, where he is tormented by perpetual hunger and thirst, in order to curse his nephews, Atreus and Thyestes. Although Tantalus initially resists, he soon gives in to the command to 'rage and fury throw' on the house of Atreus (Ker and Winston 2012: 1.1.101).[2] In *Agamemnon*, which deals with the offspring of Atreus and Thyestes, the ghost of Thyestes curses the next generation, Agamemnon and Aegisthus, looking forward to 'slaughter' and 'murder' (1.1.46).

Rage also appears in Seneca's protagonists, whose high emotions lead to terrible acts. *Thyestes* tells the story of King Atreus, who—fearing that his brother Thyestes has slept with his wife and aims to usurp the throne—lures Thyestes and his children to the palace, where he kills the children, bakes them in a pie, and feeds them to their father. He says he wants to do 'some mischief great', 'both fierce and bloody', to accomplish 'that which never shall no after age allow' (2.1.17–19). Other characters also engage in terrible acts of revenge. *Medea* presents the tale of the sorceress and spurned wife of Jason, who kills their two children (as well as Jason's new wife). She is an 'untamed tiger' that does 'rage and rave unkind' (Seneca 1566: B3^{v}). *Hippolytus* centres on Phaedra, who falls madly in love with her stepson, Hippolytus. When he spurns her, Phaedra accuses him of rape and kills herself, initiating events that lead to Hippolytus's death.

For our understanding of *Misfortunes*, a final Senecan convention involves the counsellor, servant, or nurse figure who attempts to curtail the excesses of their master. *Thyestes* involves a dialogue between Atreus and a servant who tries to restrain the king. Among other appeals, the servant asks Atreus to consider public opinion: 'Does fame of people naught / Adverse thee fear?' (Ker and Winston 2012: 2.1.205–206). Atreus rejects each of the servant's arguments and refuses to relent, settling on the cannibalistic plan. Rather than turning Atreus away from his impassioned state, the servant is reduced to helping the king plan to entrap his brother. Counsel fails in other Senecan plays. In *Agamemnon*, Clytemnestra fears the return of her husband, Agamemnon, from the Trojan War, as she is now in love with Aegisthus, with whom she has had a long affair. Her nurse urges her to 'bridle thine affections, and wisely rule thy rage' (2.1.143). But, ignoring this advice, Clytemnestra and Aegisthus make a pact to murder Agamemnon.

Misfortunes follows all of these conventions, but it also adapts and resists them. We can see how this works if we return to the character of Guenevora. She initially appears as a Phaedra- or Clytemnestra-like figure,

[2] References to plays by Seneca will be to the early English translations of the plays from the 1560s, which the authors of *Misfortunes* are likely to have known either in their original versions or in the collected edition of the plays, put together by Thomas Newton, in 1581.

engaged in an illicit affair and contemplating revenge. Consumed by fury, like Medea, she calls on furies to infect her with rage: ‘Come spiteful fiends, come heaps of furies fell, / Not one by one, but all at once’ (A3r). Like Atreus, she complains that she needs to be angrier: ‘My breast / Raves not enough’ (A3r). Guenevora emphasises the need for excess, seeking to be subsumed by the emotion. She aims at a ‘huge’ project of revenge (A3r). Also like many Senecan characters, Guenevora engages in a dialogue with a servant, in this case her lady-in-waiting, Fronia, who urges temperance and forgiveness, telling the queen to ‘repress your ire’, for ‘a lady’s best revenge is to forgive’ (A3r).

But here the similarities end. Quite unlike characters in Seneca, Guenevora listens to Fronia’s advice, agreeing near the end of their scene: ‘I can and will accept your sage advice’ (A3v). To be sure, the Queen’s resolve is short-lived. In the next scene, in dialogue with her sister, Angharat, she decides to commit suicide. Guenevora continues to emphasise her extreme emotion: ‘O gnawing easeless grief, who now can heal / My maimèd mind? It must be healed by death’ (A3r). Angharat argues against self-harm. Again, surprisingly, Guenevora relents, opting for a different and much less violent course of action, a symbolic form of death, ‘Death to the world’ (A4r). She will go to a cloister ‘to renounce the world’ (A4v).

Within the Senecan tragic tradition, Guenevora’s turnabout from revenger to cloistered nun is relatively novel. In Seneca, revengers, such as Atreus, Medea, Clytemnestra, and Phaedra never relent. Indeed, they typically become more fervent in their commitment. Thus, near the opening of *Thyestes*, Atreus works himself up, calling himself a ‘dastard’, ‘coward’, and ‘wretch’ because he has not yet sought revenge (Ker and Winston 2012: 2.1–2). Even once he accomplishes his revenge, Atreus worries that feeding Thyestes’s sons to their father was not enough, exclaiming, ‘For yet even this too little seems to me’ (5.3.85). By contrast, in *Misfortunes*, Guenevora listens to counsel, curbs her passion, reverses course, and finds another, more subdued path—one that involves neither revenge nor self-harm. Unlike Atreus, who goes on to imagine yet worse forms of revenge he should have taken, Guenevora turns away, shifting away from passion toward emotional and physical command.

A similar shift occurs in the ghost of Gorlois. At the outset of the play, Gorlois is overcome with wrath, wanting to ‘glut on revenge’ (A2r). He wants extremes: ‘Let mischiefs know no mean’ (A2r). Rephrasing lines from *Thyestes*, he aims to do a deed ‘which no age shall allow’ (A2r). And, lucky ghost, at the end of the play, all of his curses have come to pass. Gorlois gloats in triumph and declares total success.

Unlike many Senecan revengers, Gorlois does not become discontented with the method or extent of his revenge. At the end of the play, he states that he will 'rest content' (F3^{v}). Since his 'wrath is wrought', he will 'gladly thus revenged return' to the underworld (F4^{r}). As mentioned earlier, ghosts appear at the beginnings of Seneca's plays, and sometimes in the middle, but they do not return to comment on whether they are satisfied with the outcome of their curses, a move that leaves open a question about the results. Thus in many plays we see the cycle of violence continue through generations, as *Agamemnon* deals with the generation after Thyestes and Atreus, and includes the ghost of Thyestes himself seeking revenge.

Many Senecan revengers question whether the outcome was as bad as it should have been. At the end of *Thyestes*, Atreus openly mulls whether the cannibalistic banquet was enough, since Thyestes only discovered that he had eaten his own children after the fact. As Atreus thinks, Thyestes should have taken the 'blood yet warm even from the wound' so that he 'might'st drink / That lived yet' (Ker and Winston 2012: 5.3.85–88). In other words, it would have been better, if Thyestes had knowingly drunk his children's blood while they were yet alive. He regrets, 'now my wrath too lightly ended is' (5.3.98). But unlike Atreus, at the end of *Misfortunes* Gorlois has no regrets about his curses. Indeed, he is content that, as a consequence of the closure he has brought about, the future will bring a new golden age, which will be 'free of Gorlois' ghost' (F3^{v}). Britain will only see 'endless weal' (F3^{v}). There is no sense that the cycle of violence will continue.

Gorlois's arc differs slightly from that of Guenevora. Through counsel, and her own deliberation, she restrains herself. Gorlois pursues real and devastating revenge, but unlike Atreus, he does not wish to have revenged differently. He just returns to the underworld. In Seneca, characters lean into their emotion, they consistently amplify and fan their passions. Even when they seem to get what they want, they can be dissatisfied. In *Misfortunes*, there is an end to passion, and a way to reach emotional resolution.

Why does *Misfortunes* turn from Senecan tradition in this way? One response has to do with the principal audience for *Misfortunes*, Queen Elizabeth. The play praises her by presenting her reign as a time of peace. At the end of the prologue, the men of Gray's Inn state that they are performing a tragedy because there are no real tragedies in Elizabeth's times: 'For thus since your sacred majesty / In gracious hands the regal scepter held / All tragedies are fled from state to stage' (5). Likewise, in his last speech, Gorlois states that future England will be better, especially with the coming of Elizabeth I, 'that virtuous Virgo born for Britain's bliss', who will 'of all wars compound eternal peace' and 'reduce the golden age again' (F3^{v}). In this context, Gorlois's change from enraged revenger to contented shade is fitting. If he remained enraged or discontented, then there is a possibility for a continued cycle of violence that would disrupt the present peace. Queen Elizabeth's presence could also explain Guenevora's story. It might have been unseemly to represent a queen who is incapable of ultimately controlling her emotion.

Nevertheless, members of Gray's Inn could have praised Elizabeth in other ways—with other characters and plots presented in other genres. Why did members of the inns adapt Senecan tragic style to offer this flattery? To be sure, neo-Senecan tragedy was popular, but it was also most popular in the 1560s and it was a somewhat antiquated form for drama by 1587 when the play was performed. I would suggest that another possibility hearkens back to the legal profession and the representation of legal identity in the prologue. As we have seen, in the prologue, members of Gray's Inn present legal professionals as dispassionate men, who calmly interpret the law to keep the commonwealth functioning. Indeed, while Elizabeth's reign is marked by peace, at least according to the prologue, it is the legal professionals who help to keep the peace by maintaining order: 'prerogative of prince, respect of peers'. While this point is explicit in the prologue, the play itself subtly reinforces this image of the legal profession. In the play, the men of Gray's Inn not only demonstrate their high-minded interest in affairs of state, they also demonstrate their ability to subdue and curb the passions. In writing *Misfortunes*, they present a play in which they embody characters who are overcome by emotion, but—quite differently from their generic model—some of these characters are able to restrain and contain those passions, or at least to arrive at a place of contentment and satisfaction. Thus the structure of the play shows that legal men are able to inhabit many characters of high emotion, but that they are also able to back away from or control that emotion, to arrive at a place of peace (in themselves and in Elizabeth's reign) at the end. In this way, they reinforce the idea, first presented in the prologue, that legal professionals are characterised by their dispassion and their ability to control their, and others', emotions.

Although the prologue and the play seem different from the moots, it is important to recognise ways that their presentations of legal identity have a fundamental similarity. In the moots and in *Misfortunes*, legal men get close to and inhabit a persona (that of the lawyer in the moots and that of the emotional ruler in *Misfortunes*). But in both they demonstrate an ability to maintain a distance from the character that they perform. What is fundamental to legal identity is not quite, as Peters suggests, an ironised distance from the persona of the lawyer. Instead, it is the performance of a sombre distance from total emotional or intellectual investment. In this sense, in the moots and *Misfortunes*, legal professionals are not precisely either practising lawyers or Senecan characters. Looking at the construction of the moots and *Misfortunes* together points to a different, more foundational idea (or ideal). The identity of the legal professional is (or perhaps, more accurately, ideally should be) that of the stoic, someone who maintains an emotional distance from the events in which they are engaged—a distance from the vicissitudes of a particular legal exercise or the upheavals of the country. At bottom, what we see in both the moots and *Misfortunes* is the coalescence of the modern idea of the lawyer—the idea (however unlikely in reality) that to be a lawyer is to be emotionally detached.

Works Cited

Aikenhead, Ian D. 1977. "Students of the Common Law, 1590–1615: Lives and Ideas at the Inns of Court." *University of Toronto Law Journal* 27, no. 3: 243–56.

Bacon, Francis. 1642. *The Learned Reading of Sir Francis Bacon … Upon the Statute of Uses*. London.

Baker, J. H. 2000. "The Inns of Court and Legal Doctrine." In *The Common Tradition: Lawyers, Books, and the Law*, edited by J. H. Baker, 37–51. London: Hambledon Press.

Baker, J. H. and S. E. Thorne, eds. 1990. *Readings and Moots at the Inns of Court in the Fifteenth Century, Volume II: Moots and Readers' Cases*. Selden Society, vol. 105. London.

Bellot, Hugh H. L. 1922. "Some Early Law Courts and the English Bar." *Law Quarterly Review* 38, no. 2: 168–84.

Braden, Gordon. 1985. *Renaissance Tragedy and the Senecan Tradition: Anger's Privilege*. New Haven: Yale University Press.

Brown, Felicity. 2021. "Sourcing *Misfortunes* Translation and Tragedy." *Early Theatre* 24, no. 2: 157–69.

Cunliffe, John W. 1893. *The Influence of Seneca on Elizabethan Tragedy: An Essay.* London: Macmillan and Co.

Cunningham, Karen. 2002. *Imaginary Betrayals: Subjectivity and the Discourses of Treason in Early Modern England.* Philadelphia: University of Pennsylvania Press.

Dugdale, William. 1666. *Origines Juridiciales, or Historical Memorials of the English Laws ....* London.

Elyot, Sir Thomas. 1962. *The Boke Named the Governor.* Edited by S. E. Lehmberg. London: Dent.

Fraunce, Abraham. 1588. *The Lavviers Logike Exemplifying the Præcepts of Logike by the Practise of the Common Lawe.* London.

Hughes, Thomas. 1587. *The Misfortunes of Arthur Certaine Deu[is]es and Shewes Presented to her Maiestie by the Gentlemen of Grayes-Inne at her Highnesse Court in Greenewich*, London.

Ker, James, and Jessica Winston, eds. 2012. *Elizabethan Seneca: Three Tragedies.* London: Modern Humanities Research Association.

Koller, Katherine. 1940. "Abraham Fraunce and Edmund Spenser." *English Literary History* 7, no. 2: 108–20.

McGlynn, Margaret. 2003. *The Royal Prerogative and the Learning of the Inns of Court.* Cambridge: Cambridge University Press.

Nuttall, Romola *et al.* 2021. "Introduction. Changing Fortunes: Reviving and Revisiting *The Misfortunes of Arthur.*" *Early Theatre* 24, no. 2: 121–38.

Perry, Curtis. 2011. "British Empire on the Eve of the Armada: Revisiting *Misfortunes of Arthur.*" *Studies in Philology* 108: 508–37.

Peters, Julie Stone. 2022. *Law as Performance: Theatricality, Spectatorship, and the Making of Law in Ancient, Medieval, and Early Modern Europe.* Oxford: Oxford University Press.

Prest, Wilfred. 2023. *The Inns of Court Under Elizabeth I and the Early Stuarts, 1590–1640.* 2nd ed. Cambridge: Cambridge University Press.

Seneca. 1566. [*Medea*] *The Seventh Tragedie of Seneca Entituled Medea.* Translated by John Studley. London.

CHAPTER 3

A 'Fellowship in Sin': John Donne and Community in the Lincoln's Inn Pulpit

Emma Rhatigan

Addressing his Lincoln's Inn congregation in 1618, John Donne provides them with a challenge:

> It is not enough for Christ Jesus to have prepared you the balm of his bloud, not enough for us, to minister it to you, except every one of you help himself, in a faithfull application, and help one another, in a holy and exemplar conversation. (2.93)[1]

I am grateful to Mary Ann Lund and Mary Morrissey for their comments on drafts of this chapter.

[1] All quotations from Donne's sermons are from Donne 1953–1962.

E. Rhatigan (✉)
English, University of Sheffield, Sheffield, UK
e-mail: e.k.rhatigan@shef.ac.uk

E. Rhatigan, J. Watson (eds.), *Mapping the Early Modern Inns of Court*, Early Modern Literature in History,
https://doi.org/10.1007/978-3-031-77445-4_3

Conversation in this period had the broader sense of 'consorting or having dealings with others . . . society, intimacy'.[2] Donne, then, is asserting that learning to live well with others, to live in and as a community, is essential to salvation. Such a challenge is peculiarly appropriate for the members of Lincoln's Inn. The inn was deeply invested in its status as a 'fellowship'; members took pride in the society's institutional identity and self-consciously asserted it in a variety of ways, from the architectural statement of their place in London, to the conspicuous consumption which accompanied the readings and Grand Days, to the social play of the revels, and weekly attendance at sermons in the chapel.

Donne, moreover, had first-hand experience of living as part of this very community. He was appointed preacher in 1616, but his connection to the society reached back to 1592 when he was entered as a member, after spending a year at Thavies Inn (Bald 1986: 53–79; Bullough 1972: 57–94). He remained at the inn until at least 1594, possibly until 1596. Life at the inns in 1592 and 1593 was severely disrupted by plague, but Donne kept three learning vacations. He was also appointed a master of the revels in 1592 and a steward of Christmas in 1594, although in the event Christmas festivities were not held in 1592 and he declined the office as steward in 1594. Donne formed close friendships at the inn, most notably with Christopher Brooke, Rowland Woodward, and Beaupré Bell. He wrote verse letters to Brooke, Woodward, and Bell in the 1590s and his poem 'The Storm', written from Essex's voyage to the Islands in 1598, was dedicated to Brooke. After he left, Donne continued to socialise with members of the inn, in particular Brooke and William Hakewill, who entered Lincoln's Inn in 1598. Donne and Brooke are listed as members of the Mitre Tavern circle in the anonymous Latin poem *Convivium Philosophicum* (*c.* 1611) and both contributed commendatory verses to Thomas Coryate's *Crudities* (1611). Coryate's letter to the 'Sireniacal' gentlemen at the Mermaid Tavern Club from India (1616) makes reference to Donne, Brooke, and Hakewill (Shapiro 1950; Bald 1986: 190–95; Cain 1995; O'Callaghan 1998: 97–98; O'Callaghan 2006). Donne was, then, especially well placed to address the congregation at Lincoln's Inn not just as a religious auditory, but as a society, invested in the celebration of their institutional identity and acutely aware of their professional, and also social, relationships.

[2] *Oxford English Dictionary*, s.v. "conversation (n.)," July 2023, https://doi.org/10.1093/OED/1997277413.

This reading of Donne both celebrating and exhorting his congregation to maintain their corporate identity sits comfortably with the positive inflection which historians have given to community in early modern England. Alexandra Shepard and Phil Withington have, for example, noted the prevailing 'rhetorical warmth' of the term even amid the changes in its uses and applications through the twentieth century (2000: 2). However, Donne's sermons at Lincoln's Inn point to the fact that 'conversation' is not always 'holy and exemplar' and that living in community brings its own temptations. Indeed, for Donne, any celebration of community is tempered by an awareness of the sociability of sin, the impulse 'to make other mens sins ours too, by drawing them to a fellowship in our sins' (2.101). His sermons thus point to the fact that community is not just often fractured and contested, as historians have increasingly acknowledged, but intrinsically morally ambiguous. Donne warns his congregation that there are not only dangers when community fails to cohere, but dangers when it does. Thus in this chapter I want to consider how Donne uses his sermons at Lincoln's Inn not only to reflect and strengthen his congregation's status as a society, but also to warn against the moral dangers of community. Despite, or perhaps even because, of his personal connection with the society, his sermons are permeated with an awareness that living in community can be spiritually corrupting as well as potentially edifying.

'Men of Thy *Calling*, or Thy *Profession*'

Donne's awareness of the significance of community at the inns is overtly expressed in his references to his congregation's shared professional identity. His sermons at the inns can take ostentatiously 'legal' biblical texts, for example the pair of sermons on John 5. 22 ('The father judgeth no man, but hath committed all judgement to the Sonne') and John 8. 15 ('I judge no man'), and are run through with legal metaphors and analogies. Thus, in a sermon on Psalm 38. 9 he describes how Holy Communion is a seal whereby his congregation can levy a fine on their sins which 'cuts off and concludes all titles' (2.156). In other words, man can be freed from the claims of his sins by reaching a final legal agreement. Donne directly addresses his congregation as lawyers, sometimes berating them for 'the iniquities, and injustices, admitted, and committed in *Courts of justice*', other times speaking more approvingly of 'the study of your profession' (2.117, 156). Noticeably, he is frequently careful, as here, to distinguish himself from their profession; it is 'your' profession not 'our' profession. As his congregation would have known, Donne had left the inn without being called to the bar, choosing not to pursue a legal career. However, this seems more than a self-conscious autobiographical allusion. Donne's distinction between lawyers and preachers draws attention to his own ambivalent position as both a 'worthy member' of the society (as the Lincoln's Inn records, the *Black Books*, called him), and a preacher, a role requiring a degree of distance and independence (Baildon 1897–2010: 2.229–30). Donne's unique perspective on the inn came from being both within and without of their fellowship.

Donne's treatment of professional identity is, however, complex; particularly telling are his references not just to his congregation's 'profession', but also their 'calling'. For example, in a sermon to the society on Psalm 38. 4 he specifically refers to 'sins as men of thy *calling*, or thy *profession*, cannot avoid' (2.104). 'Calling' here is not just a synonym for 'profession', though that is certainly one of the meanings in play. Mary Morrissey has explored how 'calling' is a word Donne specifically uses to think about community. For example, in his 1617 Accession Day sermon he warns his auditory that 'he that dies so, by withdrawing himself from his calling, from the labours of mutual society in this life, that man *kills himself*, and God calls him not' (Morrissey 2019; 1.210). 'Calling' in that sermon is a way of thinking about how a man might contribute to society. And crucially, making this contribution is a religious imperative; God calls those who attend to their 'calling'. This sense of 'calling' as a religious duty is also the direction of travel in Donne's use of the word at Lincoln's Inn. Developing his argument about the 'sins . . . of thy *calling*', Donne insists 'he that justifies his faults by his calling, hath not yet received that calling from above, whereby he must be justified, and sanctified in the way, and glorified in the end' (2.104–05). The *antanaclasis*, repetition of a word where the meaning changes in the second instance, allows Donne to move between professional calling and religious calling, but one is not merely an analogy for the other. Donne is asserting the fact that these are, in an important sense, the same thing. Being part of a profession, contributing to society, is bound up with belonging to the Church. We receive our calling on earth and we receive our calling from above, and these two callings are profoundly interconnected: to fulfil one's duty as a lawyer is part of fulfilling one's duty as a Christian. Donne explains, 'God hath instituted Callings, for the conservation of order in generall' (2.105). Hence, as he insists in a later sermon at Lincoln's Inn, 'Men should not retire from the mutuall duties of this world, to avoid offences, tentations, tribulations' (3.169). Salvation is found not in retirement, but in active participation in the 'mutual' duties of society.

Such words would have resonated at Lincoln's Inn. Sociability was central to life at the inns. Unlike the guilds, the inns were not incorporated and consequently they had to maintain their collective status by voluntary association (Baker 1986: 45–74). As Jessica Winston explains, this necessitated 'intentional practices of social relationship that served to create community' (2016: 40). Such practices included the daily routines of living and dining together 'in commons', the professional pedagogy of the legal exercises, and the recreation and play of the revels. They also included daily offices of friendship, conversation, and social exchange (Tosh 2016). The religious practices of attending sermons and receiving communion were also significant. At Lincoln's Inn, a pulpit was first erected in the chapel in 1571. Thus by the time Donne was appointed preacher weekly sermons during term time were an accepted part of life at the inn and, alongside receiving communion each term, a key expression of the society's sense of community (Fisher 1978: 146; Baildon 1897–2010: 2.379). Bound together in space and time in their chapel, the members' professional bonds were infused with spiritual significance. Thus for Donne's congregation attending to one's calling meant not just being a lawyer, but being a lawyer within a society. And that involved active participation in a series of dynamic and ongoing processes of creating community.

But just as Donne warns against 'retiring' or 'withdrawing' from your calling, the members of Lincoln's Inn's commitment to active participation in the society's fellowship was an area of tension (Prest 2023: 147). Winston has documented the strains that could exist between members who were seriously committed to their legal training, those who were using the inns of court as a kind of 'finishing school' while navigating patronage networks, and the senior lawyers (2016: 37). Given these varying types of engagement with the society it is not, perhaps, surprising that concerns about members not living 'in commons' recur in the *Black Books*. For example, on 14 May 1603 it is recorded that

> itt appeared unto us att this Counsaill, havinge consideracion of this o^{r} Fellowshipp, that divers and sundrie gentlemen of this House having chambers therein, and lodginge in the same . . . doe notwthstandinge dyatt themselves in the towne, and sever themselves from this Societie, to the prejudice and discreditt of themselves and of this House. (Baildon 1897–2010: 2.89)

The inn's 'fellowship' is put in jeopardy by members who 'sever' themselves from the society. Noticeably, this 'severing' is not necessarily absence. The order targets those who 'lodge' in the inn, but choose not to dine, or presumably socialise, in the society. The benchers are resistant to the inn being treated like a boarding house, rather than a community. Then, again, on 27 January 1620 the *Black Books* include a complaint against the 'very many' members who live out of Commons and 'doe hereby occation the neglect and decay of exercyses, and hinder the profitt of the Howse' (Baildon 1897–2010: 2.216). 'Profitt' seems to carry a financial sense—communal dining requires a certain level of participation to be financially sustainable—as well as referring to the benefit of maintaining the legal exercises and the more general good of maintaining the inn's fellowship.

To address such absent members, benchers were appointed 'to use such perswasions and meanes as they shall thinke fitt for the reducinge [them] into commons' (Baildon 1897–2010: 2.216). Noticeably, the verb 'reducing' could carry the sense of bringing a person back from error, sin, or immorality, as well as more generally restoring them to a particular place.[3] There was, then, potentially a moral inflection to the benchers' exhortations to keep 'commons' and maintain the 'House'. Similarly, the benchers' commitment to upholding the society's 'religion and good liff' was most likely motivated by their impulse to preserve the society's reputation and corporate identity, as much as it was a response to external pressure from the bishops and privy council to demonstrate the inns' religious conformity (Baildon 1897–2010: 2.66; Fisher 1978: 145–62; Donne 2015: xxv–xxvii). The *Black Books* regularly document the benchers' attempts to monitor those who failed to attend chapel and receive communion (Baildon 1897–2010: 2.45, 82, 87). However, as with living 'in commons', it seems reluctance to receive communion was an ongoing issue at the inn, and not one limited to recusants. On 2 May 1605 the *Black Books* record that although communion had been celebrated once each term, of the 140 people present usually no more than 40 had received and, on 27 November 1615, the Council bewailed a 'greate slacknesse in many gentlemen of this Howsse for theire not receiving of the Communion in the Chappell' (Baildon 1897–2010: 2.88, 171). This 'slacknesse' is perhaps not surprising during a period in which, as Arnold Hunt argues, 'Most people . . . saw no reason to receive communion more than once a year'

[3] *Oxford English Dictionary*, s.v. "reduce (v.)," March 2024, https://doi.org/10.1093/OED/2388480309.

(1998: 45). However, it is a further indication that the society's desire for expressions of religious cohesion may not have been matched by reality. Lincoln's Inn might have done better to follow the example of the Middle Temple, which, in 1614, reduced the requirement for members to receive communion three times a year, to twice, and then just once, a year (Hopwood 1903: 22, 43; Hunt 1998: 41). The *Black Books* do not make mention of sermon attendance, but it is tempting to speculate that this too was not always as regular as the benchers might have wished. Thomas Gataker, preacher at Lincoln's Inn 1602–1611, records how after noting that 'divers of the great practisers spent a great, if not the greatest part of [the Sabbath], the Afternoon especiallie, in *entertaining* of their *Clients*' he persuaded the benchers to move the usual Wednesday sermon to Sunday afternoon in order to gain 'a more du and diligent observance of the day' (1654: 16–17). Gataker's observation provides a telling context for Donne's insistence on the interconnection of religious and professional calling. Clearly for some of the lawyers the obligations of communal religious observance ran counter to their professional commitments, rather than giving expression to a legal identity rooted in belonging to the Church.

'I Was Fain to Sin, Lest I Should Lose My Credit'

Donne's insistence on the legal profession as a form of 'calling' would thus have been as challenging to his congregation, as it was affirming. And it is further telling that his particular concern with 'calling' in the sermon on Psalm 38. 4 is with the 'sins' of the legal calling. Indeed, Donne's attention to professional sins in this sermon is part of a much more detailed exploration of the ways in which sin is bound up with man's social identity. Donne starts by describing how community can dissuade us from doing good, since

> If any good purpose arise in us, we dare not pursue it, for fear of displeasing those, with whom we live, and to whom we have a relation, and a dependence upon them. We sin, and sin, and sin, lest our abstinence from sin, should work as an increpation, as a rebuke upon them that doe sin; for this they will call an ambition in us, that being their *inferiours*, we goe about to be their *betters*, if wee will needs be *better*, that is, less vicious then they. (2.101)

In the context of Lincoln's Inn 'those with whom we live' specifically evokes the corporate life of the society, whereby members lived, dined, studied, and socialised together. However, Donne's reference to those 'to whom we have a relation, and a dependence upon' and his acute analysis of how perceived social aspiration, 'ambition', might affect social relations also points to tensions evoked by class status at the inns. Social rank and an individual's position within the hierarchy of the inn did not always correlate. For example, on 23 October 1611 Sir Francis Russell, grandson and an heir apparent to the earl of Bedford, one of the richest peers in the country, was made an associate to the bench, an honorary position which gave a member all the privileges of the bench except a vote or voice in the government of the inn (Prest 2023: 87, 91). However, the *Black Books* are emphatic that Russell should 'sit at the Bench first at the seconde messe after the first messe of Aunciente Benchers, to whome the first place at the Benche is due for the Governmente of the House' (Baildon 1897–2010: 2.140). Russell's status is recognised, but within the inn he is not given precedence over the benchers. Moreover, as Jackie Watson demonstrates in Chap. 4, the inns were home to some fiercely ambitious men who were keen to advance their social status. Watson describes how the institutional identity of the Middle Temple in the early seventeenth century was distinctive in the extent to which it was shaped by a core of men who were 'more aspirational than established', but the *Black Books* indicate that Lincoln's Inn was not immune from displays of social competition and jealousy. For instance, on 11 June 1616 they record the benchers' condemnation of 'tumultuous and uncivill strivinge for places or precedencye' at the reader's table (Baildon 1897–2010: 2.183). Such social jostling could disrupt a society's religious fellowship no less than its professional fellowship; hence a complaint from the students at the Middle Temple in 1620 that the master of the Temple had given precedence to the students of the Inner Temple by administering communion to them first (Hopwood 1903: 49; Hunt 1998: 48–49). Indeed, it was not unheard of for such tensions at the inns to break out into violence, even more extreme than 'uncivill strivinge'.[4] Most likely only the most serious instances were recorded in the *Black Books*, but there we read of Mr Wattes fined for 'strikinge' the Pannyerman 'with a cudgill' and 'drawinge his dagger' upon 'one Mr Holland, one of the Fellowes of this House', Henry Colt

[4] On the place of violence in the regulation of hierarchies of male status in this period, see Shepard 2003: 127–51.

who 'did strike the . . . Steward with a cudgell or bastinado upon the heade', Mr Johnson 'expulsed' because he hath 'stroken and beaten George Lutwich, the Chief Butler, with a cudgell, whereby one of his ribbes was broken', Mr Thomas Windham, put out of commons for 'striking a labourer on the works of the House, with his fist', John Baber and John Webbe fined for 'strikinge and stabbinge' in the hall, and Mr Edwyn Riche fined for 'beating and strikinge' the 4th Butler 'wth a baston or cudgell' (Baildon 1897–2010: 2.55, 101, 127, 135, 199, 227). Noticeably most of these incidents involved violence being perpetrated on servants in the inn. This seems, however, less likely to be because tensions between members and servants were greater in number or degree than those among members, but rather because servants took the brunt of the frustrations of a contingent of volatile young men, highly attuned and sensitive to any social slights. Such violence could be viewed as a lingering example of the aristocratic violence, which, as Laurence Stone has argued, was only just being taken into the control of the state in the late sixteenth and early seventeenth centuries (Stone 1965: 223–34). However, violence was not tolerated by the society, whether it be against servants or a fellow member (Prest 2023: 127–30). Indeed, as Penelope Geng demonstrates in Chap. 6, the inns took their moral duty to their servants seriously. In 1588, Lincoln's Inn decreed that assaults on 'any gent. of this Howse' or 'any of the officers of this Howse' would result in the offender being put out of commons and required to pay a fine before he was re-admitted (Baildon 1897–2010: 2.8) and on all the occasions described above the benchers acted quickly to fine and in some cases 'expulse' the perpetrators. However, of those expelled most were subsequently restored, leaving the inn's fellowship to contain any remaining animosities and resentments. Donne's congregation would thus have been peculiarly attuned to the risk of being accused of social 'ambition' while also, ironically, being susceptible to the danger of compromising their morality in order to maintain relationships that might facilitate social progression.

As he develops his argument, Donne proceeds to explore not just how social ties can distort man's moral compass, but how sin itself can become social. He warns that man has a 'covetousnesse' of sin, 'a way, to make other mens sins ours too, by drawing them to a fellowship in our sins' (2. 101). The deployment of the term 'fellowship' here is no doubt deliberate. Donne draws on the conventional language of community deployed by the inn, as for instance in the example discussed earlier when the benchers' 'consideracion of this o^{r} Fellowshipp' led them to take action against those not living in commons, but audaciously attributes it the opposite moral inflection. The society's 'fellowship' of professional, civic, and religious virtue is refigured as one of vice. Of course Donne's own years at Lincoln's Inn would have given him first-hand experience of just such a 'covetousnesse' of sin, as many in the congregation would have been well aware. Christopher Brooke would, most likely, have been seated prominently in the congregation as Donne preached. Brookes's friendship with Donne had led to his involvement in Donne's scandalous secret marriage less than twenty years earlier; he gave away the bride and his brother Samuel performed the ceremony. When Donne eventually confessed to the marriage, Brooke ended up being committed to prison; his loyalty repaid with a stay at the Marshalsea. The episode would have demonstrated how the very relationships celebrated within the homosocial world of the inns could put an individual on the wrong side of the authorities. To illustrate his point, Donne proceeds to analyse the different relationships which can make us vulnerable to sin. He considers 'sins of our fathers', sins which make us 'come to say, My father thriv'd well in this course, why should not I proceed in it?'; sins of 'the *Times*,' warning that we cannot blame our sins 'upon the present ill disposition that reigns in men now, and doe ill, because everybody else does so'; and 'sins of your years'; before reaching the 'sins as men of thy *calling*, or thy *profession*, cannot avoid'. He pointedly ventriloquises a lawyer's fear that 'I shall not be beleeved to understand my profession, as well as other men, if I live not by it, as well as other men doe'. Finally, he addresses sins we might seek to excuse 'upon the unjust command of thy superiour' (2.102–05). Donne thus offers a forensic analysis of the ways man is constituted by bonds of family, friendship, profession, and society and how all these relationships can lead to sin.

Such analysis could have general application, but it must have been particularly resonant when voiced by Donne at Lincoln's Inn. Donne was himself connected to the inn by his 'fathers' and by his 'superiors'. He had long-standing family connections with Lincoln's Inn. His great uncles William Rastell, justice of the queen's bench, and Richard Heywood, prothonotary of the king's bench, were both members of Lincoln's Inn, as was Richard Heywood's son, John. Thomas More, Donne's mother's illustrious great-uncle, had also been a distinguished member of the inn, together with his brother John and his son-in-law William Roper. In Donne's own generation, his brother-in-law, Avery Copley, first husband of his sister Anne, was a barrister in the society (Bald 1986: 49). His return to the inn as preacher was, moreover, undoubtedly facilitated by networks of friendship and patronage. After Donne left Lincoln's Inn his student friends, men such as Christopher Brooke and William Hakewill, continued their legal studies and rose through the society's ranks. Brooke became a bencher in 1610 and autumn reader in 1614. Hakewill was called to the bar in 1606 and would become a bencher in 1618. Such men would thus have been well placed to facilitate Donne's employment as preacher. Speaking from the Lincoln's Inn pulpit, Donne would have been living testimony to the power of familial ties and the obligations of patronage. And, of course, the innsmen in Donne's congregation would also have been negotiating their place in the webs of friendship and patronage which operated within and beyond the inns (Tosh 2016). One of the most notorious instances of violence in the inns, involving John Davies and Donne's friend Richard Martin, provides a case in point. On 9 February 1598 a series of personal attacks on Davies during the 1597–1598 revels came to a head when Davies entered the hall of the Middle Temple and struck Martin over the head with a bastinado. In Chap. 4 Watson describes how much of the tension between these men stemmed from mockery of Davies's lower class roots and social aspirations. However, as Michelle O'Callaghan has argued, the attacks may also have been 'fuelled by factional infighting between Raleigh and Essex spilling over into the inns', in other words by political and social loyalties which cut across the institutional bond the men shared as members of the Middle Temple (2007: 31–32). The inns were not hermetically sealed from the outside world and innsmen's loyalties to their community co-existed with, and had to be negotiated alongside, the bonds of family, patronage, and political alliance.

Donne concludes his taxonomy of man's social constitution by asserting that it is the fact that man is bound to Adam and humanity which makes him accountable for the burden of original sin. He explains how 'it make no difference, in this spirituall debt, of that sin, *who is first in the bond*: *Adam* may stand first, but yet thou art no surety but a Principall, and for thy selfe; and he, and thou are equally subject to the penalty' (2.105). In this 'bond' no descendant of Adam appears merely as a 'surety' or guarantor, but all are liable as 'Principalls'. The metaphor of credit is pertinent and resonates with the complexities of credit relations in the period (Muldrew 1998). In its immediate context it speaks to the debt of original sin, but it also expresses the complex web of obligations and dependence which Donne has just described as intrinsic to man's social existence. The idea of 'credit' recurs in a different form when Donne returns to think once again about the way man values himself and his social reputation. Turning to a favourite source in his early Lincoln's Inn sermons, Donne elaborates on the words of Augustine who, he says, confesses

> I was fain to sin, lest I should lose my credit, and be under-valued; *Et ubi non suberat, quo admisso, æquarer perditis*, when I had no means to doe some sins, whereby I might be equall to my fellow, *Fingebam me fecisse quod non feceram, ne viderer abjectior, quo innocentior*, I would bely my self, and say I had done that, which I never did, lest I should be under-valued for not having done it. (2.107)

Credit here is both self-worth and social standing, our 'value' among our 'fellows', what Craig Muldrew describes as 'a public means of social communication and circulating judgement about the value of other members of communities' (1998: 2). But the currency in this economy is sin. It is sin which can make us 'equall' to our peers. Again, it is striking when Donne's words are read alongside the inn's conventional rhetoric of 'fellowship'. When the benchers complained about those members who 'severed' themselves from the society's 'Fellowshipp' they were specifically concerned that they did so 'to the prejudice and discreditt of themselves and of this House'. Once again Donne is appropriating the society's language in order to challenge their assumptions. 'Fellowship' and 'credit' are re-evaluated as social imperatives which can make us susceptible to sin.

Donne's sermon on Psalm 38. 4 is particularly concerned with the ways relationships can lead to sin, but it does not stand alone. In an earlier sermon in the same series on Psalm 38 Donne describes the temptation to return to sin in very similar terms. As prompted by his text, Psalm 38. 2 ('For thine arrowes stick fast in me, and thy hand presseth me sore'), Donne's central metaphor for sin in this sermon is the arrow. Thus he tells his congregation:

> After wee have parled with a tentation, debated whether we should embrace it or no, and entertain'd some discourse with it, though some tendernesse, some remorse, make us turn our back upon it, and depart a little from it, yet the arrow overtakes us; some *reclinations*, some *retrospects* we have, a little of *Lots wife* is in us, a little *sociablenesse*, and *conversation*, a little point of *honour*, not to be false to former promises, a little *false gratitude*, and thankfulnesse, in respect of former obligations, a little of the *compassion* and *charity* of Hell, that another should not be miserable, for want of *us*, a little of

> this, which is but the good nature of the *Devill*, arrests us, stops us, fixes us, till the arrow, the tentation shoot us in the back, even when wee had a purpose of departing from that sin, and kil us over again. (257–58)

As in the sermon on Psalm 38. 4 it is specifically '*sociablenesse*, and *conversation*' which exposes man to sin. The concern 'not to be false to former promises' or to be overly respectful to 'formal obligations' suggests, once again, the various ties of professional loyalty and patronage which constituted his congregation's social lives. The reference to 'point of *honour*' brings to mind the struggles over precedence recorded in the hall at Lincoln's Inn and in the Temple Church. The betrayal of the arrow shot in the 'back' captures, moreover, the counterintuitive logic which Donne is elaborating. The danger of these sins lies in their apparent 'virtue'; '*compassion*', '*charity*' and 'good nature', the values which should underpin social living, expose us to temptation. Sin is profoundly and troublingly 'social'.

'A Scandalous Act'

Social binds can lead us to sin, but Donne also explores the more complex dynamic of social living whereby even a man who resists the social impetus to sin can be left spiritually vulnerable by the sins of his peers. Thus he explains in his second sermon on Psalm 38. 4 how 'as Christ feels all the afflictions of his children, so his children will feel all the wounds that are inflicted upon him; even the sins of other men'. Speaking not of his *own* sins, but those of *others*, Donne claims 'I cannot chuse but feel a weight, a burthen of a holy anguish, and compassion and indignation, because every one of these sins inflict a new wound upon my Saviour'. He continues, 'when my Saviour says to him, that does but injure me, *Why persecutest thou me*, and feels the blow upon himselfe, shall not I say to him that wounds my Saviour, *Why woundest thou me*, and groane under the weight of my brothers sin' (2.121–22). The complex movement between pronouns encapsulates Donne's argument. Any sin, wherever it is directed, wounds Christ, and as members of Christ's church we too 'groane under the weight' of the sins of our fellow men. At Lincoln's Inn, this argument becomes most affective when Donne frames it in the language of 'calling' and 'profession'. He describes how 'If a man of my calling, or *profession*, doe a scandalous act, I feel my self concerned in his fault; God hath made all *mankinde* of *one blood*, and all *Christians* of *one calling*, and the sins of every man concern every man' (2.122). As Donne's twentieth-century editors, George Potter and Evelyn Simpson observe, Donne's language anticipates his famous passage on the interconnectedness of mankind in his *Devotions upon Emergent Occasions*, where he meditates 'No Man is an *Iland*, intire of it selfe . . . Any Mans *death* diminishes *me*, because I am involved in *Mankinde*' (Donne 1987: 87; Donne 1953–1962: 2.122). Here, however, the emphasis on 'calling, or *profession*' attunes it to Lincoln's Inn. Donne's wider point is that any sin undermines the Church, but the specific example which he directs to his Lincoln's Inn congregation is that the sin of any lawyer implicates his professional colleagues.

It is significant that in this exploration of sin and fellow feeling Donne speaks of a member of his 'profession' committing a 'scandalous act'. 'Scandalous' here refers not to an act which generates slander or gossip, but to the specific theological term 'scandal' which, derived from the Greek *skándalon*, meaning 'stumbling block', was used for a sin which leads another to sin. These two meanings can, of course coalesce, as was the case with some of the love poetry Donne wrote during, or shortly after, his student years at Lincoln's Inn. When the speaker in the 'Elegy to his Mistress on Going Abroad' describes 'that remorse / Which my words' masculine, persuasive force / Begot in thee' he is providing an example of how he and his persuasive rhetoric have drawn his mistress into sin (Donne 2010: l. 3–5). But subsequently it seems Donne found himself navigating the scandalous reputation created by such poems. In the letters he wrote to George More defending his secret marriage to More's daughter he makes reference to 'that fault which was layd to me, of hauing deceiud some gentlewoman before' (Folger MS L.b.529). Evidently Donne had become the subject of gossip. In the pulpit Donne explains to his Lincoln's Inn congregation that

> The word from which scandall is derived (*scazein*) signifies *claudicare*, to halt; and thence, a scandall is any trap, or Engin, any occasion of stumbling, and laming, hid in the way that I must goe, by another person. (3.171–72)

Scandal is thus a distinctly social sin, a sin rooted in the interactions between two or more people acting in response to each other. As Donne himself acknowledges, it was a doctrine 'seldome touched upon' in early seventeenth-century sermons and when it was treated it tended to be in controversial writings on the Oath of Allegiance or the status of ceremonies in the Church (3.158). Thus an *Early English Books Online* search of works printed between 1616 and 1622, the years when Donne was preaching at Lincoln's Inn, reveals that the term is used by far the most frequently in Thomas Morton's *A Defence of the Innocencie of the Three Ceremonies of the Church of England* (1618). As we will see, there is a political dimension to some of Donne's remarks on scandal when he considers those who are 'scandalized' by 'forged rumours' of Catholic victories, but for the most part his attention to the doctrine is rooted in a pastoral concern with the dangers of communal living, and this is unusual. It is also striking and further evidence of his attention to his congregation's corporate identity that Donne preaches on scandal more frequently in the Lincoln's Inn pulpit than any other.[5]

Donne's most extended attention to scandal comes in the second of two sermons on Matthew 18. 7. Here he provides a characteristically detailed dissection of the sin. He starts by distinguishing between 'active scandal', 'a malice . . . in *giving* offence', and 'passive scandall', 'an easinesse in taking offence' (3.171). He then takes his congregation through a series of subcategories, drawing out the various and subtle ways in which human relationships can erode man's relationship with God. He starts with 'Active Scandall', explaining that

> to doe any thing that is naturally ill, formally sin, whereby another may be occasioned or encouraged by my example to do the like, this is the active scandall most evidently, and most directly, and this is *morbus complicatus*, a disease that carries another disease in it, a fever exalted to a frenzy; It is *Peccatum prægnans, peccatum gravidum*, a spauning sin, a sin of multiplication . . . to lead another into tentation. (3.172)

As Katrin Ettenhuber observes, Donne's understanding of scandal here is rooted in a sense of 'moral contagion' (Donne 2015: 189). Scandal is a form of 'disease' whereby one infection leads to another, 'spauning' and 'multiplying' the original fault. This sense of multiplication is then effectively replicated in the structure of Donne's sermon as he turns to consider five 'lesser degrees' of scandal. His analysis is highly forensic, taking in scenarios such as 'To doe any thing that in it selfe is *indifferent* . . . in the sight of another that thinks it not indifferent, but unlawfull, and yet because he hath a reall, or a reverentiall dependence upon me . . . does it

[5] Donne also addresses the sin of scandal in his sermon preached at Paul's Cross to the city corporation on 22 November 1629.

against his conscience by my example' (3.172). Donne's Lincoln's Inn congregation no doubt appreciated the legalistic detail of his analysis, but the subtle delineation of the webs of social dependency would have been pertinent to them not just as lawyers, but as a *community* of lawyers. The recurring circumstance throughout each 'degree' of active scandal is 'dependency'. Donne describes how it is 'dependency', whether 'reall' or 'reverentiall', expressed through the promise of 'preferment' or the 'intimidation of one in power', which can lead to the corruption of human relations. As Donne concludes, 'there is scarce any so free to himselfe, so entirely his own, so independent upon others, but that Example, or Perswasion, or Fear, or Love may scandalize him' (3.174). 'No Man is an *Island*, intire of it selfe', indeed.

Moving on to consider 'passive scandal', the sin of taking offence where none was intended, Donne's treatment of his topic becomes more politicised. Considering the spiritual dangers of being 'scandalized', Donne speaks to popular anxieties surrounding James VI and I's reluctance to support the Protestant cause on the continent and his decision instead to pursue an alliance with Spain and a Spanish bride for Prince Charles. He warns against becoming an easily scandalised Christian who 'stays not to give men their Law, to give Princes, and States time to consider, whether it may not be fit for them to come to leagues, and alliances, and declarations for the assistance of the Cause of Religion next year, though not this' (3.179). Donne's specific example looks beyond Lincoln's Inn, but the complex dynamic of passive scandal would also have spoken to the tensions surrounding religious observation at the inns. The benchers' anxieties about the low numbers of members receiving Holy Communion clearly stemmed out of an anxiety that such behaviour set a bad example, a form of active scandal. However, Donne's discussion of passive scandal raises the further risk of misinterpreting a failure to communicate as recusancy, of seeing sin where there is none. It is perhaps significant that Donne himself had been a victim of comparable misinterpretation. Following his ordination, he complained of Lady Bedford that 'she had more suspicion of my calling, a better memory of my past life, then I had thought her nobility could have admitted' (Donne 1651: 2F1^{v}).

For Donne, the response to scandal, be it active or passive scandal, can be nothing less than the removal of one's self from the social binds which have led to sin. Citing Matthew 18. 8–9, where Christ orders his followers to 'cut off' the hand or foot which leads them to sin, Donne insists,

> Though hee bee the foot upon which thou standest, thy Master, thy Patron, thy Benefactor; Though hee be thy hand by which thou gettest thy living, thy meanes, the instrument of thy maintenance, or preferment . . . if hee scandalize thee, shake thee in thy Religion at the heart, or in the ways of godlinesse in thine actions, Cut him off; that is, cut off thy selfe from that conversation. (3.179–80)

If 'conversation' and social interaction are not 'holy', but rather 'scandalising', then they must cease. The binds of dependency—'means', 'maintenance' and 'preferment'—which Donne delineated so carefully in the first half of the sermon must be ruptured. If Donne's starting point in the sermon was the infectious 'disease' of scandal, then his remedy is 'Christ's physique' of self-isolation. At Lincoln's Inn this constitutes a stark warning; no matter how strong the society's bonds of professionalism, friendship, and patronage, these cannot take precedence over their relationship with God.

Conclusion

Community and fellowship were fundamental to the inns of court, underpinning their institutional identity. At Lincoln's Inn Donne had first-hand experience of this fellowship, as both a student member and then as the society's preacher. However, preaching in the society's pulpit he also represented a further manifestation of community: the Christian community of the Church. Indeed, it seems likely that it was Donne's ability to connect these two understandings of community which helped cement his place in the society's affections; when he left in 1623 the benchers claimed they were 'loath wholly to part wth him' (Baildon 1897–2010: 2.229–30). Drawing on the language of 'calling' Donne fused professional and religious calling, developing a rhetoric of corporate identity which would have spoken directly to his congregation's conception of themselves as a community of lawyers, playing their part in the still broader Christian community of the Church. However, neither Donne, tasked with the pastoral care of leading his congregation to Christ, nor the benchers, meeting regularly to maintain their fellowship by a combination of regulation and encouragement, were naïve in their assertions of the natural good of community. Both were acutely aware that community was something which had to be actively constructed and reconstructed in the light of various changing and competing allegiances. And to participate in community, whether it be dining in 'commons' in the hall or receiving Holy Communion in the chapel meant committing to this dynamic process. Donne, however, challenged his Lincoln's Inn congregation yet further in their thinking on community, demanding that they consider the moral dangers inherent in human relationships. Indeed, by emphasising how relationships can distort our moral parameters Donne provided a counter-image of community as a 'fellowship of sin' which interrogates our contemporary assumptions about seventeenth-century celebrations of community, as much as it would have unsettled his Lincoln's Inn congregation. If Donne's sermons demanded that the benchers re-evaluated their habitual rhetoric of fellowship, then so too must scholars query any easy assumption that community was a self-evident ideal. In Donne's sermons at Lincoln's Inn, community emerges as a more ambiguous good; a centripetal force that required both critical reflection and self-conscious scrutiny.

Works Cited

Baildon, W. P., ed. 1897–2010. *The Records of the Honourable Society of Lincoln's Inn: The Black Books*. London: Lincoln's Inn.

Baker, John. 1986. "The Inns of Court and Chancery as Voluntary Associations." In *The Legal Profession and the Common Law: Historical Essays*, edited by John Baker, 45–74. London: Hambledon Press.

Bald, R. C. 1986. *John Donne: A Life*. Reissued. Oxford: Oxford University Press.

Bullough, Geoffrey. 1972. "Donne The Man of Law." In *Just So Much Honor: Essays Commemorating the Four-Hundredth Anniversary of the Birth of John Donne*, edited by Peter Amadeus Fiore, 57–94. University Park, PA: Pennsylvania University State.

Cain, Tom. 1995. "Donne and the Prince D'Amour." *John Donne Journal* 14: 83–111.

Donne, John. 2015. *The Oxford Edition of the Sermons of John Donne Volume V, Sermons Preached at Lincoln's Inn*. Edited by Katrin Ettenhuber. Oxford: Oxford University Press.

———. 2010. *The Complete Poems of John Donne*. Edited by Robin Robbins. Harlow: Pearson.

———. 1987. *John Donne's Devotions Upon Emergent Occasions*. Edited by Anthony Raspa. New York and Oxford: Oxford University Press.

———. 1953–1962. *The Sermons of John Donne*. Edited by George R. Potter and Evelyn M. Simpson. 10 vols. Berkeley and Los Angeles: University of California Press.

———. 1651. *Letters to Severall Persons of Honour*. London.

Fisher, R. M. 1978. "The Origins of the Divinity Lectureships at the Inns of Court, 1596–85." *Journal of Ecclesiastical History* 29, no. 2: 145–62.

Folger. Manuscript L.b.529.

Gataker, Thomas. 1654. *A Discours Apologetical*. London.

Hopwood, C. H., ed. 1903. *A Calendar of the Middle Temple Records*. London: Middle Temple.

Hunt, Arnold. 1998. "The Lord's Supper in Early Modern England." *Past and Present* 161: 39–83.

Morrissey, Mary. 2019. "Donne and the Church". Unpublished manuscript.

Muldrew, Craig. 1998. *The Economy of Obligation: The Culture of Credit and Social Relations in Early Modern England*. Basingstoke: Palgrave.

O'Callaghan, Michelle. 2007. *The English Wits: Literature and Sociability in Early Modern England*. Cambridge: Cambridge University Press.

———. 2006. "Patrons of the Mermaid tavern (act. 1611)." *Oxford Dictionary of National Biography*. Accessed 4 Apr. 2024. https://www.oxforddnb.com/view/10.1093/ref:odnb/9780198614128.001.0001/odnb-9780198614128-e-95279.

———. 1998. "'Talking Politics': Tyranny, Parliament, and Christopher Brookes *The Ghost of Richard The Third* (1614)." *The Historical Journal* 41: 97–120.

Prest, Wilfrid. 2023. *The Inns of Court Under Elizabeth I and the Early Stuarts, 1590–1640*. 2nd ed. Cambridge: Cambridge University Press.

Shapiro, I. A. 1950. "The 'Mermaid Club'." *Modern Language Review* 45: 6–17.

Alexandra Shepard. 2003. *Meanings of Manhood in Early Modern England*. Oxford: Oxford University Press.

Shepard, Alexandra, and Phil Withington. 2000. "Introduction: Communities in Early Modern England." In *Communities in Early Modern England*, edited by Alexandra Shepard and Phil Withington, 1–15. Manchester and New York: Manchester University Press.

Stone, Lawrence. 1965. *The Crisis of the Aristocracy, 1558–1641*. Oxford: Clarendon Press.

Tosh, Will. 2016. *Male Friendship and Testimonies of Love in Shakespeare's England*. London: Palgrave Macmillan.

Winston, Jessica. 2016. *Lawyers at Play: Literature, Law, and Politics at the Early Modern Inns of Court, 1558–1581*. Oxford: Oxford University Press.

CHAPTER 4

'Observe Him for the Love of Mockery': Revelry, Satire, and Performance in the Late Elizabethan Middle Temple

Jackie Watson

Sir Andrew: Shall we set about some revels?
Sir Toby: What shall we do else?
(1.3.133–35)[1]

Revelry is a complex term in early modern England. It encompassed the great enjoyment of the participants, as well as the lack of restraint and the transgression associated with their activities. Yet, as well as this now more usually understood concept of merry making, the verb also had alternative meanings of squandering or wasting time or money.[2] This gives an alternative sense of the expense of such enjoyments, and the lack of gain for

[1] All references to *Twelfth Night* are to Shakespeare 2008.
[2] *Oxford English Dictionary*, s.v. "revel (v.1)," March 2024, https://doi.org/10.1093/OED/4424735167.

J. Watson (✉)
Independent Scholar, Oxford, UK
e-mail: jacqueline.watson@some.ox.ac.uk

E. Rhatigan, J. Watson (eds.), *Mapping the Early Modern Inns of Court*, Early Modern Literature in History,
https://doi.org/10.1007/978-3-031-77445-4_4

financial outlay; it engages with the value Protestant England placed on work and the importance of time spent fruitfully. Revelry is thus an activity that Malvolio judges to be morally questionable, linked as revels so often were with the sinful activities of over-eating, drinking, and dancing so disapproved of by puritans (see Stubbes 1583: D6^{r}, D8^{r}, L5^{r}, M7^{v}). It is appropriate to associate it with Sir Toby or Sir Andrew, and in performance the opening quotation from *Twelfth Night* has the collusive feel of an invitation to the audience to join in, and to enjoy the revelry of the play to come. After the introduction of the romance plot and of Viola in female garb, the invitation encourages us to see the first entry of Cesario as a shift in tone: as if the revels proper are commencing. Through an examination of revelry, this chapter aims to demonstrate the importance to *Twelfth Night* of one of its earliest playing spaces, Middle Temple hall, and to show just how closely the play is connected to this institution. Connecting the play to a specific Christmas revels held at Middle Temple shortly before its first performance argues a close link between the nature of the inn at the end of Elizabeth's reign and transgression in Shakespeare's play

Innsmen and Revelry

Firstly, we must establish the nature and importance of the inns of court revels, quasi-official festivities that echoed court life. They shared many qualities of revelry more broadly, but also formed a key part of the educative process; as they are in many ways so anti-establishment, this can appear rather counter-intuitive. The official nature of the term is preserved in the title 'master of the revels', a post held by individuals at the inns as well by the official who scrutinised play scripts for the queen, but it was a pattern seen throughout Elizabethan society. Although Stubbes refers to the more lowly custom of lords of misrule throughout the land, rather than at a London institution such as an inn of court, his comments demonstrate equally his objections to the latter's Christmas revels:

> all the wilde-heds of the Parish, conuenting together, chuse them a Graund-Captain (of all mischeefe) whome they innoble with the title of my Lord of Misrule, and him they crowne with great solemnitie, and adopt for their king. This king anointed, chuseth forth, twentie, fortie, threescore or a hundred lustie Guttes like to him self to waighte vppon his lordly Maiestie, and to guarde his noble person. Then euerie one of these his men, he inuesteth with his liueries, of green, yellow or some other light wanton colour. (1583: M2^{r})

At the inns, the revels were an intermittent feature of Christmas festivities, held when plague abated and students remained in London during the vacation. At Middle Temple on 25 November 1597, five years before *Twelfth Night* was to be performed in the hall next to the parliament chamber, it was declared that 'the feast of Christmas shall be celebrated solemnly'. This gave permission for the students to engage in some very complex and expensive arrangements.

In addition to fear of plague, over which they clearly had no power, those in charge of the inns were also anxious about the consequences of uncontrolled student behaviour during the revels. Some of the leaders of the 1597/1598 activities had previously been involved in behaviour which incurred punishment. On 11 February 1592, for example, there is a record concerning Richard Martin and John Davies, whose crime, committed nine days earlier, was the violation of the inn's order forbidding official revelling:

> In spite of the orders against a Lord of Misrule on Candlemas, divers gentlemen of the House on last Candlemas night . . . broke open chamber doors and abused many gentlemen of the House, as appears by the examination of townsmen who were with them, and some of this Fellowship knew them notwithstanding their disguised attire.

The violence of their behaviour and their transgression of the rules of the inn show the men as well suited to revelry, and akin to Sir Toby Belch. Martin and another serial offender, a Mr. Fleetwood, were 'expelled for their misdemeanours and abuses to the Masters and Benchers', while it is reported that John Davies, with two others, 'shall be out of commons during the pleasure of the Masters and Benchers' (Martin 1904: 326–27).

By 1597/1598, these same men, still residing at the inn, had their wish and were allowed by the benchers to hold a 'solemn Christmas'. Martin played the Prince of Love, competing against Davies for this leading role. We know about their planning as the record of the revels, made by their friend Benjamin Rudyerd, went on to be published in 1660 as *Le Prince D'Amour*, or *Noctes Templariae*. The events recorded here demonstrate revelling's reliance on dramatic modes and show the vital nature of role-playing to law students. In a report written around 1540 by Sir Nicholas Bacon, Thomas Denton, and Robert Cary to inform Henry VIII how the inns functioned, the authors describe how at Christmas, if it is not a time of sickness, the inns:

> appoint and chose certain of the house to be Officers, and bear certain rules in the house during the said time, which Officers for the most part are such, as are exercised in the King's Highness house, and other Noble men. (Waterhouse 1663: 546)

The growth in the number of men studying at the inns in Elizabeth's reign is discussed by Philip J. Finkelpearl who estimates a 30 per cent increase over the last 30 years of the sixteenth century (1969: 5). However, it is worth remembering that students at the inns did not all aim to enter the legal profession. Rather, many were trained, through their humanist education, to work at the royal court or to become administrators or diplomats. Such a career necessitated a wide range of skills, as Sir John Fortescue commented:

> ther is in these greater Innes, yea, and in the lesser to[o], beside the study of the laws, as it were an vniuersity or schoole of all co[m]mendable qualities requisite for noblemen. There they learn to sing, & to exercise themselues in all kinde of harmony. There also they practise dauncing, & other Noble mens pastimes, as they vse to doe, which are brought vp in the kings house. (1616: 114^{v}–15^{r})

The report's authors defend participation in the revels on the grounds that the students imitate offices of state in them 'onely to the intent, that they should in time come to know how to use themselves'. As it was not possible for all young men required by the bureaucracy of the Tudor court to be 'brought up in the kings house', the inns aimed to supply the skills needed.

Despite the documented presence of a number of women in the revels audiences (see Nelson and Elliott 2012: 130), the environment where they were performed was almost wholly dependent on relationships between men. In such homosocial environments, as in grammar schools, universities, and, of course, playing companies, success relied on male friendships and patronage. With a humanist education which meant familiarity with classical texts such as Cicero's *De amicitia*, innsmen recognised both the potential emotional power of such relationships and their practical use. Gerard Legh, a member of Inner Temple, saw the ongoing importance of friendships men formed in the institutions: 'such unitie of minds and manners, as lightly never after is severed, then which is nothinge more profitable to the common-weale' (1576: fol. 119^{v}). Sir John Fortescue reinforces the importance innsmen place on male friendship when he argues that a suitable punishment for sedition is 'to be amooued from the campanye of their fellowship. Which punishment they do more feare, then other criminall offendors doe feare imprisonment and yrons' (1616: fol. 115^{v}), a commitment to community which tallies with that described by Emma Rhatigan in her discussion of the importance of 'fellowship' at Lincoln's Inn (see Chap. 3).

The Homosociality of *Twelfth Night*

The relationships between men in *Twelfth Night* should be seen in the context of homosocial spaces such as the inns of court. One relationship 'between men' draws attention to its nature by not being between men at all, and a second, the friendship of Sir Andrew and Sir Toby, is in many ways typical of those at the inns. One only has to consider John Manningham marrying the sister of his chamber mate, Edward Curle, to realise how often the quest for success and marriage into a friend's family went together. While we are privy to the greed and manipulation of Toby as he asks the knight to 'send for money' (2.3.186), and we suspect Andrew is being used, his presence at Olivia's house is quite within the bounds of typical male friendship. Equally typical is the adoption of a younger man as the favourite of an older male protector or patron, yet Viola's gender makes us consider this relationship afresh. As they enter together, the first time the audience see Cesario at Orsino's court, one of the Duke's courtiers, Valentine, draws attention to both the benefit of the relationship to the young man, and to the speed of its formation:

> If the Duke continue these favours towards you, Cesario, you are like to be much advanced: he hath known you but three days, and already you are no stranger. (1.4.1–4)

The emphasis on the exaggerated speed with which Cesario has caught the older man's affections makes the audience question the nature of such a bond. Though legitimised by the concealed gender of Viola, the relationship the Duke forms with Cesario demands that innsmen audience members re-examine aspirational patronage relationships. Orsino's immediate romantic feelings for Viola have been seen and accepted as the affection of a Duke for his young male courtier. The revelation of this error later in the play only makes an audience question the relationship further. Is the friendship between such men in a court environment not perceived as transgressive though equated to the feelings of a man for a woman?

Le Prince D'Amour is written for a largely 'in-group' male audience and demonstrates how revels performances used word play and innuendo to amuse and engage their spectators. As the revels court at the Middle Temple is that of the Prince of Love (surrounded by specially dubbed 'Knights of the Quiver' as well as the more usual Secretary, Treasurer, and so on), the opportunities for *double entendre* are manifold: the purpose clearly to create collusion between the men in the hall. While apparently flattering women, jokes betray the interests, fears, and insecurities of men. Of the many available, two will suffice to demonstrate the ubiquity of innuendo. The Prince's Lord President, undoubtedly representing the older barristers, is announced as follows:

> The President of the Councel is to give order for the Aged, that they may not be long standing; and if they urge any reason unto their Ladies, they follow it not effectually or to the point. (22–23)[3]

One can hear the echo of the schoolboy review, with unusual permission to mock their teachers and to use *double entendre* in public which is normally sniggered over in private. It continues:

> That proclamation be made, that any Gentlewoman being taken in the Armes of any Gentleman, be presumed to be his Sister, or his Cousin at the least, and that she be presumed to be no better then swowning, and he striving to put life into her . . . most of their deliberations be about the Seige of Sluce, the Battery of Brest, or sacking of Maidenhead. (23)

This coarseness also bubbles through the Sir Toby and Malvolio scenes in *Twelfth Night*. One remembers, for instance, Malvolio's apparently unconscious innuendo in his reference to Olivia's 'very Cs, her Us and her Ts', not to mention 'her great Ps' (2.5.88–89). A second example from the revels lies in the instructions to the appropriately named Knights of the Quiver, including the following:

> 2. Item, that every Knight of this Order shall still be well horsed and well armed, and have those things in readiness which Ladies desire, as the Launce for the Ring, and such like.

[3] All references to *Le Prince D'Amour* are to Rudyerd 1660.

> 3. Item, that no knight shall carry any Arrow in his Quiver, unless the head be a head of advantage, or very well steeled; and that he suffer not his Arrow heads to rust. (42–43)

This fear of 'rust[ing]' arrowheads picks up on a thread running through the revels: a fear of loss of manhood through impotence, castration, and venereal disease. Alongside the homosocial bonding of such an environment, Alexandra Shepard has argued, was a combative quality, illustrated very well through its ritualised violence (2003). In the revels, as more widely at the inns, this sat alongside the clearly collusive 'fraternal bonds which facilitated young men's inversions of patriarchal norms' and allowed them to challenge the men already embedded in positions of power. Shepard argues that '[w]hile these links were sufficiently important to overcome distinctions of social status, they were also brittle and fleeting because of fears surrounding male intimacy. An element of competition was therefore present between men even at this most homosocial phase of the life course' (2003: 16). Though presented in a humorous tone throughout *Le Prince D'Amour*, the sense of a man's need to perform, in all senses, is key.

Developing this concept of language as a form of ritualised violence, Lynne Magnusson has examined what she calls 'scoff power' at the inns, demonstrating that linguistic dexterity was used as a combative force in the 'elite male speech community [which was] a site for the production of wit as verbal injury and social classification' (2004: 197). Playing a role in an event such as the Middle Temple revels could undoubtedly provide a means to gain respect within the institution and display the linguistic merits of the performer. Not merely a way of excluding outsiders, she proposes 'there is strong evidence that mockery and verbal shaming also played an important role in shaping identity in their in-group communication' (2004: 205). One might conclude, therefore, that skill in the use of in-group language with common terms of reference, part of an innsman's habitus, both shows the supremacy of the individual and helps to bond together the homosocial actors and audience of the revels. As Middle Templar John Hoskins warned the young man for whom he wrote his manual, *Directions for Speech and Style*, 'Careless speech doth not only discredit the personage of the speaker but it doth discredit the opinion of his reason and judgment' (1935: 1–2). Again, one might think of Andrew Aguecheek, a man whose 'reason and judgement' are indeed discredited through his lack of linguistic skill. As Toby notes, with a final mocking syllable spoken aside, Andrew's epistolary challenge to Cesario is '[v]ery brief, and to exceeding good sense–less' (3.4.159–60). An innsman must use appropriate language to enact his role in society, as a man must act skilfully within a sexual relationship or in combat. Failure invited audience ridicule.

Playing His Part

Revels' roles demanded verbal skill, with named 'parts' for the Prince D'Amour's Secretary, a lord chamberlain, a lord chancellor, and a master of the horse, as well as the Lord (or Earl) Marshall, a role given by Elizabeth to the earl of Essex that very Christmas, on 28 December 1597. Sir William Dugdale's account in his *Origines Juridiciales* of a solemn Christmas, 'In the 4th year of Queen Eliz. reign' at Inner Temple, suggests that this was common (150).[4] Here the inn's ruler for the holiday season, Palaphilos, was played by Robert Dudley, with Christopher Hatton as his Master of the Game. Dugdale describes how Inner Templars contributed verbally and ceremonially while partaking in very lavish banquets. His focus on the food does not reduce his reader's consciousness of the role-play throughout; as gifts are laid before the potentate, ambassadors are presented, and Dugdale himself is created Knight of the Order of Pegasus in reward for his service to Palaphilos (152).

Dugdale's account gives a sense of the reception of such events beyond the confines of the inn. He frames his account with a description of his arrival in London, unaware of what was happening. Shocked to hear cannon fire, he asks a friendly looking citizen walking past to explain: 'It is, *quoth he*, a warning shot to the Constable Marshall of the Inner Temple, to prepare to Dinner'. Asking for further information, Dugdale is informed that the province concerned is 'A place . . . privileg'd by the most excellent Princess the high Governour of the whole Island, wherein are store of Gentlemen of the whole Realm, that repair thither to learn to rule and obey by Law, to yield their fleece to their Prince and Common weal' (151). The construction of his tale argues the esteem in which the revels are held throughout London and the admiration of a citizen achieves Dugdale's purpose here. The inns are lauded as places where men contribute to the status of England through their learning and are admired by the city on whose borders they sit. Though clearly admiration for the legal

[4] All references to Dugdale's *Origines Juridiciales* are to Dugdale 1666.

profession was not ubiquitous in early modern London, the interaction between the inns, their revels, and the wider city *was* typical. The Gray's Inn revels of 1594, recorded as the *Gesta Grayorum*, shows again the interaction between innsmen actors and a wider public audience. The Gray's Inn students, accompanied by others from Inner Temple, ride through the city streets to dinner with the (real) lord mayor:

> The next Day the Prince, accompanied with the Ambassador of *Templaria*, and attended by both Trains, took his Progress from his Court of *Graya*, to the Lord Mayor's House . . . This Shew was very stately and orderly performed; the Prince being mounted upon a rich Foot-cloth, the Ambassador likewise riding near him; the Gentlemen attending, with the Prince's Officers, and the Ambassador's Favourites, before; and the other coming behind the Prince . . . Thus they rode very gallantly, from *Grays-Inn*, through *Chancery-lane*, *Fleet-street*, so through *Cheap-side*, *Corn-hill*, and to *Cosby's Place*, in *Bishop's-gate-street*. (Greg 1914: 42–43)

After this dinner, they ride in state back again to the inn. The richness of their display suggests the immense expense of such spectacles, and the solemn Christmases held by the inns can be seen to be performed for those with influence in both city and court. The importance of performance is clear in the revelry, as is the revels' role in the students' acquisition of those skills which permitted future preferment.

The skills required by young men for success in a courtly career were in a wider sense performative. The ability to fit into an environment, verbally and visually, was vital, and playing the roles of men at the court of the Prince of Love gave Middle Templars the opportunity to practise both linguistic dexterity and the assumption of an effective appearance. As Dugdale explains, apart from learning the law, young men attend the inns 'to use all other exercises of body and mind whereunto nature most aptly serveth to adorn by Speaking, countenance, gesture, and use of Apparel the person of a Gentleman' (151), and one physical way in which this gentlemanly appearance could be fostered was through dance. The Henrician commission on the inns had commented that the gentlemen taking part in the Christmas revels 'have all manner of pastimes, as singing and dancing' (Waterhouse 1663: 546), and as Darren Royston has shown in his work on attitudes to dance and touch (2015), and Sharon Harris demonstrates in Chap. 7, the inns proved a training ground for this most courtly of skills. One well-known Middle Temple enthusiast was John

Davies, whose poem, *Orchestra*, explores in the mythological context of Penelope and Antinous the significance of dance in a court setting. But simple enthusiasm for dance was, in itself, insufficient to gain victory in the combative environment of the inns. A passion for the art was so much associated with Davies that few innsmen readers of Marston's *Scourge of Villainy* could mistake his presence behind the satirist's mockery of the dance enthusiast, 'Curio':

> Who ever heard spruce skipping Curio,
> E'er prate of ought, but of the whirl on toe . . .
> Did ever any ear e'er hear him speake
> Unless his tongue of cross-points did intreat? (H3[r–v])

Dance in this way forms another example of the appropriateness of Shakespeare's *Twelfth Night* for its Middle Temple audience, with Andrew Aguecheek's enthusiasm, as he 'delight[s] in masques and revels sometimes altogether' (1.3.111–112) and demands that 'we set about some revels' (ll. 133–34) after his demonstration of his skill in 'cut[ting] a caper' (l. 118). Toby's request that he displays his gifts in the galliard, the coranto, the jig, and the 'sink-a-pace' (ll. 125–28) while he undertakes his quotidian activities presupposes his audience's familiarity with the popular dance steps of his time. Indeed, a Middle Temple audience in 1602 was very likely to be not simply familiar with them in the abstract, but to be engaging in them during the very revels of which the play formed a Candlemas climax. The humour of the scene is only enhanced in this in-group environment, perhaps with the actor demonstrating a less-than-perfect execution of the dances. Davies's evident enthusiasm for dance in its abstract and poetic form is given the lie in Manningham's record of the verbal attack on his physical inelegance, made by one of his Middle Temple contemporaries: 'John Davies goes waddling with his arse out behind as though he were about to make every one that he meets a wall to piss against . . . He never walks but he carries a cloakbag behind him, his arse sticks out so far' (1868: 168). The likelihood of a man characterised thus performing dance steps in a pleasing fashion is as likely as the success of Andrew Aguecheek in his galliard. The ambitious young men who formed a large part of the Middle Temple audience were likely to understand the need to use dance, amongst other ways of presenting an appearance or playing a role, to affirm one's suitability for patronage and court life.

Clearly how a man appeared visually, how he used and clothed his body, was of parallel importance to his verbal dexterity. While the need to amuse others through *extempore* speaking, debating, and word play is clear, and is a key part of the 'rehearsal' encouraged by the inns, the revels also reveal the requirement to dress appropriately. Amongst many instructions to the Knights of the Quiver concerning apparel, one demonstrates the intensity of an innsman's desire to keep up with the ever-changing fashions of the time. A knight is advised to 'have the wit to mislike the fashion of his clothes before he pawn them; and . . . be always furnished with reasons for the convenience of every fashion' (45). This is accompanied by references to the ubiquity of tailors, haberdashers, and mercers, as well as the usual assumption that innsmen will have large tailor's bills. The revels, of course, rely for their humour on the mockery of behaviour which is instantly recognisable by the Middle Templars in the audience, and thus it is fascinating to see an admonishment against a man having 'his Picture . . . drawn in clothes transgressing the Statute of Apparel, himself being attired out of the compass of the Statute' (45). It appears that there were many potential pitfalls in the area of dress. Although the sumptuary laws were argued to have been more honoured in the breach than the observance, and were to be repealed by parliament in 1604, Elizabethan legal restrictions on the dress of each societal level were clear (Lublin 2011: 45). As Blessin Adams demonstrates in Chap. 5, dress was one of the regular topics of discussion amongst law students, and manuals giving advice on dress were translated by innsmen for their peers. Typically such advice can be found in Giovanni Della Casa's *Galateo*, translated initially into English by Robert Peterson of Lincoln's Inn. Here, young men are told: 'Your apparell must be shaped according to the fashion of the time . . . Euery man may applie those fashions, that be in common vse, the moste to his owne aduantage, that he can'. Della Casa warns men against wearing items which might be seen as 'Ganymedes hosen' or 'Cupides doublet', and thus cause ridicule (1576: 108–09).

That this was a period where a modish appearance was demanded by court life is demonstrated by both *Le Prince D'Amour* and *Twelfth Night*, as they show the potential peril of making the wrong choices of dress for the occasion. In a homosocial, combative context, where, as in the playhouse, one's verbal performance could secure the victory of audience approval or result in the loss of it, selecting the wrong costume could also condemn a man to be vanquished through audience ridicule. Rudyerd's account of the period leading up to the 1597/1598 revels reveals in a highly entertaining manner how the Prince's court took shape. These preliminary events expose a great deal about the *dramatis personae*. Key amongst this group is John Davies, or, as he is often labelled in the text, Stradilax. His behaviour illustrates well for our purposes an exaggerated version of the performative skills encouraged at the inns. His appearance on the Christmas Eve of the revels period, for instance, 'in a Marmelad-Colour-Taffata Gown' (82) suggests a man with the desire to attract attention. Perhaps, since we are told it 'was never seen after', the response to his flamboyance led him to believe it ill judged.

There is, of course, an echo of this misjudgement of dress in the trick played on Malvolio. Parodying the guidance on dress given by contemporary courtier manuals, Maria's letter advises the unfortunate steward to smile and wear yellow stockings, cross-gartered. As a result, he meets ridicule comparable to that experienced by Stradilax. In order to explain Malvolio's readiness to accept advice on his appearance, Shakespeare makes sure the audience see the character's grasp of the importance of performance and appearance. These will, he knows, be vital if he is to succeed in his social aspirations. In the lines preceding his finding of Maria's letter in the orchard, he is observed to be 'practising behaviour to his own shadow this half hour' (2.5.17–18), and, as the three tricksters watch, he enacts how he plans to respond when his 'kinsman Toby' is called for:

> I frown the while, and perchance wind up my watch, or play with my—some rich jewel. Toby approaches . . . I extend my hand to him thus, quenching my familiar smile with an austere regard of control. (ll. 59–67)

This rehearsal of his future behaviour, when he will 'have greatness thrust upon' him, will be key to his imagined success, and causes his ready agreement to 'be strange, stout, in yellow stockings, and cross-gartered' (ll. 171–72). For members of Shakespeare's Middle Temple audience, also socially aspirant, this is a warning not to transgress accepted sartorial norms when dressing to impress. It is clear why for one of them, John Manningham, this was key to the play. There was, he writes:

> A good practise in it to make the Steward believe his Lady widdowe was in love with him, by counterfeiting a letter as from his Lady in generall termes, telling him what shee liked best in him, and prescribing his gesture in smiling, his apparaile, &c. (1868: 18)

Manningham's focus on Malvolio is indicative of a fascination with experimentation, and an accompanying fear of error.

Breaking the Rules

A tendency towards transgression seems to have been a quality of the late Elizabethan Middle Temple. In some ways it is symptomatic of the inns as a whole, gathering together, as they do, large numbers of educated, quick-witted young men, often new to London after the relative constraint of university life and keen to make their fortunes. Yet, it is difficult to escape the impression that there was, gathered in the Middle Temple in these final years of the Queen's reign, evidence of more than average rule-breaking. There were a number of individuals with the desire to challenge institutional, cultural, and social authorities; clearly confident in their own abilities, men such as John Davies, John Marston, Richard Martin, Benjamin Rudyerd, John Hoskins, and Thomas Overbury gathered in the hall of Middle Temple to watch *Twelfth Night*, most having also taken part in *Le Prince D'Amour*. These men came from 'the middling sort' rather than the aristocracy; unlike the names such as Manners, Herbert, Cecil, Rich, Norris, Stanley, and Sidney which peppered the Gray's Inn admissions book, Middle Temple's members appear to have been more aspirational than established. Performing *Twelfth Night* at Middle Temple plays to this institutional need.

It is important to consider at this point the significance of the performance space. As a physical space, the hall has been assessed by Robert E. Burkhart to be rather like a playhouse playing stage in width, but a little shorter (1986, 1991); but the institutional power of Middle Temple is embodied in this hall. As Paul Raffield argues, their 'invisible curriculum'—from poetry and plays to masques and dining rituals—reinforces the inns' specific institutional identities. He argues that an inn's hall:

> was the setting for the continuous and undeviating repetition of legal ritual. Participation in these ceremonial rites affirmed the faith of students and practitioners in the legitimacy of the common law. Such rites were exclusive: only members of the Inn could practise them on a regular basis. (2004: 43)

That institutional identity was strongly individual. Pierre Bourdieu argues that the educative process is actually one of marking out different social groups; a process which Bourdieu calls 'acts of consecration' or 'acts of institution' (1991: 117). The men of Middle Temple in the final years of Elizabeth's reign, who witnessed *Twelfth Night* performed in the physical and symbolic centre of their own inn, were a group separated from those who were not part of the inns at all, and, to some degree, separated from those who were members of another inn. Their ability to engage in revels which transgressed the rules of Elizabethan society was secured by the protection of their institution and by the generic expectations of revelling itself. Many of the Middle Templars were ambitious to gain preferment and positions which allowed them to join those in power. Yet, there is a tension between the desire for conformity and the desire to stage a symbolic rebellion. Identification of the signifiers of power, the requirement for verbal and visual performance which would enable success at the royal court or in the wider bureaucracy, is combined with mockery of those very signifiers. Within the safety of generic expectation and within their own group, Middle Templars pushed the boundaries of rules and demanded that the audience of their revels questioned their signification.

This tension between conformity and rebellion is, as Lynne Magnusson has argued, demonstrated linguistically. By establishing in an audience a sense of its own superior perception, the revels achieve the same kind of outcome she argues for in a play such as *Love's Labour's Lost*:

> What *Love's Labour's Lost* emphasizes is not how people of different social status speak differently, but how the reception tactics of the characters operate to construct, exaggerate, and organize differences within English usage in order to index and enhance the critical listener's own social capital. (2004: 200)

That is, how the characters' respond to the language used by others identifies themselves as superior users of that language; in terms of the revels, Middle Templars are the 'critical listener[s]'. Magnusson sees *Love's Labour's Lost* as 'rooted in the experience of socially advantaged speech communities that heighten linguistic difference-making such as the London Inns of Court'. I would argue, again, that what Magnusson posits as an inns of court phenomenon is seen even more clearly in the Middle Temple of the last years of the Elizabethan regime, where the challenge to the established power structure is embodied in drama and wider performativity which is consciously presented in linguistic form. One might also see the challenge to authority lying, as this chapter has demonstrated, in the questioning of visual as well as verbal norms, with an audience encouraged to reflect upon what constitutes superiority in terms of dress and dance as well as use of language.

Twelfth Night, Middle Temple, and Transgression

Twelfth Night is thus a play particularly well designed for the Middle Temple, portraying the tension between power and revelry. Critics have seen Shakespeare's play being written with a Middle Temple audience in mind (see, for example, Arlidge 2000). Early modern playwrights had of necessity to cater for a wide range of playgoers, but as Henk Gras points out, writing with such an audience in mind simply 'mean[s] that for that selective audience the play could have had a different level of meaning from the one it would have had for the groundlings in the Globe or the nobility at court' (1989: 546). For this particular audience 'segment', then, as Manningham's diary entry suggests, the Toby and Malvolio plot would hold a specific interest, engaging as it does with issues of social mobility. Equally, we might argue that the relationship presented between Orsino and Viola/Cesario problematises male friendships, challenging assumptions of gender and, in its transgressive sexual frisson, demanding a re-evaluation of the role of *amicitia* in the homosocial environment the inns fostered.

Such an audience segment was composed of ambitious young innsmen whose political lives had daily contact with rebellion. In the year before the staging of *Twelfth Night*, one of Middle Temple's neighbours had famously met his end through the ultimate challenge to authority. The rebellion of the second earl of Essex, Robert Devereux, was formulated and staged at Essex House, lying on the western border of Middle Temple, and it is impossible that the young men of the inn were not at least witnesses to it. Essex had long been a figurehead for aspirant courtiers, leading a group whose courtly ambitions had suffered under the parsimony of the queen. Innsmen such as John Donne, and his friend, Middle Templar Henry Wotton, joined his ranks for expeditions to Cadiz and the Azores. Wotton became one of the earl's secretaries (though by 1601 he had with politic caution withdrawn from the inner group and travelled to Europe). Essex was a well-known attendee at inns of court revels, amongst the group recorded as attending the *Gesta Grayorum* in 1594, and perhaps at Middle Temple four years later; his sister, Penelope Devereux, was certainly amongst those who saw the latter revels (Nelson and Elliott 2012: xxvi).

Famously his fellow conspirators may have used drama, in the form of a Globe performance of *Richard II*, as a preliminary strike in the 1601 rebellion. The association of political transgression, the theatre, and a striking personal performance from a key court patron was very likely to appeal to the men at Middle Temple who are the focus of this chapter. The geographical proximity is suggestive, with Essex House occupying, in a similar way to Middle Temple itself, a transitional space between the court and the city: a space from which Essex had clearly hoped to draw fellow performers in his act of treason. As he rode to the house of Sir Thomas Smythe, sheriff of London—clearly expecting support from the audience of citizens as he progressed—Essex was instead to fail and, on his return to Ludgate, to find the gates closed and his rebellion defeated. His performance in 1601 may not have drawn universal applause, but that the charismatic earl was a figure of admiration for the Middle Templars is demonstrated by John Davies's adoption in the *Prince D'Amour* revels of a title the earl was accustomed to use in court pageants. Davies, Rudyerd recorded, 'would needs be called "Erophilus", in sawcy imitation of the great Earle of the time' (89). Three years after these revels, Middle Templars, standing on the edge of power and observing it, were able to judge the final performance of this actor on the political stage.

The closeness of its transgressions to those of the Middle Temple revels makes *Twelfth Night* a highly suitable play to perform at the inn. It represents the tension between conformity to the signifiers of social acceptability and the challenge to them, which is possible for those who stand outside them, perceive them, and reflect upon their authority. Indeed, the very externality of the Middle Temple, situated neither in the city nor in the court but somewhere between, becomes symbolic of the social situation of many of the inn's residents. Just as Shakespeare stages the movement from the liminal shore where Viola emerges from the sea to the commonwealth of Orsino's and Olivia's establishments, many innsmen desired to move from the social ambiguity of studentship to the court. Yet that ambition was difficult to achieve, requiring as it did daily rehearsal of the necessary performative skills and an orthodoxy which many Middle Templars may have found unpalatable. The inn, with the hall at its heart, was a sanctuary from the dangers of political reality, as well as a seat from which to observe them. Templars such as Martin and Hoskins, on the parliamentary stage, were to lose favour by arguing against the supremacy of the Jacobean royal prerogative; Hoskins and Sir Thomas Overbury were to find imprisonment and, in the latter's case, death as the reward for their political activity. Yet, in their formative years in the Middle Temple, these men developed their rhetorical skills and challenged the accepted order, alongside the cultural capital of an innsman's legal training. Their performance in public spheres appears ironically to have been tainted by the nature of the very revels which taught them those performative skills. Rehearsal was vital to the gaining of preferment; however, the questions it forced a man to ask of the system in which they had to act, laid men open, not only to ridicule from their peers as they trained, but to a future of political frustration, or worse. Intelligent, articulate, and witty, many men of the late Elizabethan Middle Temple were not 'born great' but 'achieve[d] greatness', and yet found that their training did not, after all, enable them to thrive.

This chapter ends, however, with a character who represented many of the characteristic traits of the late Elizabethan Middle Temple: the failed Prince of Love, talented and charismatic, but also belligerent and consistently transgressive, John Davies exemplifies the effects of training at such an institution. The most notably mocked of his cohort, his performance as Stradilax or Erophilus was to draw from his peers the equivalent of Maria's instruction to Sir Toby: 'observe him for the love of mockery'. One thinks of his theatrical attempt to gain the support of his peers for his bid to be Prince of the revels, describing which Rudyerd notes:

> [he] ran down amongst them, like *Laocoon ardens*, and with a most furious and turbulent action, [and] uttered these two Proverbs, the one borrowed from a Smith, the other from a Clown. *My Masters strike while the Iron is hot: Make hay while the Sun shineth.* (79)

He was immediately rejected as Prince of Love in favour of Martin, a man with whom he appears to have had a typical innsman friendship, with its mixture of affection, camaraderie, and competition. After this first performance inside the hall, he took a position on the highly visible stage outside. We are told that '*Stradilax* stept up upon the stone Staires in the Porch of the Temple-Hall, from whence nothing but Oysters ever opened their mouthes with eloquence, and spake as follows . . .'. But he is unable to complete what began as an ornate piece of oratory, for 'they went to bed, and so he did not tell them' (79).

Yet, in his love for drink and in his belligerence, Davies is not so much akin to Malvolio as to Toby. Perhaps it was through frustration at being ridiculed for his lack of wit, or the inappropriate 'Marmelad-Colour-Taffata

Gown', or perhaps the nickname of Stradilax was responsible for his behaviour. Whatever the stimulus, he fell drunk 'without a Rival' (87) as part of the proceedings, spoke insultingly of women, and had to be carried back to the inn after falling asleep in a stall. A few days later, he 'practised factiously against the Prince, and earnestly stirred enmity betwixt him and the Lincolnians' (88). Finally, in the aftermath of the 1595 revels, he attacked Richard Martin with a bastinado while the latter was at dinner in the hall: an action which was to lead to his being 'expelled, never to return' (Martin 1904: 379–80).

Yet perhaps the training was not, after all, ineffective. Despite the mockery of his Middle Temple peers, Davies was to become king's serjeant in Ireland and was chosen, just before his death, as chief justice of the king's bench. He may have been 'made the most notorious geck and gull / That e'er invention play'd on' (5.1.342–43), but in the end, perhaps, he was 'reveng'd upon the whole pack of [them]' (l. 377). With a mixture of Malvolio's social aspiration and Toby's transgressive behaviour, Sir John Davies demonstrates both the appeal and the potential of the young men of the Middle Temple. Examining his life, and that of his contemporaries, demonstrates, too, how well Shakespeare knew his inns of court audience.

Works Cited

Arlidge, Anthony. 2000. *The Prince of Love*. London: Giles de la Mare.

Bourdieu, Pierre. 1991. *Ce que parler veut dire: l'économie des échanges linguistiques*. Translated by Gino Raymond and Matthew Adamson and edited by John B. Thompson as *Language and Symbolic Power*. Cambridge: Polity.

Burkhart, Robert E. 1986. "The Dimensions of Middle Temple Hall." *Shakespeare Quarterly* 37, no. 3: 370–71.

______. 1991. "The Playing Space in the Halls of the Inns of Court." *South Atlantic Review* 56, no. 4: 1–5.

Della Casa, Giovanni. 1576. *Galateo*. London.

Dugdale, William. 1666. *Origines Juridiciales or Historical Memorials of the English Laws, Courts of Justice, Forms of Tryall, Punishment in Cases Criminal, Law Writers, Law Books, Grants and Settlements of Estates, Degree of Serjeant, Innes of Court and Chancery*. London.

Finkelpearl, Philip J. 1969. *John Marston of the Middle Temple: An Elizabethan Dramatist in His Social Setting*. Cambridge, MA: Harvard University Press.

Fortescue, Sir John. 1616. *De Laudibus Legum Angliae*. London.

Gras, Henk. 1989. "*Twelfth Night, Every Man Out of his Humour*, and the Middle Temple Revels of 1597–98." *Modern Language Review* 84, no. 3: 545–64.

Greg, W. W., ed. 1914. *Gesta Grayorum, 1688.* London: Malone Society.

Hoskins, John. 1935. *Directions for Speech and Style.* Edited by Hoyt H. Hudson. Princeton, N.J.: Princeton University Press.

Legh, Gerard. 1576. *The Accedens of Armory.* London.

Lublin, Robert I. 2011. *Costuming the Shakespearean Stage.* Farnham: Ashgate.

Magnusson, Lynne. 2004. "Scoff Power in *Love's Labour's Lost* and the Inns of Court." *Shakespeare Survey* 57: 196–208.

Manningham, John. 1868. *Diary of John Manningham of the Middle Temple and of Bradbourne, Kent, Barrister-at-Law, 1602–3.* Edited by John Bruce. Camden Society, o.s., vol. 99. London: J. B. Nichols and Sons.

Martin, C. T., ed. and trans. 1904. *Minutes of Parliament of the Middle Temple: Vol I.* London: Butterworth & Co.

Nelson, Alan, and John R. Elliott, eds. 2012. *Records of Early English Drama: Inns of Court.* Oxford: Oxford University Press.

Raffield, Paul. 2004. *Images and Cultures of Law.* Cambridge: Cambridge University Press.

Royston, Darren. 2015. "'Filthy Groping and Unclean Handlings': An examination of touching moments in dance of court and courtship." In *The Senses in Early Modern England, 1558–1660*, edited by Simon Smith, Jackie Watson, and Amy Kenny, 55–73. Manchester: Manchester University Press.

Rudyerd, Benjamin. 1660. *Le Prince D'Amour* or *Noctes Templariae.* London.

Shakespeare, William. 2008. *Twelfth Night.* Edited by Kier Elam. London: Bloomsbury.

Shepard, Alexandra. 2003. *Meanings of Manhood in Early Modern England.* Oxford: Oxford University Press.

Stubbes, Philip. 1583. *Anatomie of Abuses.* London.

Waterhouse, Edward. 1663. *Fortescutus Illustratus.* London.

CHAPTER 5

Notebooks, Play, and Legal Education at Middle Temple

Blessin Adams

It is often a surprise to those reading about legal education at the early modern inns of court to discover that these outwardly collegiate societies offered their students little direction, no tutelage, and no formal syllabus. Roger North, a student in the 1670s, wrote a discourse in which he lamented 'of all the professions in the world that pretend to book-learning, none is so destitute of institution as that of the common law' (Baker 2007: 15). Primarily, legal education at the inns was delivered through oral methods, the most advanced being readings given by recognisable members in the legal community, that were 'devoted to the exposition of a statute or part of a statute' and which exposed the audience to 'textual analysis, to historical and purposive interpretation and to some pretty intricate law' (Baker 2007: 9). Students also attended moots: elaborate vocational exercises conducted in the style of mock trials in which the formulation and debate of a hypothetical case involving one or more controversial questions of law were overseen by two or three utter barristers acting as judges. In Chap. 2, Jessica Winston explores how mooting helped to form a lawyer's legal identity.

B. Adams (✉)
Independent Scholar, Aylsham, UK

E. Rhatigan, J. Watson (eds.), *Mapping the Early Modern Inns of Court*, Early Modern Literature in History,
https://doi.org/10.1007/978-3-031-77445-4_5

One's legal education could be further supplemented by attending debates and lectures, and by observing trials where the cut and thrust of law could be seen in action. In addition to oral readings and exercises, the study of printed texts and manuscripts aided the digestion of the vast quantities of law necessary to advance in the legal profession. Manuscript copies of readings were especially valuable, the production and circulation of which were centrally important to the self-directed educations of serious-minded law students (Williams 2017: 61–79).

Attendance at readings, moots, lectures, and trials was not mandatory, and on the whole students were left to their own devices, to 'struggle on alone' (Prest 2023: 181). John Baker notes that such self-directed courses of learning were at times 'a torment', or as Blackstone put it 'a tedious and lonely process' (2007: 15). In response to a lack of formal direction, students sometimes allied themselves with older members or formed groups to provide each other with 'mutual assistance' (Baker 2007: 16). Simonds D' Ewes, admitted to Middle Temple in 1611, remarked in his diary that he read Littleton with 'a gentleman religious and honest' and 'took sweete benefitt' from discussing cases with his fellow students. Yet he too confessed that he found the arguments of senior members so perplexing that he considered abandoning his legal studies altogether (cited in Prest 2023: 181). Studying law at the early modern inns was a hard business and students often found themselves overwhelmed and distressed by a lack of institutional direction.

Legal Notebooks

Many students kept notebooks to support themselves as they embarked on an education that was predominantly self-driven. Unlike the typically miscellaneous academic commonplace books composed at grammar schools and universities, these notebooks were defined by their primary legal function. They were practical, textual objects that recorded and facilitated a distinct process of legal education. While each notebook uniquely reflected the author's individual course of study, there nonetheless were similarities of style, content, and method which suggests that their composition fit a generic, albeit flexible, form. Ranging in size from portable octavos to larger folio volumes, largely written in Law French with a smattering of Latin and English, they contained materials that directly related to learning law: copies of readings, moots, and lectures; records of cases; notes on statute law; abridgements of law; law reports; and extracts copied from printed digests, treatises, and commentaries such as Bracton's *De Legibus et Consuetudinibus Angliae* (1569) and Littleton's *Tenures* (1502). From these notebooks legal historians such as John Baker and Wilfrid Prest have meticulously reconstructed the day-to-day business of legal education at the inns.

The majority of surviving notebooks contain materials from these strictly legal sources. Yet there are some notebooks that incorporate a broader selection of texts that on first view appear to be of a decidedly non-legal nature. These materials include sonnets, couplets, songs, rhymes, dance steps, music, and jests, alongside lengthier extracts copied from classical and humanist literature, Scripture, contemporary histories, and varied works of philosophy. Some of these materials may have been no more than ephemeral jottings, however not all can be dismissed as mere distractions. By the inclusion and framing of so-called non-legal texts within their legal notebooks, I argue that some law students perceived a productive, legal relationship between these diverse texts. I am especially interested in the question of whether the authors of these notebooks treated play as an important part of their legal educations.

This chapter examines the notebook of an anonymous Middle Templar, dated *c.* 1611, in which the author and his friends composed, *in medias res* of serious legal notes, a series of jests and stories titled 'Joco Seria' (CUL Dd.5.14). Through this case study I consider how an institutionally organised group of serious law students used low-brow play as a part of their professional development, to enhance their broader legal educations and also to ease the overwhelming burden of stress that was seemingly endemic within their chosen field of study. I argue that these records of play are evidence of an adaptive style of learning and composition entirely unique to the inns of court. Before we turn to examine that notebook, however, it is important to review our current understanding of the relationship between legal education and play.

Legal Education and Play

The early modern inns were widely considered to be the equivalent of finishing schools. Members of the gentry and merchant classes attended to make connections in London, seek opportunities outside of the legal profession, and perhaps absorb a little law along the way. The inns were largely treated as 'courtly academies' that were 'devoted to the cultivation of gentlemanly accomplishments and liberal studies . . . with perhaps a subsequent dash of Renaissance humanism' (Prest 2011: 88, 92). Ostensibly the inns were law schools, yet the majority of members did not commit to undertake legal study or pursue legal careers.

Working from the rolls of the common pleas, alongside the membership records of the four main inns, Baker concluded that 'fewer than ten percent of inns of court men in the fifteenth and sixteenth centuries took to the legal profession as a career' (2011: 9). Contemporary reports attest to the tensions that existed between those who were learners or 'plodders', and non-learners or 'revellers'. An account from the late 1530s bemoans that amongst the members of Middle Temple '[t]here is none there that be compelled to learn, and they that are learners . . . are much troubled with the noise of walking and communication of them that be no learners' (O'Day 2000: 129).

If the lay majority had little interest in studying law, then what did they get up to? Drama, play, and revels, especially around Christmas, were important intellectual and cultural traditions within the inns. Jessica Winston in *Lawyers at Play* argues that poetry, translation, and performance were not only recreational pastimes but 'defined and elevated the status of Inns of Court men' (2016: v). Chapters in this volume explore many of these pastimes (see Arthur Marotti on the composition and sharing of poetry; Winston, Felicity Brown, and Jessica Apolloni on dramatic productions; and Renae Satterley on translation). These civilised forms of play and revelry were integral to the professional, social, and personal development of inns members.

Alongside traditions of high culture there also flourished a great deal of mischievous play and bawdy behaviour. John Spellman, who joined Gray's Inn around 1500, described how the Christmas revels included feasts, music, dancing, and mock fights, along with the less salubrious pastimes of cards and dice-play. During the second half of the sixteenth century barristers and students 'were perfectly free to attend plays or sermons as they chose, to drink in taverns . . . and to patronise dicing houses or stews [brothels] at their pleasure' (Prest 2023: 124). Winston observes that many rowdy types of play, such as flyting, table talk, libels, and contests of wit, were combative and disruptive to the community, even suggesting they may inevitably overspill into physical violence (2016: 20). These modes of play were considered oppositional to serious legal study and proper gentlemanly conduct.

Cultural, literary, and intellectual forms of play elevated inns' members, while lower, disorderly forms debased them. Yet these modes of play were not wholly distinctive, nor mutually exclusive. Revels and high drama went hand in hand with feasting, drinking, and gaming. Serious-minded law students were not so puritanical as to wholly reject rebellious or disruptive play. We shall presently see this blurring of lines between play and serious study within the notebook of our anonymous Middle Templar.

The Notebook

At Cambridge University Library there is a portable quarto notebook written in English, Law French, and shorthand, measuring 199 × 155 mm, containing 136 pages (CUL Dd.5.14). It is a typical example of a legal notebook specifically composed to support a legal education. On fol. 3^{r} the contents of the notebook are titled 'Divers & uncertayne discourses del ley', followed by copies of readings and moots given at various inns of court and chancery. On fols. 1^{r}–7^{r} are legal notes including a series of moot exercises dated 1611–1612. Following this, on fols. 8^{r}–69^{r} there is a record in Law French of Anthony Benn's reading on the statute of H8.6, dated 2 March 1611. Benn's reading is interspersed with records of moots at Clement's Inn, New Inn, Clifford's Inn, and Middle Temple. From fol. 32^{v} there are notes from the Year Book dated Elizabeth 31 (1589). The reverse of the notebook continues with records of readings dated between 1613–1614 given by Mr Trattman at Clifford's Inn, Mr Jenckenson at Barnard's, and Mr Wootten at no given place.

On fols. 70^{r}–76^{v} there are written 29 humorous stories titled 'Joco Seria, Of Divers Subts'. Unlike the legal records throughout the rest of the notebook, the *joco seria* show a keen interest in human nature, sociability, and play, ranging in theme from the prescience of death to the hubris of scholars. They contain a colourful cast of characters, some fictional and some based on well-known figures, such as John Foxe and Richard Mulcaster. Some are crude, bawdy, and defamatory and others sensitive, inventive, and joyfully competitive. Many of the *joco seria* appear to be original compositions, while others are reimagined stories taken from common printed jest books such as *A Hundred Mery Tayls* (1548) and *The Jests of Scogyn* (1570).

The identity of the notebook's author is unknown, however, he notes the names of his social circle who participated alongside him in moots and the telling of *joco seria*. These men were: Ellis Swayne, Thomas Gallop,

Anthony Gulson, Richard Grovesey, Mr Dennis, Mr Clotworthy, Mr Fisher, Mr Clarke, Mr Gibbensen (possibly John Gibbes), Robert Browne, Mr Bull, and Mr White. Many of these names are recorded in the *Register of Admissions to the Honourable Society of the Middle Temple* (Sturgess 1949) and in the *Minutes of Parliament of the Middle Temple* (Martin 1904). Of these 12 named members, seven (58 per cent) were called to the bar: John Gibbes in 1602; Henry Fisher in 1608; Henry Clarke, who was called to the bar in 1611 and made a master of the bench in 1628; Ellis Swyane and Robert Browne in 1614; and Anthony Gulson in 1615. At a time when only 15 per cent of students at Middle Temple were called to the bar, these men represented an academic elite (Prest 2011: 89).

As these men gathered for moots and storytelling, they had to hand the legal notebook ready to record their activities. The presence of several hands implies communal use, and the partial recording of moots and *joco seria* in shorthand demonstrates that verbal contributions were most likely recorded *in tempore loquendi*. The notebook was a practical, material object, central to the business of work and play within this select group. It not only allowed them to record their studies and jests, but it was also a tool that enabled them to strengthen the institutional and social bonds between them, reinforcing the sense of 'fellowship' which Emma Rhatigan discusses in Chap. 3.

Play as a Form of Legal Exercise

One way we can address the question of whether our anonymous Middle Templar perceived a relationship between sessions of legal study and sessions of play is to examine how he recorded those exercises in his notebook. There are striking similarities of form, style, and theme between the recording of moots and the *joco seria* that suggests these serious-minded students organised, conducted, and documented legal study and play in much the same way.

The moot cases recorded on fols. 119^{v}–135^{r} are titled 'Divers & uncertayne discourses del ley'. Individual moot sessions are headed by centrally aligned titles with the dates, names of the participants, and the locations in which the moots took place, for example: 'Moote case Feb: 27 1611 Per Mr Parker & Mr Townsend' or 'Le moote case en le mieu Temple March 5 1611'. These titles are followed by a brief introduction of the legal matter in hand and salient points to be discussed. The text recording the moot proper is aligned to the right, leaving a generous marginal space to the left for writing the names of speakers and other miscellaneous notes such as Year Book numbers, dates, textual markers, and general comments on the points of law being argued. Where speakers make multiple points, '*idem*' ('the same') is annotated in the margin to signal continued speech.

Now compare to the *joco seria*. They are titled 'Joco Seria of Divers Subjects', recalling the previous legal title of 'Divers & uncertayne discourses del ley'. The individual titles of the *joco seria* are likewise aligned to the centre of the page above the relevant body of text. Like the moots, these titles provide the names of the present speakers, the date, and the location of the story-telling session such as 'By one Mr Clarke at Mr Gibbenses att dinner Feb: 7th 1611 compleate' and 'By Mr Robt Browne the 7th of April in the ye Temple Garden to younge Mr Bull & my selfe'. The main body of the text is aligned to the right, leaving the left-hand margin free for annotations. These annotations are largely the names of speakers and other general notes on the theme of the story, such as '*Audaces fortuna iubet*' ('Fortune favours the bold') or 'Mr Gallop: Good souldiers against yeyr wills'. Stylistically, there is almost no difference between the recording of moots and *joco seria*.

Also evidenced are striking similarities of methodology between sessions of mooting and *joco seria*: both sustained practices held over several months or years. The moots took place between March 1611 and December 1614. The notebook was, of course, on hand to record proceedings. The first session of the *joco seria* is dated 27 November 1611, and they continue to 22 July 1612. The same members attended the moots and the sessions of *joco seria*, and the same notebook recorded activities. The *joco seria* were not spontaneous moments of play; like the moots they were organised meetings.

The arrangement and preparation of moots required time and effort. Simonds D' Ewes, for example, spent nearly a month preparing for his first moot (Prest 2023: 155). Moots dealt in hypothetical cases, with the theme and subject agreed upon beforehand. The limits and precedents of law were examined through the structured argumentation of fictional cases. These communal exercises tested law students' abilities beyond the memorisation of the common law, while the cut and thrust of legal argument also tested students' skills in invention, argument, and reply.

As with moots, these same law students planned and organised their sessions of play to fit certain themes or subjects. The first five tales in the *joco seria* were presented within the chamber of Ellis Swayne on 27 November 1611, with Gulson, Grovesey, and the author of the notebook present. The theme that day was the prescience of death. The title of the first story, told by Swayne, is 'Of Death', in which a wealthy yet dangerously sick man sent for one Dr Grey to tend upon him. Grey's grim diagnosis was imminent death, and within a quarter of an hour the wealthy patient dropped dead. As indicated by the marginal note 'idem et eode temp' ('at the same time and place'), Swayne immediately launched into another tale, titled 'Of ye knowledge that many have of yeyr end and the tyme'. This brief tale recounts how Swayne's grandfather predicted his own death and then expired shortly afterwards. After Swayne had delivered these two stories, another speaker expanded on the theme. The next tale, 'By Richard Grovesey at ye same tyme & place', is only six lines in length and simply tells of a man who put his legal affairs in order before shutting himself in his room with a Bible and promptly falling dead. Then Gulson, at 'ye same tyme', described how a fit and healthy 92-year-old man efficiently predicted his own death. The final story of this session is once again given by Swayne and is titled 'Of Doctor Grey'. At 59 lines this is the longest tale in the session and features the aforementioned Dr Grey who not only predicted the death of a local duke, but also swindled him out of his precious plate, beat a pedlar with the handle of his dagger, stole a cloak, and was arrested before making a bold escape.

Each speaker contributing a story to the session was working within the established theme of the prescience of death. The individual tales were similar, yet members took pains to expand, embellish, and create new variations upon the theme. There was an element of reactive and imaginative competition as each story appears to outdo the last in inventiveness and humour before Swayne closed the session with what was, arguably, the most absurd and entertaining story of all.

After this first session of 'serious jest', the same group of members met several times to exchange stories upon a pre-arranged theme: one session held at Middle Temple 'in ye hall at supper' was on the theme of melancholy and madness, another about executions, and another on the apprehension of thieves. Some of the stories were recollections of personal experiences, some were evidently the result of spontaneous invention, and others lifted from popular works of literature, medicine, and jest books. But did these law students view their pre-arranged sessions of *joco seria*—as the title 'Serious Jest' may suggest—as being *more* than just play? And what benefit could they have expected beyond simply having fun?

Through organised play they practised skills of argument, memory, invention, oratory, rhetoric, and wit: the same auxiliary skills that were also practised in moots. This was not coincidental; these sessions of play were deliberately intended to function in concert with their wider legal educations, as we shall see in those *joco seria* that deal with jurisprudential themes.

Jurisprudential Themes in the *Joco Seria*

Today we recognise that legal ethics are centrally important to the teaching of law. The early modern inns did not formally teach ethics, however this did not mean law students did not concern themselves with subjects such as legal philosophy, criminality, justice, and equity; all of which were important to their professional development. In Chap. 11 Jessica Apolloni considers how the plays staged at the inns explored these very issues. In this section I examine how the anonymous Middle Templar and his friends incorporated a wider kind of jurisprudence, common law thought, legal ethics, and philosophy into their play in their self-directed legal educations.

In 'Of Lidford Lane' on fol. 72^{v}, Mr Clotworthy recounted a proverb: 'Hange him first & judge him afterwards'. He immediately followed this with a tale titled 'Of Hallifaux', in which he described a guillotine known as the Halifax gibbet. With relish Mr Clotworthy explained the operation of this device: men, who 'any fault committed in veine deserving death', were put 'upon a block with a pully pullainge up a thinge like ye gron of an axe they let it fall againe & cut of there heade'. The so-called 'gibbet law' of Halifax was described by William Bently in 1761 as being 'by some persons in that age, judged to be too severe' (Midgley 1789: 417). According to historian A. V. Judges, the law in Halifax was a relic of an ancient Anglo-Saxon custom in which 'Sixteen jurors, selected by the four local constables, recorded in writing their verdict of the guilt of the accused; and further without the intervention of a magistrate, they gave their "determined sentence"': accused men were summarily executed without trial, often on the same day or following market day (Judges 2002: 59). Anecdotes about ancient methods of execution would have been of interest to men whose professional mindset was rooted in the common law. Relics of Anglo-Saxon customs and legal language were frequently drafted into service by legal antiquarians such as Edward Coke, as evidence supporting the existence of a pre-conquest English legal system, drawing authority from the ancient origins of Anglo-Saxon laws (Schoeck 1954). The Halifax 'gibbet law' was an ancient custom becoming increasingly intolerable to a society that viewed its practice as unjust.

By pairing 'Of Lidford Lane' with 'Of Hallifaux', Clotworthy may have been voicing his own discomfort towards the injustice of these summary beheadings. As future lawyers and judges in training these men were readying themselves for a profession where such judgements were to become regular procedures. They would be directly involved in the administration of justice, with the power and position to effect change. Indeed, the gibbet law was abolished 39 years later in 1650. It is not surprising that upcoming legal professionals were interested in tales of injustice and execution, nor that they chose to write about these subjects in their legal notebooks. What is different here is that Clotworthy explored these themes during a playful session of *joco seria*, and in doing so deliberately used play to attend to a far more serious kind of legal and ethical thought.

The theme of law continues in 'Of wearing gold and silver', a humorous tale in which a heated parliamentary debate concerning sumptuary laws is resolved through clever use of precedent. The argument at hand had become stuck on the question of who should be permitted to wear gold and silver: 'some would saye some punishment and others penaltye for all [that] wore' them, while 'some would have none but let every man weare according to his calling goe apparelled as best liketh'. There seemed to be a stalemate, until a man called Martin came forward to recount a 'pretty history' in which a king, not having absolute power to raise an army, passed a law in which any man could call another a coward if he failed to do his martial duty. The same stratagem, Martin argued, could easily be applied to the matter of wearing gold and silver. The solution was not to pass complex sumptuary laws, but rather to make it 'lawfull to call any man that goeth apparelled with gold and silver prodigall foole as to say looke there goeth one of the prodigal asses'. This tale of an absurd yet effective solution to a convoluted legal problem touched upon a range of subjects: the legal authority of kings and parliament, the power of precedent, and the moral question of how lawmakers were to compel free men against their wills to comply with unpopular laws. Innsmen too would have been deeply interested in dress, and the complex rules surrounding it; as Jackie Watson comments in Chap. 4 modish appearance was vital for a man to rise socially and innsmen were acutely aware of 'the potential peril of making the wrong choices of dress for the occasion'.

Other tales in the *joco seria* are focused on crime and detection. In 'Of a poore woman that had lost her brood goose' the owner of a stolen goose petitioned the parson of the parish to help her recover it. The parson assured her that he would. On the following Sunday he brought a stone with him to church and brandishing it with intent he warned his congregation that 'he would nowe throw the stone at him that did it'. The thief ducked down in his seat and gave himself away. The goose, swiftly recovered, was restored to its rightful owner. This story is nearly identical to 'Of him that had his goose stole', in the 1567 *A Hundred Mery Tayls*, where the victim is a man who petitioned the local curate to help him retrieve his stolen goose. During Sunday service the curate bade everybody to sit down, and when they sat he berated them for not sitting. The confused congregation protested that they were indeed sitting, to which the curate replied, 'he that stealeth the goose sitteth not'. A defiant voice shot back 'yes that I do', and the thief was exposed and punished. The *joco seria* version placed a greater emphasis on those parts describing the victim's petition for aid. The sex of the victim was changed from male to female, perhaps to better suit the humour of the all-male inns audience, and the parson's trick was changed from a somewhat unbelievable application of reverse psychology to that of a threat of violence. Both versions focus upon legal petition, clever resolution, and equitable outcome, demonstrating how these law students were not only interested in sharing jests of a legal nature, but also delighted in imaginatively reinventing them to fit their own purpose.

As part of this thematic session of storytelling, a similar tale titled 'How a master found that a servant had stolen from him' was shared by Thomas Gallop. Here the titular master reveals the identity of a thief in his household by announcing to his gathered servants that 'I knowe who had it [the stolen item], he hath a feather there on his nose'. The culprit then unthinkingly reached to wipe his nose, thus exposing himself as guilty. In this tale, and that of the brood goose, justice is reached through absurd and unlikely trickery. Outwardly these two *joco seria* do not seem to meditate upon weightier themes of legal philosophy, but they nonetheless demonstrate that these students used inventive storytelling to explore legal subjects: crime, petition, detection, conviction, and equitable outcome.

The law students' playful sympathy towards condemned criminals is shown in the tale of a man who had been sentenced to death for stealing a mare. The condemned man lamented that 'he was to be hanged for a matter of nothinge: as onely for stallinge of a 2d haltar'. This short and rather bleak tale revisits the students' concern with injustice, seen in 'Of Halifax'. Another story on this theme recounts the final journey of a man on his way to be hanged at Tyburn. Desperate to be spared from pain and humiliation, he called out to a friend in the crowd that he hoped to be put out of his misery by being shot in the neck with an arrow. The friend, mishearing 'arrow' for 'narrow' does not catch the meaning of the request, and so stands by, musing 'if the rope had been wider he had not been hanged'. This tale of misunderstanding and death is a dark species of comedy, for Mr Browne and his audience would have been aware of (and perhaps not indifferent to) the agonies suffered during executions by hanging. Yet another story on this same theme, as told by Mr Bull, describes a man in court who had just been condemned to death. The judges ordered that he should give thanks for the sentence, and pray to the king, to which the condemned man replied that he 'might have been prayine for all the kinge but he had lapse to prayse God for him that caught & prompted him'. His witticism is but a futile moment of defiance in the face of his inevitable death.

The criminals are comedic and sympathetic characters whose good-humoured attempts at self-preservation are doomed to failure. Their plights are situated alongside a series of tales that delight in detection and fair resolution. In the case of the brood goose, for example, the crime of theft is answered with recompense rather than corporal or capital punishment. Along with the earlier session of *joco seria* that included 'Of Lidford Lane' and 'Of Halifax', it seems that these law students were using their sessions to explore the moral and legal themes of justice, equity in the courts, and the ethics of judicial execution and torture. The subject matter chosen for these *joco seria* is not incidental; their pointed legality allowed the participants to explore playfully a broader kind of legal ethics that was essential to their professional development.

Play and legal ethics are not mutually exclusive. Indeed, the early moderns well understood that there was wisdom in folly. Joel Altman argues that there existed within the play and drama of early modern England a strong tradition of rhetorical enquiry through which authors and audiences alike explored fundamental questions concerning love, justice, sovereignty, and nature (Altman 1978: 2). Such work is evident within the legal notebook of our anonymous Middle Templar; within its pages we can see the diverse nature of play between members of an institutionally contracted group as they participated in a social performance grounded in legal and humanist traditions of discourse. Themes of justice, law, and equity were explored through a type of play that was purposely ludic and serious.

Restorative Play

So far, I have discussed how the author of the notebook and his social group used play as a tool to enhance their legal educations. However, they also recognised the value of play for play's sake. For this group, play served a restorative function that relieved the stresses and strains of legal study. Awareness of the restorative value of play is clearly communicated within their shared stories, indeed five consecutive *joco seria* are wholly centred on the theme of scholar's melancholy. These particular tales were shared between Mr Dennis and Mr Gallop 'in ye hall at supper' at Middle Temple and recorded by the author of the notebook who was in attendance for this humorous exchange. These law students were especially concerned with the mental and physical strains put upon them by prolonged periods of study, and how relief could be attained through play that was, according to pedagogical and humanist models of the time, practically restorative as well as fun.

The image of the scholar as an isolated and depressed figure was popular in early modern England. Indeed, excessive melancholy was sometimes fashionably enlarged and affected by those who wished to present themselves as scholastic martyrs. Expressions of despair concerning extreme workloads and social isolation at the inns of court were not uncommon, as we have seen in the introduction to this chapter. Robert Burton, in *The Anatomy of Melancholy*, placed overmuch work and isolation as the chief causes of melancholy. Burton's 'Abstract of Melancholy' specifically cautions his readers against the dangers of solitude:

> When I lie waking all alone, Recounting what I have ill done, My thoughts on me then tyrannise, Fear and sorrow me surprise, Whether I tarry still or go, Methinks the time moves very slow. All my griefs to this are jolly, Naught so mad as melancholy. (2017: 8)

Timothy Bright, in his 1586 treatise on melancholy, recognised that study and exercises of the brain were to be managed in 'great moderation'. All things must be in balance; thus, extremes of 'idleness' and 'solitariness' were checked by 'over vehement study' and 'excessive labour' with the caveat 'only take you no lesse care in the one then in the other' (1586: 250). If one were to subscribe to these medical theories, then the pairing of serious legal study with outrageous play was simply sensible practice.

The importance of play as part of a serious course of study was championed by many of the leading pedagogues of the time. Richard Mulcaster, the famous headmaster of the Merchant Taylor's School (who was himself the subject of a tale in the *joco seria*), insisted that his students participated in strenuous physical exercise alongside their studies to balance body and mind (1581). Erasmus wrote in the *De Pueris Instituendis* that children's study should be intermixed with play, and that education itself should be treated like a game: 'Such study' he wrote 'may hardly be distinguished from play, and is a source of enjoyment to the child' (Erasmus 1985: 202). Play was not spontaneous nor bacchanalian, rather it was deliberately incorporated into the academic lives of children and young adults as an aid to learning and as a release from the pressures of study. Within the notebook we shall see how our anonymous Middle Templar used rowdy, low-brow play to bring balance to his own studies. We are inclined to believe that serious-minded law students, those 'plodders' who sneered from within the confines of their stuffy chambers at the lay 'revellers' outside, would not debase themselves by engaging in lewd and bawdy kinds of play. But why not? Forms of educative and restorative play need not always be of the elevated variety.

In the tale, titled 'Of Melancholicke Conceyts', Mr Dennis tells of one Mr Edward Band who, in a state of shock, had confined himself to his chambers at Middle Temple to 'lay in the glume' throughout the vacation period. This apparently was a true story, as both Gallop and Dennis jump in to claim that they had to summon a sergeant to break down Band's door with a halberd. There, 'with grief', they beheld their friend's awful condition. The cause of Band's melancholy, they concluded, was 'to much study'. Here we have a warning to the group as they recollected how their mutual friend's mental illness and social isolation was occasioned by excessive legal study. The same cautionary theme continued in the tale 'Of one that was perswaded that he was an owle', in which a scholar at Corpus Christi College became convinced that he had been transformed into an owl. Fearing that he would be attacked by his fellow students he locked himself in his room where he festered in a state of delusion. This story is immediately followed by a recollection by Gallop from his days at Oxford, in which a scholar suffering from a form of body dysmorphia steadfastly refused to leave his chambers, until the wit and intervention of his friends cured him of his mania. The common theme in these stories is mental illness in students occasioned by excessive study and social isolation.

The causes and remedies for scholars' melancholy are featured in the following *joco seria*. In 'Of one that feared to drowne the world by pissinge', as told by Gallop, a scholar at Brasenose College believed that were he to urinate then the flow would never cease, and the world would be drowned in the deluge of his piss. His delusion was cured through the clever intervention of his friends, who ran into his chambers crying that the city was on fire and only he, with his infinite stores of water, could douse the flames. The hapless scholar fled from his rooms into the city to do his duty, and upon discovering that his urination was in fact finite, he was cured of his disorder. The matter of the story is base, but the message was one of great importance: it was by the witty intervention of friends that this student was drawn out of self-imposed isolation and restored, in body and mind, to his proper health. Gallop almost certainly had a medical motivation behind this story, considering that his source was most likely Burton's *Anatomy of Melancholy*, wherein a version of this tale is featured under the subsection 'Help from friends by counsel, comfort, fair and foul means, witty devices . . . &c.' (472).

The longest tale on the theme of melancholy, once again told by Gallop, was titled 'Of Foxe who thought himself glasse'.[1] While at college in Devon young Foxe, through a 'greatness of study', fell into a mania in which he believed himself to be made out of glass. So 'deeply was he oppressed with that humor' he shunned the company of friends and hid in his chambers, for fear that should he venture outside he might knock himself and shatter into pieces. During a moment of panic, he ran out of his chambers and into the college gardens, where he by chance met a friend. As this friend reached out to embrace Foxe, he cried out 'that by no meanes he should touch him for he was made of glasse' and would certainly break. Sensitive to Foxe's condition, his friend gently led him back to his rooms, suggested that he lay in a feather bed, and with company and good cheer the patient was soon cured of his glass delusion. Once again, we see the recurring theme of madness and isolation brought on by study that is subsequently remedied through wit and friendship.

The restorative purpose of the *joco seria* was noble, yet the content of these stories was base, bawdy, and rude. Such play may be outwardly crude, yet it worked entirely in accordance with the advice of medical and

[1] So-called 'glass delusion' is discussed several times in Burton's *Anatomy* as a symptom of melancholy and may well have been the inspiration behind this tale (2017: 328, 335, 343, 350).

pedagogical experts who advocated balance by integrating play and society into the educative lives of their students. Through the sharing of low-brow tales, these law students not only demonstrated their awareness of the dangers of excessive study, but they also sought to engage in deliberately beneficial modes of communal play as a means to support their mental-wellbeing throughout their long years of serious academic study.

Conclusion

The legal notebook featured in this chapter was uniquely a product of the early modern inns of court, most likely adopted from the notebooks composed in the classrooms of grammar schools and universities and adapted to manage the overwhelming volumes of law that one was expected to digest as part of a self-directed legal education. In this case study we can see how an anonymous law student at Middle Temple and his contractual group of fellows used his notebook to record both their legal studies and their play. Traditional scholarship relating to play at the early modern inns of court holds to the compelling image of the 'reveller' majority conflicting with a minority group of stodgy, play-adverse 'plodders'. In this model play falls into distinct categories of high and low, or cohesive and disruptive. Yet recent scholarship in the areas of play, culture, and community at the early modern inns, such as that of O'Callaghan (2007) and Winston (2016), look beyond these simplified models to suggest that the lines between play—in particular bawdy or rowdy play—and legal education are not as defined as once thought.

My own study reveals how rude, base, and at times libellous play was deliberately used by a group of serious-minded law students to develop auxiliary skills such as rhetoric, invention, and argument; to explore legal ethics and a broader kind of jurisprudence; and to put into practice humanist and medical methods of restorative play. The notebook not only recorded these efforts, but its materiality facilitated the organisation and execution of these legal and playful practices. Here I argue that play was not incidental to a serious course of study at Middle Temple; on the contrary, it was integral.

Of course, this is but a single notebook, and alone it can only ever be suggestive of a broader genre of legal writing in which law students supported their studies through a wider range of non-legal texts, materials, and practices. However, during my research I have uncovered many other such notebooks in which diverse literary, humanist, and playful materials are situated side by side with serious legal texts. Baker's catalogues of legal manuscripts, in which he details the inclusion of many such materials in legal notebooks, are an excellent starting point for any scholar interested in expanding upon my own ideas (Baker 1996; 1990; 1975). Continued research into the presence of non-legal texts in these notebooks would be valuable in enlarging our understanding of legal education and play at the early modern inns of court. Furthermore, such work may well challenge our perceptions of what constituted a legal text in the early modern period. This legal notebook is an example of a unique and practical genre of legal writing at Middle Temple. By decompartmentalising the diverse contents of these legal notebooks, we can examine them anew, and consider how even the most outlandish materials were composed and arranged in a manner that facilitated and supported a serious course of legal education.

Works Cited

Altman, Joel B. 1978. *The Tudor Play of Mind: Rhetorical Inquiry and the Development of Elizabethan Drama*. London: University of California Press.

Baker, John H. 1975. *English Legal Manuscripts Vols. I and II: Catalogue of the Manuscript Year Books, Readings, and Law Reports in the Library of the Harvard Law School.* Zug: Inter Documentation Company.

———. 1990. *English Legal Manuscripts in the United States of America, A Descriptive List Part II: Early Modern and Modern Periods 1558–1902.* London: Selden Society.

———. 2007. *Legal Education in London, 1250–1850.* London: Selden Society.

———. 2011. "The Third University 1450–1550: Law School or Finishing School?" In *The Intellectual and Cultural History of the Early Modern Inns of Court*, edited by Jayne Elisabeth Archer, Elizabeth Goldring, and Sarah Knight, 8–24. Manchester: Manchester University Press.

Baker, John, and J. S. Ringrose. 1996. *Catalogue of English Legal Manuscripts in Cambridge University Library.* Woodbridge: The Boydell Press.

Bracton, Henry. 1569. *De legibus et consuetudinibus Angliae*. London.

Bright, Timothie. 1586. *A Treatise of Melancholie*. London.

Burton, Robert. 2017. *The Anatomy of Melancholy.* Memphis: General Books.

Cambridge University Library. Dd.5.14.

Erasmus. 1985. *Collected Works of Erasmus: Literary and Educational Writings - 3 & 4.* Edited by J. K. Sowards. London: University of Toronto Press.

Judges, A. V., ed. 2002. *The Elizabethan Underworld—a collection of Tudor and Early Stuart Tracts and Ballads.* London: Routledge.

Littleton, Thomas. 1502. *Tenures.* London.

Martin, C. T., ed. and trans. 1904. Minutes of Parliament of the Middle Temple: Vol. I. London: Butterworth & Co.

Midgley, Samuel. 1789. *The History of the Town and Parish of Halifax*. Halifax.

Mulcaster R. 1581. *Positions, Wherin Those Primitive Circumstances Be Examined, Which are Necessarie for the Training up of Children, Either for Skill in Their Booke, or Health in Their Bodie*. London.

O'Callaghan, Michelle. 2007. *The English Wits: Literature and Sociability in Early Modern England*. Cambridge: Cambridge University Press.

O'Day, Rosemary. 2000. *The Professions in Early Modern England, 1450–1800*. Harlow: Longman.

Prest, Wilfrid. 2023. *The Inns of Court Under Elizabeth I and the Early Stuarts, 1590–1640*. 2nd ed. Cambridge: Cambridge University Press.

———. 2011. "Conflict, Change and Continuity: Elizabeth I to the Great Temple Fire." In *History of the Middle Temple*, edited by Richard O. Havery, 81–110. Oxford: Hart Publishing.

Schoeck, Richard. 1954. "The Elizabethan Society of Antiquarians and Men of the Law." *Notes and Queries* 199: 417–21.

Sturgess, H, ed. 1949. *Register of Admissions to the Honourable Society of the Middle Temple*. London: Butterworth & Co.

Williams, Ian. 2017. "Common Law Scholarship and the Written Word." In *The Oxford Handbook of English Law and Literature, 1500–1700*, edited by Lorna Hutson, 61–79. Oxford: Oxford University Press.

Winston, Jessica. 2016. *Lawyers at Play: Literature, Law and Politics at the Early Modern Inns of Court, 1558–1581*. Oxford: Oxford University Press.

PART II

Without the Inns

CHAPTER 6

The Mad Butler of Gray's Inn: Service, Mental Disability, and the Limits of Institutional Care

Penelope Geng

I am grateful to Andrew Bozio, Rivi Handler-Spitz, David Luck (Bethlem Museum of the Mind Archive), Andrew D. McIntyre, Avi Mendelson, Wilfrid Prest, Jenifer Barclay, Ashley M. Williard, Michelle O'Callaghan, and Emma Rhatigan and Jackie Watson for their generous aid during the writing and research process. Many thanks to Gray's Inn archivists Katherine Gwyn and Francesca Tate for sharing digital images of Gray's Inn Ledger A (FIN/1). Additional thanks go out to the press readers, the Mapping Inns online group, and the organisers and audience of the Consortium for the History of Science, Medicine, and Technology: Disability and Mad Studies Workshop.

P. Geng (✉)
English, Macalester College, Saint Paul, MN, USA
e-mail: pgeng@macalester.edu

E. Rhatigan, J. Watson (eds.), *Mapping the Early Modern Inns of Court*, Early Modern Literature in History,
https://doi.org/10.1007/978-3-031-77445-4_6

On 14 May 1593, the pensioners of Gray's Inn were presented with an urgent matter: what should they do about John Somerscales, the fourth butler, who was 'now visyted with sicness' (Fletcher 1901: 100)?[1] The men took turns speaking, starting with the most junior member (likely Francis Bacon) and ending with the most senior (Prest 2023: 113). The 14 men who participated in the meeting differed in age and experience, but they shared a common desire to preserve the honour of their society.[2] They understood very well the importance of embodying the practical as well as spiritual side of magistracy. They had all heard preachers intoning that a 'good magistrate must be a father of the people' (British Library [Yelverton? 1592–1621]: fol. 31^{r}).[3] In the end, as one unified body and speaking with one voice, the pension ordered the steward to pay Somerscales '5s by the weke during hys sicness . . . out of thadmyttance [the admittance] money': that is, out of the money collected from new matriculants (Fletcher 1901: 100).

The lawyers could not have anticipated the prolonged nature of Somerscales's illness—or the ultimate scope of their financial obligation. At their 31 January 1594 meeting, after seven months, the pension was forced to acknowledge that Somerscales's condition had not improved. In fact, he had lost 'hys perfect sence & memorye' and had fallen into a state of 'lunacy' (Fletcher: 102).[4] Another butler was promoted to his place. They put Somerscales on what we would today call medical leave. But whereas today, workers are rarely offered their full salary when they take extended leave, Somerscales would receive a sum of £3, 6s, 8d as well as the year's 'stock' (more discussion of this in the next section). His annual salary was only £2, 17s, 6d at the time (FIN/1: fol. 24^{r}).

[1] Somerscales was hired in July 1590 (Fletcher 1901: 88). All dates have been changed to the New Style Calendar.

[2] The 14 men at the meeting were John Brograve,* Richard Anger (or Aungier),* William Whiskins,* William Cardinall,* John Penruddock, Richard Kempe,* William Daniell,* Nicholas Fuller,* Francis Bacon,* Edmund Pelham, John Lancaster,* Jeremy Bettenham,* John Lany,* and Geoffrey Nightingale (multiple candidates). Starred individuals served as treasurers; see "Historical List of Recorded Treasurers"' Gray's Inn Archives, https://www.graysinn.org.uk/app/uploads/2023/06/Grays-Inn-Archives-and-History-Treasurers-1.pdf, accessed 15 March 2024.

[3] For a longer discussion of judicial conduct and compassionate magistracy, see Geng 2021: Chap. 2.

[4] In this chapter, I use madness, no quotation marks, in place of 'lunacy.' Mad and madness have been recovered as non-stigmatising terms in mad studies and disability studies.

In February or early March 1595 (approximately two years after his initial collapse), the pension committed Somerscales to Bethlem Hospital, then England's only hospital specialising in the treatment of madness. Again, the pension paid. An entry in the Ledger states, 'payd the 3 of Marche 1594 [1595] to m[aste]r Slifford the Master of Bethelem' in the amount of 13s, 4d (FIN/1, fol. 35^{r}). Institutionalisation at Bethlem was extremely rare. As Michael MacDonald points out, Bethlem was a 'tiny' hospital and '[o]nly a handful of the insane in a nation of five million souls were cast into an asylum before the English Revolution' (1981: 4). It is possible the pension used their influence to secure a place for Somerscales. Months turned into years, and years into decades. From 1595 to 1611, the pension sent regular sums to the master of Bethlem for Somerscales's maintenance.

The case of the mad butler of Gray's Inn, which is little known even to specialists, raises a number of questions pertaining to the innsmen's conception of their obligation to their servants and the role of lawyers in shaping cultural perceptions of madness.[5] On the question of service, Wilfrid Prest encourages scholars to conduct 'further research across a range of records, including those of neighbouring parishes and the city of London, as well as central government and the courts of law' to increase our knowledge of the experience of service at the inns (2023: 17). I answer that call by attempting to reconstruct Somerscales's journey from Gray's Inn to Bethlem using evidence drawn from administrative documents from both institutions as well as from cultural texts (such as drama). My chapter contributes to the historical study of madness and mental disability 'from below' and introduces a conversation about ableism at the inns of court. During Somerscales's monthslong confinement at Gray's Inn, the society played host to a lavish series of Christmas revels for members of their society, members of the Inner Temple, and the elites of Elizabethan London. Their celebration on Innocents' Night (28 December 1594) culminated in the first recorded performance of Shakespeare's *The Comedy of Errors*. The play's staging of the involuntary confinement of Antipholus of Ephesus for madness on the diagnosis of Dr Pinch occurred under the very roof that sheltered Somerscales. What do we need to ask about this strange juxtaposition of pretend and real madness?

[5] I wanted to understand just how unique a case this was, so I asked Prest. He did not know off-hand of any other such cases ('Email,' 3 March 2024).

In Sickness and in Health

When the pension paid Somerscales's wages during his initial period of illness and confinement, it was operating within a set of contractual protocols governing master-servant relations. The phrase 'in sickness and in health'—which implies reciprocity between parties—appears in some apprentice indentures from this period (Pelling 1998: 124). This pledge of reciprocity, however, was more of an ideal than a reality. As Margaret Pelling shows through her detailed analysis of Norwich legal and hospital records, masters routinely sought to get out of their obligations by any means possible—including flat-out chicanery. Many disempowered child-apprentices suffered in silence, but a few successfully took their masters to court. Their testimonies provide historians with a glimpse of the experience of illness from the servants' perspective. In 1655, for example, the Norwich master Lionel Hargrave 'was bound over to [quarter] sessions on the complaint of his apprentice . . . Charles Spendlove. The justices agreed that Spendlove was to be discharged from his master, and that Hargrave was to pay Spendlove's father 40s. for the keeping of Charles during his sickness' (1998: 128–29).[6]

Examples of masters failing to perform their legal and moral duties provide a historical context for understanding the pension's decision. Workers today expect very little in the way of financial long-term support from their employers. From a modern vantage, it is natural to marvel at the pension's generosity. But in the context of what Prest calls 'cradle-to-grave paternalism,' the pension's action should not surprise (2023: 111). The question to ask is not why the pension acted as it did it, but what the pension stood to lose if it did not dole out sick pay. These men were the elites of the inns of court; they viewed themselves as a cut above the rest. As Jessica Winston has illuminated, in the sixteenth century, the four inns of court spent enormous amounts of money and human resources (time and energy) to consolidate their authority as magistrates; they strove to 'present themselves as possessing a social and professional decorum that matched their image of the ideal magistrate and wise counsellor' (2016: 215). As 'ancients' (senior lawyers of their society), pensioners needed to set a sterling example for younger members. Turning Somerscales out of

[6] Masters rarely nursed their servants personally. Pelling cites Paul Slack's discovery of 'the case of a London gentleman who dealt with the illness of a servant by boarding her up in a separate part of the house and employing a stranger to look after her. This master was observing the letter of his obligation towards his servant but not its spirit' (1998: 198).

door was just not an option. Magistrates were appointed to curb vagrancy; the pension could hardly be seen to increase it.

Beyond the powerful tug of legal ethos and paternalism, there were perhaps medical and pragmatic reasons shaping the pension's decision. Earlier, I hinted that the pension might have hoped that Somerscales could be cured of his illness. Madness, in this period, was often framed as curable with the right intervention—dietary, physical, or spiritual (or all three). 'Foolishness' and 'idiocy' were understood as congenital and permanently disabling, and madness as a 'temporary state' (MacDonald 1981: 5; see also Metzler 2016; Equestri 2021). The language that the pension used to describe Somerscales's initial illness suggests as much: he was 'visyted with sicness' (Fletcher 1901: 100). The Ledger repeats that word: 'his first visitac[i]on' began on 'j of marche An° 35 [1 March 1593]' (FIN/1, fol. 34^{v}). According to the *Oxford English Dictionary*, 'visitation' in this period signified 'the action of going to a place'.[7] Like an unwelcomed guest, the illness could leave Somerscales with the right encouragement.

In hoping for Somerscales's recovery, the pension could have been thinking of household management as well as the sick man's own comfort. Inns' administrators struggled to find and keep high-performing servants. They faced competition in London from elite and non-elite households for able-bodied and competent servants. If Somerscales had served well—there is no indication of him being scolded for dereliction—then it would have been in the pension's own interest to keep him. To appreciate this facet of Somerscales's relationship with the pension, it is helpful to consider the pension's response to news of the illness of the steward of the house. In October 1596 (after Somerscales had been committed to Bethlem), the pension learned that John Draper the steward had fallen ill and had petitioned the pension to be 'discharged of his office' because his 'sickness' prevented him from 'perform[ing] the said office.' The pension agreed to his terms. It promoted Draper's subordinate, triggering a cascade of promotions and room swaps: 'Buck is chosen to be Steward from and after Saturday next, and Parry to be chief butler and Casson to be in his room, and Catmar to be in Casson's room.' The order ends with the hope of Draper's recovery: 'If, however, Draper shall recover, he shall continue his stewardship or shall be chief butler if he like thereof, and the

[7] *Oxford English Dictionary*, s.v. "visitation (n.)," https://doi.org/10.1093/OED/9281252594, accessed March 2024.

other butlers to take their former places' (Fletcher 1901: 128). The proviso ('if … recover … shall continue') speaks to the pension's desire for the steward's healing—a desire no doubt also motivated by a pragmatic interest in household stability.

When Somerscales's condition remained unimproved, the pension permitted the disbursal of further wages to him. As previously mentioned, at their 31 January 1594 meeting, the pension ordered that Somerscales be paid £3, 6s, 8d 'yearly duringe hys lunacy' and, further, that he should also have £6, 8s, 4d 'of the stock of the howse for this yeare' (Fletcher 1901: 101–02). Should Somerscales be cured of his madness, he would be welcomed back to his position:

> yf yt shall please God at any tyme hereafter to restore the sayd John Somerscales to hys perfect sence & memorye agayne that then the said John yf he shall lyke thereof shall & may com & execute hys place agayne in the buttyre & shall have soch fees & commodyties as heretofore he hath had. (Fletcher 1901: 102)

Until that time, Somerscales's duties would be assumed by Anthony Catmer (Fletcher 1901: 102). The sum £3, 6s, 8d carries symbolic weight. The admission fee for a new matriculant to Gray's Inn (a person who had no prior training at one of the preparatory inns, such as Staples Inn) was £3, 6s, 8d. The 'stock of the house' refers to the remainder left over after the reconciliation of recurrent expenditure by a tax or levy. Any surplus money remaining after the payment of the annual expenditures became part of the stock (Prest 2023: 119; see also Nelson and Elliott 2010: xxxv–xxxvi). 'Stock' in the context of elite households could also mean a retirement pension on the completion of decades of satisfactory service (Hindle 2023: 314). Thus, the payment to Somerscales during his illness was the equivalent of a new member's admission fee. The 'stock' brings to mind the concept of 'public stock': money or property held by the society for the good of its institution. By allocating a fraction of the stock to Somerscales, the pension affirmed the voluntary nature of their society. As Emma Rhatigan discusses in Chap. 3, the inns of court, in a manner not unlike medieval confraternities and the London guilds, required fellowship from its members (performed in the taking of meals in the hall, residency in chambers, and participation at readings), as well as many acts of voluntary fellowship. To quote Michelle O'Callaghan, 'rituals and cultural fictions' were needed to enforce the 'voluntary contract' (2007: 10).

Finally, the phrase 'such fees' likely signified standard payments shared among servants gathered from all members (a kind of service tax) while 'commodities' likely meant food, linens, and other incidentals.

Gray's Inn's sick pay to Somerscales constituted not a minor but a significant expense. Like many of the other inns, it operated by a slim revenue margin. While individuals at the inn may have been personally wealthy—the law could be an extremely lucrative profession, as the career of Sir Edward Coke attests—inns as voluntary societies were barely solvent. Because of the voluntary status of the inns of court, each inn's income was dependent on 'current income,' principally fees from members (Nelson and Elliott 2010: xiii). Prest describes the situation thus: 'the societies . . . failed to enjoy a comfortable affluence based on substantial annual surpluses of income over expenditure' in spite of efforts by their governors (2023: 119). An ongoing expenditure such as the pension's sick pay to a non-working servant would have had an impact on the accounting.

What kind of medical attention Somerscales received during his confinement at Gray's Inn cannot be fully determined, only conjectured. It is almost certain that he was kept to his room. Beyond that, it is hard to say. In this period, those who were diagnosed with madness were subjected to involuntary confinement, corporal punishments (flogging), bloodletting, and drugging delivered in the form of 'opium grains, unguents, and laudanum' depending on the severity of the symptoms (MacDonald 1981: 190, 196). The treatment could have been calibrated to fit the diagnosis. Medical and religious authors theorised a complex array of mental disorders which they indexed by external signs premised on non-normative social behaviours such as disordered speech, hair, or dress, and irregularities of pulse and body temperature. A popular medical author of this period, Nicholas Culpeper, stated that signs of madness may include 'laughing, sighing . . . doting, crying out, threatening, skipping, leaping' (cited in MacDonald 1981: 139). Laughter and tears were not in themselves signs of madness, rather, they constituted evidence when they were judged excessive by the socially accepted norms. In other words, madness was sometimes spoken of as being internal to the individual, but, viewed historically, it was also clearly socially, as well as religiously, constructed. In Peter Rushton's study of quarter session records, the initial diagnosis of madness often originated in the family unit; labelling was 'conducted by friends and relatives rather than local officials' (1996: 38). In a time when medical professionals had yet to consolidate their monopoly over diagnosis, an imputation of madness against a person constituted a communal verdict. Keeping in mind the social context of madness, which resonates with the social model of disability, it is conceivable that Somerscales was declared mad on the strength of communal testimony. Perhaps his fellow servants, the chief butler, and students at the inn provided eye-witness testimony.

The payment of 5s a week—a sum reflected in the treasurer John Lancaster's account from 1593–1594 (FIN/1, fol. 34^{v})—could have been sufficient to pay for female caregivers or watchers from the neighbourhood (Harkness 2008). It had become common practice in this period for masters or parish overseers to hire 'goodwives' to visit, board, or heal the sick in their home. Women earned small wages as watchers, nurses, and keepers. There is evidence of Gray's Inn engaging in this practice. At their 31 January 1603 meeting, the pension asked Francis Bacon as treasurer to pay 10s 'unto Alice Pryce & goodwife Chappell for keeping of Mr Whiskins,' although Whiskins died shortly thereafter (Fletcher 1901: 489). A goodwife might have watched Somerscales. Additionally, Somerscales might have received spiritual attention from a clergyman. In *Twelfth Night*, Malvolio is visited by Feste masquerading as Sir Topaz the curate, a reminder of the entwining of medical and spiritual care work in this period. As Hannah Newton explains, 'the care of the body and soul were connected, and ministers were often well versed in medical theory' (2021: 535). Could Somerscales have received attention from the preacher, Dr Crooke? In several places in the Ledger, we find payments of wages to Somerscales near payments to Dr Crooke. Although the proximity of these payments does not necessarily prove a connection, it is just possible that Dr Crooke exchanged words with Somerscales. Furthermore, did Somerscales receive personal attention from his fellow servants or from John Draper, the steward? Interpersonal relations between servants could be fraught as *Twelfth Night* well reminds us, but even allowing for the occasional strife, the men could have developed a bond from the shared experience of working and living together at Gray's Inn. Finally, even if Somerscales was shunned by his fellow servants, he was at least housed in a familiar environment. Newton's study of the phenomenology of the sickchamber underscores the emotional value of familiar objects (such as bedsheets) to those who experienced illness (2021).

Somerscales's time at Gray's Inn came to an end in early March 1595. An entry dated 3 March records the first of many payments to 'Mr Slifford [Rowland Sleforth] the Master of Bethelem.' Someone at the inn (perhaps Draper) paid 6s to hire a 'cariage' to take Somerscales to Bethlem. Just prior to this, however, the Ledger records an attempt—coordinated by Draper—to temporarily rehome Somerscales in the 'country' (FIN/1, fol. 34^{v}):

It[e]m payd to the carriage of Somerscales down into the Norths	20s
It[e]m geven the carrier to paye for his board in the Countrye till I might convenient send by some other	20s
It[e]m sent to Somerscales towardes the payment of his diet and other things in the Country	26s, 8d
It[e]m paid to Sharples for John Somerscales	£3, 6s, 8d

There are a couple of ways to interpret this evidence. The first is that Somerscales was sent home to his kin, but his family was not equipped to care for him.[8] The second is that the country trip was always intended to be temporary. He could not be sent straight to Bethlem, perhaps because of a lack of space. During his stay in the country, whoever was in charge of Somerscales (perhaps Sharples?) received payments from Gray's Inn for the sick man's room and board. Despite being sent away, Somerscales was still tethered to his original place of employment, which speaks to the inn's dynamic definition of fellowship and household.[9] The arrangement must have been very temporary, for immediately following these entries begin a stream of payments in the amount of 13s, 3d per month to the 'said m[aste]^{r}' of Bethlem (FIN/1, fol. 35^{r}) (Fig. 6.1). At their 11 February 1596 meeting, the pension confirmed a payment of 40s (or £3, 9s, 9d) to the 'masters of Bethlem' for 'iii monethes' (Fletcher 1901: 113).

[8] Charmian Mansell explains that the '1601 poor law clearly set out that direct descendants (children) and first-generation ascending relatives (parents) were expected to economically support those unable to work, including the sick' and that '[s]iblings did not—at least in theory—bear the weight of such expectations' (2023: 11). I have not been able to determine Somerscales's place of origin. My guess is that he hailed from Lincolnshire (which lies north of London). Two families, both bearing the last name Somerscales, flourished in the late sixteenth century in Lincolnshire: the Somerscales of Brigsley and the Somerscales of Grimsby. According to Prest (2023: 58–59), between 1590 and 1639, 261 members of Gray's Inn hailed from Lincolnshire; Lincolnshire was the third best represented region after London (392 members) and Yorkshire (387 members).

[9] I am grateful to Emma Rhatigan for helping with this part of the transcription and the interpretation of the evidence.

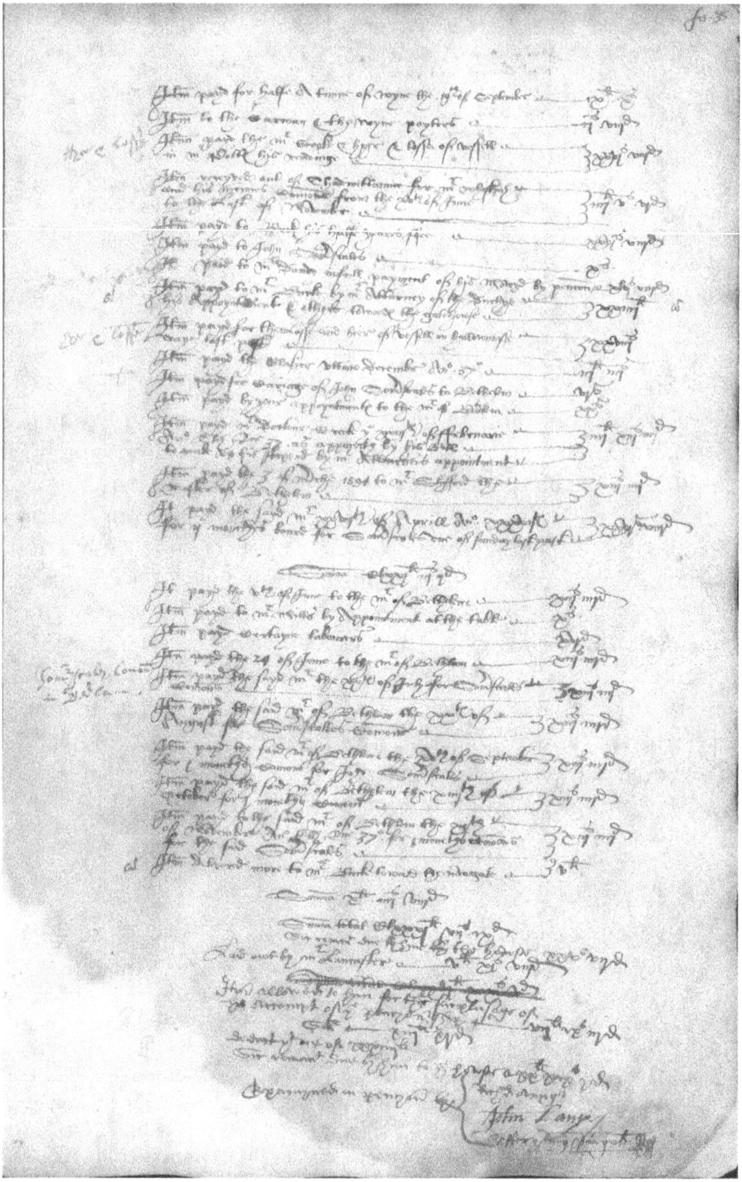

Fig. 6.1 Gray's Inn Ledger, fol. 35[r]. By kind permission of The Honourable Society of Gray's Inn

Surviving Bethlem Hospital

In the late sixteenth century, Bethlem was located in Bishopsgate (now the site of Liverpool Street station). Founded in the thirteenth century as the priory St Mary of Bethlehem by the London citizen Simon FitzMary (son of Mary), Bethlem was only 1.6 miles from Gray's Inn yet a world apart. Whereas Gray's Inn was entering an era of beautification and expansion, Bethlem was experiencing an irreversible decline.[10] It was a dehumanising environment. A centuries-long jurisdictional struggle between the city and the crown over the patronage of Bethlem had left the hospital in dire financial straits (Allderidge 1979: 147; Andrews *et al.* 1997: 42). In the 1590s, Bethlem came under the administration of the governors of Bridewell Hospital (Andrews *et al.* 1997: 62). These governors, in Patricia Allderidge's words, 'took little interest in the supervision of Bethlem,' leaving the day-to-day business to an appointed master or keeper (1979: 149). With a maximum capacity of roughly 20 residents, Bethlem was Bridewell's small, neglected, and overlooked sister.

The governors of Bridewell left the administration of Bethlem largely to the discretion of the keeper. A few historically notable individuals enjoyed the title of keeper, including George Boleyn (Anne Boleyn's brother), Edward Alleyn (the father of the actor of the same name), and Helkiah Crooke. Most were unremarkable citizens whose worst trait was negligence. Two keepers intersected Somerscales's story: Rowland Sleforth, a clothworker appointed in 1579, and John Parrott, a draper, who assumed the office in 1598 after Sleforth. Sleforth is remembered down to this day for his mismanagement of the institution (Allderidge 1979: 150). In December 1598, a commission sent by the governors of Bridewell to survey Bethlem—a rare surprise audit whose exceptionalism underscores the general pattern of inattention—discovered that Sleforth had allowed the hospital to fall into a state 'not fitt for anye man to dwell … so loathsomely and filthily kept not fitt for anye man to come into the sayd howse' (BCB-04, fol. 52^{r}).[11] In this 1598 survey we encounter a familiar name: 'John Somerskall sent in by m[aste]^{r} Swaldell when he was Treasorer

[10] On the magnificence of Gray's Inn Great Hall, especially its strapwork, see Girouard 2011: 147. On the expansion of Gray's Inn famous 'walks,' see Jacques 1989: 41–67.

[11] The 1598 survey begins on fol. 51^{r} and concludes on fol. 52^{r}. While I have transcribed from the original document, the survey is partially transcribed and printed in Allderidge 1979: 151–53. I am grateful to David Luck for allowing me to consult and photograph the original Minute Book.

at the request of the Benchers of Grayes Inn about three years past and is allowed for by them' (Fig. 6.2).

There is little evidence to suggest that the Bethlem keepers were interested in applying the latest theories for the curing of madness. MacDonald's magisterial study of the casebooks of Richard Napier shows that physicians like Napier, 'one of the last Renaissance magi,' deployed a variety of approaches to treat their patients (1981: 16).[12] In *The Physitian's Library* (1663), a compendium of the writings of the period's most famous doctors, the first book provides detailed aetiology and cures for 'Weakness of the Mind,' 'consternation of the mind,' 'Alienation of the Mind,' and 'Defatigation of the Mind' (C1^r) (Anon. 1663). Outside of England, Sara Scalenghe's research on mental disability in the Ottoman Arab Empire opens a view to what was possible in terms of mental health care in another part of the world in this very period. She points out that Ottoman-era hospitals should not be romanticised—'hospitals were viewed as fearful places: if they appeared in a dream, they indicated death and hell, "because the hospital is the place of chains and shackles."' Yet, she continues, 'the hospitals of Cairo, Damascus, and Aleppo were impressive buildings with pools, fountains, and gardens, where music therapy was sometimes employed' (2016: 99). Contrast this to Bethlem where, instead of the sound and sight of splashing fountains, there was only the noise of a rapidly urbanising precinct and the nauseating smell of a poorly draining 'open ditch' (Andrews *et al.* 1997: 50). Bethlem's pattern of institutional negligence established a historical precedent for the warehousing of patients. The Bethlem model would, in time, pave the way for the rise of private and public asylums in the nineteenth and twentieth centuries.

As a further indication of neglect of 'prisoners' at Bethlem (or so they were called in the 1598 survey), there is little to suggest the keepers sought to improve the health of those under their authority through 'dietics' (Pelling 1998: 38). Since at least the time of Galen, food was imbued with curative properties for both physical and mental disorders (1998: Chap. 2). The diet at Bethlem kept a person alive, but it was not modified to improve their health. Bethlem inmates likely ate the kind of meal provided to the non-working population at Bridewell hospital: a daily diet of bread (12 oz.), beer (1 quart), beef on non-fast days (6.5 oz.), and dairy on fast

[12] Napier's casebooks have been digitised; see Simon Forman and Richard Napier, *The Casebooks of Simon Forman and Richard Napier, 1596–1634: A Digital Edition*. Edited by Lauren Kassell *et al.* https://casebooks.lib.cam.ac.uk, accessed 20 March 2024.

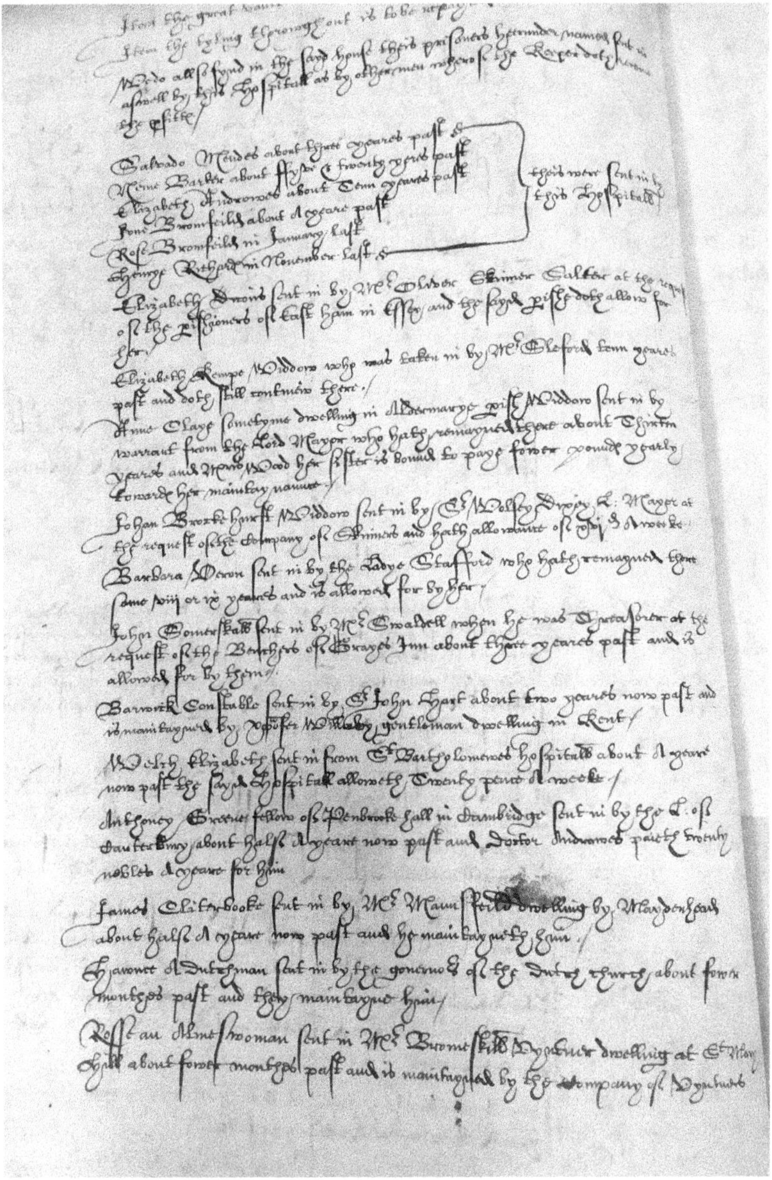

Fig. 6.2 'John Somerskall,' BCB-04, fol. 51v. Author's photo, 2023. By kind permission of the Bethlem Museum of the Mind

days (4 oz. cheese or 2 oz. butter) (Archer 1991: 191; Andrews *et al.* 1997: 127, no. 9).[13] Anything beyond the standard diet would need to be arranged—and paid for—by neighbours, kin, or charitable patrons.

Theatricalising Madness at Gray's Inn

The uncanny parallel between John Somerscales and Malvolio inspired Basil Brown, one of the first twentieth-century editors of *Gesta Grayorum* (1688), to speculate that Somerscales might have been the prototype for Shakespeare's 'mad' steward. Writing shortly after the end of the First World War, Brown posited a friendship between Shakespeare and Francis Bacon and argued that it was through Bacon that the playwright learned of the case of Gray's Inn's mad butler:

> if, as I believe, Bacon befriended the poet, he would have known all about Somerscales; and, as Bacon took a sympathetic interest in the poor butler, perhaps Shakespeare would drop in to see him [at Bethlem] now and then and report to Bacon how he was getting on. (1921: 2)

It goes without saying that scholars do not subcribe to the theory. My research does not indicate any sympathy on Bacon's part to Somerscales. Bacon devoted far more attention to improving the walks of Gray's Inn than to the welfare of its servants. While I would shelve Brown's fanciful theory, I want to acknowledge the rightness of Brown's instinct to concentrate on understanding the meaning of the staging of madness at Gray's Inn during Somerscales's initial period of confinement.

In this final section, I argue that innsmen used dramatisation of madness to foil intellectual virtuosity, and that this practice enabled a regime of intellectual ableism. In his famous account of the inns, Sir George Buck praises the inns as the 'third universitie' of England, and he called Sir Edward Coke 'not onely a most learned professor, but also a singular Antecessor, a chiefe Judge, and a principall interpreter' (1615: 4M1^{r}). Men like Coke monopolised the production of legal knowledge. They also actively shaped the ideology of ability (intellectual, mental, and to a certain extent, physical). In my previous study of the rhetoric of legal expertise, I was intrigued by lawyers' remarks about the uniqueness of the legal 'brain' (2021: 16). I interpreted such boastful expressions as a rhetorical

[13] I am grateful to Andrew Bozio for helping me to think through this entire section.

defence against a lay movement that sought to reclaim legal judgement and authority as the birthright of every conscience-bearing individual. Reading these remarks again, I notice that these assertions of intellectual superiority strongly anticipate the Enlightenment discourse of rationalism.

Stephanie Elsky explains, 'unlike civil law, which was based on a set of authoritative texts, common law was considered "general custom" or the "custom of the realm"' (2020: 3). The lack of a code or digest meant that while certain local legal customs were indeed engrained in local memory, the bulk of legal knowledge (or what jurists called the 'matters of law' as opposed to 'matters of fact') remained in the hands of a highly concentrated elite: common lawyers who had trained at the inns of court. Compounding the inaccessibility of legal knowledge was the fact that centuries of legal innovation (especially in land law) had created a confusion of precedents and exceptions. Some publicly minded individuals like Bacon tried to systematise legal learning, but these attempts never came to fruition. The point is that those who dedicated themselves to the study of law at the inns valued such intellectual traits as a keen memory and verbal playfulness—characterised by the use of 'innuendo, allusion, flyting and rhetorical point-scoring' (Watson 2015: 7). The innsman differentiated himself from the ordinary man by his unimpeachable mastery over all faculties controlled by reason. As Jackie Watson discusses in Chap. 4, in addition to his supreme intelligence and linguistic prowess, an innsmen (in this period) also cultivated a courtly physique. Ongoing work on the performance of dancing and fencing at the inns reveals that innsmen admired balance, strength, and quick-footedness. Not everyone had the body to meet such strict standards. John Davies (before his knighthood and promotion to solicitor-general for Ireland) was shamed for his ill-shaped form. According to John Manningham, 'Jo[hn] Davys goes wadling with his arse out behinde as though he were about to make every one that he meetes a wall to pisse against. (B. Rudyerd, or Th. Overb[ur]y). He never walkes but he carries a clokebag behinde him, his arse stickes out soe farr' (1976: 255).

The celebration of intellectual (and at times, physical) virtuosity found a powerful outlet in the Christmas revels. These were the occasions when lawyers patronised, promoted, and participated in the staging of both scripted and improvised theatrical performances (Rhatigan 2011: 154). These celebrations enabled lawyers to further index their mental and physical abilities. To understand how lawyerly theatricality aided intellectual ableism, it is helpful to consider disability theatre's theorisation of 'cripping up' or 'disability drag' (see Fox and Sandahl 2018; Sandahl 2008; Siebers 2004). As explained by Katherine Schaap Williams, there is an established tradition in Hollywood which sees Oscar-seeking, able-bodied actors vying to play severely disabled characters. The act of impersonation indexes the actor's virtuosic capacity. This insidious form of impersonation—which treats the non-disabled body as the neutral form of embodiment, one capable of chameleonic changes—is reflected and complicated by early modern theatre, which, according to Williams, often foregrounds the 'contingent vulnerability of the actor in real time' and 'implicates every body in that vulnerability too' (2021: 9).

The question that I want to ask is whether the 'unfixing' (Williams's term) power of early modern drama is neutralised when it is staged in spaces designed to show off intellectual prowess like the hall of Gray's Inn. If an audience is bent on intellectual and physical conformity, is it still possible to understand theatre to be staging an ethical 'beholding' of bodymind non-normativity (Hobgood 2021)? While this is not a question that can be answered fully or proven historically, it cannot be dismissed because it orients us to be critical, not merely descriptive, of the inns' penchant for welcoming mad spectacle into their hallowed halls, as Gray's Inn did in 1594–1595, and of their delight in counterfeiting physical disability and poverty, as the four inns did in their performance of James Shirley's masque *The Triumph of Peace* in 1634. According to the eyewitness account by the lawyer Bulstrode Whitelocke, 'the personall beauty & gallantry of the handsome young gentlemen,' was set off by the 'first Antimasque, being of Cripples & Beggars'; the 'variety & change from noble musicke, & gallant horses as went before them, unto their proper musicke & pitifull horses, made both of them the more pleasing' (Nelson and Elliott 2010: 1.274, with a summary of *The Triumph of Peace* at 503–04). The beautiful body is thrown into high relief by the juxtaposition to the impoverished and disabled body.

In what remains, I posit that the staging of madness at Gray's Inn helped to cement lawyers' virtuosic ability to turn madness on and off. As mentioned, the Christmas revels of 1594–1595—the revels extended 'over the full Christmas season (1 November to 2 February and beyond)'—was an elaborate and expensive event that Gray's Inn co-produced with the Inner Temple (Nelson and Elliott 2010: 2.363). Participating in this theatrical extravagance served as an 'opportunity for self-creation' (Rhatigan 2011: 156). The hierarchical nature of the Christmas court mimicked the hierarchal *status quo* of the 'real' court—the Queen's court—and thus the revelry may be understood to reinforce deeply conventional and traditional views on rank and status.

Scholars of early modern drama primarily remember the revels for their connection to Shakespeare. *The Comedy of Errors* was staged on 28 December 1594, Innocents' Night, in the hall of Gray's Inn. In the play, the merchant-traveller Antipholus (of Syracuse) is mistaken for his twin Antipholus (of Ephesus). The comedy of mistaken identity leads to confusion, culminating in Adriana, the wife of Antipholus (of Ephesus), declaring her husband demonically possessed and mad, a diagnosis confirmed by Dr Pinch. Antipholus is bound and confined to quarters. Eventually, he wiggles out of his prison and makes his appeal before the Duke of Ephesus, complaining, 'They fell upon me, bound me, bore me thence, / And in a dark and dankish vault at home / There left me and my man, both bound together' (2016: 5.1.247–49). Both the initial diagnosis of madness and its eventual resolution depend on the testimony of the community. As Jessica Apolloni explains, '[t]he play resolves with community members exerting their own power, a power that is reliant on communal connections and social relationships' (2022: 11). The play's exploration of madness and community recalls the social dimension of madness as explored by historians such as MacDonald, Rushton, and others.

For the lawyer, watching this comedy of mistaken identity during a sanctioned time of misrule could have been a way to reinforce his superior status as a potential judge of fact. Antipholus and Dromio (the former's enslaved servant who is haplessly caught up in the confusion) are baffled for the gratification of a knowing audience. On the very night of this performance, the lawyers in the audience indulged in a bacchanalian revelry so extreme that it threatened to eclipse the action of the comedy. As told in the *Gesta*, guests of the Prince of Purpoole generated such a 'disordered Tumult'—rushing 'upon the Stage'—that the Inner Temple's 'Lord Ambassador and his Train' fled, being 'discontented and displeased' (Nelson and Elliott 2010: 2.397). Yet this mayhem was temporary. The end of festival paved the way for the beginning of a new legal term. The revels served to reinforce not only the sense of fellowship among the revellers, but reminded lawyers of their ability to dabble in mad antics without becoming permanently impaired. The 'Night of Errors' did not so much transform the culture of reason at the inn as reinforce it. The lawyers, in other words, cripped up.

The staging of theatricalised madness at Gray's Inn has a cognate in the European folly tradition in which fools (very broadly conceived) were displayed for the amusement and edification of readers. Tomaso Garzoni's *L'Hospedale de' pazzi incurabili* (1586), translated into English by Edward Blount as *The Hospitall of Incurable Fooles* (1600), declares that 'discovering other mens follies, you may shew your selves the wiser' (Garzoni 1600: A4^{v}). Garzoni's emphasis on beholding 'people enchanted in brained, and transformed with brutish Metamorphoses into unreasonable and sottish folke' as a way to be assured of one's good senses speaks to authors' use of literary devices, such as the *exempla*, to re-entrench the binary of reason/madness. Watching madness from the safety of the audience position allowed innsmen to cement their superior hold on rationality.

It is impossible to say how many members (besides the pension) were aware of John Somerscales during this Christmas period. The servants knew, but did many of the student-learners? What passed through the minds of those who knew of Somerscales's 'lunacy' when they watched Dr Pinch diagnose Antipholus? Did the drama remind them of their own responsibility as magistrates? Did it affirm their desire to police the boundary of rationality and madness?

Conclusion

Sometime before 1611, Somerscales was discharged from Bethlem. Because of the limited space available at the hospital, keepers (and Bridewell governors) were in the habit of discharging inmates as soon as they were found to be sane enough to return to society. Having been institutionalised for more than a decade, Somerscales was hardly equipped to succeed in finding employment. Not surprisingly, then, in October 1611, Somerscales returned to Gray's Inn—now much altered—for alms. The pension once again gave him money:

> Att this penc[i]on [30 October 1611] it pleased the Benche to bestowe on John Somerscales one of the Butlers of this house the som of 20 marks in comiserac[i]on of his poverty & in recompence of his service done to this societie which som the said Somerscales did thankful lie accept in recompence of his place & full satisfacc[i]on of all pretence to be restored to the said office. (Fletcher 1901: 195)

The amount £13, 6s, 8d (the equivalent of 20 marks) was noted in the treasurer's accounts: 'To Jho[n] Somerscalles p[er] order of Penc[i]on 30 october 16ii' (FIN/1, fol. 76^{r}). The rhetoric of reciprocity and mutual pleasure—'it pleased the Benche to bestowe' and 'Somerscales did thankfulie accept'—smooths over troubling questions of Somerscales's future prospects. The payment effectively put an end to any 'pretence to be restored to the said office.'[14]

Somerscales's story reveals the possibilities (and limits) of institutional care in an era defined by communal obligation. While we should remain sceptical of the quality of the care Somerscales received, we cannot deny that the pension of Gray's Inn fulfilled their duty as magistrates according to the letter, if not the spirit, of the law. In my effort to reconstruct John Somerscales's experience, I have asked questions about the cultural attitudes towards madness and mental disability. I have been interested in the documentary evidence of disease and disability at the inns of court, as well as the role of the inns in making or shaping cultures of ableism. The practice of theatricalising madness at the inns arguably furthered the marginalisation and stigmatisation of mentally disabled subjects like Somerscales. The picture of Gray's Inn which emerges in my account is contradictory: capable of demonstrating benevolence and compassionate fellowship, the institution also participated in the production of ableist ideals of body-mind normativity.

Works Cited

Allderidge, Patricia. 1979. "Management and Mismanagement at Bedlam, 1547–1633." In *Health, Medicine and Mortality in the Sixteenth Century*, edited by Charles Webster, 141–64. Cambridge: Cambridge University Press.

Andrews, Jonathan, *et al.* 1997. *The History of Bethlem*. London: Routledge.

Anonymous. 1663. *The Physitian's Library*. London.

Apolloni, Jessica. 2022. "'A Night of Errors': Chaos, Comedy, and Comparative Law at the Inns of Court." *Law, Culture and the Humanities*. https://doi.org/10.1177/17438721221080785

Archer, Ian W. 1991. *The Pursuit of Stability: Social Relations in Elizabethan London*. Cambridge: Cambridge University Press.

[14]An online search in The National Archives uncovers items pertaining to "Somerscales, John, (idiot): Lincoln" dated 8 James I (1610–1611, under WARD 7/34/49 and C 142/313/56), and "Somerscales, John, (lunatic): Lincoln" dated 14 James I (1616–1617, under WARD 7/55/202 and C 142/355/3). The 1616–1617 record is a *post-mortem* inquest, which leads me to think that Somerscales died sometime between 1616 and 1617 (assuming this Somerscales is the same man). I have not had a chance to view these records.

Museum of the Mind. Bridewell Court of Governors Minute Books. BCB-04, February 1598–November 1604. https://archives.museumofthemind.org.uk/image_viewer.htm?BCB-04,947.

Brown, Basil. 1921. *Law Sports at Gray's Inn (1594) Including Shakespeare's Connection with the Inn's of Court … Together with a Reprint of the Gesta Grayorum*. Privately Printed.

Buck, George. 1615. "The Third Universitie of England." In John Stow and Edmund Howes, *The Annales, or Generall Chronicle of England*. London.

Elsky, Stephanie. 2020. *Custom, Common Law, and the Constitution of English Renaissance Literature*. Oxford: Oxford University Press.

Equestri, Alice. 2021. *Literature and Intellectual Disability in Early Modern England: Folly, Law and Medicine, 1500–1640*. New York: Routledge.

Fletcher, Reginald J., ed. 1901. *The Pension Book of Gray's Inn (Records of the Honourable Society), 1569–1669*. Vol. 1. London: Chiswick.

Fox, Ann M., and Sandahl, Carrie. 2018. "Beyond 'Cripping Up': An Introduction." *Journal of Literary and Cultural Disability Studies* 12, no. 2: 121–27.

Garzoni, Tomaso. 1600. *The Hospitall of Incurable Fooles: Erected in English, as Neer the First Italian Modell and Platforme, as the Vnskilfull Hand of an Ignorant Architect Could Deuise*. Translated by Edward Blount. London.

Geng, Penelope. 2021. *Communal Justice in Shakespeare's England: Drama, Law, and Emotion*. Toronto: University of Toronto Press.

Girouard, Mark. 2011. "The Halls of the Elizabethan and Early Stuart Inns of Court." In *The Intellectual and Cultural World of the Early Modern Inns of Court*, edited by Jayne Elisabeth Archer, Elizabeth Goldring, and Sarah Knight, 138–56. Manchester: Manchester University Press.

Gray's Inn. FIN/1: Ledger A, 1586–1703.

Harkness, Deborah E. 2008. "A View from the Streets: Women and Medical Work in Elizabethan London." *Bulletin of the History of Medicine* 82, no. 1: 52–85.

Hindle, Steve. 2023. *The Social Topography of a Rural Community: Scenes of Labouring Life in Seventeenth Century England*. Oxford: Oxford University Press.

Hobgood, Allison P. 2021. *Beholding Disability in Renaissance England*. Ann Arbor: University of Michigan Press.

Jacques, David. 1989. "'The Chief Ornament' of Gray's Inn: The Walks from Bacon to Brown." *Garden History* 17, no. 1: 41–67.

MacDonald, Michael. 1981. *Mystical Bedlam: Madness, Anxiety, and Healing in Seventeenth-Century England*. Cambridge: Cambridge University Press.

Manningham, John. 1976. *The Diary of John Manningham of the Middle Temple, 1602–1603*. Edited by Robert Parker Sorlien. Hanover NH: University Press of New England.

Mansell, Charmian. 2023. “Reconstructing the Labour of Care in Early Modern England.” *The Historical Journal* 67, no. 1: 21–41.

Metzler, Irina. 2016. *Fools and Idiots? Intellectual Disability in the Middle Ages.* Manchester: Manchester University Press.

Nelson, Alan H., and John R. Elliott, eds. 2010. “Bulstrode Whitelocke’s ‘Annals’” (BL, Add. MS 53726). In *Inns of Court: Vol. 1: Introduction and the Records*, 1:270–80. Records of Early English Drama (REED). Cambridge: Brewer.

Newton, Hannah. 2021. “Inside the Sickchamber in Early Modern England: The Experience of Illness through Six Objects.” *The English Historical Review* 136, no. 580: 530–67.

O’Callaghan, Michelle. 2007. *The English Wits: Literature and Sociability in Early Modern England.* Cambridge: Cambridge University Press.

Pelling, Margaret. 1998. *The Common Lot: Sickness, Medical Occupations and the Urban Poor in Early Modern England.* London: Routledge.

Prest, Wilfrid R. 2023. *The Inns of Court under Elizabeth I and the Early Stuarts, 1590–1640.* 2nd ed. Cambridge: Cambridge University Press.

Rhatigan, Emma. 2011. “Audience, Actors, and ‘Taking Part’ in the Revels.” In *Imagining the Audience in Early Modern Drama, 1558–1642*, edited by Jennifer A. Low and Nova Myhill, 151–69. New York: Palgrave.

Rushton, Peter. 1996. “Idiocy, the Family and the Community in Early Modern North-East England.” In *From Idiocy to Mental Deficiency: Historical Perspectives on People with Learning Disabilities*, edited by Anne Digby and David Wright, 44–64. Abingdon: Routledge.

Sandahl, Carrie. 2008. “Why Disability Identity Matters: From Dramaturgy to Casting in John Belluso’s Pyretown.” *Text and Performance Quarterly* 28, nos. 1–2: 225–41.

Scalenghe, Sara. 2016. *Disability in the Ottoman Arab World, 1500–1800.* Cambridge: Cambridge University Press.

Shakespeare, William. 2016. *The Comedy of Errors.* Edited by Kent Cartwright. London: Bloomsbury.

Siebers, Tobin. 2004. “Disability as Masquerade.” *Literature and Medicine* 23, no. 1: 1–22.

Watson, Jackie. 2015. “Satirical Expectations: Shakespeare’s Inns of Court Audiences.” *Actes Des Congrès de La Société Française Shakespeare* 3. https://doi.org/10.4000/shakespeare.3352.

Williams, Katherine Schaap. 2021. *Unfixable Forms: Disability, Performance, and the Early Modern English Theater.* Ithaca: Cornell University Press.

Winston, Jessica, 2016. *Lawyers at Play: Literature, Law, and Politics at the Early Modern Inns of Court, 1558–1581.* Oxford: Oxford University Press.

British Library. [Yelverton, Christopher?]. “Notes of Sermons, 1592–1621.” Additional Manuscript 48016.

CHAPTER 7

From Inns of Court Revels and Masques to John Playford's *The English Dancing Master*

Sharon J. Harris

No artistic genre is more closely associated with the Jacobean and Caroline English court than the masque. Martin Butler numbers 139 masques and masque-like entertainments during the Jacobean and Caroline periods, 1603–1642, most of which were presented at or for the court (2008: 358–76). The inns of court produced masques as well, however; an exception to the common notion that the masque was an exclusively aristocratic affair. As such, the inns were harbingers of increased appropriation of the masque in popular culture by the end of the seventeenth century. By the mid-1640s with the start of the Civil War and eventual end of the court and execution of the king, any masques were necessarily performed outside a court context. The inns of court were one such outside context, and one publication in 1651, *The English Dancing Master* (hereafter *Dancing Master*), demonstrates how gentlemen of the inns continued and extended dances from masques during the Interregnum to make them more widely

S. J. Harris (✉)
English, Brigham Young University, Provo, UT, USA
e-mail: sharon_harris@byu.edu

E. Rhatigan, J. Watson (eds.), *Mapping the Early Modern Inns of Court*, Early Modern Literature in History,
https://doi.org/10.1007/978-3-031-77445-4_7

known. This collection reveals dancing practices that were in vogue at the inns of court and points to court-like practices of dancing and revelry from those not at court. I focus on the cultural and social contexts of the dances in *Dancing Master* and show how the inns of court served as motivation for the volume's production.

In the 1650s printer and publisher John Playford inaugurated a new fashion of commercial music publications. The success of his first popular music book, *Dancing Master*, seems to have been catalysed by revels at the inns of court.[1] These revels were an adapted courtly practice which, like court masques, included a prescribed set of dances, or measures. At the inns, revels were held weekly during Christmas festivities. The term 'revels' was also used more specifically to describe the informal dancing that took place after the 'solemn measures' at the inns of court or after the formal masque proper at court entertainments, when masquers would take dancing partners from the audience. These revels involved a variety of less formal dances including country dances, though country dances seem to have been more common and more popular at the inns than in revels at court.

Playford taps into the popularity of country dances with his commercial hit, *Dancing Master*, which was the first printed collection of English country dances, subtitled *Plaine and easie rules for the dancing of country dances, with the tune to each dance*. In his prefatory address to the 'ingenious reader' Playford refers to 'the Gentlemen of the Innes of Court, whose sweet and ayry Activity has crowned their Grand Solemnities with Admiration to all Spectators' (Playford 1651: A1^{v}). Country dances are closely linked to the inns of court, and their intersection illuminates how the masque was reconfigured after the court was gone.

Over time, masques were excerpted and consequently democratised as portions of them such as songs, dances, spectacle, theatrical effects, design and set technology, vizard masks, and costumes spread into popular practices and entertainment forms. One example of this democratisation is in the reception of Playford's *Dancing Master*. Extremely popular, it was

[1] The second and subsequent editions of *The English Dancing Master* were known simply as *The Dancing Master*. Most dancing masters working in England in the first half of the seventeenth century were French. Perhaps the success of the first edition eliminated the need to emphasize the collection as a home-grown cultural product. I use the abbreviated *Dancing Master* to refer to the 1651 first edition *The English Dancing Master* not the subsequent editions called *The Dancing Master*. To disambiguate, any reference to subsequent editions will specify the date of publication.

reprinted in 18 editions well into the eighteenth century. It contains 104 songs; each song sports a title (and sometimes an alternative title), a musical score, dance notation showing the formation of male and female dancers, and written instructions for the movements of the dance. Besides being Playford's earliest success in printed music, this collection of dances was unusual in that it was the first English music publication to include several dances and dance instructions, rather than vocal or instrumental music like most of Playford's publications, such as *The Musicall Banquet* (1651) (Jocoy 2005: 409; Carter 2016: 95–129). Unlike the creators of printed songbooks in the early seventeenth century, Playford had no sponsors. He started a trend of commercial music publications targeted to a mass market that, as Stephanie Carter says, 'provided the amateur musician with an introduction to the art of music without dependence on musical connections and networks of manuscript circulation that dominated the transmission of music in earlier decades' (2016: 96). *Dancing Master* in particular conveyed country dances as a specifically English mode of recreation. Even the title, 'English Dancing Master,' took a continental trope (most dancing masters were French) and adapted it for specifically English dance authority, style, and instruction.

The success of *Dancing Master* indicates that there was wide interest in country dances. Where did this interest come from, and who were Playford's customers? Rebecca Herissone acknowledges that we know few details about Playford's customers but that 'he seems to have known them well, since his music books have a remarkably consistent profile, suggesting that he knew what would sell' (2010: 250). Peter Lindenbaum, Stacey Jocoy, and Keith Whitlock read *Dancing Master* as the work of a royalist publisher who sent political messages through music (Lindenbaum 2001: 124–38; Jocoy 2005: 406–07, 409; Whitlock 1999: 548–78). Ian Spink identifies a weekly music meeting of 'shopkeepers and foremen' as the commercial impetus and a possible source of materials for several of Playford's songbooks (1967: 35). In like manner, Carter connects Playford's publications to a variety of social activities including music meetings, sometimes even hosted in Playford's home; music teachers and their lessons; music making in bookshops; collectors acquiring presentation copies; and the activities of inns of court members (2016: 98–116). Examining the cultural and social contexts that Spink and Carter emphasise suggests a new account of the genealogy of English country dances. Namely, the masque practice of dancing measures followed by revels made its way to the inns of court and from there it spread widely among the English public.

This reading of *Dancing Master* ties into ongoing scholarly conversations about dramatic activity during the Interregnum. Susan Wiseman (1998), Janet Clare (2002), and Rachel Willie (2015) have challenged the inherited assumption that English drama generally ceased from 1642–1660 when the theatres were closed. Many scholars focus on the relationship between stage and page during the period. Lauren Shohet demonstrates that masques were popular not just in performance but also in print and notes that performance and print audiences of inns of court masques were 'especially likely' to overlap (2010: 110). Heidi Craig argues that rather than serving merely as a consolation prize to the closure of the theatres in 1642, printed drama helped build plays' popularity (2023).[2] She observes that printed drama was not just politically motivated, as some have presumed, but, like Playford's savvy sense of the market, Interregnum mid-century playbooks cultivated an 'interest in drama *as* drama' (2023: Chap. 1). Performance genres were thus taken up by a greater number and variety of consumers. Laura Estill confirms this popularity by showing how passages of plays and masques were quoted in commonplace books across the seventeenth century (2015). In a similar vein, innsmen recorded dances in their personal notebooks for many years, as Adams shows in Chap. 5 (Ward 1993: 2–6).

Playford's customers came, at least in part, from the inns, though this has not received much attention in scholarship. In what follows, I discuss the relationship between country dances in *Dancing Master* and the inns of court, first by discussing the traditions of dance at the inns as well as the Caroline era practice of weekly revels there. Next, I lay out Playford's career and relationship with the inns of court and how these contributed to the creation of *Dancing Master*. The popularity of *Dancing Master* connects to shifts in the masque genre and its accessibility to a wider audience in the mid- to late-seventeenth century. Then the chapter turns to a case study; the inns of court masque *Triumph of Peace* (1634) illustrates the democratisation of the masque and how this process relates to country dances, showing that the inns were positioned in the cross currents of these changes. Finally, I consider how Playford's dance volume is part of a larger trend of printed performance genres in the mid-seventeenth century. It is one of many works printed after their performance venues, such

[2] I am grateful to Heidi Craig for sharing her pre-publication manuscript with me.

as theatres and the court, were shut down. What makes *Dancing Master* different from the other works is that it was not a masque, a play, or conventional reading material. It was instruction for performance which did not require an audience, only dancers and musicians. The number of potential customers who had sufficient musical literacy and access to make use of Playford's publications probably would have been small, but the dances were accessible and his customer base grew over time (Carter 2016: 105; Ravelhofer 2005: 41–45). By codifying and dispersing dances, *Dancing Master* democratised revelry practices and further fragmented and distributed the masques and measures that had been their source material.

Dancing at the Inns of Court

Long before Playford addressed the inns of court gentlemen in *Dancing Master*, the inns had an extensive history of dancing and revels. What follows is an overview of dancing customs as the inns of court developed a tradition of revels and became a focal point for dancing, including country dances. Individual members had long been recording dances for their own use. A Lincoln's Inn manuscript book from sometime during the reign of Henry VII or Henry VIII records instructions for a dance that seems to have been part of Christmas festivities (CUL MS Ll.1.11 fol. 33^{r}).[3] Several manuscript copies of social dances known as 'the old measures' have been identified. John M. Ward cautions that only Butler Buggins's copy as '"taught by Robert Holeman a Dancing-Master before 1640 and continued ever since in the Inner Temple hall" can be directly associated with one of the Inns of Court' (1993: 2). But authors of other copies were students of law, whether or not they were recording dances specifically as they were performed at the inns. In the last few decades of the sixteenth century, dance measures which had been taught in London dancing schools 'became the ritual measures of the Inns of Court,' forming a 'courtly trivium' with fencing and music (1993: 8). These dance measures came to be known as the 'old measures,' referring to their provenance from the Tudor period. The sections of these measures, primarily pavans and almains, remained consistent and stayed in the same sequence across centuries (Ravelhofer 2005: 38–40). They comprised the formal rituals of

[3] Transcribed in Baker (1986: 26, 30); cited in Ravelhofer (2005: 37).

the inns, to be followed by a variety of other dances such as corantos, galliards, and country dances.

As rituals, the solemn measures were always performed at the beginning and the end of the revels season, which ran for a quarter of the year from All Hallows Eve (31 October) to Candlemas (2 February), with weekly revels on Saturdays during that period.[4] In Chap. 4 Jackie Watson explores the possible echoes of these revels and their dancing in *Twelfth Night*. London's broader legal network joined for feast days: an unknown author from Middle Temple, *c*. 1634–1638, notes 'the Judges & Serjeants at law formerlie fellowes of these Societies [the Inns],' showing how the practice of dancing spread in its frequency and number of participants (Brerewood MS, Middle Temple Library, 82, cited in Ward 1993: 8). When Bulstrode Whitelocke took over as Master of the Revels of Middle Temple in 1628, he described how, at the beginning of Christmas, the Master entered the hall with 16 revellers, and they danced 'the old measures, after that they daunced the Branles, then … the Revellers daunced Galliards, Corantoes, & french daunces, then countrey daunces till it grew very late' (Nelson and Elliott 2010: 1.224). William Prynne described just how late the revelry might go:

> When I was a Student and Puny Barrester in Lincolns Inne, it was the constant custome of that House and all other Inns of Court from All-Saints Eve, to Candlemas night, to keep open Revels, Dancing, Dicing and Musick in their Hals every Saturday night (as we usually call it) till eleven or twelve of the clock, and many times till 4. In the morning or later (1655: A2[r]).

Accounts of regular Saturday evening revels at the inns can be found in 1628, 1633, and 1635, and Buggins's quotation above indicates that Inner Temple was using a dancing master in 1640. Innsmen needed to know courtly skills in order to lead and participate in the inns' culture of revels. As Michelle O'Callaghan writes, 'Those who led the grand revels had to be highly skilled in courtly accomplishments – singing, dancing, music' (2009: 14). The tradition of dancing measures and revels at the inns became still more established during the Caroline period.

[4] Due to an incident the previous year, Alan Nelson notes restrictions placed on Inner Temple revels during the 1628 Christmas season, limiting celebrations to three weeks with additional limits on alcohol use and tobacco sales (2011: 307–10).

At least two important differences distinguished the old measures from country dances at the inns of court.[5] The first is that the solemn measures were compulsory while the country dances were elective. In a retrospective printed in 1660, the antiquarian William Dugdale wrote of Lincoln's Inn members, 'Nor were these Exercises of Dancing meerly permitted; but thought very necessary,' so much so that

> the Under-Barristers, were by Decimation put out of Commons, for examples sake, because the whole Bar offended by not Dancing on Candlemass day preceding, according to the antient Order of this Society, when the Judges were present: with this, that if the like fault were committed afterwards, they should be fined or disbarred. (1660: 246)

Some were chastised and 'put out of Commons' for not participating in the old measures. Unlike the mandated solemn revels enforced by punishment and fines, however, the country dances and additional entertainments were undertaken primarily by the most skilled and enthusiastic dancers, often younger lawyers.

The second distinction between post-revels and the old measures at the inns is that the post-revels, country dances, and the like could include women. In 1632, some junior Middle Templars were chastised for admitting prohibited guests and were reminded that they were not allowed to 'bring downe anye Ladie or Gentlewoman to see their ordinary revells, or at anye time to daunce with anye such in the Hall in the absence of the Benche' (Williamson 1925: 356). From that same inn, however, Whitelocke described the 'Court Ladies & other Grandesses' and visiting dignitaries who participated in the post-revels festivities, listing the old measures first and then numbering several other kinds of dances: 'the old measures, after that they daunced the Branles, then . . . the Revellers daunced Galliards, Corantoes, & french daunces.' Whitelocke continued, '*then* countrey daunces till it grew very late' (Williamson 1925: 224). Old measures may have been required, but country dances were the hot-ticket after-party, and many 'gentlemen & Ladies, and some of them of great quality' participated.

[5] Skiles Howard understands country dancing as being opposed to courtly dancing, and the two are distinct in formality, tone, and choreography. I am interested in how the country dances that follow formal measures at the Inns mimic a court-like practice at the Inns while also demarcating a publicly accessible, popular dancing practice (1998: 1–25, esp. 6).

Thus, to the extent that the inns of court were influential in cultivating a culture of dancing, the portion that reached the greatest number of people was the less-formal and less-prescribed post-revels—the portion with country dances. It is worth noting that while *Dancing Master* marketed itself as a collection of country dances, it was, as Barbara Ravelhofer has pointed out, a broad umbrella that included various kinds of dances (2005: 41–45). Some titles are casual like 'Jog on my honey,' or they may evoke a more formal continental dance style like 'Saraband.' Some seem to be named after upper class people or trained dancers, like 'Lady Cullen' or 'Confess, his Tune,' named after French dancing master, Nicolas Confesse. Country dances were a capacious category distinct from formal, exclusive measures.

This practice of revels and dancing at the inns of court shows how the choice to create a collection of country dances marketed to innsmen was savvy and practical. Some have identified Playford primarily as a publisher who wished to produce royalist publications, and many of Playford's early publications are royalist in inclination, intended audience, and source material (Lindenbaum 2001: 130). But there were political and pragmatic reasons at the beginning of the Interregnum for Playford to emphasise the country dance aspect of *Dancing Master* rather than foregrounding court masques or other royalist associations with the dance music. If he was to create successful commercial music publications, he needed to craft them to appeal to a large customer base including men and women, and he needed to strike a balance of appealing to both royalists and parliamentarians. The inns provided a ready cross-section of these categories, especially through their weekly holiday revels. The old measures made up the backbone of formal English dances, and those at the inns could 'assume that most if not all of their members would know how to perform the eight measures' (Ward 1993: 8). In contrast to those eight old warhorses, Playford presented 104 dances in his first edition. Country dances represented a 'newer bucolic country-dance style of music,' as Ian Payne writes, and were in vogue for those who were familiar with court masques and those who yearned for greater access to masques (2003: 70). Country dances allowed for a continuation of a kind of courtly ritual while also being non-courtly, masking their masque associations. A volume that was both a compilation and tutorial of the mixed-gender, post-revels dances in their sprawling variety was a safer option in the political turbulence of the mid-seventeenth century. It was what Playford's buyers wanted and needed.

Playford and the Inns of Court

The inns of court provided a customer base for Playford to produce a popular English dance manual, but this was not his only connection to the inns. Playford's training, the location of his shop, and his access to musical content also positioned him to understand the demographic around the inns of court and target his publications to their members. Playford was apprenticed to John Benson, located next to St Dunstan-in-the-West. The same year that Playford began his apprenticeship in 1640, his master Benson published the notorious collection, *Poems: Written by Wil. Shake-Speare. Gent.* Scholars have lambasted Benson for altering, obscuring, or omitting elements of Shakespeare's poetry (Shakespeare 1997: 41–42; Shakespeare 2004: 118–19). As Faith Acker points out, however, Benson was using 'nearly every popular feature that a desperate young publisher could' and crafted it to be 'a product of the tastes of the 1630s and 1640s' (2017: 90). Put another way, one of the first projects Playford saw as a stationer's apprentice was Benson repurposing older, popular work to make it attractive to contemporary readers. Playford would do the same with his music publications.

When Playford branched out on his own in 1647, his shop was located not near St Paul's, like so many other printers and booksellers, but in the heart of the inns, in or near the porch of Temple Church on Inner Temple Lane, in Inner Temple and near Middle Temple. Playford was not just proximate to but also involved with the inns; in 1653, two years after publishing *Dancing Master*, he was appointed clerk of Temple Church (Thompson 2004). Given his location and connections from his church position, music from the inns of court must have been among the content most readily available to him. A pragmatic businessman, Playford cultivated an entire music market not limited to music books but including ruled music paper and, according to a late eighteenth-century source, musical instruments as well (Thompson 1995: 605–08, 610–18). Playford dominated the music publishing business in England for over 30 years and was a significant influence on all aspects of the music industry during that time. A major centre of music in London during the Interregnum and Restoration was in the middle of the inns of court.

One of the practical exigencies Playford faced in publishing dozens of music books was coming up with source material. Beyond dance manuals, he used songs that had been developed and circulated across the first half of the seventeenth century and earlier, drawing on ballads, dances, catches, canons, songs used in dramatic interludes, and other music from a variety of contexts. Examples of songs from *Dancing Master* that were several decades old include 'Grayes Inne Mask' from the 1613 *The Masque of the Inner Temple and Gray's Inn*, and 'Kemps Jegg,' referring to Will Kempe, a former clown of the Lord Chamberlain's Men. In short, many of Playford's selections were older and well known, their familiarity helping his new venture into music publishing to succeed financially. Accordingly, much of the music from Playford's 1650s publications hails from the 1630s. As an example, a broadside, *The little barly-corne*, was registered in 1632 and indicated that it should be sung to the tune 'Stingo,' a tune also known as 'Cold and Raw.' We cannot date the origin of the Stingo tune, but it was well-enough known in 1632 to be a reference for the broadside, suggesting that it had been in circulation for decades by the time Playford included it in *Dancing Master* under the title 'Stingo, Or the Oyle of Barly' (Williams 2020: 73).[6] As this one example illustrates, the entries in *Dancing Master* represented an intersection of multiple media and contexts. Playford's customers were acquainted with the works through balladry, theatre, dancing, or related songs.

Attention to Playford's dedicatory address at the beginning of *Dancing Master* suggests that he expected members of the inns of court to be his primary readers of the 1651 first edition of *The English Dancing Master*. Scholars have sometimes mentioned Playford naming the 'Gentlemen of the Innes of Court' in his prefatory address 'To the ingenious reader,' but only in passing and as one group of the larger readership intended for the volume. I suggest that for this first edition of the dancing manual Playford considered innsmen to be his main audience. Details from the prefatory address indicate as much: Playford begins by invoking the ancient Greeks' regard of dance, specifically calling it a 'commendable and rare Quality fit for yong Gentlemen,' perhaps a nod to innsmen (1651: A1^{v}). Then he recites how it 'has been formerly honoured in the Courts of Princes, when performed by the most Noble Heroes of the Times! The Gentlemen of the Innes of Court, whose sweet and ayry Activity has crowned their Grand Solemnities with Admiration to all Spectators.' Perhaps this refers to the court ladies Whitelocke described who enjoyed the inns' holiday

[6] Some version of the tune may have been circulating at or before the turn of the seventeenth century, as the alternate title of the tune, 'Cold and Raw' begins in much the same way as the song 'Cold's the Wind and Wet's the Rain' in Thomas Dekker's *Shoemaker's Holiday*, published 1600. See Duffin (2018: 297–98).

revels, or possibly in the Interregnum Playford viewed the inns of court as a kind of surviving remainder of the dissolved royal court. Whatever the relationship implied, he names the inns right after he associates dancing with courtly activity. As if to acknowledge dancing as an outlet for students, he goes on to 'commend it to be Excellent for Recreation, after more serious Studies' and submits this book to 'ingenious Gentlemen lovers of this Quallity,' designating himself as 'a faithfull honourer of your Virtues.' All of these passages imply that Playford has a specific group in mind as his readers, and the only group he identifies is the 'Gentlemen of the Innes of Court.'

The contrast between the address in the 1651 first edition and that in the 1653 second edition makes the argument that it was directed to members of the inns all the more persuasive. In the first edition, Playford writes, 'I have ventured to put forth this ensuing Worke to the view, and gentle censure of all ingenious Gentlemen lovers of this Quallity' (1651: A1^{v}). In the second edition, however, he places his venture in the past tense and adds a critical adjective: 'I did venture this ensuing Work to the *publick* view' (1653: A3^{r}, emphasis added). Playford may have attempted the first edition as an experimental venture, expecting that it would at least appeal to some customers from the inns, but unsure of its success beyond that. He may even have been printing a compilation of dances that was regularly used at the inns of court, as he says he only printed the first edition because of a 'false and surrepticious Copy at the Printing Presse, which if it had been published, would have been a disparagement to the quality and the Professors thereof, and a hinderance to the Learner' (1651: A1^{v}). Taking matters into his own hands, Playford says he had 'an Excellent Copy' and the 'assistance of a knowing Friend,' and so he determined to publish his own version instead. In the 1653 second edition, he acknowledges that the collection's reach has expanded beyond the inns by presenting the updated version not only to the Gentlemen addressed in the first edition but also to the 'publick view.'

Playford's *Dancing Master* volumes helped carry dancing and revels that had been part of court masques and old measures to a wider English public. Although Stuart masques were generally regarded as a courtly genre, after the Caroline court was gone, the term 'masque' was applied more flexibly to a variety of popular entertainment contexts including William Davenant's through-composed *Siege of Rhodes* (1656), drollery excerpts in Francis Kirkman's *The Wits* (1662), and Henry Purcell's entertainments inserted between acts of *Fairy Queen,* which was Thomas

Betterton's adaptation of *Midsummer Night's Dream* (1692). This democratising shift in the genre predated Playford's *Dancing Master*. In an inns of court masque 17 years earlier we can see tensions and shifts within the genre and another instance of how the inns invoked the country to mediate their relationship with court.

Tensions in the *Triumph of Peace* Masque

The only masque presented by all four inns of court, James Shirley's *Triumph of Peace* (1634), provides one example of how those not at court understood their access to masques and courtly conventions. Shirley, who lived near the inns and was admitted to Gray's Inn in 1634, wrote his eye-catching dramatic work in consultation with inns of court members. This work's interest in the country and country dances shows how some of the non-elite could imagine their relationship to the masque in these terms. *Triumph of Peace* exposes the artificiality of the masque by featuring laypeople breaking through the masque's façade. The masque stages a meeting of city and country, but the only country dance in the masque proper, following the anti-masques, is more Londoners' urban cosplay of the country than an earnest portrayal of rural England. It portrays city folk who conceive of their relationship with and access to the masque via the more casual anti-masque and its country dances. In so doing *Triumph of Peace* makes an implicit case for the value of anti-masques and laypeople in holding up the fantasy of the masque proper.

Shirley's *Triumph of Peace* was the inns' attempt to return to the crown's good graces, following the offence caused by William Prynne's aggressively puritan antitheatrical tract, *Histriomastix* (1633). At face value the unparalleled spectacle of *Triumph of Peace*—its expense; hundreds of participants; and, not least, its elaborate procession through London—seems at odds with the supposed simple life of the country. The Folger manuscript cast list calls for nearly 900 people in the procession including 42 musicians and singers, 143 singers and coachmen, 25 'Gentlemen Riders' from each of the four inns, 300 attending grooms and torchbearers, 200 halberdiers, and 16 Grand Masquers, four from each Inn (Elliott 1992: 198–99). After years of Saturday night dances at Christmastime, the innsmen paraded their festivities to the London public directly. The cost totalled approximately £21,000, making it the most expensive English masque that had yet been produced (Whitted 2009: 7).

In the Caroline period the idea of the country was emerging from various sources including country house poems, cavalier writing that cultivated the idea of 'merry olde England,' and the development of country dances. In contrast to the pastoral, which was often an aristocratic fantasy of lowly shepherds in bucolic landscapes, the country was populated with real-life workers such as mowers, farmers, and couriers—with laypeople who were uninitiated in the sophisticated decorum of the elite. The country lays bare the labour that undergirds aristocratic and pastoral settings (see Orgel 1975: 49–58; Britland 2006: Chaps 3, 6, 8). When the pastoral masque appears as only a device, the realism of the country comes into view.

Although *Triumph of Peace* was, in part, the inns' attempt to make peace with Queen Henrietta Maria, its rustic characters are not like the classical shepherds in the Queen's entertainments. The masque shows a meeting between a London gentleman named Confidence and a family from the country, led by Opinion, all of whom are preparing to attend a masque. Opinion wears decidedly dated garb including a 'Doublet of blacke Velvet, and truncke hose,' casting country characters as removed from the fashionable dress of their city cousins (Shirley 1634: 1). Another character, Phansie, is to furnish anti-masques for the event. As Brent Whitted observes, Phansie is the 'personification of the Inns in that his role is to stage, in short order, a performance at court that fashions political corrective as *entertainment*' (2009: 15). More pointedly, Phansie produces anti-masques, raucous foils to order and sophistication in the masque proper. Like the inns, Phansie creates revelry and invokes the country as a contrast with the formal dances. When he first learns that there are no anti-masques unless he produces them, Phansie exclaims that they should sooner tear down all the timbers and façade of the masque scenery than go without anti-masques. He declares that someone must provide such entertainment, or 'they will bee jeerd to death else for their ignorance' (Shirley 1634: 3). According to Phansie, anti-masques are indispensable to maintaining the court's triumph of peace. So, he takes on the task.

Phansie's sequence of anti-masques features many groups that could be found in the English countryside, such as a dance of birds; another of nymphs, satyrs, and hunters; one of bird-catchers; and one of beggars who, after cozening people of their money, throw away their false prosthetics and dance. Another anti-masque revises the possibilities of the English country as a 'country fellow' embraces technology to carry out his farming duties. He purchases a 'queint wheele' so that he can thresh his corn 'without helpe of hands ... and now he lays about him'—except for when he merrily jumps up and dances, presumably some kind of country dance (Shirley 1634: 7). Here the country dances that punctuated revels on Saturday nights at the inns are placed in anti-masques, suggesting that these were dances for both the upper class in their revels and lower classes in quotidian life. *Triumph of Peace* is facilitated by dozens of unnamed servants and amateurs, many who were not professional performers, and the blending of the high and low, rich and poor is presented as part of the masque text.

This dynamic of real-life workers behind the scenes of the masque is acted out in *Triumph of Peace*'s masque proper. Phansie and his anti-masquers leave the stage, and the masque begins, led by three women, Irene (Peace), Eunomia (Law), and Diche (Justice), the children of Jove and Themis (King Charles I and Queen Henrietta Maria). They represent peace's triumph, honouring the court as a champion of these values. After five songs, the scene changes to a green hillside with a 'delicious Arbor' and 16 masquers who are the sons of Peace, Law, and Justice, arranged as a posed set piece (Shirley 1634: 17). At the end and culmination of the pastoral masque, they sing and perform the main dance, the highlight of the device.

Suddenly, just before the taking out, that is, before the final dance when masquers invite participants from the audience, 'a cracke is heard in the workes, as if there were some danger by some piece of the Machines falling,' and various masque craftsmen and some of their wives 'rush in' (Shirley 1634: 19). Eight people break into the masque: a carpenter, painter, scullery worker, tailor, the tailor's wife, an embroiderer's wife, a feather maker's wife, and a prop-master's wife. The carpenter demands, 'D'ce thinke to keepe us out?' (19). After a confrontation with the guards, the prop-master's wife declares, 'My husband is somewhere in the workes, I'me sure I helpt to make him an Owl and a Hobbihorse, and I see no reason but his Wife may bee admitted in *Forma paperis*, to see as good a Maske as this.' The others agree, all wanting to see the masque, when they decide to 'dance a figary our selues,' making it a 'peece of the Plot,' saying ''twill seem a new device too' (21). As they perform their 'lively friske' and exit the stage, they resolve, 'let us goe off cleanely, and some body will thinke, this was meant for an Antimasque' (21). *Triumph of Peace* stages a growing tension inherent to masque production: as more people from all walks of life contribute to making masques, they feel a sense of connection and wish for greater access to them. Blurred boundaries between anti-masques and the masque proper naturally follow.

The point of access between the London masque artisans and their unwitting performance in the masque is when they dance 'a figary' and pass it off as an anti-masque, like those Phansie prepared earlier in *Triumph of Peace*. Various characteristics connect the labourers' interruption with the country dances that proved so popular in Playford's publications. First, *Triumph of Peace* was conceived and staged by innsmen. It seems probable that dances in *Triumph of Peace* would have deliberately and explicitly alluded to dances, practices, and styles common to the inns' revels, perhaps with familiar choreography or tunes. 17 years later Playford drew on these tunes and dances in creating *Dancing Master*, marketing it to innsmen. Second, because the characters in this scene are from the lower classes, the dance they performed was most likely popular and accessible enough to be widely known, like those that could be learned from *Dancing Master*. Finally, *Dancing Master* included symbols of crescent moons and circles with each dance to show the arrangement of the men and women; it said these 'Characters' expressed 'the Figure of the Dance,' using the same term of 'figary' found in *Triumph of Peace* (1651: A4^{v}). If 'figure' was the common way to describe the setup of country dances, perhaps the word also suggests that they performed a country dance in this scene.

It is important to note that the craftspeople engaging in the country dance here are not from the country. Their characters are a nod to a cavalier ideal of jovial, rustic workers, but they themselves are city dwellers. Country is more a fantasised aesthetic than a rural import. The artisans' 'lively friske' is probably a country dance, danced with women and men together, especially because formal dances usually were not done with mixed company until the taking out. Thus, a country dance is the workers' and wives' manner of imitating and participating in the masque. It represents their version of revels and doubles as a more accessible masquing form.

Moreover, country dances are framed as distinctly English. Playford's *Dancing Master* features country dances in the service of a nationalist view of England and Englishness rooted in the country. The country dance was a kind of replacement of continental dance traditions that had become popular in England and abroad with decidedly English festivities. In the inns of court masque, *Triumph of Peace*, a country dance replaces the convention of finishing the masque with the pastoral form. If, as Orgel says, the culmination of the pastoral is the court and state, a masque that culminated with labourers' interruption and a country dance presages not only a democratisation of the masque but also a redistribution of courtly practices and the power of the state itself (1975: 50, 53). When English workers break into the stylised *Triumph of Peace*, they physically crack open the constructed façades of masque settings and lay bare the artificiality of the court in favour of a more democratic and workaday English reality beneath. This shift is enacted in the masque produced by all four inns, suggesting that they inhabit the borders of tensions and transitions within the masque. At those borders we find English laypeople doing a country dance.

Conclusion

The freedom and festivity of country dances may seem an unlikely subject to translate into print, but in this Playford's *Dancing Master* was part of a larger mid-century trend. Especially after the court dissolved and the theatres closed, performance genres rerouted to other venues, including the printed page. Milton's *A Maske Presented at Ludlow Castle* was printed in 1637 and the second edition of Jonson's *Works* with his masques appeared in 1640. Humphrey Moseley published James Shirley's *Poems*, which included a reprint of *Triumph of Peace*, in 1646 and the Beaumont and Fletcher folio in 1647, which included the *Masque of the Inner Temple and Gray's Inn* performed in 1613. Each of these works appeared in print after the occasion for its performance was long gone. Likewise, *Dancing Master*, addressed to the 'Gentlemen of the Innes of Court' seems to have been published after the practice that made its dances popular was forbidden. On 28 November 1649 parliament issued the following:

> *Ordered*, That the Benchers of the several Inns of Court, and the Heads of the Inns of Chancery, be enjoined not to permit any publick Revelling or Gaming in any of the said Inns of Court or Chancery. (1802: House of Commons Journal 28 November 1649)

The records of Lincoln's Inn show that the inns of court understood this prohibition to be directly related to dancing. They describe the order and their response to it:

> Upon the reading of an Order from the Parliament for suppressing of Revellinge and Dancinge in the Inns of Courte and Chancery, It was ordered that there should be no more Revills, Dancing, nor Musique in the common

> Hall of this House, untill further Order taken; and that the Order of Parliament be sett upon the skreene tomorrow att dinner time, that the gent. may have notice of it. (Baildon 1898: 385)

As with the court and the theatres, the time-honoured tradition of revels, dancing, and music at the inns had come to a halt. Craig argues that theatre closure produced the paradoxical, or at least unintended outcome of cultivating interest in and desire for dramatic entertainments (2023). I suggest that parliament's prohibition of dancing at the inns of court provoked a similar effect: less than one year later, Playford entered *Dancing Master* in the Stationers' Register, 7 November 1650 (Thompson 2004).

When the inns lost their performance venue for dances in 1649, their court-adjacent, masque-like practices became democratised further, entering England's book market. *Dancing Master* and the music books that followed it democratised masque music and dancing practices beyond the purview of the court, forever altering the social associations of masques and revels. And the inns of court sat at the fulcrum of these changes.

Works Cited

Acker, Faith. 2017. "John Benson's 1640 *Poems* and Its Literary Precedents." In *Canonising Shakespeare: Stationers and the Book Trade, 1640–1740*, edited by Emma Depledge and Peter Kirwan, 89–106. Cambridge: Cambridge University Press.

Baildon, W. P, ed. 1898. *The Records of Honorable Society of Lincoln's Inn. The Black Books*. Vol. 2. London: Lincoln's Inn.

Baker, John H. 1986. *The Legal Profession and the Common Law: Historical Essays*. London: Hambledon Press.

Britland, Karen. 2006. *Drama at the Courts of Queen Henrietta Maria*. Cambridge: Cambridge University Press.

Butler, Martin 2008. *The Stuart Court Masque and Political Culture*. Cambridge: Cambridge University Press.

Carter, Stephanie. 2016. "'Yong Beginners, Who Live in the Countrey': John Playford and the Printed Music Market in Seventeenth-Century England." *Early Music History* 35: 95–129.

Clare, Janet. 2002. *Drama of the English Republic 1649–1660*. Manchester: Manchester University Press.

Craig, Heidi. 2023. *Theatre Closure and the Paradoxical Rise of English Renaissance Drama in the Civil Wars*. Cambridge: Cambridge University Press.

Duffin, Ross W. 2018. *Some Other Note: The Lost Songs of English Renaissance Comedy*. Oxford: Oxford University Press.
Dugdale, William. 1660. *Origines Juridicales*. London.
Elliott, John R. 1992. "The Folger Manuscript of *The Triumph of Peace* Procession." In *English Manuscript Studies 1100–1700* 3: 193–215.
Estill, Laura. 2015. *Dramatic Extracts in Seventeenth Century English Manuscripts: Watching, Reading, Changing Plays*. Newark: University of Delaware Press.
Findlay, Alison. 2006. *Playing Spaces in Early Women's Drama*. Cambridge: Cambridge University Press.
Herissone, Rebecca. 2010. "Playford, Purcell, and the Functions of Music Publishing in Restoration England." *Journal of the American Musicological Society* 63, no. 2: 243–90.
Howard, Skiles. 1998. *The Politics of Courtly Dancing in Early Modern England*. Amherst: University of Massachusetts Press.
"House of Commons Journal 28 November 1649." 1802. In *Journal of the House of Commons*. Vol. 6. 1648–1651. London: His Majesty's Stationery Office. British History Online. http://www.british-history.ac.uk/commons-jrnl/vol6/pp326-327.
Jocoy, Stacey. 2005. "Decoding Musical Resistance: English Vocal Music in the Service of the King, 1625–1660." PhD diss., University of Illinois Urbana-Champaign.
Lindenbaum, Peter. 2001. "John Playford: Music and Politics in the Interregnum." *Huntington Library Quarterly* 64, nos 1/2: 124–38.
Nelson, Alan, and John R. Elliott, eds. 2010. *Records of Early English Drama: Inns of Court*. Cambridge: Brewer.
Nelson, Alan H. 2011. "New Light on Drama, Music, and Dancing at the Inns of Court to 1642." In *The Intellectual and Cultural World of the Early Modern Inns of Court*, edited by Jane Elisabeth Archer, Elizabeth Goldring, and Sarah Knight, 302–14. Manchester: Manchester University Press.
O'Callaghan, Michelle. 2009. *The English Wits: Literature and Sociability in Early Modern England*. Cambridge: Cambridge University Press.
Orgel, Stephen. 1975. *The Illusion of Power: Political Theater in the English Renaissance*. Berkley: University of California Press.
Payne, Ian. 2003. *The Almain in Britain, c. 1549–c. 1675*. Burlington, VT: Ashgate.
Playford, John. 1651. *The English Dancing Master*. London.
———. 1653. *The Dancing Master*. London.
Prynne, William. 1655. *A briefe polemicall dissertation*. London.
Ravelhofer, Barbara. 2005. *The Early Stuart Masque: Dance, Costume, and Music*. Oxford: Oxford University Press.
Shakespeare, William. 1997. *Shakespeare's Sonnets*. Edited by Katherine Duncan-Jones. Arden Shakespeare, 3rd ser., London: Thomson Learning.

Shakespeare, William. 2004. *Shakespeare's Sonnets*. Edited by Paul Edmondson and Stanley Wells. Oxford: Oxford University Press.

Shirley, James. 1634. *The Triumph of Peace*. London.

Shohet, Lauren. 2010. *Reading Masques: The English Masque and Public Culture in the Seventeenth Century*. Oxford: Oxford University Press.

Spink, Ian. 1967. "The Old Jewry 'Musick-Society': A 17th-Century Catch Club." *Musicology* 2, no. 1: 35–41.

Straznicky, Marta. 2004. *Privacy, Playreading, and Women's Closet Drama, 1550–1700*. Cambridge: Cambridge University Press.

Thompson, Robert. 1995. 'Manuscript Music in Purcell's London'. *Early Music* 23, no. 4: 605-608+610-18.

———. 2004. "Playford, John (1621x23–1686/7), music publisher.' *Oxford Dictionary of National Biography*. Accessed 27 January 2023. https://www.oxforddnb.com/view/10.1093/ref:odnb/9780198614128.001.0001/odnb-9780198614128-e-22374.

Ward, John M. 1993. "Apropos 'The Olde Measures'," *Records of Early English Drama* 18, no. 1: 2–21.

Whitlock, Keith. 1999. "John Playford's *The English Dancing Master* 1650/51 as Cultural Politics", *Folk Music Journal* 7, no. 5: 548–78.

Whitted, Brent. 2009. "Street Politics: Charles I and the Inns of Court's *Triumph of Peace*." *Seventeenth Century* 24, no. 1: 1–25.

Williamson, J. Bruce. 1925. *The History of the Temple, London: From the Institution of the Order of the Knights of the Temple to the Close of the Stuart Period*, 2nd ed. London: William Clowes and Sons.

Williams, Sarah F. 2020. "An Intermedia Approach to Seventeenth-Century English Popular Song Culture." In *Open Access Musicology*, edited by Daniel Barolsky and Louis Epstein, vol. 1, 61–84. Ann Arbor: Lever Press.

Willie, Rachel. 2015. *Staging the Revolution: Drama, Reinvention, and History, 1647–72*. Manchester: Manchester University Press.

Wiseman, Susan. 1998. *Drama and Politics in the English Civil War*. Cambridge: Cambridge University Press.

CHAPTER 8

Mapping Selden's Library

Joshua Eckhardt and Julian T. S. Neuhauser

As he compiled 'The Discourse of Iohn Selden, Esq.' (later printed under the title *Table Talk*), Richard Milward decided to place first Selden's comments on 'Abbeyes, Prioryes .&c~.' The approximately alphabetical order of the topics that Milward assigned to Selden's statements may suggest that this starting point was random. In the more or less alphabetical arrangement of a commonplace book, didn't the section on 'Abbeyes' have to come before Selden's comments on the '39 Articles' and 'Baptisme'? No, Milward could have easily placed this section elsewhere by naming it 'Prioryes' instead, or 'Monasteries', or y^e 'Dissolution of the Monasteries'. For in this section, Selden made remarks about the 'vnwillingnesse of the Monkes, to part wth their Lands' and on 'taking from ye Abbotts, & Priours their Lands, & their Houses' (Houghton Library MS Eng. 1211.2: 1–2). Yet placed at the beginning of the collection, Selden's

J. Eckhardt (✉)
English, Virginia Commonwealth University, Richmond, VA, USA
e-mail: jmeckhardt@vcu.edu

J. T. S. Neuhauser
Independent Scholar, Hastings, UK
e-mail: jtneuhauser@gmail.com

E. Rhatigan, J. Watson (eds.), *Mapping the Early Modern Inns of Court*, Early Modern Literature in History,
https://doi.org/10.1007/978-3-031-77445-4_8

comments on confiscated monastic property could serve the same purpose that they may have originally served in person. When Selden welcomed Milward or anyone else to his home later in life, he welcomed them to the home that he shared with and then inherited from Elizabeth Grey, countess dowager of Kent. Upon the death of Henry Grey, earl of Kent, in 1639, Selden had moved just a few minutes' walk eastward from his chambers in the Inner Temple to the countess' London home. That home had once been a Carmelite friary; it still went by the name of Whitefriars (Toomer 2009: 1.10, 313–14; Clapham 1910: 15–31).

By foregrounding Selden's comments on the confiscation of such monastic houses, Milward was arguably sharing first with readers the sort of comments that Selden may have made to a visitor to his home upon arrival. That home could easily have raised questions for a visitor. What was this lawyer and member of parliament doing, after all, living with a dowager countess in a former friary? How could all of these buildings, originally designed for communal religious life, have become private property, where Selden could amass his own private library and share such liberal comments with his guests? You can hear Selden answering such questions, perhaps pre-emptively, right at the beginning of 'The Discourse':

> Att the tyme of ye Dissolution they were very tender in taking from ye Abbotts, & Priours their Lands, & their Houses, till they surrendred them [as most of them did]. (Houghton Library MS Eng. 1211.2: 1–2)

According to Selden, those in charge of confiscating monastic houses and lands had been 'tender' about the operation; most abbots and priors eventually 'surrendred' them. Who wouldn't like to believe that their home, or university campus, had been voluntarily and ethically surrendered by its former occupants? Selden was not making detached historical observations here. He was coming to terms with how he and his guest could possibly have come to occupy their present location, Whitefriars.

Any guest whom Selden welcomed indoors at Whitefriars would have seen a lot of books. Shortly after he died, and probably in 1655, Selden's executors had a catalogue of his library compiled (Toomer 2009: 2.795). This hand-written library catalogue (itself now catalogued as Bodleian MS Selden supra 111) identifies not only the books at Whitefriars but also their locations in particular rooms and even on particular shelves. The Whitefriars catalogue, in other words, enables readers to map Selden's library even to the minute detail of shelf order. As with any good map, this catalogue provides a representation of the relevant terrain—which in this case is both physical and bibliographical. But a map may also be used as a tool for navigation. This chapter employs Selden supra 111 as just such a tool, using the catalogue to think about one innsman's work in terms of both his writing and his reading. This chapter will consider a single extended example of the relationship between Selden's 'Discourse' and his library. It will then turn to two authors found in Selden's library also connected to the inns, John Donne and Thomas Coryate. Though Selden collected very little of these authors' work, the books that he did add to his shelves helped to form and inform the material and intertextual context of the Whitefriars library. The latter two-thirds of this chapter will use Selden supra 111 as a map to explore the books that literally surrounded the work of these authors. Doing so allows us to investigate Donne's and Coryate's texts in a specific and important material context so that we might draw conclusions about their use, reception, and afterlives.

Selden at Whitefriars

When Selden's 'Discourse' turns to particular authors, the library catalogue tells us where Selden and his guests could have physically turned to retrieve Selden's copies of the works of those authors. On the subject of the 'Bible, Scripture', Selden reportedly told Milward (who, by the way, was a rector), 'Lay-men haue best interpreted y^{e} hard places of y^{e} Bible, such as Iohannes Picus, Scaliger, Grotius, Salmasius, Heinsius .&c$^{\sim}$' (Houghton Library MS Eng. 1211.2: 7). The Whitefriars catalogue records the fact that, if he had wanted to illustrate this point, Selden could have directed Milward or any guest to the sixth shelf in the primary library room (Bodleian MS Selden supra 111, fol. 24^{r}). That shelf contained a nice cluster of books by Salmasius—some of them apparently still shelved together at the Bodleian Library:

> Salmatius de Calculo: 8°: L: Bat: 1640:
> Bartholnius de Cruce x^{ti}: 8°: Hafniæ 1651:
> Salmatius de fenore 8°: L: Bat: 1640:
>   De vsuris 8°: L: Bat: 1638:
>   De modo vsurarū 8°: L: Bat: 1639:
>   De Testamentis 8°: L: Bat: 1648:
>   Defensio Regia: 12°: 1650: (fol. 25^{r})[1]

[1] Claude Saumaise, *Cl. Salmasii Interpretatio Hippocratei Aphorismi* (Bodleian 8° S 7 Med. Seld.). Thomas Bartholin, *Thomæ Bartholini… de cruce Christi hypomnemata iv.* (Bodleian 8° B 23 Th.Seld.). Claude Saumaise, *Dissertatio de fœnore trapezitico* (Bodleian 8° S 3 Th.

Farther down this shelf, Selden kept his copy of 'Cæsaris Scaligeri liber Poetices 8°: Comelin: 1607:' (fol. 25v).[2] The shelf also contained a group of books by Heinsius:

> Henisij Orationes 12°: Lug: Bat: 1612:
> Herodes 8° L: Bat: 1632:
> In Arestotelem Poetica 8°: L: Bat: 1620:
> Orationes 8°: L: Bat: 1627: (fol. 26r)[3]

As Selden progressed along this shelf (walking away from the 'North doore'), he would pass additional books by Scaliger, scattered among the work of others: 'Iosephi Scaligeri opuscula gr: & Lat: 8°: Par: 1605:' (fol. 26v);[4] 'Iulius C: Scaliger de subtilitate 8°: ffort 1607:'; 'Iuliius C: Scaliger de Causis L: Latinæ 8°: 1597:' (fol. 27r);[5] 'Iulij C: Scaligeri Poemata 8°: Comelin: 1621:' (fol. 28r).[6] Soon he would reach work by Grotius: 'H: Grotius his Discourses: 12°: Lond: 1653:' (fol. 28r);[7] 'Hugonis Grotij

Seld.). ___, *De usuris liber* (Bodleian 8° S 4 Th.Seld.). ___, *De modo usurarum liber* (Bodleian 8° S 6 Th.Seld.). ___, *Specimen confutationis animadversionum Desiderii Heraldi sive Tractatus de subscribendis & signandis testamentis* (Bodleian 8° S 8 Jur.Seld.). ___, *Defensio regia, pro Carolo i* (Bodleian 8° S 39 Art.Seld.).

[2] Giulio Cesare Scaligero. *Iulii Cæsaris Scaligeri … Poetices libri septem* (Bodleian 8° S 16 Art.Seld.).

[3] The first of these four books may have gone to Gloucester Cathedral. The benefactors' book there lists, among the books that it received from Selden's library, a copy of 'Heinsius Orationes' (Gloucester Cathedral Library, Kirby MS 71, fol. 20v). No book matching this description appears in the online catalogue of the cathedral library. The Bodleian retains at least two of the others: Daniel Heinsius, *Danielis Heinsii Herodes infanticida, tragœdia* (Bodleian 8° Z 28(1) Th.Seld.). ___, *Danielis Heinsii orationum editio nova* (8° H 5 Art. Seld.). The Bodleian has given 'Seld.' shelfmarks to two copies of a Heinsius work on Aristotle's poetics, but both were produced in 1611, not 1620: ___. *Aristotelis de poetica liber* (Bodleian 8° A 62(1) Art.Seld.; 8° A 33 Art. Seld.).

[4] Joseph Scaliger. *Iospehi Scaligeri … opuscula diuersa Græca & Latina* (Bodleian 8° S 44 Art.Seld.)

[5] Giulio Cesare Scaligero, *Iulii Caesaris Scaligeri Exotericarum exercitationum liber quintus decimus, De subtilitate* (Bodleian 8° S 38 Art.Seld.). ___. *Iulii Cæsaris Scaligeri de causis linguæ Latinæ libri tredecim* (Bodleian 8° S 47 Art.Seld.).

[6] Giulio Cesare Scaligero, *Iulii Cæsaris Scaligeri … poemata in duas partes diuisa* (Bodleian 8° S 36 Art.Seld.).

[7] The Bodleian associates with Selden neither of its copies of the 1653 edition of *Hugo Grotius his discourses* (Bodleian 8 ° C 22 Th.BS.; Vet. A3 f.588). The closest match in *SOLO* is the 1654 London edition of *The illustrious Hugo Grotius of the law of warre and peace* (8° G 3 Jur.Seld.).

Epistolæ ad Gallos 12°. L: Bat: 1648:' (fol. 28ᵛ).[8] Continuing in the same direction, Selden would approach a book by the first lay interpreter that he recommended to Milward: 'Picus Mirandula de Auro: 8°: vrsellis: 1598:' (fol. 29ʳ).[9] Then he would pass Grotius' edition of Lucan's *Pharsalia*: 'H: Grotius in Lucanū 8°: Raphelengij: 1614:' (fol. 29ʳ).[10] Way down on the sixth shelf was a run of works by Scaliger and Grotius (fol. 31ʳ). Many more works by Grotius, Scaliger, and Selden's other favourite lay biblical interpreters appeared throughout his library.

That library extended well beyond the room originally designated for a library at Whitefriars. Once the catalogue reaches the end of the sixth shelf, it proceeds to 'the Bookes In the 1:ˢᵗ Roome:/' (fol. 34ʳ). Next, it lists 'the Bookes in the third Roome from the Librarie:/' (fol. 38ᵛ). Much later in the manuscript, the catalogue records the books 'In the 2ᵈ Roome As yoᵘ Come from the Librarie:/' (fol. 86ʳ). Clearly, Selden's books had exceeded the considerable space available in the library proper. Later the catalogue enumerates Greek manuscripts 'In the roome at the long end of the Librarie' (fol. 103ʳ). Is this the same 'Roome at the End of the Long Librarie' (fol. 116ᵛ)? In any event, the catalogue includes Talmudic sources that, in 1655 (but almost certainly not in Selden's lifetime), were 'On the ground In the Corner in the same roome'; it lists other Hebrew manuscripts in more than one numbered 'Heape' (fol. 120ᵛ–121ʳ). Gerald Toomer has made the entirely reasonable presumption that it was not Selden but the 'emissaries' from Oxford University who had assembled these heaps of Greek and Hebrew manuscripts on the floor in the process of selecting them, since they transported these very manuscripts to the Bodleian Library in 1655, well before they agreed to accept other parts of the library on Oxford's behalf (Toomer 2009: 2.795). Indeed, the part of the Whitefriars catalogue that includes these Greek and Hebrew manuscripts, which bears a distinct series of folio numbers, is attributed to Oxford's representatives, 'Dʳ: Langbaine' and 'Mʳ: Pocock' (Bodleian MS Selden supra 111, fols. 103ʳ, 116ᵛ). Either these Oxford librarians or someone else found books even in 'the Roome next the Euidence house West:' (fol. 112ᵛ). They followed Selden's collection into 'the Furthermost

[8] Hugo Grotius, *Hugonis Grotii epistolæ ad Gallos* (Bodleian 8° G 30 Art.Seld.).

[9] Pico della Mirandola, *Ioannis Francisci Pici Mirandulæ … domini, libri iii, de auro* (Bodleian 8° M 1 Med.Seld.).

[10] Hugo Grotius, ed., *M. Annæi Lucani Pharsalia siue De bello ciuili Cæsaris et Pompeii libri x* (Bodleian 8° L 12 Art.Seld.).

Roome but one Westwards:' (fol. 121^{v}). Finally, the cataloguers reached 'the Furthest Roome in the Librarie Southwest' (fol. 128^{v}). Clearly, Selden had collected more books than the original library could hold and found space for them in multiple rooms at Whitefriars.

As Tara Lyons has shown, the Whitefriars catalogue also includes the books that the countess of Kent had collected and left to Selden along with the lease to Whitefriars and considerable wealth. Not unlike Selden's, the countess's books were distributed among distinct physical spaces (Lyons 1992: 324). The Whitefriars catalogue turns to the countess' collection with the heading, 'A Catalogue of the Bookes in Folio in the Countess her Librarie' (Bodleian MS Selden supra 111, fol. 99^{r}). After her folios, the catalogue proceeds to the octavos 'In the Countess her Librarie on the 2^{d}: shelfe on the Right hand:/' (fol. 100^{r}). It continues with 'the Bookes in 4:° In the Countess her studdie, as they stand on two shelues In the Little Roome on the left hand:/' (fol. 100^{v}). Lyons explains that these are three separate spaces: the countess' library, her study, and a little room in the study.

Its details about individual rooms and shelves make the Whitefriars catalogue a remarkable early modern document of a remarkable early modern library. This hand-written book list makes it possible to map most of Selden's library room by room, shelf by shelf, and even book by book. With the exception of the books that the executors and librarians initially selected for themselves or their institutions, the catalogue allows us to see which books Selden kept beside one another at the end of his impressive lifetime of collecting, reading, and using books. Awareness of how Selden ordered his books might also tell us something of how he used his library. While Selden supra 111 sometimes contains runs of manuscripts, quartos, folios, and so on, it more often mixes formats and media together: manuscripts are beside printed books, octavos are beside quartos, and so on. This apparent lack of an obvious organisational scheme structured around bibliographical features provides us with an exceptional level of material context. If Selden did not arrange his books along neat but ultimately coincidental rules, then perhaps he arranged them in a more meaningful way.

The suspicion, obvious as it might sound, that we want to bear out here is that Selden may have organised his books in a manner that would be useful to him. If he did, we can think of his library as a literary technology that he employed, one that was designed to assist him in his work as a lawyer or in his writing. Connections that Selden saw between texts might result in those texts being stored beside one another. If Selden's books didn't find permanent homes alongside related topics, then there is also the possibility that Selden grouped books together as he used them. Perhaps the reason that any given book was found next to any other is because Selden had used both of them in his work, and then returned them to the shelf together. Either way, it is our hypothesis that considering books that Selden supra 111 cites as appearing near each other can give us some indication of how Selden used his library.

To that end, this chapter moves into its subsequent parts, investigating the material contexts that Selden provided for the works of two contemporary English writers connected to the inns, John Donne and Thomas Coryate, by looking at the books that he kept beside them on shelves in his library at Whitefriars. Selden invested much more in the works of ancient and foreign authors than he did in contemporary English ones. And he invested more in other contemporary English writers than he did in either Donne or Coryate. Indeed, like Robert Ashley (the subject of Renae Satterley's chapter in this volume), he acquired far more of the foreign books from Donne's library than books that Donne had written—as one of the present authors has pointed out elsewhere: this chapter corrects an error in the brief account of Selden's library that appears in *Religion Around John Donne* (Eckhardt 2019). It surveys the books with which Selden surrounded the writings of Donne and Coryate—just beyond the physical bounds of Inner Temple. It thereby explores historical contexts that are also local, bibliographical, and material contexts.

Donne at Whitefriars

The Whitefriars catalogue names only two books by John Donne. It describes the first merely as 'A sermon by Dr Donne:' (Bodleian MS Selden supra 111, fol. 8^{v}). This vague reference occurs in the first part of the catalogue. This part of the hand-written book list is not divided by room or shelf. Gerald Toomer explains why:

> The first eleven folios of the catalogue (enumerating some 680 items) are not arranged by shelf, and clearly contain those books and manuscripts which had been picked out by the executors to be retained for themselves. These reflect the interests of the lawyers Vaughan and Hale (for it is likely that the other two took few or no books), and comprise almost all the rich

> collection of manuscript Year Books and other legal texts assembled by Selden, as well as the notebooks in which he excerpted material for his researches and (presumably annotated) copies of his own publications. (2009: 2.795)

Like Donne, Hale belonged to Lincoln's Inn. Like Selden, Vaughan belonged to Inner Temple. Consistent with Toomer's interpretation of the catalogue's arrangement, no single Donne sermon associated with Selden appears in any subsequent Bodleian catalogue. Without additional information, the Whitefriars catalogue indicates neither which Donne sermon Selden owned nor where he kept it before one of his executors selected it for his own use.

His executors left unclaimed the other Donne book named in the catalogue: his treatise on suicide. This book therefore appears in the large part of the catalogue organised by shelf. In particular, the book shows up as one of 'the Bookes of the 5^{t} shelfe Begining att the North doore:/' (Bodleian Selden supra 111, fol. 44^{v}). Precisely ten volumes away from the door in Whitefriars' primary library room sat 'A Declaracon of selfe Homicide by Dr Donne Lond'. Unlike the Donne sermon that Selden had owned, this book appears in subsequent Bodleian catalogues. In 1659, the bulk of Selden's library joined his choice manuscripts in Hebrew and other languages at Oxford. Over the next few years, Thomas Lockey re-catalogued Selden's books for the Bodleian's purposes. Lockey included 'Donne. Biathánatos.' as the first item under the letter 'D' in 'The Catalogue of M^{r}: Seldens bookes at the west end of S^{r}: Th: Bodleys Library' (Bodleian MS Library Records b.474, fol. 15^{r}.). The book appears in much the same place in 'A Catalogue of the books giuen by Mr Seldens Executors to the Library of the vniuersity of Oxford.//' (although the copyist placed it above the subheading 'D.' by mistake): 'I. Donne. Biathanatos' (Bodleian MS Add. c.40: 52). In 1663, the Bodleian donated more than 200 of Selden's books to Gloucester Cathedral Library; Donne's *Biathanatos* does not appear in the benefactors' book at the cathedral, suggesting that it stayed at the Bodleian (Gloucester Cathedral Library, Kirby MS 71, fols. 19^{v}–21^{r}). Perhaps ten years after Lockey had completed his catalogues of Selden books at the Bodleian, in 1672, the Bodleian fulfilled its duty to send copies of its Selden catalogue to both of Selden's surviving executors, John Vaughan and Sir Matthew Hale. Vaughan's copy of the executors' catalogue eventually made it back to the Bodleian. Hale's copy is now at Houghton Library at Harvard. Both copies of the executors' catalogue duly record Selden's copy of 'I. Donne. Βιαθάνοτος' (Bodleian MS Broxbourne 84.10: 29; Houghton MS Eng. 1328, sig. G[2]^{r}).

In 1674, the printed catalogue of the Bodleian included a copy of *Biathanatos* with a 'Th.Seld.' shelfmark:

> Βιαθανατος, that Self-murther is not so naturally a Sin, that it may never be otherwise. *Lond.* 1648. 4° G. 11. *Th. BS.* Et — 1664. 4° D. 6. *Th. Seld.* (Bodleian Library 1674: 212)

Despite the inexplicable year erroneously printed before it ('1664'[11]), the second copy of *Biathanatos* recorded here ('4° D. 6. *Th. Seld.*') would seem to be the very same copy of the book that appears in the executors' catalogue, Lockey's catalogues, and the Whitefriars catalogue.

The digital search tool *Search Oxford Libraries Online* (*SOLO*) has not been able to find the Th.Seld. copy of *Biathanatos* for years. Nevertheless, *SOLO* designates another Donne book, with the same volume-level shelfmark, as a Selden association copy: *Six sermons upon severall occasions* (4° D 6(2) Th.Seld.). (The parenthetical number 2 indicates that *Six sermons* is the second item in the volume, even though *SOLO* cannot currently access the number (1) item in the same volume.) A Bodleian reader who calls up this copy of *Six sermons* finds that the first item in the *Sammelband* is indeed the 1648 copy of *Biathanatos*, with the same base shelfmark written inside. One also finds that Selden's distinctive Greek motto does not appear in this volume, and that another reader's signature does, both on the title page of *Biathanatos* and on the front paste-down of the entire volume: 'Margaret Bowles'. Sir Geoffrey Keynes identified this early owner as Donne's daughter (Keynes 1973: 119). *Biathanatos* was printed in 1648; Selden died in 1654. This leaves only six years for Margaret Bowles to proudly inscribe her name in a *Sammelband* of her deceased father's works and then to decide to sell it, or give it away, or lose it, so that Selden

[11] The incorrect year printed in the 1674 Bodleian catalogue—'1664'—would be changed to the more defensible year 1644 in the Bodleian's 1738 catalogue of printed books:

> Βιαθανατος, that Self-Homicide is not so naturally Sin, that it may never be otherwise. — 1644. 4° D. 6. *Th. Seld.* Et *Lond.* 1648. 4° G. 11. *Th. BS.*

Bodleian Library. 1738. *Catalogus Impressorum*. Oxford, vol. 1, p. 369.

could acquire the volume (without adding his personal motto to it). This is a strong possibility. In this possible scenario, Selden must have owned not only two Donne books but three—and not only one Donne sermon but seven.

The only other possibility is that the Bodleian lost or deaccessioned Selden's copy of *Biathanatos* and acquired Bowles' *Sammelband* at least five years before she died, in time to assign it a 'Seld.' shelfmark and include it in the 1672 printed catalogue.

Regardless of whether or not the Bodleian's 'Seld.' copy of *Biathanatos* was the same one that Selden actually owned, the Whitefriars catalogue records which books he placed beside Donne's treatise:

> A Catalogue of the Bookes of the 5[t] shelf
> Begining att the North doore:/
>
> The Italian Schoolemaster: 12°: Lond: 1608:
> Le Ceremoniall de France 4°: Paris 1619:
> Papinius Statius Crucei &[ca]: 4°: Woll Par: 1618:
> Tragedie of Cleopatra 12°: Lond: 1639:
> The European Mercurie by I: W: Lond: 1641:
> The Standard of Equallitie Lond: 1647: 12°:
> A Relacōn of the Earle of Nottingham wth many others
> Into Spayne: 4°: 1605:
> Wallers Poems 8°: London: 1645:
> Cento Nouelle Scelte de Sansouino 4°: Ven: 1610:
> A Declaracon of selfe Homicide by Dr Donne Lond
> The first parte of Churchyards chips 4°: Lond: 1575:
> Les Biggarures de Seigneur des Accords 12°: Rouen: (1616)
> The warrs of Swethland 4°: London 1609: &[ca]:
> Nonni Dyonisiaca 8°: Græce Antw: 1569: (Bodleian MS Selden supra 111, fol. 44[v])

These references in the Whitefriars catalogue correspond to the following:

1. Claudius Hollyband, *The Italian school-maister*—untraced beyond Gloucester Cathedral Library, Kirby MS 71, fol. 21r.
2. Théodore Godefroy, ed., *Le cérémonial de France*—4° G 44 Art.Seld.
3. P. Papinius Statius, *Publii Papinii Statii opera*—4° S 64,65 Art.Seld.
4. Thomas May, *The tragedie of Cleopatra queen of Ægypt*—8° M 72(1) Art.Seld. (bound with Thomas May, *The tragedy of Julia Agrippina; empresse of Rome*—8° M 72(2) Art.Seld.)

5. James Wadsworth, trans., *The European Mercury. Describing the high-wayes and stages from place to place, through the most remarkable parts of Christendome*—8° W 14 Art.Seld.
6. Philo-Dicaeus pseud., *The standard of equalitie in subsidiary taxes & payments*—8° S 7 Art.Seld.
7. Robert Treswell, *A relation of such things as were obserued to happen in the iourney of the right Honourable Charles Earle of Nottingham, L. High Admirall of England, his highnesse ambassadour to the King of Spaine*—4° R 21(1) Art.Seld. (bound with Marius Bettinus, *Rubenus* - 4° R 21(2) Art.Seld.; *The most delectable history of Reynard the fox*—4° R 21(3) Art.Seld.; Sir John Tindall, *A true relation of a most desperate murder, committed vpon the body of sir Iohn Tindall*—4° R 21(4) Art. Seld.; A.R., *True and wonderfull. A discourse relating to a strange and monstrous serpent (or dragon)*—4° R 21(5) Art.Seld.; Thomas Harman, *A caueat for commen cursetors, vulgarely called vagabones*—4° R 21(6) Art.Seld.; John Lambe, *A briefe description of the notorious life of Iohn Lambe, otherwise called doctor Lambe, together with his ignominious death*—4° R 21(7) Art.Seld.; Thomas Harman, *The fraternitye of vacabondes. whereunto also is adioyned the .xxv. orders of knaues*—4° R 21(8) Art.Seld.; S.E., *The discouerie of the knights of the poste*—4° R 21(9) Art.Seld.)
8. Edmund Waller, *Poems, &c.*—8° W 8 Art.Seld.
9. Francesco Sansovino, *Cento nouelle scelte da piu nobili scrittori della lingua volgare*—4° S 7 Art.Seld.
10. John Donne, *Biathanatos*—4° D 6(1) Th.Seld. (bound together with *Six sermons upon severall occasions*, 4° D 6(2) Th.Seld.)
11. Thomas Churchyard, *The first parte of Churchyardes chippes*—4° C 48 Art.Seld.
12. Estienne Tabourot, *Les bigarrures et touches du Seigneur des accordes*—8° A 66 Art.Seld.
13. Anthony Nixon, *The warres of Swethland*—4° S 58(1) Art.Seld. (bound with "Nota bene. / Cum Luna fuerit discendens"—[4° S 58(2) Art.Seld.]; Albert and Isabella, Sovereign of Netherlands, *A proclamation or edict. Touching the opening and restoring of the traffique, and comerce of Spaine*—4° S 58(3) Art.Seld.;[12] *Certaine consid-*

[12] Like the Donne *Sammelband*, the one that begins with Nixon's *The warres of Swethland* also includes items that *SOLO* cannot currently recall (the second and fourth items of 4° S 58 Art.Seld.).

erations drawne from the canons of the last sinod—4° S 58[(4)] Art. Seld.; Sovereign of England and Wales, *A declaratioun of the kings maiesties intentioun and meaning toward the lait actis of parliament*—4° S 58(5) Art.Seld.; Thomas Cartwright, *A brief apologie of Thomas Cartwright against all such slaunderous accusations as it pleaseth mr. Sutcliffe in severall pamphlettes ... to loade him with*—4° S 58(6) Art.Seld.; *Certain arguments to perswade ... parliament ... to promote ... the sincere ministry of the gospell*—4° S 58(7) Art.Seld.; Robert Browne, *An answere to master Cartwright his letter for ioyning with the English Churches*—4° S 58(8) Art.Seld.; Hugh Broughton, *Two little workes defensiue of our redemption*—4° S 58(9) Art.Seld.; ___, *Declaration of generall corruption of religion . . . wrought by d. Bilson*—4° S 58(10) Art.Seld.; E.D., *The copy of a letter . . . The former part conteineth rules for the perseruation of health*—4° S 58(11) Art. Seld.; James I, *Dæmonologie*—4° S 58(12) Art.Seld.; *Albrecht VII, archduke of Austria, A proclamation of the truce between his majesty of Spayne, and their most illustrious highnesses on the one party, and the states generall of the vnited Netherlands on the other party*—4° S 58(13) Art.Seld.; *Articles of a treatie of truce made and concluded in Antwerp, the 9. of April 1609. betweene the commissioners of the archdukes Albert and Isabella Clara Eugenia . . . Together with the commissioners of the estates generall of the Vnited prouinces of the Low-countryes*—4° S 58(14) Art.Seld.)

14. Nonnus, of Panopolis, *Nonni . . . Dionysiaca*—4° N 16 Art.Seld.

Several of the books that surrounded *Biathanatos* at Whitefriars likewise begin *Sammelbände*. Further research would be required to determine whether the multi-title volumes listed here could have been bound together before, or only after, they reached the Bodleian. Nevertheless, in each of the cases presented here, only the lead item in a multi-item volume appears in the Whitefriars catalogue; this very short part of the catalogue records no items that appear later in a *Sammelband*. This suggests the strong possibility that, with so many books to record, the cataloguers were citing only the first item in a volume, even if that meant skipping an item (or 13). This means that the 'Totall Number' of books recorded in the Whitefriars catalogue ('7,466') may account only for individual volumes and that the total number of publications in Selden's library could be much higher.

The volume of two works by Thomas May offers something of a parallel to the volume of two works by Donne. Yet Thomas Walkly published both of these plays by May in 1639 and could have certainly sold them together. By contrast, the two Donne books were produced 14 years apart in different cities. Selden's library was intimidatingly multi-lingual and his facility with languages reflects innsmen's interest in translation, explored further in this volume in the chapters by Jessica Winston, Felicity Brown, and Renae Satterley. But Donne and May were both vernacular English writers and not the only ones owned by Selden. He did not collect Donne's poems, but he did collect Edmund Waller's. He also had copies of *Reynard the fox* and *Churchyardes chippes*, which sat on one side of the Donne volume. This may amount to a higher proportion of English literature than one can usually discern in broader surveys of Selden's library.

No other sermons or treatises on suicide accompanied Donne's works of these sorts on their shelf at Whitefriars. It may be worth mentioning, however, that the first two of Donne's *Six sermons* were addressed to royalty, specifically King Charles I. Does the royal audience of those sermons resonate with the royal author of James VI and I's *Dæmonologie*, or perhaps with the treaties involving Spain and the Netherlands? In general, Selden kept these books in an order that neither the Bodleian nor many others would affirm.[13]

This part of the fifth shelf would seem to resonate less with Donne than with Coryate. Wadsworth's account of the highways and stages throughout Christendom could certainly interest a reader of Coryate's travels, which extended even beyond Christendom. So too could the account of the earl of Nottingham's journey to Spain, and Thomas Harman's books on vagabonds. Selden famously did not travel beyond England; instead, he compiled one of the most linguistically and geographically diverse collections of books that his country had yet hosted in a single location. Even just this end of one shelf, with its uncharacteristically high proportion of vernacular English writing, arguably demonstrates Selden's commitment to seeing, and arguably even to mapping, much of the world in impressive geographic and linguistic detail from his library.

[13] Or did Selden collect the Cambridge collection of Donne's sermons because of its relation to the inns of court? The final two sermons in the volume had been preached at Lincoln's Inn and address relatively legal biblical texts, insofar as they deal with judgement: 'John 5. 22. The Father judgeth no man, but hath committed all judgement to the Sonne'; 'John 8. 15. I judge no man'. We owe this point to Emma Rhatigan.

Coryate at Whitefriars

As the record of the shelves that house Selden's Donne volumes indicate, Selden supra 111 does not yield a clear organisational structure to Selden's library. Rather, what it might do is provide us with a better view as to how Selden used his books. Drawing conclusions about Selden's book use may reveal something about the reception of those books; if the inns of court were an early modern literary centre, then surely considering a book's position in an important innsman's library can tell us something worth knowing about that book. To test this hypothesis, we will now turn to another leaf of Selden supra 111, fol. 39^{v}. We have chosen this leaf in particular because it includes a peculiar and notable book, Thomas Coryate's 1611 European travelogue, *Coryats Crudities.*

Crudities stands out from Selden's erudite collection because it is a text that, since its publication, has had the reputation of being a frivolous, self-aggrandizing book that flaunts the author's own foolishness as a selling point. A large factor in the development of this reputation is the collection of mock-commendatory verses that preface the main text. Penned by nearly 60 friends and acquaintances of Coryate, the so-called Panegyricke Verses mocked the book's size, the bombastic personality of its author, and its tedious descriptions of continental sights, cities, and cultures.

When we spotted this book in Selden's collection, we questioned why it might have been included. Tara Lyons' catalogue of the countess of Kent's library, which was eventually combined with Selden's, does not include *Crudities* despite the countess's interest in what we might think of as more literary books.[14] It appears that Selden acquired this book on his own. Since several of the contributors to the 'Panegyricke Verses' were innsmen, one reason why Selden might have acquired this book could be that he was interested in the literary heritage of the inns of court. For instance, one author of this chapter has argued that there existed a close friendship between Coryate and the lawyer (and later Sergent at Law), John Hoskins; not only were both members of the Right Worshipful Fraternity of Sireniacal Gentlemen—a literary club that took the form of a mock-guild and was administered in part by Coryate—but manuscript evidence has been discovered that shows Hoskins to have defended Coryate's

[14] *Crudities* falls within a genre of early modern books designed for pleasurable reading. Katherine Craik points out that Coryate directs his diverting text to a male audience exclusively (Craik 2004: 44, 84).

family in a legal battle while Coryate was abroad (Neuhauser 2023). In total, 27 of the contributors to the 'Panegyricke Verses' were confirmed, or are suspected of having been, innsmen. From Lincoln's Inn were William Austin, Christopher Brooke, Sir Roland Cotton, John Donne, Robert Halswell, Sir Henry Poole, and Sir Robert Yaxley. Michael Strachan suggests that Richard Hughes was also associated with Lincoln's Inn (Strachan 1962: 280). Middle Temple's contributors included Sir William Clavel, John Hoskins, Inigo Jones, Sir Lewis Lewknor, Richard Martin, Thomas Momford, John Pawlet, Sir Robert Phelips, Sir John Strangewayes, George Sydenham, and Laurence Whitaker. In addition to raising the possibility that William Baker and John Chapman were also members of Middle Temple, Strachan's identification of the two contributors who used Greek pseudonyms (Edward Phelips as 'Αποδημουντόφιλος and James Montague as Tò 'Ορὸς-ὀξύ) shows them to be members of Middle Temple, as well (Strachan 1962: 270, 272, 284). The only contributor that was sure to have been a current member of Gray's Inn at the time of submitting his verse was John Sutclin, though Sir Dudley Digges was associated with Gray's Inn from 1631, and the Nicholas Smith who contributed a verse was likely either of Gray's or Lincoln's Inn (Strachan 1962: 288). The sole contributor suspected of being from Selden's home inn, the Inner Temple, was John Gyfford (Strachan 1962: 278).

Despite the good showing of innsmen here, Selden's own work suggests that he might have been more interested in the main text of *Crudities*: the description, reports, and judgements that Coryate placed on the continental cultures that he came across. As Satterley and Working and Stevenson observe in their chapters in this volume, innsmen had a keen interest in travel and foreign cultures. Toomer documents Selden's specific curiosity noting that he knew Samuel Purchas, the author/compiler of *Purchas His Pilgrimage*, a lengthy folio that included reports and observations of several cultures and countries, derived primarily from the work of other writers (Toomer 2009: 1.18). He observes that in the first, 1613 edition of *Pilgrimage*, Purchas thanks Selden for allowing him to see a manuscript in his collection, and that Selden supplied that edition of *Pilgrimage* with two commendatory verses, one in Greek and one in Latin (1.19). The latter of these included a marginal note that took up the better part of two pages (Purchas 1613). Subsequent editions of *Pilgrimage* noted contributions from Selden on the subject of Jewish tithes and on ancient records relating to Jews living in England (Toomer 2009: 1.19–20). It is therefore possible that *Crudities*, a book famously derided for its perceived frivolity, was not received as something quite so frivolous. Rather, Selden may have been more interested in Coryate's narrative than in the disparaging verses that prefaced it.

This idea, that Selden collected Coryate's book because of the contents of its main text, is reinforced by considering what books he shelved around it. Starting from the top of Selden supra 111 fol. 39^{v}, and going through to ten entries past *Crudities*, we find the following titles:

> Velleius Paterculus 16°: Fort: 1607:
> Meibomii Musica 4°: one volume Amst: 1652:
> Besleri Hortus Eystettensis 1613: fol:
> Montebrū Ephemerides: 4° Bononiæ 1645:
> *Croyats* [sic] Crudities 4°: Lond: 1611:
> Iustiniani Index vniuersalis fol: Romæ: 1612:
> Curopolate Historiarū Compendiū fol: Ven: 1570:
> Voisin Theologia Iudeorū 4°: Par: 1647:
> Sebei Index Homeri 4° græce Comelin 1604:
> Pentateuchus Hebr: Lat: 4°: Ven: 1551:
> Io: Cumani Historia Imperat Constant: 4°: Vltra=(iectini 1652)
> Duck de Iure Ciuili 8°: Lond: 1653:
> Willeramus in Cantico 8°: Lugd. Bat: 1598:/
> Nonnus de Re Cibaria 8°: Ant: 1627:
> Lopius de Re Medica 8°: Ant: 1564: (Bodleian MS Selden supra 111, fol. 39^{v})

Below is a list of these same books as we know them today, with shelfmarks corresponding to their current homes at the Bodleian:

1. Gaius Velleius Paterculus' *Historiae Romanae ad M. Vinicium cos. Libri Duo*, which discusses both Greek mythology and Roman history—8° P 91 Art.Seld.
2. Marcus Meibom's *Antiquae Musicae Auctores Septem Graece et Latine*, a work of scholarship on ancient Greek Music—4° M 32,33 Art.Seld.
3. Basilius Besler's *Hortus Eystettensis*, a richly illustrated florilegium—MS. Arch. Selden. B. 1.
4. Franciscus Montebrunus' *Ephemerides nouissimæ motuum cœlestium*, a detailed astrological book that provided dates, positions of the sun, astrological symbols, tables, figures, etc. for the year 1646—4° M 11 Art.Seld.

5. Thomas Coryate's *Coryats Crudities*—4° C 28 Art.Seld.
6. Fabianus Justinianus, bishop of Ajaccio, *Index vniuersalis alphabeticus materias in omni facultate consulto pertractatas, earumq. scriptores, & locos designans*, an index to the Bible—F 1.1 Th.Seld.
7. Johannes Curopolates' *Historiarum Compendium*, covering the history of Byzantine Emperors from the Nikephoros I in the ninth century to Isacc I Komnenos in the eleventh century—C 2.10(1) Art.Seld. (bound with Giovanni Pietro Maffei's *Historiarum Indicarum libri xvi*, on the Portuguese in India and the Indies—C 2.10(2) Art.Seld.).
8. Joseph de Voisin's *Theologia Iudæorum*, a Latin text with printed marginal notes in Greek and Hebrew about Jewish Theology—4° V 18 Th.Seld.
9. Wolfgang Seber's *Index Vocabulorum in Homeri*, a Homer concordance spanning more than 500 pages, containing citations for all the words used in Homer's *Illiad*, *Odyssey*, and other works—4° S 36 Art.Seld.
10. A version of the Torah, or as it is referred to here, the Pentateuch, printed in Hebrew and Latin in parallel columns—4° P 8 Th.Seld.
11. Dutch scholar Cornelius Tollius' edition of *Ioannis Cinnami de Rebus Gestis*, John Kinnamos' history of Emperor John II Komnenos and his son, Manuel I Komnenos' reigns—4° C 65 Art.Seld.
12. Arthur Duck's *De Vsu & Authoritate Juris Civilis Romanorum in Dominiis Principum Christianorum*, a book that criticised the English Monarchy through its consideration of how Roman civil law might work in England—8° D 2 Jur.Seld.
13. A printed version of Benedictine Abbot Williram of Ebersberg's Old Dutch paraphrase of the Song of Songs, edited by Paulus Merula—8° W 2(1) Th.Seld. (bound with Bonaventura Vulcanius' survey of languages, *De literis & lingua Getarum, siue Gothorum*—8° W2 (2) Th.Seld.).
14. Ludovicus Nonnius' *Diæteticon, siue De re cibaria*, a book concerned with eating and drinking, treating food in an almost medical manner—8° N 2 Med.Seld.
15. Garcias Lopius' medical book, *Commentarii de Varia rei Medicae Lectione*—8° L 2(1) Med.Seld. (bound with Balduinus Ronsseus' *De magnis Hippocratis lienibus*—8° L 2(2) Med.Seld.; Auger Ferrier's book on syphilis, *de pudendagra*—8° L 2(3) Med.Seld.; and Nicolás Bautista Monadres' work on pleurisy, *de secanda vena in pleuriti inter Græcos & Arabes concordia*—8° L 2(4) Med.Seld.).

There are plausible reasons as to why *Coryats Crudities* might have been stored next to any of these books. Throughout his relations of his travels, Coryate digressed into commentary on the historical significance of the places he encountered, often harkening back to ancient Greek and Roman history. Perhaps Selden thought of *Crudities* as a companion to Paterculus', Meibom's, Curopolates', or Kinnamos's historical works. *Crudities* may have been something more than just a reference book for Selden: he could have spent time contemplating Coryate's commentary. Coryate was not only interested in observing foreign cultures but he was also quick to pass an English and Protestant-minded judgement on them as he worked his way through the continent. It could be that he offered Selden a perspective on ancient Roman laws to complement Duck's consideration of Roman laws in the early modern English setting. Coryate's commentary and judgements on Catholic religious practices in France and Italy might have prompted Selden to verify Coryate's claims in his copy of Justinianus' Italian-made biblical index. One of the most frequently noted passages of *Crudities* is Coryate's observations of the Jewish Quarter in Venice, thought to be the first Jewish ghetto in Europe. Selden possessed a keen interest in Jewish thought, and he may have kept Coryate's work near his copy of the Pentateuch and Voisin's theological book to serve as a more contemporary perspective on the politics and religious practices of one group of European Jews.

Of course, there is the possibility that Selden's interest in Coryate was, like so many of his readers, rooted in his enjoyment of the overall strangeness of *Crudities.* Coryate's presence on this shelf could be due to his book's metaphorical core, which suggested that, by reading the book, the reader was participating in the ingestion of Coryate's 'crudities', raw morsels that Coryate had already partially digested by writing them down in the first place. And finally, there are the mocking prefatory 'Panegyricke Verses', wherein Corayte was teased for his tendency to make up new words. Might Coryate's love of neologisms have led Selden to set this book nearby Williram's complicated linguistic paraphrases? Similarly, several of the contributors to these verses criticised Coryate over his casual overuse of Greek words, making his proximity to Seber's Homeric concordance fitting.

Whether or not the 'Panegyrcike Verses' are the primary reason that we would have found Coryate near Williram and Seber, *Crudities*' mere presence in Selden's library raises an intriguing question about the commendatory verses that he provided for the 1613 edition of *Purchas his Pilgrimage*. Toomer reports that Selden's commendatory sonnet written for Micheal Drayton's *Poems* in 1610 was full of nigh-impenetrable 'allusions', 'archaisms', and 'elaborate conceits' that would result in his poetic attempt laying in 'desperate obscurity' (Toomer 2009: 1.20). Toomer's next examples of Selden's commendatory verses are from 1612—for Arthur Hopton's *A Concordancy of Yeares*—and for Purchas' 1613 *Pilgrimage*, both of which contain 'huge notes (far greater in length than the poems to which they are attached)' (1.21). While there is no definitive proof that Selden was inspired by the mock-commendatory verses found in the 1611 *Crudities*, one of the major innovations of the 'Panegyricke Verses' was their form-challenging tendency to include ludicrous marginal notation. Of course, where Selden's verses and notes differed from those directed to Coryate was that they were intended to clarify his verse to the reader, not to abuse his subject.

We may not be able to determine definitively what the connections were between *Crudities* and the books with which it shared shelf space at Whitefriars. Despite this, its placement within Selden's library helps us understand more about the book itself. Selden's copy of *Crudities* offers an excellent example of how a book's material context can help reframe the way that we think about individual early modern books. Selden's ownership of Coryate's book has the potential to reshape our approach to it. Despite its reputation as a trifling thing, one of the most learned and respected innsmen of the seventeenth century placed *Coryats Crudities* in a rather heady space.

Since they took up so little space on his shelves, the books that Selden owned by Coryate and Donne offer the opportunity to consider very briefly the local, material context of his library at Whitefriars. It would take much more space, for instance, to trace the books by any one of his favourite lay interpreters of the Bible (such as Salmasius, Scaliger, and Grotius) throughout Selden's library. Such a survey would also be more revealing and more demanding. Our concluding point is that such a study is possible since the Bodleian retains the Whitefriars catalogue, a number of subsequent catalogues of Selden's books, and a vast quantity of those books themselves. While it would require enormous work, the materials survive to produce a documentary edition of Selden supra 111 that cross-references several subsequent catalogues, including *SOLO*, and the surviving items from Selden's library as well. Combined with Selden's published scholarship and the considerably more welcoming 'Discourse of Iohn Selden, Esq.', a complete edition or study of Selden's library at Whitefriars could reveal a great deal about what was becoming possible in early modern England for a gifted scholar with resources.

Works Cited

Bodleian Library. 1674. *Catalogus Impressorum*. Oxford.

Bodleian Library. 1738. *Catalogus impressorum*. Oxford.

Bodleian. Manuscript Add. c.40.

Bodleian. Manuscript Broxbourne 84.10.

Bodleian. Manuscript Library Records b.474.

Bodleian. Manuscript Selden supra 111.

Clapham, A. W. 1910. "The Topography of the Carmelite Friary in London." *The Journal of the British Archaeological Association*, 2nd ser., 16: 15–32.

Craik, Katharine A. 2004. "Reading 'Coryats Crudities' (1611)." *Studies in English Literature, 1500–1900* 44, no. 1: 77–96.

Eckhardt, Joshua. 2019. *Religion Around John Donne*. University Park, Pennsylvania: Pennsylvania State University Press.

Gloucester Cathedral Library. Kirby Manuscript 71.

Houghton Library. Manuscript Eng. 1211.2.

Houghton Library. Manuscript Eng. 1328.

Keynes, Geoffrey. 1973. *A Bibliography of Dr. John Donne*. 4th ed. Oxford: Clarendon Press.

Lyons, Tara. 1992. "Lady Elizabeth Grey (née Talbot), Countess of Kent. Writer (attributed), literary patron: Inventory. 1654." In *Private Libraries in Renaissance England: A Collection and Catalogue of Tudor and Early Stuart Book-Lists*, vol. 10, edited by Robert J. Fehrenbach and Joseph Black, 324–61. Binghamton, NY: Arizona Center for Medieval & Renaissance Studies.

Neuhauser, Julian T. S. 2023. "Sirenaicks, Guilds and a New Coryate Manuscript." *The Review of English Studies* 74: 31–46.

Purchas, Samuel. 1613. *Purchas His Pilgrimage*. London.

Strachan, Michael. 1962. *The Life and Adventures of Thomas Coryate*. Oxford: Oxford University Press.

Toomer, Gerald. 2009. *John Selden: A Life in Scholarship*. Oxford: Oxford University Press.

CHAPTER 9

Lewiston Fitzjames and Other Stray Poets of the Inns of Court

Arthur F. Marotti

While he was working on his edition of the poetry of Sir John Davies 64 years ago, Robert Krueger published a two-part article on Bodleian MS Additional B.97 (1975). This was mainly because it was compiled by someone at the Middle Temple, where the compiler and poet were in close proximity, and because it contains a large portion of Davies's verse: a collection of his epigrams, a unique manuscript copy of his epithalamion for the marriage of Lady Elizabeth Vere and William Stanley, earl of Derby, and the only surviving manuscript copy of the long poem *Orchestra* (Krueger 1962a, b). The compiler of this composite manuscript, whose contents were assembled, according to Krueger, in two separate periods (1595–1598 and 1607–1609) was Lewiston Fitzjames of Dorset, who moved from Balliol College, Oxford, to the Middle Temple and who got access to Davies's work while at the inn before the poet was expelled for his violent attack on his former close friend Sir Richard Martin during the

A. F. Marotti (✉)
Emeritus, Wayne State University, Detroit, MI, USA
e-mail: a.marotti@wayne.edu

E. Rhatigan, J. Watson (eds.), *Mapping the Early Modern Inns of Court*, Early Modern Literature in History,
https://doi.org/10.1007/978-3-031-77445-4_9

1597–1598 Christmas Revels.[1] The copy of *Orchestra* in this manuscript is prefaced by Davies's original dedication to Martin (fol. 24^{v}). Understandably, Krueger concentrated his attention on the verse in this document attributed to Davies, but I would like to broaden the focus to examine the other features of this composite manuscript, both as an inns-of-court collection and as a compilation, like other such collections, originating at the university and continued in the metropolitan political environment of late Elizabethan and early Jacobean London. I would also like to direct some attention to the verse composed by Fitzjames and use this as an entry to an examination of the poems written by what I choose to call 'stray poets' who functioned in the inns and its urban environment.[2]

Lewiston Fitzjames's Manuscript

Bodleian Add. B.97 is a true miscellany, containing prose as well as verse. It includes the following prose items:

'Of Behemoth & Leviathan' (fol. 1^{v})
'Examples of Pestilence' (fol. 2)
'Part of the Conference betwine Reynolds & Harte' (fols. 2–4)
a refutation of anti-monarchical political theory (fol. 4$^{r–v}$)
a narrative about the visit of King James to Sir Francis Tresham (fol. 11$^{r–v}$)
sermon notes on 'Doctor Lavall at Saint Clements on All Saints daye. 1605' (fol. 11^{v})
'A Prayer for the faithfull understandinge of Scripture' (fol. 12^{v})
a medical receipt (or 'Charme') for the cough (fol. 12^{v})
some short quotes 'At the Arraignment of Sir Walter Ralegh' (in 1603) (fol. 12^{v})
a description of part of Somersetshire about Axbridge (fol. 13)
a Latin item 'Quaritur AEgistus quare sit factus adulter' (translated as 'By what occasion Aegistus turned Lover and Souldier' [fols. 13–15^{v}])

[1] *Alumni Oxonienses* records Fitzjames matriculation at Balliol on 5 March 1590/91 at the age of 17 and entry to Middle Temple in 1594 ("Fitzjames, Leweston", in *Alumni Oxonienses 1500-1714* (Oxford 1891). British History Online, accessed May 11, 2024, https://www.british-history.ac.uk/alumni-oxon/1500-1714). Sturgess records his admission on November 6 (1949: 67).

[2] This chapter uses some material presented in a different form in my book (Marotti 2021: 220–50).

a short item about 'Folish pittie' (fol. 15^{v})
'Variety of Judgment in bewtye' (fol. 18^{v})
a quote from Sidney's *Arcadia* (fol. 19)
'The copie of the letter sente by one of the conspiracie in the Blowinge up the Parliament howse to L[ord] Mountegle: wherby the Treason was discovered & prevented' (fol. 23^{v})
'A charme for an Ague' (fol. 24)
the anti-papal piece, 'Peeter not cheife of the Apostles' (fol. 24)
two prose pieces, 'Pacis mala' and 'A Conceit' (fol. 40^{v})
a prose discourse on a passage from Paul's Epistle to the Romans (fol. 48)
a discussion of the law of primogeniture (fols. 51^{v}–55^{v})
discussion of scriptural matters, particularly the blessing of Esau (fol. 55^{v})
several letters in Latin and English written by Fitzjames and his friends John Mayo and Thomas Chafie (the latter a minister) (fols. 57^{v}–62^{v})
another 'charme' or medical receipt, 'To take away the spotts of the small Pockes' (fol. 64^{r}).

The interests reflected in these various prose entries in both English and Latin are religious, political, medical, literary, and personal. Fitzjames was compiling a miscellany in a manner similar to that used by educated individuals who were recording important items from their lives and reading in their commonplace books. His collecting took place at the university, at Middle Temple, and in the broader sociocultural context of late Elizabethan and early Jacobean London, illustrating the interconnecting communities inhabited by innsmen. It is thus not surprising that Fitzjames mixed such disparate materials as folk medical cures (in the 'charms' to treat the cough, the common cold, and smallpox), notes on sermons he heard, political information and gossip, a theoretical discussion of the relative merits and flaws of monarchy and of aristocratic rule, and religious controversy between Protestants and Catholics. As, first, a student at Oxford and then as member of Middle Temple, he was in the midst of sophisticated discussions of a wide range of contemporary intellectual, religious, and political issues (O'Callaghan 2007; Prest 2023; Archer, Goldring, and Knight 2011; Nelson and Elliott 2010: 1.xiii–xlvii).

The poetical collection also has items deriving from Fitzjames's university years, as well as some from his post-inns period in the first decade of the seventeenth century. The ones related to Oxford include the very first piece in the collection, a very long pastoral dialogue ('Jenkin? why man? Why Jenkin? Fie for shame' [fols. 5–10^{v}]) by the poet-wit Thomas Bastard denying his authorship of the libel that may have been the cause of his expulsion from New College (May and Bryson 2016: 370–401). A song, beginning 'When Phoebus did fayre Daphne love' is found in a form that contains a supplementary stanza by a fellow Balliol student from Dorset, Charles Ryves, an example of the kind of literary freedom readers had to alter the texts they received through the system of manuscript transmission. Late in the manuscript, there is an English translation of the Latin insignia of the university, 'The horned Oxe our Athens once did beare' [fol. 39]). Finally, there is an apparently unique manuscript copy of a poem by James Mabbe, of Magdalen College, who matriculated in 1588: 'To Sir G. T. K.' (fols. 56^{v}–57), a witty poem listing flowers and herbs, most of which have traditional medical uses. Mabbe would have overlapped with Fitzjames at the university (see Appendix).

Several misogynistic poems are part of Fitzjames's collection. A unique copy of a piece on the theme 'Fewe Woemen good' ('Amongst 1000 men sayth Solomon I found one good' [fol. 18^{v}]) accompanies another, apparently unique, poem on women, 'Woemen we knowe were made of bone' (fol. 18^{v}). The next poem seems to be about the widowed Lettice Knollys, who continued to style herself the countess of Leicester after the earl's death in 1588. She was the mother of the second earl of Essex, had a scandalous reputation, and, in the reign of James VI and I, was in a legal battle with Robert Dudley, the bastard son of her late husband. A viciously witty couplet about her is recorded in this manuscript:

> Is it not the tricke of an arrant Whore,
> To washe her Arse in milke & give it to the poore.
> written in Essex gallerie by the doore
> of my Ladie of Lecesters Chamber
> (fol. 19)

Two other poems ('It is a question in heraldry' [fol. 20^{v}] and 'If any ask why Tarquin meant to marry' [fol. 20^{v}]) deal with the indiscreet marriage of Richard Fletcher, bishop of London, to the morally problematic Lady Mary Baker in 1594/95, an act that caused Queen Elizabeth to suspend the bishop (Davies 1975: 398–99). Gossip about the marriage in the inns environment obviously accounts for the presence of these two poems in Fitzjames's collection.

Some of the other poems in this manuscript are pieces freely circulating in the broader social world in which Fitzjames functioned. This larger metropolitan environment, discussed by many of the chapters in this collection, extended to the world of taverns, such as the Mermaid and Mitre, in which innsmen mingled with members of parliament and fellow literati in an atmosphere in which (often competitive) verse was composed. Fitzjames's collection includes two epigrams by Sir John Harington, 'Ludicrum of marriage' ('A fine young Preist a kin to Friar Frapper' [fol. 38^{v}]) and 'Of Othes' ('In elder tyme the ancient custome was' [fol. 39^{r}]), the second here attributed to Ben Jonson ('Authore: Ben: Jonsonio'),[3] and copies of two poems by John Donne, the epigram on a licentious person ('Thy sinnes and haires may no man equall call' [fol. 39^{v}]) and the elegy 'The Anagram' ('Marrie and love thy Flavia' [fols. 55^{v}–56^{r}]), the latter apparently the most widely circulated of that poet's love elegies and an example of the poetry which, as Rhatigan discusses in Chap. 3, made him the subject of gossip later in life. The Donne elegy is followed by what looks like schoolboy verses that may have circulated in a university setting:

> Verba infinita
> Amare, placere, studere, ambire
>
> To Love's to runn a Maze of hopes & feares,
> To please's to varie with the winde & weather,
> To studie's, to be restles as the Spheares,
> To woe's, to sue & seeke to gaine a Feather.
> For who so ere Doth Love, please studie woe
> When all is Donne shall finde some thinge to doe.
> (fol. 56)[4]

The collection also has a unique copy of a Latin epigram about hangings being worse than marriage, 'In Connubium: worse than hanging' (fol. 39^{v}), which appears along with its English translation.

Although university and inns pieces express the anti-Petrarchan, Ovidian, or misogynistic attitudes associated with these homosocial environments, other poems in Fitzjames's collection deal with love in a more polite idiom. Fitzjames reproduced 'A Poesie, written by a gentleman in

[3] The first, entitled 'Ludicrum of marriage', appears in three other manuscripts (BL Add. MS 25707: fol.128; BL Add. MS 12409: 90–91; Folger MS V.a.249: 121). It is attributed in several manuscript and print documents to the Jesuit Henry Fitzsimon (see Kilroy 2009: 169–70, who prints the piece with the title 'Of the commodities that Priests have by their marriadge').

[4] This poem also appears in BL Additional MS 15226, fol. 3^{v} and Stowe MS 962, fol. 171.

the ende / of a booke, which he gave to his Mistress': 'Deere but remember it is I: / That for thy love will love, & dye' (fol. 19). There are three sonnets, the first of which is a palinode ('Read in my face the fortunes of my youth' [fol. 19ᵛ]) (see Appendix). The second and third, which politely express frustration in love, are labelled 'An other dependinge on this' (fol. 20) and 'An other on this' (fol. 20). They seem part of the same sequence, rather than two answer poems.

We find another group of poems in the sonnet form written in a neat italic hand, each headed 'Canto', but the fifth is marked as incomplete ('Desunt multa: for it was a Dreame' [fol. 23]) and it is followed by another (unnumbered) love poem identified as unfinished ('An other also Imperfecte' [fol. 23]), followed by the prose explanation: 'He described his mistresse walkinge, observinge how the grasse assoone as she tooke up her feete arose as seeming to follow them, the ayre blewe about her, the sonne pirrd in at her maske, & small pinkes in her gloves &c.' (fol. 23). This whole series looks like the in-progress work of a single poet, perhaps Fitzjames himself. After the fourth of these poems, there is a prose note that could suggest that the author was Fitzjames: 'At his frendes request that was falling in liking of a Gentle-woman he made this Prosopopeia' (fol. 22ᵛ).

As Sharon Harris demonstrates in Chap. 7, innsmen had a keen interest in songs and music, so it is, perhaps, not surprising that the miscellany also includes songs related to the early seventeenth-century London musical culture Mary Hobbs has identified (1992: 105–15). One song, 'What if a day or a night or a year?' (fol. 16), is found in many manuscript and print copies, and dubiously attributed to Thomas Campion in one print publication.[5] Shortly after this is a rare poem that was probably also sung ('What shal a man desier in this World' [fol. 16ᵛ]) (see Appendix). Two other songs follow. The first is an apparently unique copy of a persuasion to love imitating the well-known eighth song of Sidney's *Astrophil and Stella* (see Appendix). A couplet labelled 'Injurie, Contumelie, & Reproche wislye passed over', refers irreverently to James VI and I and Queen Anne: 'The lyke were never yet in England seene / Unto our huntinge kinge & Dauncinge Queene' (fol. 47). This is followed by the statement 'So wrotte Anonymos' and the explanation that King James, despite being urged to punish the writer, decided to treat the piece as innocuous because it was

[5] See the list in the Folger Index: https://firstlines.folger.edu/advancedSearch.php?val1=if+a+day&col1=firstline#results.

true. A further prose explanation cites the case of the king being asked to punish 'Players for traducing Certeine of the Nobility on the Stage' to which he answered, 'No no Lett them first leave these vices for which they are taxed & then they will never be touched' (fol. 47).

Fitzjames, in using his initials, claims authorship of several poems in the collection, but he may also have written other unattributed pieces. His first poems appear early in the collection. The first is an epigram attacking a poet who praises Sidney and Spenser, but who scorns lesser writers, 'In Calvum Poetam' ('Well didst thou prayse the noble high conceit' [fol. 17]) (see Appendix). A second piece, 'In eundem' ('Calvus is pleasd with none but with the best' [fol. 17^v]) (see Appendix), attacks the same individual and is subscribed with Fitzjames's initials.

Fitzjames translated a number of Latin items in his collection into English. For example, he took a short dialogue between 'Philosophus' and 'Justitia' from the expanded version of Elizabeth Grymeston's *Miscellanea* (1606) (see Hughey and Hereford 1934) and produced an English version (fol. 47^v). He followed this with the translation of a Latin poem on the theme of the transitoriness of life, 'Out of the same Booke as the former' (fol. 48) (see Appendix). The schoolboy habit of translating from Latin to English carried over into Fitzjames's adult life; as other contributors in this volume demonstrate, the same intellectual habit contributed to the popularity of translations of classical drama at the inns. Latin correspondence comes at the end of the collection, whose final item is a Latin poem presented before the king at court.

Other Stray Poets of the Inns of Court

Historically, Fitzjames has had a very low profile as a poet, but many other individuals in the inns environment who turned their hand to verse have also largely escaped notice. These include John Grange, Nicholas Hare, John Vaughan, Richard Clarke, Robert Ellice, Henry Blount, Sir Thomas Salusbury, and William Austin.[6] Their activities were spread over a number of decades, testifying to the importance of the inns world as a rich sociolitrary environment in which the writing of verse was encouraged.

[6] In his section of the Introduction to our in-progress edition of the poems of Dr Richard Andrews, Steven W. May notes the social connections of Austin with Andrews as well as with John Bill and Sir Nicholas Smith.

John Grange (1587–1622), whose poems appear in manuscripts associated with the inns (such as Folger MSS V.a.96 and V.a.245 and Huntington MS HM 198.2), like FitzJames at Balliol College, moved to Lincoln's Inn in 1604, received a B.A. in 1606, and was ordained as a priest in 1610 (Krueger 1961: 93). John Grange's poems, some of them quite popular in manuscript transmission, managed to enter later printed collections, for example, song books such as Lawes's *Select Ayres and Dialogues* (1653; 1659; 1669) and Playford's *The Musical Companion* (1672). They were also printed in miscellanies and poetical anthologies such as Benson's edition of *The Poems of William Shakespeare* (1640) (which has a section of miscellaneous poems by other, mostly Caroline, poets), *Wits recreations* (1640, 1641), and *Parnassus Biceps* (1656). In addition, they were published in books identified as belonging to the social networks centred in the inns of court, later published volumes such as Benjamin Rudyerd's account of the 1597/98 Middle Temple revels, *Le Prince d'Amour* (1660) and, in misidentified form, in *Poems . . .by Pembroke . .* [and] *Ruddier* (1660). The last has an address to the reader with the claim that the poems in the book 'were chiefly preserved by the greatest Masters of Musick' (A4) including Lawes and Lanier.

Peter Beal, who includes Grange among the authors in his online *Catalogue of English Literary Manuscripts* (*CELM*), lists 15 poems by or ascribed to Grange that survive in manuscript and print versions:

1. 'Not that I wish my mistress' (26 copies)
2. 'Black Cypress veils are shrouds of night' (25 copies)
3. 'Since all [or 'every'] men [or 'man']that I come among' (13 copies) (a song)[7]
4. 'A lover once I did espy' (ten copies)
5. 'Be not proud 'cause fair and trim' (seven copies)
6. 'Blind beauty! If it be a loss' (seven copies) (Krueger 1961: Appendix II, 93)
7. 'Come, ye swarms of thoughts and bring' (six copies)
8. 'To the world I'll now discover' (five copies)
9. 'The world created God made man' (three copies)

[7]See Krueger (1961:79–80). In Folger MS V.a.96, fols. 38^{r-v} and 74, it is titled in the second transcription 'Mr. John Grange his ballet', while in the Pembroke and Rudyerd edition, it is titled 'B.R. his ballet' (p. 53). Both Bod. MS Malone 13, p. 57 and National Library of Wales MS Peniarth 500B attribute the poem to Grange.

10. 'Sir, such my fate was, that I had no store' (three copies) (See 1961: 81)
11. 'Sure thou framed were by art' (two copies)
12. 'What is rude nature hath less care exprest' (two copies) (1961: 81)
13. 'Why do we love these things which we call Women' (two copies) (1961: 80)[8]
14. 'O bury not this dead child: lett him lie' (one copy)
15. 'On this swelling bank, once proud of its burden' (one copy)

There is another poem attributed to 'Granger' in Bodleian MS Malone 13, 'I said the thing for which I woe'.[9] In his edition of the poems of Pembroke, Robert Krueger claims that as many as seven of the poems in the 1660 Pembroke and Rudyerd collection were written by Grange, while only four were by Pembroke's close friend from the same environment, Benjamin Rudyerd (Krueger 1961: 93). In her edition of the Stoughton manuscript, Mary Hobbs states that 'six of his fourteen recorded poems were set to music by Henry Lawes' (1990: 311). A couple of Grange's poems were obviously quite popular. The first, 'Not that I wish my mistress' (see Appendix) was published in its longest version (fourteen stanzas) in *Le Prince d'Amour*. The second most popular of Grange's poems goes back to his years at Oxford, an answer poem to Richard Corbett's much-circulated 'To the Ladies of the New Dress', beginning 'Black cypress veiles are shrouds of night'. This poem is an example of university-inns connections. Other poems by Grange survived in manuscript and print, some as songs.

The next stray inns poet is Nicholas Hare. Although John Carey has done a great scholarly service in providing an introduction to, and edition of, this poet's verse, Hare still is below the literary-historical radar (1960). Carey identifies Hare as a student at Christ's College, Cambridge, a fellow commoner who matriculated in 1598–1599 and was admitted to Inner Temple in June 1596. He was the son of prominent inns figure, John Hare, master of the bench of Inner Temple, and was known to the inns diarist John Manningham by 1603. He was later much travelled, familiar, for example, with Dudley Carleton at Venice. He had his will witnessed by

[8] This is found in the Conway Papers, BL Additional MS 23299, fol. 53; in Morgan Library MS MA 1057, 144; in *The Harmony of the Muses* (1654: 26) and in Pembroke and Rudyerd (1660: 55–56).

[9] On the page following Grange's 'Since every man I come among' (57), listed by Krueger (1961: 58).

Isaac Walton, and John Donne, recently made Dean of St Paul's, oversaw his posthumous charitable donation to the poor. Carey states: 'Nicholas was well known among his contemporaries as a man of letters, and . . . had been accepted into literary and learned circles on the Continent' (1960: 372). He was, however, not included in Peter Beal's *CELM*.

The Folger Index lists only one poem by him ('Here do repose, but in lamented waste'). Carey, however, identifies him as the author of nine poems, one found in the 1618 publication mostly comprising the verse of a fellow innsman, Henry Fitzjeffrey, *Certaine Elegies done by Sundrie Excellent Wits, With Satyres and Epigrams.* One of his poems appears in Huntington MS HM 198.2, a collection that has been identified by Mark Bland as originating in the inns environment (Bland 2005: 158). Other poems are found in BL Egerton MS 923 and Stowe MS 962, University of Edinburgh Laing MS III.493 and the collection of the Skipwith family (BL Additional MS 25707) and Nicholas Burghe (Bod. MS Ashmole 38). The misleadingly marketed *Poems . . . by Pembroke* [and] *Ruddier* (1660) contains one of Hare's poems, 'Why with unkindest swiftnes doest thou turne' ($E4^v$), presented without authorial ascription. It is clear, from his biography, from the notice by John Manningham in his *Diary*, from his association with fellow innsman Henry Fitzjeffrey, and from the appearance of his work in a manuscript with inns provenance, that Hare was, in the loose sense of the term, an inns poet. The later inclusion of one of his poems in the Pembroke and Rudyerd collection is unsurprising, given the fact that Hare and they were part of the same social network. Carey's analysis of Hare's appropriation of the conventions of the Roman elegy, also adapted by fellow inns poets John Donne and Thomas Campion, and his fondness for satiric and epigrammatic modes put him culturally and socially in tune with his inns contemporaries in his poetic practice. Before Carey's 1960 article, however, Hare's work was neglected.

The next stray poet I would like to highlight is John Vaughan (1572–1634). Mary Hobbs has written about him, along with Robert Ellice and Henry Blount, as someone who moved from Oxford (Christ Church) to Inner Temple (Hobbs 1992: 45). She has associated him, along with William Davenant and Thomas Carew, with the late 1620s circle around Edward Hyde, later earl of Clarendon (1992: xiii). The account of him in *The Dictionary of Welsh Biography* notes that he served under the earl of Essex in Ireland in 1599, was a member of parliament in 1601 (in which his contemporary John Donne also served), and was again an member of parliament in 1620–1622. He was comptroller of the household to Charles, prince of Wales, and went to Spain with him in 1623 to arrange the Spanish Match. He was later created Baron Vaughan of Mullengar (1621) and earl of Carbery (1628; an Irish title).[10] Born in the same year as John Donne, he wrote and circulated verse while at the Inner Temple and his poems appear in several manuscripts with inns provenance: for example, BL Additional MS 25303 and Additional MS 21433 and Sloane MS 1446. His most transcribed poem, beginning 'Why fair vow-breaker hath thy sin thought fit', has various titles such as 'Upon a gentlewoman inviting her old friend to her wedding' (Bod. MSS Ashmole 38: 7; Malone 16: 46; Rawl. Poet 84, fol. 89 rev.; Yale MS b.52/2: 168), 'On a perjured lady' (BL Additional MS 21433, fol. 159 and Additional MS 25303, fol. 177), 'On his mistres inviting him to her marriage' (BL Sloane MS 1394, fol. 174), or 'An Elegy on an invitation to a wedding. It appears in 14 manuscripts.[11] It also appears in two Commonwealth-era printed collections: *Wit and Drollery* (1656: 103–107) (where it is titled 'To a Gentlewoman from her formerly betrothed, but deserted servant, he being invited to the celebration of her Nuptials') and *Wit Restor'd* (1658: 73–76) (where the title is simply 'An Elegie'). The length of the text in its various appearances runs from 48–86 lines. A long version is found in Yale Osborn MS b.205 (see Appendix). The situation is not merely that of a man's angry response to his mistress's marrying someone else, but also of her choosing a higher status or 'place' (l. 12) than would have come with marrying him. Innsmen, who were audience members of romantic comedies in which Shakespeare dramatised young men's twin successes of love and upward social mobility, were especially sensitive to the connection between love and social status, so this poem would have hit home (see Watson's chapter on the inns context of *Twelfth Night* in this volume). Its long life in manuscript and print transmission was thus not just due to its being the complaint of a rejected lover but also testimony to readers' engagement with a vengeful misogynistic rant that expressed social as well as amorous frustration: a complaint found in Ovid's love elegies, but reiterated in a contemporary English context. Four of Vaughan's other poems also made it into print publication: 'Upon the battle of Agincourt, written

[10] See https://biography.wales/article/s-VAUG-JOH-1603.

[11] Yale Osborn MSS b.205, fol. 82ᵛ, and b.52/2: 168; Bod. MSS Ash. 38: 7; Eng. Poet. c.50, fol. 131ᵛ; Malone 16: 46; Rawl. Poet. 84, fol. 89ᵛ rev.; Folger MSS V.a.319, fol. 54ᵛ; V.a.322: 44; V.b.43, fol. 15; BL Additional MS 21433, fol. 159; Additional MS 25303, fol. 177ᵛ; Sloane MS 1394, fol. 174; and 1446, fol. 67; Huntington HM 198.1: 40.

by his dear friend Michael Drayton' ('Had Henry's name been only met in prose') (*English Short Title Catalogue*, 7190); 'An ode' ('Rise, laurell'd shade, from peaceful seats'); 'Upon this unequalled work, and the author' ('Rome had been still my wonder: I had known')—a commendatory poem prefacing Thomas May's translation of Lucan's *Pharsalia* (1627; *English Short Title Catalogue*, 16887); and 'On love' ('When I do love I would not wish to speed'), the last appearing in an anthology into which much manuscript-circulated verse migrated, *Parnassus Biceps* (1656).

Henry Blount (1602–82), the next poet to whom I would like to call attention, moved from Trinity College, Oxford, to Gray's Inn in 1620: an inn that generally had a more socially elevated group of residents than the others. He is the author of ten poems, many of which are found in manuscripts rooted in the inns of court and other London social networks, including Henry King's social circle. Mary Hobbs says that these pieces 'are found almost exclusively in the Stoughton group of manuscripts', in which she includes the Skipwith collection (BL Additional MS 25707), the Calfe manuscripts (BL Harley MSS 6917–18), the collection of Thomas Manne (BL Additional MS 58215), BL Sloane MS 1446 (an inns collection), St. John's College, Cambridge MS 423, and Folger MS V.a.125 (Hobbs 1992: xvii). Blount's work was circulated in both inns' collections and in those associated with what Hobbs has identified as musical circles. John Aubrey describes him as 'pretty wild when young, especially addicted to common Wenches' and as someone who socialised in the 'Pallsgrave-head taverne', which was 'much frequented by parliament men and gallants' (Aubrey 2015: 1.336–37). He was an inns of court resident who was involved in the conversations and recreations of London's political and intellectual elite in an environment in which erotic poetry was common social currency.

Clark Library MS 1950.024, a Wyrley family collection that contains unique copies of poems by Francis Wyrley, includes a group of seven poems by Blount (5–8):[12] 'On kisse of a fayre Ladys muffe in a church by stealth' ('They who peculiar saints implore'), 'Behold those pure eyes in whose light' (5), 'A lovers meditation in the country being absent from his

[12] See the Clark Library's catalogue description of this manuscript https://search.library.ucla.edu/discovery/fulldisplay?docid=alma9962990373606533&context=L&vid=01UCS_LAL:UCLA&lang=en&search_scope=ArticlesBooksMore&adaptor=Local%20Search%20Engine&tab=Articles_books_more_slot&query=any,contains,Clark%20Library%20MS%201950.024&offset=0. For the poems by Wyrley, see Maule (2000: 150–53).

Mistress' ('My restlesse howres call to mind' [6]), 'Fie cruell glasse didst thou not see' (6),[13] 'To his Mistress' ('They who gainst Loves Kingdome raile' [7]),[14] 'A Gentlemans repentance for his behaviour being drunke at the Revells in Grayes Inne' ('When the proud juise had reacht my head' [7]), and 'A Gentleman staying too long at a Taverne could not get [seats] at Paules church, and thereby lost that opportunitie of seing the sight of some fayre Ladys' ('Zounds Gentlemen how now; shutt out?' (8)).[15] The first of these, 'They who peculiar saints implore', survives in most copies and is found in five other manuscripts with inns connections.[16] Echoing the riotous descriptions of inns revels discussed by Watson in Chap. 4 is the penultimate one, 'A Gentlemans repentance for his behaviour being drunke at the Revells in Grayes Inne', that appears only to have been preserved in the Clark manuscript. It describes his bad behaviour as a wine-soused dancing man who gets cudgelled by constables and swears off drinking (see Appendix).

Another inns poet whose work is found in the Clark Library manuscript is Richard Clarke, admitted to Lincoln's Inn in 1627 (Lincoln's Inn 1896: 202), two of whose poems appear in that collection: 'On the death of a young maid' ('Beneath this stone, which thou must love' [18]) (see Appendix) and 'In scorne of a Mistress' ('Cannot I love except she love, or date' [18]) (see Appendix). The first poem, according to the Folger Index, only survives in one other manuscript (Folger MS V.a.125, fol. 2ᵛ), but the second appears in four inns of court manuscripts.[17] Four other poems by Clarke are found in both manuscript and print: Both BL Additional MSS 25303 and 21433 contain 'Her eyes which all the world

[13] This appears in Folger MSS V.a.276.2, fol. 35ᵛ, and V.b.43, fol. 23; BL Additional MS 21433, fol. 157, and Additional MS 25303, fol. 171; and in two later printed books, *Wit Restor'd* (1658) and *Female Poems on Several Occasions Written by Ephelia* (1679).

[14] This poem appears in two related inns manuscripts, BL Additional MS 21433, fol. 157, and Additional MS 25303, fol. 171.

[15] The Folger Index has copies of some of these poems by Blount, but there are other poems in archives not indexed there. See: https://firstlines.folger.edu/advancedSearch.php?val1=Blount%2C+Henry&col1=au#results.

This poem is found in Sir John Mennes's and James Smith's printed anthology, *Musarum Deliciae* (1655), and may have been composed either by Blount or by one of the editors of that volume.

[16] BL Additional MS 25303, fol. 170ᵛ; Additional MS 21433, fol. 156ᵛ; and Additional MS 25707, fol. 22; Harley MS 6917, fol. 41ᵛ; and Sloane MS 1446, fol. 60ᵛ.

[17] Folger MS V.a.245, fol. 19ᵛ, and BL Additional MS 25303, fol. 170, and Additional MS 21433, fol. 155, and Sloane MS 1446, fol. 88.

but me',[18] 'Sure 'twas the spring went by for th'earth did waste',[19] 'To her whose beauty doth excel'[20] (see Appendix), and 'Why should I live but while she loves', the last also appearing in another inns manuscript, Sloane 1446 (fol. 88). The third of these poems, a drinking pledge to health, seems to have been the most popular: part of the innsmen's tavern culture and the wider social 'play' discussed by Adams in Chap. 5.

Alumni Oxoniensis tells us that a contemporary of Clarke, Robert Ellice, moved from Merton College, Oxford, to Gray's Inn in 1627.[21] One of his poems, beginning 'Religion bids mee pause or else ide paye' (see Appendix), follows several of Clarke's poems in BL Additional MS 25303 and precedes a poem by Henry Blount in that manuscript, 'Kissing a Ladies Muffe in the Churche' (fol. 170^{v}). Few of Ellice's poems have survived, but their proximity to pieces by other innsmen is suggestive.

The next 'stray' poet of the inns is William Austin (*c.* 1587–1634), who moved from St John's College, Cambridge, in 1604 to Lincoln's Inn. He was obviously part of a social network centred in the inns and one of his poems, 'mr Austinn to his friend Benn Johnson' (see Appendix) memorialises an evening of drinking with fellow wits with whom he has just come from a theatrical performance, thus mapping an innsman's movements between the social and cultural spaces of the theatre, the tavern, and the inns. It describes a contest in composing extemporaneous poems on set themes, which seems similar to the *Joco Seria* discussed by Adams in Chap. 5. This performance was apparently sent to Jonson (from one of whose plays the revellers might have just come) to maintain epistolary contact with someone who was part of the tavern culture Austin portrays. This is also the context of Austin's contribution to the game of wit played in the facetious celebration of Thomas Coryate's travels found in *The Odcombian Banquet* (1611: L2^{v}–L4); Austin was among the wits who wrote

[18] BL Additional MS 25303, fol. 169, and Additional MS 21433, fol. 154. This poem also appears in BL Harley MS 6917, fol. 36, and Henry Lawes's music manuscript, BL Additional MS 53723, fol. 70^{v}.

[19] BL Additional MS 25303, fol. 169^{v}; Additional MS 21433, fol. 154^{v}; and Additional MS 25707, fol. 42^{v}.

[20] BL Additional MS 25303, fol. 170; Additional MS 21433, fol. 155^{v}; Additional MS 25707, fol. 93^{v}; Additional MS 14047, fol. 5^{v}; Additional MS 15227, fol. 82; and Harley MS 6057, fol. 7^{v}.

[21] "Ellis, Robert", in *Alumni Oxonienses 1500-1714* (Oxford, 1891). British History Online, accessed May 11, 2024, https://www.british-history.ac.uk/alumni-oxon/1500-1714.

commendatory verses for *Coryat's Crudities* (see Eckhardt and Neuhauser in Chap. 8 on these contributors). The next poem in the manuscript in which this piece is found looks like Austin's contribution to the game being played: a riff on the word 'whereby' (see Appendix).

Austin's nine religious poems, however, were composed after he left the inns' environment for a London residence in which he lived with his family. Some of these poems appear in manuscript collections: for example, the Christmas carol 'Hark hear you not a cheerful noise' is found in two manuscripts[22] and 'Here we must rest; and where else should we rest?' is found in five.[23]

The last stray poet I'd like to highlight is Sir Thomas Salusbury, of the Welsh Salusbury family of Lleweni. He moved from Jesus College, Oxford to the Inner Temple in 1631, where he stayed for less than a year before returning to his family estate in Wales upon the death of his father. The *Oxford Dictionary of National Biography* notes that Anthony à Wood called him 'a most noted poet of his time', but that only one of his poems was published in his lifetime, *The History of Joseph* (1636) (Bowen 2004). His poems and dramas, however, are found in the National Library of Wales MS 5390D. In this manuscript, we find several poems apparently written while Salusbury was at the Inner Temple—for example 'An Elegie upon the death of Mr. Beke gent[leman] of the Inner Temple written to his Sister now great with child'[24] (see Appendix)—a poem each of whose lines is numbered. Two pages later, the manuscript offers an alternate text for lines 25 and following, expanding the poem to 66 lines (see Appendix). Writing a poem on behalf of a friend, Salusbury engages in the conventional praise of the deceased but indicates how unusual it is to find 'worth and honesty in a lawyer' (l. 18). He relates his dead colleague to the man's pregnant sister by raising the possibility that, through the transmigration of the soul, he will come to inhabit the child to be born. This exasperatingly rambling poem is a rather unusual elegy.

Another one of Salusbury's poems refers to his legal activities between the inns of court and Westminster, 'An Exposulaton with my Muse and a

[22] BL Additional MS 34752, fol. 5, and Bod. MS Rawl. Poet. 61, fol. 80.

[23] Bod. MSS Lat. misc. fol. 445: 209; Rawl. D. 301, fol. 20; Rawl. Poet. 61, fol. 25; BL Additional MS 34752, fol. 27v; and Yale Beinecke MS b.65: 64.

[24] *Alumni Oxonienses* lists a Jeremiah Beke from Norfolk, who matriculated at Magdalen College in 1639 at age 15, but who was a student at the Inner Temple in 1638. "Beke, Jeremiah", in *Alumni Oxonienses 1500–1714*, (Oxford, 1891). British History Online, accessed May 11, 2024, https://www.british-history.ac.uk/alumni-oxon/1500-1714.

'Defiance of Poetry' (see Appendix). In this ambitiously long poem, Salusbury first laments the loss of his poetic identity and then rejects contemporary poetry as corrupt and corrupting, since poets have chosen to express their 'witt' as 'railing' (l. 90) rather than as heartful amorousness. Playing with the contrast of poetry writing and legal business visible in the work of some other inns writers, such as John Donne, Salusbury laments that he is 'buisilie enforc't to stirre betweene the inns-of-court & westminster' (l. 48) and admits that 'the tender Nymph more willinge meets / the Satyrs lust, then in the loathed sheetes / o'th crabbed law my mind yeeldes up consent' (ll. 59–61). He admits that he once used 'sportive wit' (curiously, the title later used for a midcentury poetic miscellany) to purge his 'folly' (l. 79) and he used 'devotion' as a cure for 'Malancholly' (l. 80). He tells Apollo, the god of poetry, that he was able to 'yeild releif / and soderd'st up my broken hart, when greife / oppreset my Soule' (ll. 81–83). At the end, however, he rejects a medium he feels has abandoned him. He claims he has outgrown the amorous verse of his youth and accepts the pains and frustrations of his maturity—and, perhaps, the purgatory of the legal profession. This poem steps outside the love poetry, epigrams, and satires of earlier young inns-of-court writers and the fashionable Cavalier verse then in circulation in the Caroline period to deal with the problem of how to reconcile the serious business of the mature man with the urge to continue writing poetry.

Salusbury did, however, write occasional social verse in his maturity—for example, 'To the good Gentlewoman of Thornton: upon the rope shee sent me instead of a ribbon for my Codpiece, which shee promist mee, together with the Sirrop of Mulberries for my sore Throate: May: 16: 1640' (see Appendix). Salusbury was 'a poore member of parliament' (l. 2) who was a staunch royalist during the English Civil Wars. The 'pride' (l. 26) with which the speaker swells at the end of the poem is an erection provoked by a mistress's tying a ribbon on his codpiece. Another poem to women on a specific occasion, 'Upon the thunder & rayne that overtooke the Ladyes at Keven y Werne upon Wednesday the 18th of may. 1643' (NLW MS 5390D: 303) (see Appendix), was left incomplete.

A few of the late poems Salusbury wrote were elegies, some on behalf of friends: 'To my especiall freind C:C: upon the Death of his beauteous Mistris Mistris G:S: 1640' (NLW MS 5390: 300); 'An Elegie upon the Doceas, of that Patterne of virtue, and Noblenes Rich[ard] Bulkley of Barnhill in the Countie of Anglice Esq. To my verie good freind Mr

Michaell Evans' (301–02); 'An Epitaph upon Captaine William Robinson who received his deaths wound at Brainford & dyed at Reading' (305–06); and 'Upon the Death of the right Honorable the Lord Daubignie prepard against his funerall at Oxford' (307–08). In the same section of the manuscript are several elegies on his own death by other poets.[25] Salusbury did write an elegy paying tribute to Ben Jonson, who had longstanding connections with his family, particularly with his grandfather, Sir John Salusbury (of 'The Phoenix and the Turtle' volume fame). Jonson, he says, inspired him and others to take poetry seriously, although they could never rise to his aesthetic heights.[26] Salusbury's own dramatic and masque writing, influenced by Jonson and other dramatists, is preserved in the NLW family manuscript, but it was not printed. One scholar, however, has called him 'the leading literary figure in the region of the North Welsh Marches . . . for a whole generation, 1632–1642' (Gair 1968: 77).[27] The gesture Salusbury makes of distancing himself from his earlier poetic productions and the contemporary work of Cavalier poets makes sense in terms of the kinds of cultural change taking place in mid-century England. It is only one further step to the rejection of fashionable poetry by a much greater writer, John Milton.

In an age in which many literate men who were members of the inns of court found it natural to compose verse as a means of social bonding and as a sign of their political awareness and cultural sophistication, many writers other than the ones who, like John Donne, John Marston, and Sir John Davies, made it into the English literary canon turned to and circulated their verse within and beyond the social networks of which they were part. Lewiston Fitzjames, who compiled a manuscript miscellany that contains his own as well as the more famous poetry of Davies, and the other

[25] 'Upon the death of the honorable Sir Thomas Salusbury who was buryed at Whitchurch the [ ] day of [ ] (309) by 'Will[iam] Lloyd'; 'To his ever honoured Aunt the Lady Ursula loy'd upon the death of her onely Brother Sir Thomas Salusbury' by 'Cousen George Evans' (310); 'On the death of that noble & illustrious Knight & Baronett Sir Tho[mas] Salusbury' by 'Cosen George Evans' (311–12), the last of which refers to Salusbury's long published poem, *The History of Joseph*.

[26] See 'An Elegie meant upon the death of Ben: Johnson' ('Shall I alone spare paper? in an age' [NLW MS 5390D: 289]). On the connections between the Salusbury family and Jonson, see Gair (1968: 73–79).

[27] Brown (1977: 83), suggests that Salusbury, whose family had ties to Jonson, read the 1616 folio edition of Jonson's works.

inns poets whose verse I have highlighted were important parts of the inns world and its social dynamics, which included the manuscript transmission of their work. Because most of this work never made it into print or only did so in poetical anthologies and miscellanies, however, it has been excluded from the narrative of English literary history and has remained virtually invisible.

Appendix

To Sir G. T. K.

I give not (though I love them well) the Lillies,
The fayrest flower that our Colledge yealdes:
Nor the Couslipp, which beawtifies the feelds,
nor dish deckinge Daffadoun dillies.
        nor Carnations, Violetts nor Roses
        whereof the Ladies make their sweetest posies.

Nor Cardus Benedictus which now raignes
& makes this Iland happie in her growth,
nor Opium the nourisher of sloth,
nor Pennie-royall op'ner of the vaynes.
        nor Rewe, that's good against infeccion,
        nor yet Eringoes, wreker of exertion.

I give not Testes Vulpis nor Potatoes,
Terra sigillata, nor Cariophilla
nor Galangal, nor sursa-perilla
nor Polipedium, nor Steuchados,
        nor yet Eupohorbius, nor Oposanx.
        nor scabiosa, nor the Sasaphrax.

I give not Soldanella nor Borax.
Trifolius, nor Diagridium,
Ichthiogella nor Olybannum,
nor Elleborus Albus nor storax.
        nor powerfulll fearne-seede, that will opne Lockes,
        nor Guacum that is good against the poxe.

I give not Sebesten, nor Scordium,
Filpendula, nor Decormicus,
nor Dictamus, nor Hermodactilus,

nor Asa-fedita, nor Hordeum.
    nor Cerusse, nor Capillus Veneris,
    nor yet shred parsley that will make one pisse.

I give not Bayes that healpes to cureth Itche,
nor Sagapenum, nor the Agarce
nor yet Nux vomica, that make Crowes sicke,
nor fomentacions to ridd away the sticke.
    nor Potions, Lotions, nor Electuaries.
    the riche revenoowes of Apothecaries.

But I (o Muse) what shall I saye, I give,
Inriche my brayne & teache me what to write,
Alas she answers me, its past my might
And then but center powrst into a sive.
    Then breifely thus, Tobacco I presente
    The holsomst Herbe, under the firmament.
        J. Mabb.
    (Bod. MS Add. B.97, fols. 56^{v}–57^{r})

Read in my face the fortunes of my youth,
where care imprints deepe furrowes of dispayre:
A lowe ansackg head, in tymes of ruth,
like wasted towres, that whilome cheackt the ayre.

Beholde myne eyes, howe they repents their faulte,
That gave free entrance to that Tyrant Love;
*deepe an — in recompence presents the *greate assaulte,
(ans with their blud, salt teares which nowe I prove.

Read howe my harte (the city of my lyfe)
*or sides — consumes in endlesse fyer; my *flesh (her walls)
(ansack by thy disdayne, & my thoughts strife,)
to thee (aye mercylesse) for mercy calles.

But teares seilde° perseth Rocks, cease eyes your payne, °seldom
Ye write on water, oh you waite in vayne.
    (Bod. MS Add. B.97, fol. 19^{v})[28]

[28] See the left-hand margin for alternative readings in the manuscript marked by asterixis.

What shal a man desier in this World
When there is nought in the world that's worth desieringe,
Shal then a man case his thought to the Earth
And to the Heavens with his Eyes so high aspiringe.

Thinke that livinge thou must dye
Assure thy selfe thy dayes are tolde,
*yet believe Thought on Earth thou seem'st to be.
Assure thy selfe thou art but molde
All our Wealth
Bringes no health,
But returnes from whence it came
So shall we
All agree,
For we are the verie same.

Goe sillie Notes to the Eares of my Deere,
Make thy selfe blest, & Patience swetly languish,
Laye thee to sleepe in the bed of her Harte,
Give her delights though thy selfe be full of anguish,
There when thou art then speake of me
That from thence am banisht,
Saye that once I had contente,
Though it nowe be vanisht.

Yet when Tyme
shall runn backe
And never more renewe,
She shall cease
To be fayre
But I will live to be trewe.
(Bod. MS Add. B.97, fol. 16^{v})

A songe

since Kisse me sweete now we are heere,
thou neede not All is hush't, nay never feare,
The whole House doth soundlie sleepe,
Come lett us our Loves-watch keepe.
Come cole° me & clipp me & kisse me to
So should wanton Lovers doe So, so, so should Lovers doe.

2 Twentie dayes are past & gonn
our hartes were both. Since our two Harts were/made one
Twentie pleasaunt Nights are spente
Since my Love did give consent
To cole me &c.

3 Blessed be that happie Tyme
Which did first our Harts combine,
Maye this night be ended never
That thus joynes our Lipps togeather,
O cole me &c.

5[*sic*] Out, alas the daye appeeres,
And my voyce my mother heeres
Soone when Night shall showe her face
Sweete, then reste me in this place
And cole me &c.

4 Last longe Night & bannish Daye,
*bewray Which will all our Joyes *betraye/
When Night comes, Come Forth trewe
That we maye our Loves renewe.
Then will I cole thee &c. ./.
finis
(Bod. MS Add. B.97, fol. 17^{v})

In eundem.

Calvus is pleasd with none but ^with the best^ ~~best & worst~~
To those his pen affordes some michell° ~~paynes~~ prayes °great
he nought esteemes of any of the age,
but on their idle witts his witt displayes.
Fye Calvus, fye man hate thou not thy selfe
Thou art not best make not thy eye corrupt
Thus may thy wordes be true saye foolish selfe
Thou art in love with none but best & worst.
So Calvus maye be lov'd amongst the rest,
For he is worst, who ever prove the best.
LF
(Bod. MS Add. B.97, fol. 17^{r})

Is thy howse faire, thy table full of plate?
hast thou of gold & silver Coyne great store?
Is thy wyfe fayre, or borne of high estate?
Doth this world smile on thee for ev'more?
All theise so soone ^to soone^ doe slide away
No good att all they doe I saye.
we cannot call them trewly good I saye.
(Bod. MS Add. B.97, fol. 48r)

Not that I wish my Mistris
Or more or lesse then what shee is,
Write I these lynes: for 'tis too late
To prescribe Rules unto my fate.

But yet as tender stomaches call
For some choice meates, that brooke not all
Soe a queazie Lover doth impart
What Mistris 'tis must take his hart../

First I would have her richely sp^r^ed
with Natures blossomes white and redd;
For flaming heates will quickely die
That have noe fewell from the eye./

Yet these alone will never wynn
Unlesse some treasure lye within
For where the spoile's not worth the stay
Men raise the seidge and march away./

I'de have her wise enoughe to knowe
When and to whome a grace to showe
For shee that doth at randome chuse
Shee will her choise assoone refuse./

And I will wish her true to bee
(Mistake me not, I meane to mee.)
Shee that loves one, and loves one more
Will love the kingdome ore and ore./

And yet methinks I'de have her mynde
To a flowing Curtesie inclyn'd,

And tender harted as a mayde
Yet pittie onely when I pray'd./

And I could wish her full of witt
Soe shee knewe howe to howsewife itt;
But shee whose insolence makes her dare
To try her witt, wil sell her ware./

Some other thinges delight will bring
As if shee dance, or play, and sing,
If hers be safe what though her partes
Catch ten thousand other hartes?/

But lett mee see; should shee be proud?
A little pride must be allowed;
The Amorous Youth will pray and prate
Too freely, if hee finde noe state./

I care not much if shee lett downe
Sometimes a chiding or a frowne;
But if shee wholly quench Desire,
It's hard to kindle a newe fire./

To smile and toy 'tis not amisse.
Sometimes to interpose a kisse
But doe not cloy; sweet thinges are good
And pleasant, but are nought for food./

But stay Nature hath overwrought my Art
In her to whom I offer upp my hart,
And cunning Passengers shall sooner trace
The wanton beames that dance on Thames smooth face

Or find the tracks wheron the Fowle did stay
Or the wast sands which tydes have washt away.
Then men shall finde my love with taint or spott
Soe a revolt of hers procures it not..

Mr Jo[hn] Grange
(Folger MS V.a.96, fols. 63^{r}–64^{v})

An Elegy on an invitation
to a wedding.

why fayre vow breaker hath thy sin thought fit
that I be damd example of thy wit
as well as scorne? bad woman have not I
deservd as much as quiet misery
Be wise & trouble not my suffering fit
for every sin I have repentance yet,
unles for loving thee, doe not thou pres
my easy madnes to a wickednes
as deepe as it, least I be driven so
as far from heaven as thou art, which I know
Is not thy ayme, for thou has sind to be
In place as in affection far from me.
Intreate a man to catch the plague, or be
A witnes to his mothers infamy
bespeake me to be shamd, or else to bring
Myselfe an Eunuch to a gosseping
upon record how desperat was thou bent
to envite me for a wedding complement
Am I thy freind or kinsman? have I ought
that is familiar with that bating° thought   contending
A dreame, some letters to perhaps that lie
neglected recordes of my injury.
know this, nor yet my silent sorro moves
to beg a bridall kis or payre of gloves
those are the slighter duties which they seeke
whose sleepe is sound, as constant as the week
is to the nightes, who never met the chance
of love amis but in a dreming trance.
and wakt with gladnes, lie not so with me
who have no nature left but misery.
should I come thither while the holy man
his spirituall Magicke had once began
to tie thee from me I might leape into
a rage, & safely all our lives undoe
when heaven would be so courteous to disgy[se]
that bloodshed to the name of sacrifice.
private as sorrowes loding had I dwelt
fellowd with my despayre, & never felt
Anger unles of living hadst thou bin

content with my undoing, is a sin
my love could not forgive thee to unbrayd
a wretchednes which thou thy selfe hast made
heaven knowes I sufferd & I sufferd so
that by me twas infallible to know
how passive man is, fate knew not a curs[e]
bating thy new device, to make me worse
and that I felt, when I so low was brought
I knew not that I liv'd, but that I thought
And counted sighes & teares as if to scan
the ayre & water which make up a man
I was diseasd, diseasd past thine owne ^care^ [emend: "cure"]
and wouldst thou kill, what made me to endure
My patience, oh strange murder wouldst thou prove
whither it wer as dying as thy love.
hath woman such a way that she can give
to man deniall as of love, to live
why then the abhorred reason meeteth why
succesles lovers doe so quickly dye
and so be it with me but if a curse
may first be fastned on thee, that is worse
then thy unwept for now breath, may it com
as my greife heavy, may the tedious sunn
of thy great sinnes stand sentinell to keep
Repentance from thy thoughtes, wretch may thy sleepe
be broken as my hopes, may I be plact
before thy mind when thou shalt be disgract
by some mans hate thou lovst, bore all may be
thou chusest husband grow to Jealousy
and find it true to kill thee may the
on which thy sleepe dith paraphrase in dreams
be my sad wrongs, & when soe other shall
when chance hath made with me apocriphall
In loving stories search an instance forth
to dam his lady for her litle worth.
May thy name meete him under which must be
the common place of womans perjury.
May heaven make all this true, & if thou pray
may heaven regard thee as thou didst to say
thy last lost promises, I have sayd be free
this penance don my day of destiny,
by thee is antidated, but 3 sighes

I must first pay admission to the skies
one for my madnes to love woman so
that I coud thinke her true, the next must goe
for wronged lovers that ile breathe anew
the third shall beg my curses be made true.
(Yale Osborn MS b.205, fols. 82v–84v)

A Gentlemans repentance for his behaviour being
drunke at the Revells in Grayes Inne.

When the proud juice had reacht my head
It sent my witts, not me to bedd;
And carried me as in a traunce,
To see our youthfull Gallants daunce.
Where I the greatest dauncer prov'd
Each stepp like to a passage mov'd.
In stead of Musick heard a dinne
Of o gods Zounds, my Toe, my Shinne.
I wonder calling this to mind,
Daggers and Torches were soe kind
To spare me, nay I must to thinke,
How I could scape a very linke.
Thanks honour'd Plush; thou sav'st my locks
From whistling flames, thou from the stocks
Secur'ds my reeling feete, and thou
Mad'st surly Officers to bowe.
Else had there by some cruell fate,
A busie cudgell mett my pate:
Whose hotter discipline might well
have turn'd my sacke to Coller fell.
Till with some Porter in a close,
Ide chaung blew eye for blowdie nose.
Which triumph might have rais'd more high
My creditt, then a Pillorie
Or loftie Gallowes: For which scape
Te Deum: Ile beware the grape.
Hen[ry] Blunt
(Clark Library MS 1950.024, p. 7)

On the death of a young maid.

Beneath this stone, which thou must love
More beautie lies then lives above.
Ere foure yeeres old she hence did part
When death in envie of Cupids dart
First strooke her: By fances truest tongue
The childish God was sold, as younge
She was as he is fain'd and faire,
That both togeather seeme a payre
And Twinns might seeme, at which he cryes
Till then he never mist his eyes.
Yet if, he had them, twere in vaine,
for he would weepe them out againe.
Thy teares, which if thou pittie hast
Thou canst not chuse but sheede or wast.
For if a sinne could taint her yeeres
Tis cleane washt in her Mothers teares.
Richard Clarke
(Clark Library MS 1950.024, p. 18)

A health to a mistris

To her whose beautie doth excell
Storie,we tosse these Cups, and sell
Sobrietie a sacrifice,
To the bright luster of her eyes,
Each soule that sipps heere is divine,
Her beautie deifies the wine.
Richard Clarke
(Clark Library MS 1050.024, p. 17)[29]

In scorne of a Mistris

Cannot I live except she love? or date
Sadd funeralls to my joyes, because her hate
Darts it selfe at me? Cannot I persist

[29] This also appears in *The Academy of Complements* (1640: 174).

Active and capeable except she list
To breath her smile upon me? Cannot I
Be wanton but in cupletts weare and lie
In truth exceeding Poetry but when
to make her face my subject? Shall I then
be blind to errore when her starrlike eyes
Shall cease to light? me to her falcitys?
Shall I when shees forgott want where to buy
At a hard rated price credulitie?
Or will my wine which I most feare of all
If I not drinke her health, deay and pall?
Heres the deare losse of Love: who butt attaines
To loose a mistris, in those losses gaines.

Richard Clarke
(Clark Library MS 1950.024, 18)

Religion bids mee pause or else ide paye
Devotions unto that glasse every Daye
wherein I sawe your face; o there did I
veiwe that white forhed & that peircing eye
which can with one looke make more love sicke hartes
then toyinge Cupids Quyver full of dartes
I veiwde those lipps which nature crownd with blisse
greateste of all when they eache other kisse
eache parte I sawe with such perfection fraughte
with natures beste of skill and wisdome wroughte
as wanton Poetts in theyre flowinge witte
coulde never fancie out a beautie gett
aequall to yours but let that glasse bee throwne
into some place that never maye bee knowne
for if once more yowe loke in't yow must prove
Narcissus-like with your fayre selfe in love
and then more cruell Fate will make yow bee
my Foe in beinge Ryvall unto mee

Rob[ert] Ellice
(BL MS Add. 25303, fol. 170^{v})

mr Austinn to his friend
Benn Johnsonn

Sir you desire to see in writing

A love you heard of my inditing,
I sent it, and on your perswasion
Have adde to it the occasion
I that am but a very Zane
In poetrie, as eare was any
May blush to do my lame tricks bouldly
Where judgment sitts and viewes me
But since you bidd me I will venter
To show one gamball, so I enter.

One evening of a sommers daye
Som six of us came from a play
And by consent wee tooke our waye
To Mansells
He presently was at our backe
And that wee stomacks should not lacke,
he gave us each two cupps of sack
For Hansells
when wee had warmd us with this drinke
on supper wee begann to thinke
Thorne backe came up and did not stinke
As chansel
And while it on the bord did stand ten
Each man on each side plac'd his friend,
Blence was to the lower end
Devancel
I think the matter be not greate
To sett you downe our other meate.
In sommer men drinke more then eate,
you know it.
But truth to say eare wee did rise
wee bore the busines in such wise
The reckning (and lett that suffice)
Did show itt
well supper done, and cloth tane upp,
The pipe began succeede the cupp
Shall wee to nought but sipp and supp
Quoth Chettwoode
Bring penn and incke and let's provoke
Our witts to purge, that else will choke
And here ly smothering in the smoke
Like wettwood.

A match quoth Browne, quoth Blinco stay,
you ever fly to fast that waye
Your Muse hath gott a laske they say
She runns so
write not at rovers, com those too't.
Lett one with sheames set all on foote,
Are you content that I shall doo'te,
Tis don soe.
Then Arlling forth like Polipheme
He gives but one word for the theame
A thing that wee did never dreame
On before.
Quoth Bryan what shall taske my penn
your theame quod Blencow shall be when
And yours to Chettwood shall be theme,
yo do it and nomore
And Browne quod he now show the creame
of your invention, lett it streame,
For notwithstanding is your theame.
yo do itt
At last on me he cast his eye
what is your will with me quod I
Quod he your theame shall be whereby.
Falle to it.
wee do so, but with vexed harts.
For Blencow getts the pintes and quarts,
And clinks and whistells tooke in parts
Lavalta,
Sometimes he maks as he would spewe,
Sometimes he farts (whats trew is trew,
And somtimes dunces like the Jewe
Of Malta
He makes his fingers play the organ
And rores as lowde as Demogorgon
Then robbs himselfe like Justice Morgan,
And wollows;
Then takes a penn and in that fitt
Cries cease all penns till I have writ
And then a stoole came from his witt
As followes.
Heliogabulus that renowned Prince
Being often lickt with pleasure us'd [?] to winch

while they were laughing loud at this
I that for slownes feard the hisse
wrote finis, and was glad I wisse
To end it
How they did each their theames excell
I should but mar if I should tell
But heere is mine, or ill or well,
Befriend itt.
(St. John's Col., Cambridge MS S.23, fols. 15–16v)

To John Blencow
whereby

Whereby by what or who
how shall a man write of whereby
Thou that this word whereby hast writt,
I thinke woldst heerby trye my witt,
Or thereby make me weave a scaine
wheerby my Muses I might shame
For with the piping and the clinking
The dancing, farting, and the stinking,
unles our subject were a turde,
I thinke no man could write a worde,
But since thy Heliogabulus
Smeles not of Taverne, but of Alehouse
I thinke my selfe I well do quitt
If I make rime though show noe witt

To thee then John whereby it may appeare,
or as a man would say even as it were
whereby it may be thought to seeme to bee
So do these verses runn to rime to thee
To thee they com for thee they fittly lye,
Since thou wert even the very cause whereby.
(St. John's College, Cambridge MS S.23, fol. 17)

An Elegie upon the death of Mr. Beke gent[leman] of the Inner Temple written to his Sister now great with child

1 In whome noe wanton Subjects of the tyme
2 Nor mirth nor mistris could produce a rime

whoe neither indignation, nor fond love
the spurrs to Poetrie could ever move
to him greife lends a quill, greife, that I thinke
would change the cullour of our teares to inke
that they might mourne more perfect, this did yeild
mee Muse, and method, this it was that fild
mee with Poetick furie, onelie sadnes
could give a Muse that gave mee almost madnes
or else this sorrow havinge causd to raine
in showers the moisture that did clogg my braine
hath purifide them soe, that now I can
raile on the fates as badd as anie man
and call them blind, and cruell both to us
virtue and nature havinge crossed thus
all possibilitie, that wee should ere
find worth or honesty in a Lawyer
him thought were borne to vindicate all shame
and blotts that tyme hath layde upon theire name
of his profession: to those hopes adeu
lets think upon our losse, and weepe anew
and yet not soe, I have more neede to keepe
my wordes for comfort, then to bidd yow weepe
y'have too much sence of sorrow, this I say
not that I think, wee either doe or may
too much lament his [death] with whome did dy
such store of worth, and virtue, but I spy
a comfort bringing cure to this our losse
let not greife unasswagde in yow prove crosse
fate to the second hopes wee look should come
from or the fruitfull treasure of thy womb
If faith of the Philosophers bee true
of the soules transmigration, taking new
bodyes of old ones death, why may not I
beeleeve his spiritt by some Dietie
preservd till thy childs birth, that hee may then
reenter his owne flesh and blood agen:
for tis impossible that whene hee went
soe soone but that his second part was mean[t],
in this thy offspringe: by this hope doe wee
digest our sorrow, and tis onelie hee
whome thy womb promiseth the world can dry
my teares engag'd to further obsequi

45 for my dead freind, still to weepe o're his herse
46 but those hopes stopp my greife and soe my verse
Tho[mas] Salusb[ury
This coppie was altered from the 24
verse, at the gent[leman's] request for whome
they were made: vide infra:
(NLW MS 5390, pp. 263–64)

[alternate text]

25 y'have too much sense of sorrowe, that my feares
26 are, lest you make a'dluge [sic] with your teares
27 and spendinge all your moysture with your moane
28 like Niobe growe dry, and turne t'a stone
29 and when with greife, thus farr at last y'are spent
30 save him the charges of a'monument
31 by beinge yourselfe a'statue, and by this
32 means, make's tombe richer then a'Pyramis
33 Husband your teares more carefully, and keepe
34 some of them still in store, that yow may weepe
35 as oft as worth in any man may call
36 him to your mind, for that was repleate with all
37 virtue, and goodnes, if yow chance to see
38 a man thats young and hopefull, such was hee
39 think soe, then dropp a'teare, if of the store
40 of grace hee had, able to rescue more
41 then thousandes from damnation, did it fall
42 like holy water sprinkled mongst them all,
43 one chance to meet thee then may his death bee
44 renewde in thy still wakinge memorie:
45 then mayst thou weepe a'fresh to think upon
46 what graces liv'd with him, which hee beinge gone
47 whoe soe's a'freind to virtue must lament
45 then mayst thou weepe a fresh to think upon
48 his losse, and whoe soe knowes the detriment
49 th'whole countrie felt in his death, I dare sware
50 if then hee weepe not, hee's not worth a'teare
51 or merites punishment, such as a slave
52 or traytor to the common wealth must have:
53 But what neede I urge teares our weepinge eyes
54 might wash him from his grave, could hee but rise

wee have soe manie that his losse lament
as could dissolve a'marble monument.
Hold rather dry your eyes, for my beleife
tells, that his leavinge us requires noe greife
more then some teares at partinge, for wee knowe
hee's gone before but whether wee me goe
If wee but trace his stepps, by this hope wee
digest our sorrow; beinge assur'd to see
him once againe is onelie it can dry
my teares ingag'd to further Obsequy
for his deare losse, still to weepe o're his herse
but this hope stoppes my greife, and soe my verse.

(NLW MS 5390, pp. 266–67)

An Expostulacion with my Muse
and a Defiance to Poetry

And wilt thou leave mee soe my churlish muse?
not biddinge once farewell; I pray thee use
mee like a'freind, and e're thou gett thee gone
give mee a parting Cupp of Helicon.
Pretend not kindnes thates a double sinne
the stupid dullnes, that thou leavest mee in
take not away, but addes unto my paine
whilest I have sence to feele none to complaine
Or art thou not indeede unkindlie flyinge
but with unwholesome cares, choakt up, and dyinge
Singe like a Swanne then first. that all may know
thy losse, and share the burthen of my woe
I tooke thee for my Soule, yet thou art gone
mee thinkes I feele a'transmigration
for sure I am not dead, but dispossest
of my old Genius, my forsaken brest
new tennanted, and such my memory is
now of tymes past, when thou wert myne as his.
That being a'sage Philosopher could say
hee had binne Captaine, and was slayne at Troy
I can remember since my mind hath binne
soe different from the state it now is in
it cannot bee the same, I could have spent
my greife in verse, and cur'd my discontent,

in flowinge Elegies have drownd all care
and with my numbers charme'd away dispaire.
But thou beinge gone, soe standes the case with mee
I know not how to waile the losse of thee.
but as the ruder kernes, when thryre freindes dye
in stead of lamentation; aske them why!
What did they want they should bee soe unkind?
to goe to Heaven, and leave them all behind?
Soe I must question thee to know the cause
thou left'st mee, did I breake Apollo's lawes?
was I not proud enough of every line?
or was it that I drank too little wine?
Did I grow rich, and putt out gold to use?
that were a'fault indeede to fright a'Muse,
what is't that might my humorous saucy move
I am not growne soe old but I can love
my beard pretendes not to Philosophy
Apollo, and Cupid have as much as I
nor want I indignation toward those
that use to flatter, or to raile in prose.
why wilt forsake mee then? was it because
I've orderd binne of late by other lawes
then thine? and buisilie enforc't to stirre
betweene the Inns of Court & westminster
Canst thou like Pallas for th'offence of one
that thought all Poetry prophonation,
hate all the brothers of the gowne; yet feare
mee not, though I bee troubled often there
What e're I bringe I'me sure I've noe pretence
to everie broken french, or gould from thence,
both which are poyson to thee, but my head
thou seest with other studyes busied
then thou allowst, let not thy jealousy
think theise can winne mee from the love of thee
But know the tender Nymph more willinge meets
the Satyres lust, then in the loathed sheetes
o'th crabbed law my mind yeeldes up consent
O then my Muse bewayle the ravyshment
whoe happie in theire loves what man and wife
enjoyd like us the sweetenes of a'life,
in theire accomplisht wyshes, every toy
thou rendredst in an extasie of joy

unto my heightned fancie; not a'glance
or smile, but lull'd mee in a pleasing trance
Thou madst my sences subtile, & didst teach
my hopes to tast of sweetes beyond my reach,
past pleasures thou recallst and those at hand
thou mad'st mee learned in, to understand
my blisse, and not with brutysh appetite
but gav'st my soule a'rellish of delight
Thou didst my passions spend without offence
my verie anger cloth'd in innocence
Thou taughtst mee wronges to suffer like a'saint
and study noe revenge, but beare complaint
My mirth in sportive witt, was purg'd from folly
and in devotion past my Malancholly
in feare, and faintnes thou didst yeild releife
and soderd'st up my broken hart, when greife
opprest my Soule, teares gave not speedie vent
to my swolne eyes, then thou my discontent
with ease disburthenest. Now for want of thee
see how my passiones tryumphs over mee
First try my anger I am growne in rage
and like the furious Poetes of this age
whoe for a'Mistres losse theire Muses faylinge
would utter that for witt, which is but railinge
I vowe, as they have cause to love noe more
a'Mistres that still keepes her servantes poore
and when shee sees, theire youth, or peace [?] decay
(for all's the same) care makes a'younge man gray)
seekes for a greener head, [ ] thou vaine
and bastard yssue of an idle braine:
Lust of such youthfull fancies, as committ
folly in verse, Adultery of witt
Traytour, that whilst o'th soule thou dost derive
thy essence, art a'stronge provocative
temptinge the flesh to sinne, thou thinge of nought
and chac'd away by every serious thought
prophane Idolater, that dost adore
the Heathens painted Dietyes, and more,
by all thy varnisht Mistresses farewell
cares are but Purgatories, thou a'hell:

T[homas] S[alusbury]
(NLW MS 5390, pp. 293–95)

A Challenge of her promise

Fy Madam could yow bee soe cruell bent
gainst a'poore member of the Parliament
as to prepare such bondes for him that scap'd
both house, and Towne unquestion'd nor was apt
ever to raise commotions, or rebell
though hee hath stood off there, yet noe word fell
to such lowd purpose from him, but y'have gott
perchance the trick on't, and will say yow not
for any thinge there said, or done confine
him to Captivity, in soe strong a line
but for some rude act since, th'unrulie joynt,
hath broke two buttones, and a'Codpeice point,
his prison lock, and boltes, yet let me say
this for him, hee were ment to runne away.
Longe use hath made him ever best content
with the most narrow, close, imprisonement
If youle beleive this madam, and assure
mee that yow sent this Cordage as a'cure
for my sore throate, if t'other I receavd
together with't should faile, this nere deceav'd
them of theire endes that tryde it, I'le confesse
your bountie, but must challenge nere the lesse
your promise, my requestes unsatisfied
and my poore Codpeice Gapes to bee supplide
with a'faire ribon from yow, which being tyde
by such a'hand would make mee swell with pride.
(NLW MS 5390D, pp. 295–96)

Upon the thunder & rayne that overtooke the Ladyes
at Keven y Werne upon Wednesday the 18th of may. 1643

Thunder and rayne at once what meanes the Sky?
Like a vext huswife to scold & Cry
here are no shrewes aload, but virgines fayre
Whose ey beames might uncloud and cleare the ayre
sure heavenes in kindnes weepes but to repay
The Dayrry back the Creame they eat to day.
Why hides the ^sunne^ his face, What were his feares
his rayes should Injure, or Compare with theyres

Twas wisdome soe to Cover his extreames,
the earth he knew ^then^ needed not his beames,
and loath like fonder loveres to become
by his officious presence troublesome
Hee for a tyme withdrawes, but Courts meanwhiles
them in his teares, more Welcome ^then^ his smiles
For these were wealthy & perfumed showers
Exhald in morning Maye Dewes from the flowers
And payd againe with use, for all hee drew
from every playnt producing more and new
of fresher sent, those dames to intertayne
with fragrant ayres, as those, they breath agayue,
Heavens sultry heat thus quell'd, & earth made sweet
The stubborne Cloddes dissolv'd beneath their feet
Delicious was the walk, no dust did rise
to vex theyr Nostrilles, or offend their eyes
This Courtship much prevayld, which to requite
The Ladies each unmaskd, and soe one sight
The fasting sunn in favour was allow'd
of all theyr beautyes, from behind a Cloud
(NLW MS 5390D, p. 303)

Works Cited

Archer, Jayne Elisabeth, Elizabeth Goldring, and Sarah Knight, eds. 2011. *The Intellectual and Cultural History of the Early Modern Inns of Court*. Manchester: Manchester University Press.

Aubrey, John. 2015. *Brief Lives*. Edited by Kate Bennet. 2 vols. Oxford: Oxford University Press.

Bland, Mark. 2005. "Francis Beaumont's Verse Letters to Ben Jonson and 'The Mermaid Club.'" *English Manuscript Studies 1100–1700* 12: 139–79.

Bodleian. Manuscript Ashmole 38.

Bodleian. Manuscript Additional B.97.

Bodleian. Eng. Poet c.50.

Bodleian MS Lat. misc. fol.445.

Bodleian. Manuscript Malone 13.

Bodleian. Manuscript Malone 16.

Bodleian. Manuscript Rawl. D. 301.

Bodleian. Manuscript Rawl. Poet 61.

Bodleian. Manuscript Rawl. Poet 84.

Bowen, Lloyd. 2004. "Salusbury [Salisbury], Sir Thomas, second baronet (1612–1643), poet and politician." *Oxford Dictionary of National Biography*. Accessed 10 May 2024. https://www.oxforddnb.com/view/10.1093/ref:odnb/9780198614128.001.0001/odnb-9780198614128-e-24545.

British Library. Additional Manuscript 12409.

British Library. Additional Manuscript 14047.

British Library. Additional Manuscript 15226.

British Library. Additional Manuscript 15227.

British Library. Additional Manuscript 21433.

British Library. Additional Manuscript 23299.

British Library. Additional Manuscript 25303.

British Library. Additional Manuscript. 25707.

British Library. Additional Manuscript 34752.

British Library. Additional Manuscript 53723.

British Library. Additional Manuscript 58215.

British Library. Egerton Manuscript 923.

British Library. Harley Manuscript 6057.

British Library. Harley Manuscripts 6917–18.

British Library. Sloane Manuscript 1394.

British Library. Sloane Manuscript 1446.

British Library. Stowe Manuscript 962.

Brown, Cedric C. 1977. "The Chirk Castle Entertainment of 1634." *Milton Quarterly* 3: 76–86.

Carey, John. 1960. "The Poems of Nicholas Hare," *Review of English Studies*. n.s. 44: 365–83.

Clark Library. Manuscript 1950.024.

Davies, John. 1975. *The Poems of Sir John Davies*. Edited by Robert Krueger, with introduction and commentary by the editor and Ruby Nemser. Oxford: Clarendon Press.

Folger. Manuscript V.a.96.

Folger. Manuscript V.a.125.

Folger. Manuscript V.a.249.

Folger. Manuscript V.a.245.

Folger. Manuscript V.a.276.2.

Folger. Manuscript V.a.319.

Folger. Manuscript V.a.322.

Folger. Manuscript V.b.43.

Gair, W. R. 1968. "The Salusbury Circle at Lleweni." *Research Opportunities in Renaissance Drama*. 11: 73–79.

Harrington, John. 2009. *The Epigrams of Sir John Harington*. Edited by Gerard Kilroy. Burlington VT: Ashgate.

Hobbs, Mary, ed. 1990. *The Stoughton Manuscript: A Manuscript Miscellany of Poems by Henry King and his Circle, circa 1636*. Aldershot, U.K. and Brookfield, VT: Scolar Press.

———, ed. 1992. *Early Seventeenth-Century Verse Miscellany Manuscripts*. Aldershot: Scholar Press.

Hughey, Ruth, and Philip Hereford. 1934. "Elizabeth Grymeston and her *Miscellanea*." *The Library,* n.s., 15: 61–89.

Huntington. HM 198.1.

Huntington. HM 198.2.

Krueger, Robert, ed. 1961. "The Poems of William Herbert, Third Earl of Pembroke." BLitt diss., University of Oxford.

———. 1962a. "Sir John Davies: *Orchestra* Complete, *Epigrams,* Unpublished Poems." *Review of English Studies*, n.s., 113, no. 49: 17–29.

———. 1962b. "Sir John Davies: *Orchestra* Complete, *Epigrams,* Unpublished Poems." *Review of English Studies*, n.s., 113, no. 50: 113–24.

Lincoln's Inn. 1896. *The Records of the Honorable Society of Lincoln's Inn*, vol. 1, *Admissions from A.D. 1428 to A.D. 1796*. London: Lincoln's Inn.

Marotti, Arthur. 2021. *The Circulation of Poetry in Manuscript in Early Modern England*. New York and London: Routledge.

Maule, Jeremy. 2000. "'To the memory of the late excellent Poet John Fletcher,' A New Poem by John Ford." *English Manuscript Studies* 8: 136–59.

May, Steven W., and Alan Bryson, eds. 2016. *Verse Libel in Renaissance England and Scotland*. Oxford: Oxford University Press.

Morgan Library. Manuscript MA 1057.

National Library of Wales. Manuscript 5390D.

National Library of Wales. Manuscript Peniarth 500B.

Nelson, Alan, and John R. Elliott, eds. 2010. *Records of Early English Drama: Inns of Court*. Cambridge: Brewer.

O'Callaghan, Michelle. 2007. *The English Wits: Literature and Sociability in Early Modern England*. Cambridge: Cambridge University Press, 2007.

Prest, Wilfrid R. 2023. *The Inns of Court under Elizabeth I and the Early Stuarts, 1590–1640*, 2nd ed. Cambridge: Cambridge University Press.

St. John's College, Cambridge. Manuscript 423.

Sturgess, H., ed. 1949. *Register of Admissions to the Honourable Society of the Middle Temple*. London: Butterworth & Co.

University of Edinburgh. Manuscript La. III. 493.

Yale. Beinecke Manuscript b. 65.

Yale. Osborn Manuscript b.52/2.

Yale. Osborn Manuscript b.205.

PART III

Beyond the Inns

CHAPTER 10

George Gascoigne's Proliferative Poetics

Felicity Brown

The collective voice of early Elizabethan literature has been characterised as 'that of the schoolmaster exhorting … wayward youths' (Panofsky 1975: 7). While the centrality of the inns of court, as both a professional community and a vibrant literary epicentre, spanned the long century from 1550 to 1660, the moralising legacy of the humanist schoolroom is particularly prominent in texts produced at the inns in the 1560s. This decade saw the first vernacular plays in blank verse written and performed. Despite being staged during a festive season associated with institutionally sanctioned performances of misrule, the first inns drama, Thomas Norton and Thomas Sackville's *Gorboduc* (*c.* 1561–1562), is a didactic tragedy. In performance and then print, George Gascoigne and Francis Kinwelmersh's *Jocasta* (*c.* 1566–1567) is framed by paratexts, dumbshows, and choral odes that heavy-handedly direct moral interpretations of its action. Even *The Misfortunes of Arthur* (*c.* 1587–1588), the *terminus ad quem* of this kind of performance, begins with five law students justifying their creative writing to the muses and the queen. The value of imaginative English literature was still being established (Helgerson 1976).

F. Brown (✉)
English, Christ Church, University of Oxford, Oxford, UK

E. Rhatigan, J. Watson (eds.), *Mapping the Early Modern Inns of Court*, Early Modern Literature in History,
https://doi.org/10.1007/978-3-031-77445-4_10

No writer experimented more prolifically with the delights and dangers of English literature in this period than George Gascoigne. Born *c.* 1534, he studied at Trinity College, Cambridge, before being admitted to Gray's Inn in 1555. Gascoigne returned to Gray's a decade later, having appeared in Elizabeth I's coronation, conducted a failed farming experiment in Bedfordshire, married a widow (who may still have been married to someone else), and spent time in parliament, the army, and debtors' prison (Pigman III 2010). On his return, he collaborated in the authorship of *Jocasta*.[1] A veritable compendium of the Theban saga, *Jocasta* retells the story of Euripides' *Phoenissae*. It was translated from Ludovico Dolce's Italian *Gioasta* (Venice, 1549) by Gascoigne and Kinwelmersh (Christopher Yelverton contributed the Epilogue, Kinwelmersh translated Acts One and Four, and Gascoigne did the rest). Its argument, written by Gascoigne, encourages *Jocasta*'s audience to identify a 'type' of tyranny in Creon and a 'myrror' of misery in Oedipus. Dumbshows at the beginning of each act animate didactic emblems, and the play's final speech reinforces man's powerlessness in the face of Fortune, encouraging the viewer to: 'Example here, loe take'.[2] These framing devices not only reinforce the moral of the play, but they complicate it by positioning *Jocasta* within Gascoigne's real and imagined literary communities.

Gascoigne repeatedly wrote in the voice of the reformed-prodigal-turned-moralist.[3] His success in this guise has, as Gillian Austen notes, eclipsed his reputation as a courtly poet. However, his moralising should be seen as a part of the complexity of this courtliness, which 'is often a mixture of seriousness and playfulness' (2008: 2, 4).[4] When Gascoigne assures you that something is dutiful rather than profligate, you cannot necessarily take his word for it—the court of high commission did not when they recalled *The poesies of George Gascoigne Esquire* (1575), despite

[1] Marie Axton (1977: 54) assumes that *Jocasta* and *Supposes* formed part of the Christmas revels of 1566; G. W. Pigman (2000: xxvii) proposes the 'Christmas to Lent revels, 1565–6 or 1566–7'; Katherine Duncan-Jones (1991: 48) suggests the 'New-Year-to-Shrovetide festivities in 1565–6, or those of 1566–7'; Austen (2008: 48) notes that there were also revels at All Hallows, Candlemas, and Accession Day.

[2] In manuscript (BL MS Add. 34063), and print (1573), commonplace marks also alert the reader to *sententiae* ripe for extraction and reflection, see Suthren (2020: 59–84).

[3] On Gascoigne as prodigal, see Helgerson (1976: 44–57).

[4] Before his return to Gray's Inn, he had spent a few 'extravagant' years on the periphery of the court which are the subject of the eroticised narrative of his 'seven Sonets in sequence'; on the games Gascoigne plays with his reader, hiding in plain sight, see Skura (2008: 168–196).

its claim to have been purged of 'sundrie wanton speeches and lascivious phrases' (Winston 2016: 226; Hughes 1997: 1). Accordingly, a sceptical critical turn has scrutinised the importance of accidents, seriocomic performances of failure, narrativisations of authorial intent, and Gascoigne's position within an early modern poetics of 'discomposition' (Pfeiffer 2022: 249–98; Braden 2022: 38–81; Hetherington 2016: 29–59; Desai 2023: 28-68).

Jocasta, meanwhile, has been examined for its complex intertextual genealogy, in particular the use made, not just of Dolce's *Giocasta* but of multiple Latin translations and Euripides' original Greek (Dewar-Watson 2010: 22–32; Pyré 2020: 44–58). The expansion of female roles in *Jocasta* has also been a subject of study, as has the way in which it was read in Elizabethan England as a model tragedy (Norland 2009: 83–89). For Tanya Pollard, *Jocasta* provides an example of a broader mother–daughter dyad that models a shift in authority from classical literary sources to their modern descendants (2017: 43–88); for Tania Demetriou, Gabriel Harvey's annotations reveal *Jocasta*'s value for early modern readers as a kind of composite tragic collection (2021: 757–87). While the topicality of the play and its engagement with Elizabethan politics have been fruitfully discussed by both Lorna Hutson and Jessica Winston, this chapter considers the play's position within Gascoigne's wider oeuvre (Hutson 2023: 245–78; Winston 2016: 193–212). *Jocasta*, a play whose characters are all too deeply entangled with one another, has remained isolated in this respect. By focusing on proliferation—in Gascoigne's use of *polyptoton* (the repetition of words derived from the same root), his sonnets, and their occasional contexts—I argue that didactic writing at Gray's Inn provided opportunities not only for earnest reformation and reflection but for play.

Roots and Resemblances

Euripides' *Phoenissae* is a tragedy preoccupied with growth. It appropriates Aeschylus' depiction of an Oedipus 'who sowed the sacrosanct soil / of his mother, where he had been nurtured, / and suffered a bloodstained progeny' ('ὅστε ματρὸς ἁγνὰν / σπείρας ἄρουραν ἵν' ἔτραφη / ῥίζαν αἱματόεσσαν / ἔτλα') (Aeschylus 2014: 11.753–56). Aeschylus' Apollonian oracle uses the verb '*σπείρω*' ('to sow') when warning Laius: 'do not keep sowing the child-begetting furrow' ('μὴ σπεῖρε τέκνων ἄλοκα') (Euripides 1994: 1.18). In *Phoenissae*, Antigone is a 'shoot' ('θάλος'), a noun that 'transforms itself into the cognate verb when discord ('ἔρις') is said to 'sprout' ('θάλλει') (1994: 1.88, 11.811–12; see also Pyré 2020: 52)'. Moreover, the repetition of the adjective 'δεινός' ('terrible' *and* 'wonderous') yokes this vegetative imagery to the procreative quality of suffering and art. This effect is further reinforced by the conflation of crime and generation in the double meaning of 'αἷμα' ('the blood that is spilled' and 'the blood that is transmitted') (1.61, 1.179, 1.374, 1.1051). Euripides' Theban tragedy is one of excessive productivity.

The fertility of the suffering of the house of Laius, so potent in Euripides' play, was recreated, to varying degrees, by three early modern Latin translators: 'Dorotheus Camillus', the pseudonym of Rudolphus Collinus (or Ambühl); Philip Melanchthon; and Stiblinus (Kaspar Stiblin), respectively.[5] As Yves Pyré observes, only Collinus sees the 'advent of discord as a bitterly ironical efflorescence ("contentio floret")' and it is from Collinus that Dolce worked when translating *Giocasta*. Jessica Apolloni notes in Chap. 11 on *Gismond of Salerne* (written by members of Inner Temple and performed for Queen Elizabeth in the same year that *Jocasta* was staged) how innsmen in this period were heavily engaged with Italian literature and culture. The same year that Dolce's Italian text served as Gascoigne's primary model for *Jocasta*, he translated Ludovico Ariosto's *I Suppositi* (1509) into the comedy *Supposes*. In *Giocasta*, Dolce further expands on the negative fertility imagery he found in his source:

> Ma, si come da verde & fresca pianta
> noui rampolli un sopra l'altro nasce;
> Cosi a l'interno mio graue tormento
> Vn se n'aggiunge, & forse ancho Maggiore (1549: 15).
>
> [But, yes, as from a green and fresh plant
> nine offspring one above the other is born;
> So inside my grave torment
> One is added, and perhaps even greater.]

[5] As John W. Cunliffe established (1912: xxxvi–xxxvii), Dolce did not translate directly from Euripides but used Collinus (1541). By the time Gascoigne and Kinwelmersh staged their play, however, both Melanchthon (1558) and Stiblinus (1562) had been printed by Joannes Oporinus' press in Basel: the latter a bilingual Greek and Latin edition. On the Latin translations, see Pyré (2020), and on the use made of Seneca, see Dewar-Watson (2010).

Gascoigne translates Dolce's formulation:

> And as the growing greene and pleasant plante,
> Dothe beare freshe braunches one above an other,
> Even so amidde the huge heape of my woes,
> Dothe growe one grudge more greevous than the rest (1573: 95).

Dolce's 'perhaps' ('forse') is abandoned for the conviction of the alliteration and *polyptoton* of growth. Here, Gascoigne embraces the challenge of translating Dolce into English, a language without the aural affordances of a highly inflected language like Italian ('a' in the first line given above, 'o' in the third) which comes close to constituting something like internal rhyme. He does this by creating a rhetorical pattern that encodes the action of the plot at the level of the sentence. Rather than clustering sounds at the end of words and lines, he emphasises shared etymological roots.

Jocasta's eponymous queen is elided throughout the play with the native soil of Thebes, over which Pollynices and Eteocles fight, and from which Oedipus and Antygone are ultimately banished. This preoccupation with the 'natyve soil' that elides the queen and city permeates all five acts of the play, but no examples of *polyptoton* occur in the two acts translated by Kinwelmersh; it is a distinct feature of Gascoigne's sections. In his acts, it is striking how often the same word is repeated in a different case, inflection, or voice within a line or across a single speech. Pollynices regrets that '[he] must departe, and parting must' (108). Once he is dead, Antigone recalls that 'Whyle [he] yet livedst, I had a lively hope … But now, hastie death hath done to dye, / This dying hope of mine' (153). Eteocles assures his brother that the man who would shed his own blood to spill Pollynices', 'By thee he standes, and thou standst him before' (107). Creon reveals to Meneceus 'That this devine of thee devined hath' (124). This rhetorical pattern sits uncomfortably between repetition and progression, echoing the confused consanguinity of the characters. In *The Arte of English Poesie* (1589), George Puttenham would describe how this device 'do pleasantly encounter, and (as it were) mock one another by their much resemblance' (170). It is that *much resemblance* that makes Gascoigne's *polyptoton* the perfect figure for the of the House of Laius.[6]

[6]In 'Certayne notes of instruction concerning the making of verse or ryme in English', Gascoigne stresses the centrality of *inuentio*, and the importance of using figures that 'lead you not from your first invention' (1575: 581).

Gascoigne's *polyptoton* not only proliferates its source word, it also repeatedly calls it into question. The opening speech of Act Two ends with the question: 'Where resteth now the restless queene of Thebes?' (93) and it is answered with further negation. The Chorus hope that Pollynices will 'Some quiet bring to this vnquiet realme' (93). Jocasta's rest is complicated by her restlessness just as Pollynices' army un-quiets his homeland. These antitheses multiply across the play: there is no rest from restless grief and no quiet ends to unquiet lives (119). Nobility and worth become the 'Vnoble' and 'vnwoorthie' (146) actions that fuel the tragic plot. Reiteration does not reinforce meaning; just as Thebes' two princes do not make the city twice as strong, they almost destroy it.

The same principle is at work in *The poesies of George Gascoigne Esquire* (1575) in which *Jocasta* was printed for the second time, having first appeared in *A Hundreth sundrie flowres bound up in one small Poesie* (1573).[7] Because the first book was 'doubtfully construed, and (therefore) scandalous', Gascoigne abandoned the fiction of an anonymous anthology, restructured the material, and added three dedicatory epistles.[8] Each of the epistles addresses a different audience and makes a different claim for the book's content and significance (Pfeiffer 2022). The first and longest of these letters is addressed to 'To the reuerende Diuines', in which Gascoigne mounts a forensic defence of the accused book by playing the trial lawyer and pre-emptively refuting the objections of 'grave and graye headed Iudges' (1575: 1, 3). The second is addressed to 'al yong Gentlemen, and generally … the youth of England'—it is tempting to suspect he had his fellow innsmen in mind—which, in exploring how questionable parts of *A Hundreth sundrie flowres* have been misread, admonishes his readers to exercise greater caution in reading (and so advertises the book's lewd qualities) (15). The third appeals to 'the Readers generally' and promotes the variety of the work included (27). In his book, he suggests, there is something for everyone. Yet in providing multiple epistles, the nature of the volume's contents becomes more, not less, obscure: is it serious, scandalous, or all of the above?

[7] A manuscript of *Jocasta* dated 1568 survives in BL MS Add. 34063.

[8] In the tripartite horticultural structure of *The poesies*, *Jocasta* is positioned as useful, even curative, one of the 'good hearbes' rather than 'fresh flowres' or 'holsome weedes' (Gascoigne 1575: 33).

Posies and Poses

Gascoigne, who had written one of the earliest English sonnet sequences and perhaps the second corona of English sonnets, uses them to further complicate the tone of *Jocasta*. While Petrarch's recuperation of frustrated desire as poetic glory in the sonnet was already well established by this time, the 'huge and hungry crocodile' of sexual desire, associated with the sonnet form from Philip Sidney's *Astrophel and Stella* (printed 1591) onward, was still to come (Kuin 1998: 89). But it was Gascoigne who authored the first prescriptive definition of the sonnet in one of the additions he made to *The poesies*. In 'Certayne notes of instruction concerning the making of verse or ryme in English', he specifies that sonnets 'serue aswell in matters of loue as of discourse' (1575: 587). 'Discourse' encompassed both 'reasoning' and 'conversation' at the time, revealing a dual tradition in which sonnets were used both for love and 'a less emotive and introspective purpose' (Shrank 2008: 35). Cathy Shrank's examination of mid-Tudor sonnet collections—including Richard Tottel's *Songes and Sonettes* (1557), Barnabe Googe's *Eglogs Epytaphes, and Sonettes* (1563), George Turbeville's *Epitaphes, Epigrams, Songs and Sonets* (1567), Thomas Howell's *Newe Sonets and Pretie Pamphlets* (1567–1568), and Gascoigne's 'The deuises of sundrie Gentlemen' in *A Hundreth sundrie flowres* (1573)—reveals recurrent attempts to demystify love. In these sonnets (broadly defined), both the rejection of the female subject by the male speaker and the poem's circulation amongst men fortify male sociability. The sonnets' didactic quality, proffering ponderous advice, emerges, at least in part, as a pose; the moralist, like the prodigal young man, is only one persona among the many adopted by the speakers. These sonneteers are not just earnest lecturers, they are prolific and 'gregarious' impersonators (Shrank 2008: 40).

Jocasta begins and ends with a sonnet. Where Dolce's *Giocasta* starts with a 55-line prologue, 'A Sodisfattion De Gli Spettatori recitato da un fanciullo' ['To the Satisfaction of the Spectators recited by a child'], Gascoigne's begins with '*The argument of the Tragedie*': a sonnet in rhyming couplets. What starts like a classical invocation, 'To scourge the cryme of wicked Laius, / And wrecke the foule Incest of Oedipus, / The angry Gods styrred up theyr sonnes', moves to a *de casibus* conclusion, 'Creon is King, the type of Tyranny, / And Oedipus, myrrour of misery' (1575: 71), familiar from Italian and then English texts, such as John Lydgate's *The Fall of Princes* (*c.* 1431–1438) and the recently published *Mirror for*

Magistrates (1559, 1563).[9] This vernacularisation is reinforced by the distinctly English sound of the verse, its rhyming couplets, alliteration, and the predominance of monosyllables (Gascoigne explains in 'Certayne notes of Instruction' that 'the more monasyllables that you use, the truer Englishman you shall séeme, and the lesse you shall smell of the Inkehorne') (1575: 581).[10] While it is possible that he performed his own prologue in 1566, or that a written copy was circulated with the arguments of the dumbshows in advance of the play, it may also have been a later addition for publication.[11] However the sonnet-argument was disseminated, Gascoigne also transformed Dolce's final 11-line choral ode into an English sonnet. In it, the abstract 'Cosi ingegno & uirtu cede a fortuna' ('So ingenuity & virtue yields to fortune') of the Italian is reimagined as an active and embodied 'dame Fortune' (162), hoisting men up on her wheel with typically English phrasal verbs that proclaim she has not only been '*translated and digested into Acte*' (71) but into English (Dolce 1549: 53). The sonnet form of *Jocasta*'s argument and its conclusion make Gascoigne's contribution to the commonweal explicit, while also gesturing to the contrived and socially performative nature of the moral lesson being delivered.

The sonnet argument of *Jocasta* ends with the Latin tag: '*Fortunatus infœlix*' ('fortunate then unhappy' or 'the lucky unfortunate') (1575: 71). A fitting tag for the fate of the eponymous heroine, this motto also concludes several other texts in both *A Hundreth sundrie flowres* and *The poesies*. These include a series of poems which, we are told, were composed upon a particular 'occasion' by their author:

> Hee had (in myddest of his youth) determined to abandone all vaine delightes and to returne unto Greyes Inne, there to undertake againe the

[9] The main repository of *de casibus* narratives in English, *A myrrour for magistrates* (1563), carries in most of its editions the motto '*Felix quem faciunt aliena pericula cautum*' ('happy are they made cautious by the plight of others').

[10] He may be echoing 'A Letter of syr I. Cheekes' in Thomas Hoby's translation of *The courtyer of Count Baldessar Castilio diuided into foure books* (London, 1561). Despite being a competent Latinist and a liberal coiner of words derived from both Old English and Latin, Gascoigne anticipates later poets by recognising English's potential as a literary language.

[11] See Austen (2008: 55). Dieter Mehl (1965: 11); '*The argument of the Tragedie*' would not be 'best allowe[d]' to be termed as a sonnet by Gascoigne's definition in 'Certayne instruction', which limits the form to the English sonnet (1575: 585).

> studdie of the common Lawes. And being required by five sundry Gentlemen to write in verse somewhat worthye to bee remembred, before he entered into their fellowshipped, hee compiled these five sundrie sortes of metre upon five sundrye theames, whiche they delivered unto him [.] (1573: xxix; 1575: 356–69)

This is one of the few instances in *A Hundreth sundrie flowres* when the names of real men are used: John Vaughan, Alexander Neville, Richard Courtop, Francis Kinwelmersh, and his brother Anthony, were all Gascoigne's contemporaries at Gray's Inn. Each provided a prompt to which Gascoigne responded. Anthony Kinwelmersh's suggested '*Satis suffit*' ('enough is enough', 1573: 357), which may have been an allusion to Gascoigne's extensive financial and legal difficulties (Pigman III 2010). The 'sudden surfeit of contradictory proverb lore' in Gascoigne's response, characteristic of the answer poem genre, disrupts 'the gravity of the moral stance' set up in the serious exemplarity of his rhyme royal opening (Austen 2008: 40). The exercise is a jocular one and its morality a flexible posture (Hart: 1956: 19–20). In response to an Erasmian prompt, '*Audaces fortuna iuvat*'—translated by Gabriel Harvey as 'Fortune advaunceth hazaders' but more commonly taken as 'fortune favours the bold' (1575: 356)—Francis Kinwelmersh, *Jocasta*'s co-author, received an English sonnet in which Gascoigne not only plays with the relative audacity of the classical figures Caesar, Menelaus, and Aeneas but also with his own.[12] Written within a year of 'Gascoynes five notable devises', *Jocasta* is the product of further collaboration by this irreverent coterie.

Gascoigne makes these responses more than the sum of their parts by dramatising their occasion and so turning the challenge he was issued, to write 'something worthy to be remembered' (1575: 357), into the foundation of his conceit. He devised these poems, we are told, while:

> ryding by the way, writing none of them until he came at the ende of his journey, the which was no longer than one day in ryding, one daye in tarying with his friend, and the thirde in returning to Greyes Inne: and therefore called Gascoignes memories. (Austen 2008: 1)

[12] Malone 792, B7. The proverb can be traced to Erasmus via Taverner, '*Audaces fortuna juvat.* Fortune helpeth men of good courage. He that feareth yt his matters shall not have good successe: shall never bringe his matters to passe', in *Proverbes or Adagies. Gathered out of Erasmus* (1539, 1552, B2). It originates with Seneca; see A. Otto, *Die Sprichwörter und sprichwörtlichen Redensarten* (Leipzig: 1890), *ad fortuna*, 9.

He did not just write but memorised 259 lines of verse. A similar centrality (and the same motto) appears in the occasional framing of another series of poems included in both *A Hundreth sundrie flowres* and *The poesies*, 'The devises of sundrie Gentlemen' (1575: 294–308). Likely circulated around Gray's Inn in manuscript years earlier, these poems are interspersed with details of the occasions of their composition:

> whiles he sat at the dore of his lodging, devising these verses above rehersed, the same Gentlewoman passed by againe, and cast a long looke towards him, whereby his left his former invention and wrotes thus[.] (306)

The occasion transforms the amorous verses into a coherent narrative and the poems themselves become performative as a result. The poetic sequence looks increasingly like a dramatic script.

Occasion itself is always both rooted and boundless in Gascoigne's work. The 'sundrie' speakers of these verses are identified not only by their mottos but their initials. Each is linked in some way to Gascoigne and the other alter egos he used throughout his career. As well as sharing a motto with *Jocasta*, 'F. I.' is linked by the printer's convention (that made I and J interchangeable) with the eponymous protagonist of *The Adventures of Master F.J.* As Austen has argued, Gascoigne peoples *A Hundreth sundrie flowres* with 'plausible figures from the nascent world of literary publishing'. In this light, we can identify H.W. as the publisher, G.T. as an aspiring editor and narrator, and F.J. and his friends as the group of writers whose work is published with (or without) their consent in this fictional coterie (Austen 2013). The occasion of 'Certayne notes of instruction', meanwhile, makes Gascoigne's poetic manual part of an epistolary response to a fictive Italian friend, Signor Eduardo Donati, who is desperate to be instructed in the mysterious ways of rhyme. These connections recall the structures of Italianate experimental prose fiction, such as the story-telling games of Boccaccio's locked-down house party and Chaucer's Canterbury-bound pilgrims. While distinctions between the occasional contexts and fictional content are similarly confused, if not completely collapsed by Gascoigne, he always keeps multiple occasions in play.

More Is More

The importance of Fortune in *Jocasta* can be traced back to the various notions of fate that permeate the *Phoenissae*. Euripides creates lexical patterns around fate, chance, and providence (τύχη) as well as fortune, both good (εὐτύχής) and bad (δυστυχής). His Latin translators carry this over in words such as 'calamitas', 'fortuna', and 'infoelicitas', as well as the corresponding adjectives 'felix', 'infelix', 'fortunatus', and 'miser'. But it is Dolce who significantly expands the role of fortune in light of the trends of the period in which he wrote. *Giocasta* traces the influence not only of Petrarch's *Il Canzoniere* (*c.* 1327–1374) and *I Trionfi* (c. 1351–1374) but also of Boccaccio, who introduced Jocasta in his *De Claris Mulieribus* (*c.* 1361–1362) as 'the queen of Thebes that was made famous more by her mishap / misfortune than by her reign and merits' ('Jocasta Thebarum regina fuit magis infortunio suo clara quam meritis, aut regno'), and who was the first woman to appear in his *De Casibus Virorum Illustrium* (*c.* 1355–1374). Dolce's prologue opens with reference to the affliction of 'Fortuna', and it is the final word of his play (1549: 3, 53).

As well as absorbing the significance of fortune introduced by Dolce, *Jocasta* expands upon it, exaggerating the pose. This is apparent in the most spectacular addition made by Gascoigne and Kinwelmersh to their sources: the dumbshows. The Egyptian King Sesostris, representing ambition, is wheeled onstage in a chariot drawn by four kings for the first dumbshow (1573: 73). In the final dumbshow, the chariot returns in a visual *polyptoton*. This time it is driven by Fortune, who is pulled by four 'noble personages' while leading two kings by a string in her right hand and two slaves by a string in her left (144). She then proceeds, by redistributing their crowns and rags, to invert their statuses. The parallel implies a close connection between the two shows: ambition represents the ascending movement of Fortune's wheel. As well as inspiring Christopher Marlowe's iconic 'pampered jades of Asia' in *Tamburlaine, Part II* (1588), these dumbshows have a clear connection with the action of the play, in which Antigone drives (presumably the same chariot) on stage, bearing the bodies of her dead mother and brothers (152). Pyré notes that the emblem of Sesostris as Fortune's ambitious fool—first proposed by Menander Protector (1851: 4.210), made popular by John Tzetzes' *Chiliades* (*Book of Histories*) (1826: 3.8, 83–84), and taken up by Henry Peacham (1612: 76)—provides an emblematic frame that emphasises the wheel of Fortune as the source of tragedy (Pyré 2020: 46). But there is also an inns-specific context at play in these elaborate pageants. In *Jocasta*, the weighty political and moralistic form of the dumbshows in *Gorboduc* (performed at Inner Temple in 1561–1562) are echoed and their sober lessons reimagined. The split flames of *Jocasta*'s second dumbshow and Curtius' leap into the 'great Gulfe' (1575: 116) in its third are both special effects as bold as the play's two stately chariot sequences. An inns audience would surely have had to smile as these played out in Sesostris's wake. Fortune, after all, favours the bold.

The fourth dumbshow goes even further, magnifying *Gorboduc*'s opening sequence in which six wild men tried and failed to break a faggot of small sticks until they had divvied them up. In *Jocasta*, this lesson is performed as a fight scene:

> Trumpets, drummes and fifes sounded, and a greate peale of ordinaunce was shot of: in the which ther entred vpon the stage .vj. knights armed at al points ... either parte beeing accompanied with .vij. other armed men: and after they had marched twice or thrice about the Stage, the one partie menacing the other by their furious lookes and gestures, the .vj. knights caused their other attendants to stand by, and drawing their Swords, fell to cruell and couragious combate, continuing therein, till two on the one side were slayne. The thirde perceiuing, that he only remayned to withstand the force of .iij. enimies, did politiquely rūne aside: wherewith immediatly one of the .iij. followed after him, and when he had drawen his enimie thus from his companie, hee turned againe and slewe him. Then the seconde also ranne after him, whom he slewe in like mãner, and consequently the thirde, and then triumphantly marched aboute the Stage wyth hys sword in his hand. (129–30)

As in *Gorboduc*, those who hold together cannot be overcome, but 'being once disseuered by any meanes, are easily ouerthrowen' (130). Unlike *Gorboduc*, however, *Jocasta* features eight central characters—Jocasta, Antygone, Pollynices, Eteocles, Creon, Meneceus, Tyresias, and Oedipus—and it also requires 17 interlocutors. Moreover, the proliferation of participants in the dumbshows make it difficult to stage with fewer than 46 people, even if the extras double their roles (Austen 2008: 37). The original production, then, must have involved a significant proportion of the total membership of Gray's Inn, which Austen estimates comprised 220 men at most in the period (53). The size of the show is surely part of the fun; enough is *not* enough. Christopher Yelverton's epilogue is wise to this performance context. Winston has noted how the 'we' of its moral interpretation of the action performed, 'See, ruin grows when most we reach to rise' (1575: 163), might target the personal and professional ambition of the play's innsmen performers and audience (2016: 193–212). But this self-awareness is not confined to a cheeky wink at the play's end, it is a structural principle.

A similar approach is apparent in the next classical tragedy performed by the gentlemen of Gray's Inn, *The Misfortunes of Arthur* (discussed further by Winston in Chap. 1). As well as sharing a collaborator with *Jocasta*, *Misfortunes* recalls it by portraying Arthur as a British Oedipus, describing Curtius' leap in its third dumbshow, and by revisiting Creon's conflict—a father who must choose between the welfare of a beloved child and that of his country—in Arthur's new found fondness for Mordred.[13] *Misfortunes* also follows *Jocasta*'s approach to the moralising dumbshows of *Gorboduc*, restaging *Gorboduc*'s fourth as its first one. As well as three furies emerging 'from under the stage' in the same way, wearing the same costumes, and carrying the same snake, firebrand, and whip, three additional emblematic props (a 'snake athwart a cup', a 'Cupid', and a 'Pegasus') are added, as are three nuns to mirror the three furies (Hughes *et al.* 1587: A1^{r}). Both *Jocasta* and *The Misfortunes of Arthur* play with the notion of excess while warning against it. By making, remaking, and even unmaking meaning in this polyptotonic way, inns drama cultivated the opaque and unpredictable energy that would go on to flourish in the commercial theatre.

By playing with didactic drama, Elizabethan innsmen helped to establish the legitimacy of creative compositions in the vernacular. In the 1580s and 1590s, as purpose-built playhouses came to dominate English drama, the inns would increasingly be associated with other forms of literary innovation, notably verse satire. Just as Sidney's crocodile of frustration would break the 'well-banked river' (Kuin 1998: 89) of the sonneteering tradition outlined in Gascoigne's 'Certayne notes of Instruction', so, the young men who followed Gascoigne into the inns of court would develop his aggregative approach and unleash something of even greater linguistic virtuosity and viciousness. Gascoigne had charted a new kind of career as an author of imaginative English literature and it proved to be fertile ground.

[13] Inns of court circles had shown interest in this type of conflict before *Jocasta*, when the recusant common lawyer Edmund Plowden had used the dilemma to exemplify his theory of the king's two bodies, albeit by referencing Agamemnon and his sacrifice of Iphigenia.

Works Cited

Aeschylus, 2014. *Persians. Seven Against Thebes. Suppliants. Prometheus Bound.* Edited and translated by Alan H. Sommerstein. Cambridge, MA: Harvard University Press.

Austen, Gillian. 2008. *George Gascoigne.* Woodbridge: D. S. Brewer.

———. 2013. "The Adventures Passed by Master George Gascoigne: Experiments in Prose." In *The Oxford Handbook of English Prose 1500–1640*, edited by Andrew Hadfield, 156–71. Oxford: Oxford University Press.

Axton, Marie. 1977. *The Queen's Two Bodies: Drama and the Elizabethan Succession.* London: Royal Historical Society.

Braden, Gordon. 2022. *Petrarchan Love and the English Renaissance.* Oxford: Oxford University Press.

British Library. Additional MS 34063.

Cunliffe, John W. 1912. *Early English Classical Tragedies.* Oxford: Clarendon Press.

Demetriou, Tania. 2021. "How Gabriel Harvey Read Tragedy." *Renaissance Studies* 35: 757–87.

Desai, Adhaar Noor. 2023. *Blotted Lines: Early Modern English Literature & the Poetics of Discomposition.* Ithaca, NY: Cornell University Press.

Dewar-Watson, Sarah. 2010. "*Jocasta* 'A Tragedie Written in Greeke'." *International Journal of the Classical Tradition* 17: 22–32.

Dolce, Ludovico. 1549. *Giocasta: Tragedia di M. Lodovico Dolce.* Venice.

Duncan-Jones, Katherine. 1991. *Sir Philip Sidney: Courtier Poet.* London: Hamish Hamilton.

Euripides. 1541. *Phoenissae, Euripidis Poetae Antiquissimi … Tragoediae XVIII.* Translated and edited by Collinus. Basel.

———. 1558. *Euripidis Tragoediae, quae hodie extant, omnes.* Translated and edited by Melanchthon. Basel.

———. 1562. *Euripides Poeta Tragicorum princeps, in Latinum sermonem conversus adjecto eregionè textu Graeco.* Translated and edited by Stiblinus. Basel.

———. 1994. *Euripides Phoenissae.* Edited by Donald J. Mastronarde. Cambridge: Cambridge University Press.

Gascoigne, George. 1573. *A Hundreth Sundrie Flowres.* London.

———. 1575. *The poesies of George Gascoigne Esquire.* London.

———. 2000. *George Gascoigne, A Hundreth Sundrie Flowers.* Edited by G. W. Pigman III. Oxford: Clarendon Press.

Grafton, Anthony, and Lisa Jardine, 1986. *From Humanism to the Humanities.* Cambridge, MA: Harvard University Press.

Hart, E. F., 1956. "The Answer Poem in the Early Seventeenth Century." *Review of English Studies* 7, no. 25: 19–29.

Helgerson, Richard. 1976. *The Elizabethan Prodigals.* Berkley: University of California Press.

Hetherington, Michael. 2016. "Gascoigne's Accidents: Contingency, Skill, and the Logic of Writing." *English Literary Renaissance* 46: 29–59.

Hughes, Thomas, *et al.* 1587. *Certaine deuises and shewes presented to her Majestie by the Gentlemen of Grayes-Inne at her Highnesse Court in Greenewich, the twenty eight day of Februarie in the thirtieth year of her Majesties most happy Raigne*. London.

Hughes, Felicity A. 1997. "Gascoigne's Poses." *Studies in English Literature* 37: 1–19.

Hutson, Lorna. 2023. *England's Insular Imagining: The Elizabethan Erasure of Scotland*. Cambridge: Cambridge University Press.

Kuin, Roger, 1998. *Chamber Music: Elizabethan Sonnet-Sequences and the Pleasure of Criticism*. Toronto: University of Toronto Press.

Mehl, Dieter. 1965. *The Elizabethan Dumb Show: The History of a Dramatic Convention*. London: Methuen.

Norland, Howard. 2009. *Neoclassical Tragedy in Elizabethan England*. Newark: University of Delaware Press.

Panofsky, Richard. 1975. "A descriptive study of mid-Tudor short poetry, 1557–1579." PhD diss., University of California, Santa Barbara.

Peacham, Henry. 1612. *Minerva Britanna or A garden of heroical deuices*. London.

Pfeiffer, Douglas S. 2022. *Authorial Personality and the Making of Renaissance Texts: The Force of Character*. Oxford: Oxford University Press.

Pigman III, G. W. 2010. "Gascoigne, George (1534/5?-1577), author and soldier." *Oxford Dictionary of National Biography*. Accessed 10 May 2024. https://www.oxforddnb.com/view/10.1093/ref:odnb/9780198614128.001.0001/odnb-9780198614128-e-10421.

Pollard, Tanya. 2017. *Greek Tragic Women on Shakespearean Stages*. Oxford: Oxford University Press.

Protector, Menander. 1851. *Fragmenta Historicorum Graecorum*. Edited by C. Müller. 5 vols. Paris.

Puttenham, George. 1589. *The Arte of English Poesie: Contriued into three Bookes: The first of Poets and Poesie, the second of Proportion, the third of Ornament*. London.

Pyré, Yves. 2020. "Eclectism and Syncreticism in Gascoigne and Kinwelmersh's *Jocasta*." *Translation and Literature* 29: 44–58.

Shrank, Cathy. 2008. "'Matters of Love as of Discourse': The English Sonnet, 1560–1580." *Studies in Philology* 105: 30–49.

Skura, Meredith Ane. 2008. *Tudor Autobiography: Listening for Inwardness*. Chicago: Chicago University Press.

Suthren, Carla. 2020. "Translation Commonplace Marks in Gascoigne and Kinwelmersh's *Jocasta*." *Translation and Literature* 29: 59–84.

Tzetzae, Joannis. 1826. *Historiarum Variarum Chiliades.* Edited by Theophilus Kiesslingus. Leipzig.

Winston, Jessica. 2011. "Lyric Poetry at the Early Elizabethan Inns of Court." In *The Intellectual and Cultural World of the Early Modern Inns of Court*, edited by Jayne Elisabeth Archer, Elizabeth Goldring, and Sarah Knight, 223–44. Manchester: Manchester University Press.

———. 2016. *Lawyers at Play: Literature, Law, and Politics at the Early Modern Inns of Court, 1558–1581.* Oxford: Oxford University Press.

CHAPTER 11

Gender, Revenge, and Legal Performance at the Inns of Court

Jessica Apolloni

The first known English play based on an Italian novella, *Gismond of Salerne* (1566), is an example of the popularity of classical translations and Italian adaptations at the inns of court. Writers in this collection, including Felicity Brown and Renae Satterley, offer interesting insights into the rich, intertextual environment at the inns. This chapter builds on such intertextual analysis to demonstrate how comparative influences became crucial to the development of revenge tragedy, connecting the origins of this popular genre to a legal setting. Jessica Winston's work, including a chapter in this collection, has demonstrated in detail how earlier plays at the inns such as *Misfortunes of Arthur* and *Gorboduc* employed Senecan-style

I wish to acknowledge Alexandra Sears's work as a research assistant in the initial stages of this project through Christopher Newport University's Summer Scholars Program.

J. Apolloni (✉)
English, Christopher Newport University, Newport News, VA, USA
e-mail: jessica.apolloni@cnu.edu

E. Rhatigan, J. Watson (eds.), *Mapping the Early Modern Inns of Court*, Early Modern Literature in History,
https://doi.org/10.1007/978-3-031-77445-4_11

tragedy, a form that was 'at that point native to the inns' (Winston 2016: 17). Winston's work has established the significant influence of Seneca and classical authors in the literary production of the inns, as well as innsmen's attraction to Senecan political ideas (Winston 2006). While members of the inns were actively translating classical texts, they were also absorbing Italian literature and culture. The first English plays based on Italian short stories—including *Gismond of Salerne* (1566) and Gascoigne's *Supposes* (1566)—were staged at the inns of court. Scholars have detailed how this interest in classical and Italian materials was a strategy of the innsmen to elevate their social status and illustrate their involvement in 'high culture' literary activities and knowledge (Domenichelli 2019). I argue a result of this phenomenon is the extent to which classical and Italian legal contexts frame revenge narratives at the inns and circulate comparative understandings of law in both legal and popular environments.

Examining the sources of inns of court plays also reveals a long-standing fascination with gender and revenge. *Gismond of Salerne*, like the inns plays *Gorboduc*, *Jocasta*, and *The Misfortunes of Arthur*, dramatises the close link between gender and vengeance at the heart of revenge narratives. This chapter explores the comparative, intertextual development of revenge narratives within and outside the inns of court by first tracing the genealogy of the genre to the legal spaces of the inns. In this broader view of revenge tragedy, gender dynamics central to plays' portrayals of retribution bring to light a recurring interest in legal performance and the legitimacy of violence. By analysing the longer trajectory of gender and revenge at the inns, I argue *Gismond* is an illustrative example of the way such narratives challenge key ethical issues in the performance of law. Specifically, the chapter considers how women like Gismond question who has the authority to perform law; what gives legal acts, especially violent acts, legitimacy; and how much emotion should be tied to legal performance.

Performing Classical Revenge

Composed by Robert Wilmot, Christopher Hatton, Henry Noel, and other members of the Inner Temple, *Gismond of Salerne* was performed for Queen Elizabeth during a Christmas celebration around 1566. Like *Jocasta*, *Gorboduc*, and *Misfortunes*, the play is highly influenced by Senecan tragedy popular at the inns during this period. The plot follows the first story on the fourth day of the *Decameron*: the widow Ghismonda (Gismond in the play) is forbidden to remarry by her father, Tancredi

(Tancred). Ghismonda initiates a secret affair with Guiscardo (Guishard), who is an earl in the English version. Tancredi takes a nap hidden away in Ghismonda's bedroom and discovers the lovers. This twist of fate occurs because of fickle fortune in Boccaccio and through the more menacing forces of Cupid and Megaera in the English play. Tancredi orders the execution of Guiscardo, placing his heart in a cup to be delivered to Ghismonda. She commits suicide to avenge Guiscardo's death and punish her father. The two lovers are then buried together in the same tomb. While Boccaccio's version concludes by discussing the noble afterlife and reputation of the lovers, the English play highlights Gismond's act of revenge on her father and King Tancred's plans to kill himself and be placed in the same tomb as his daughter.

Ghismonda's story and its heightening of Senecan revenge in *Gismond* anticipates the more official 'revenge tragedy' genre on the popular English stage. In addition to Winston's scholarship, Bradley J. Irish also traces the genealogy of revenge tragedy to the Senecan dramas of the 1560s at the inns of court, looking at the influence of revenge in early plays to the more established genre as it is later adopted in *The Spanish Tragedy* and meticulously detailing the Elizabethan interest in vengeance as a key thematic and structural element of early theatre at the inns (2009). While analysis of popular revenge tragedy often relies on the perceived binary, as Derek Dunne explains, between public law and justice, and private revenge and vengeance, work in the field of law and literature has shown the deep connections between the performance of revenge and the performance of law (2016). Classical and Italianate revenge narratives are crucial to this connection and offer a fascinating textual history and memory that repeatedly conflates revenge and justice.

While the style of *Gismond of Salerne* is often described as a mix of Senecan elements applied to Boccaccio's novella, scholars have also noted how much Boccaccio was building from classical features of tragedy in the tales told on day four of the *Decameron*. For example, James C. Kriesel details how Boccaccio's tragedy was influenced by Ovid and Seneca and demonstrates that Ghismonda's story embodies theatrical elements such as the narrative staging of different scenes and the performative role of an audience operating in a similar fashion to a classical chorus (2016). Kriesel argues that Boccaccio was especially interested in the synthesis of politics, violence, and fortune in classical texts (426). This synthesis, intensified and transformed to an English context, is particularly relevant to gender and revenge at the inns of court. Comparing Boccaccio to *Gismond* establishes the significance of gender dynamics in classical revenge imagery as well as the narratives' larger performance of (in)justice through supernatural forces.

Boccaccio's tale is representative of classical reception in Italy, synthesising ideas on fortune, authority, and violence that became prevalent in Italian Renaissance literature. The inns play further intensifies and dramatises these crucial classical concepts within a legal context. Specifically, the play's dominant characters of Cupid and Megaera establish a revenge motif linking representations of fortune to divine retribution. The vital link between these two characters creates a critical view of divine retribution and participates in gendered representations of fortune, justice, and revenge—which often overlap in intriguing ways. The play opens with Cupid describing his motives for violence as an attempt to restore his own honour, a frame narrative very common to revenge plays:

> But now the world, not seing in these dayes
> Such present proues of myne almighty power,
> Disdaines my name, and seketh sondry wayes
> To conquer and deface me euerie houre.
> My name supprest to raise againe therfore,
> And in this age myne honor and renome
> By mighty act intending to restore,
> Down to the earth in spite now am I come.
> (1.1.49–56)[1]

Scholars have highlighted the overarching change to Ghismonda's story stemming from Cupid's vindictive character. Frederick Kiefer states the inns writers 'profoundly alter the spirit of Boccaccio's novella, for their Cupid is a savage creature, bristling with hostility and fury' (1977: 38). Kiefer then demonstrates the importance of Cupid's stated purpose of regaining his own reputation through violent means as a stark contrast to the representation of love and fortune in Boccaccio's tale. Jane Kingsley-Smith (2008) similarly notes how the opening lines illustrate Cupid as both a Senecan revenger and consumptive disease infecting the play, pointing to the lines 'I drink the louers blood, / and eate the liuing hart within his brest' (1.1.11–12). Significantly, Kingsley-Smith details how Cupid's lines are at times borrowed almost verbatim from the opening of Lodovico

[1] All quotations from *Gismond* are taken from Cunliffe (1912).

Dolce's *Didone*, a text and author essential to the 1566 inns play *Jocasta* (203), which is discussed in this volume by Felicity Brown. Cupid's lines consequently reflect an ongoing interest in Senecan violence at the inns that stems from classical translations as well as classically inspired Italian texts that were becoming increasingly popular among innsmen. Cupid's violent characterisation in the play develops out of such Senecan interest and adds a critical layer to Boccaccio's representation of love and fortune.

Cupid's actions in the play transform Boccaccio's portrayal of love as an ennobling force into one where the lovers are cynically unable to avoid their disastrous fate (Ruggiero 2014). While characters in *Gismond* certainly feel like 'unwitting puppets in a bloody demonstration of Love's power', Cupid's violence is specifically tied to the personified force of revenge (Kingsley-Smith 2008: 203). After Cupid has 'enflamed' Gismond and the two lovers have begun their secret affair, Cupid's revenge plot relies on one of the classical furies, Megaera. At the beginning of Act 4, Megaera rises out of hell and states that she brings 'Vengeance and blood' to Gismond's cursed house. While the chorus often criticises the affair and moralises on feminine virtue, Megaera interestingly explains the reason she has been sent from Pluto's realm in relation to Cupid's cruel aspirations. She details how Mercury reported to the underworld that Cupid filled Gismond's heart with 'fickle ioy' because he was 'hyely disdaining his renomes decay', and wanted to 'shew by profe of woefull end / some terror vnto those that scorne his name' (4.1.20–25). She then reminds the audience of Pluto's friendship with Cupid, before detailing how Pluto decided on this course of action after receiving advice from Minos and others, including the vengeful ghost of Gismond's former husband: a layer of revenge absent from Boccaccio. Cupid and various forces of revenge and divine retribution are thus linked in this critical moment and throughout the remainder of the play. Megaera and Cupid even have the shared imagery of a serpent: the Chorus describes Cupid as a 'slye snake' lying in wait under flowers and Megaera claims she will throw a 'stinging snake' into the breast of Gismond and her father so that they cause each other's death (Stallybrass 1991–1992). Significantly, she states she will accomplish this in order to make 'Cupid Lord of his will' before claiming Furies send pain to those who cannot restrain themselves from sin (4.1.37). Megaera does not simply moralise the affair but also illustrates how the lovers' downfall is a part of Cupid's plot that no one can prevent.

Linking Megaera's divine vengeance to Cupid's plot creates a hostile image of fate, fortune, and divine retribution in the play. Cupid punishes characters for a desire he creates so that the play develops a peculiarly self-fulfilling sense of retribution (Kingsley-Smith 2008). In comparison to Boccaccio, Kiefer details how the divine force of fortune becomes vengeance in *Gismond*: 'Justice in the shape of revenge informs the play from beginning to end; practically every character is either an executor or victim of revenge' (1977: 42). Kiefer also points out the Senecan logic or mathematical reasoning in the play's representation of revenge as a balancing force, a concept which connects to scholarship on revenge embodying ideas of fairness and numeric equality—most notably work by Linda Woodbridge (2010). While she focuses on popular revenge narratives, *Gismond of Salerne* fits into Woodbridge's fascinating study of the overlapping images of justice, fortune, and revenge in early modern perceptions of equality. For example, she synthesises common Aristotelian and biblical views of justice embedded in the iconographic image of scales to demonstrate how revenge narratives often unite numeric and retaliatory justice. Cupid's opening lines in *Gismond* specifically draw the audience's attention to the imagery of scales; he claims he rules the world with one hand that bears 'vain hope, short ioyfull state' and the other holding 'repentance all to late' and 'paines without recure' (1.1.5–8). Yet Cupid's self-fulfilling divine retribution distorts the balance or fairness implied by this imagery of a scale and speaks to a more cynical view of fortune and justice as subjects to the whims of Cupid's wrath.

Cupid's link to fortune and justice in the imagery of balancing scales becomes even more critical when considering the representation of his character as a blind force throughout *Gismond* (Kingsley-Smith 2008: 202). Cupid's blindness correlates with Woodbridge's discussion of cynical perceptions of fortune and justice in the early modern period that led to the popularity of revenge narratives. The blindfold common to representations of the female Justitia and Fortuna has often been interpreted in terms of neutrality, and Woodbridge describes how this extends even to representations of Cupid as hooded. Yet Woodbridge illustrates how Fortuna's blindfold, often perceived as the 'callous indifference as to who prospers and who plummets', became increasingly tied to Justitia's iconography (2010: 111). In this overlap, the apathetic or careless balance of fortune could be conflated with the balance of justice. When the Chorus is told of Guishard's execution, the messenger describes 'false fortune' multiple times, and claims his death is a result of 'injust fortune, that so seld upheaues / the worthy man, hath blindly turned her whele' (5.133–34). These crucial lines exemplify Woodbridge's larger claim that 'even when doomed, revengers are existential heroes in a culture which, seeking justice, found chance and fortune' (2010: 115). The violent representation of fortune in *Gismond of Salerne*, as well as Cupid's self-fulfilling divine retribution, anticipates this larger phenomenon in popular revenge tragedy and creates a similar sense of heroism for the doomed lovers. Divine forces are not merely apathetic but antagonistic, and this disparaging portrayal amplifies the relationship between fortune, justice, and revenge in this play. The gendered imagery connecting Fortuna and Justitia is further complicated by the play's specific design to intersect these concepts with the character Megaera—pointing to a larger, often conflicted, history of linking gender and vengeance.

The overlay of fortune, justice, and revenge in *Gismond* exemplifies the complex history of gender and revenge iconography. Vengeance has long been a part of traditional honour-based customs where it has often been perceived as the social or even moral obligation of men. Male characters such as Odysseus, Beowulf, and Hamlet star in revenge narratives, reinforcing their reputations as heroes. But there is equally a long tradition of female characters in revenge narratives—including classical female avengers such as Medea and Clytemnestra—with varied afterlives. The gendering of revenge and its ability to function as both a repressive and disruptive force is detailed in fascinating length in Lesel Dawson and Fiona McHardy's edited collection, which states that there is still much to uncover in this field of study (2018). Scholars such as Marguerite Tassi have also described the powerful iconography of revenge as female in linguistic terms; where Latin and romance languages gender revenge as feminine; in the classical representation of Furies and the gender connotations of the word 'fury'; and in numerous other mythical female figures of revenge such as Nemesis who, like the Furies, persecutes the guilty (2011).[2] As we turn to inns of court plays like *Gismond*, they appear 'haunted' by supernatural and classical revenge icons embodying and performing the memory of past wrongs (Brown 2021).

Megaera's character in *Gismond of Salerne* adds to this complicated iconographic history and is also representative of a larger pattern of furies appearing in inns of court plays. Both *Gorboduc* and *The Misfortunes of Arthur* have stage directions at critical moments utilising Furies as spectres of vengeance. In such moments, Furies perform classical memory and gendered images of revenge but also represent a performative act of

[2] On the gendered connotations of furies, see Steenbergh (2012: 123).

justice. Throughout the classical and neoclassical drama, Furies play an important role in 'making death matter in living relationships', where they act upon the resentments of the dead to personify memories of past harm (Tassi 2011: 37). Supernatural vengeance recording historical and even legal memory is similarly represented by Nemesis in Francis Bacon's *The Wisdome of the Ancients* (1619), where Nemesis is 'a Goddesse venerable vnto all' and her name 'doth signifie Reuenge or Retribution' (cited in Tassi 2011: 35). This powerful equation of revenge and divine retribution is likewise performed by the Furies of inns of court plays. Megaera's appearance in *Gismond* exemplifies how supernatural and gendered forces of vengeance at the inns of court began to conflate a simple binary of performing justice versus revenge.

In addition to the Furies, inns plays continually translate and perform classical tales of women avengers. These plays are haunted, to use Felicity Brown's term for the ghosts of other texts in revenge narratives, by both supernatural forces and intertextual memories that are performed in scenes centred on representations of authority, emotion, and the legitimacy of violence. Queen Videna echoes Medea in *Gorboduc* and characters in *Jocasta* (1566) similarly re-perform classical myths amplifying a narrative of revenge and violence (Steenbergh 2012: 127). In *The Misfortunes of Arthur*, another play interested in ideas of law, legitimacy, and violence, Guenevora contemplates revenge by ventriloquising classical wronged wives at moments when they wrestle with and accept their roles as avengers (specifically Clytemnestra, Deianira, and Medea).[3] In addition to performing past female icons and vengeance, female characters are also taken over by the force of Furies. In *Gorboduc*, Queen Videna takes revenge on her remaining son 'moved by Furies'. Megaera similarly claims she will possess Gismond's body to fill her with wrath. While Guenevora in *Misfortunes* ultimately decides not to take revenge, she initially invites avenging furies to her breast, claiming 'wrong cannot be reveng'd, but by excesse' (1.2).[4] Moments like this illustrate the embodied performative aspect of classical Furies, where it was a common convention for supernatural forces to overcome an avenger's body to call out and act on past wrongs. Collectively, the performance of these avenging women includes

[3] Brown (2021: 162) details how Guenevora's lines are mostly composed of translations from *Thyestes*, *Hercules Oetaeus*, and *Agamemnon*; Steenbergh (2012: 130) notes that Mordred actually continues Clytemnestra's lines after Guenevora leaves the stage as well.

[4] See Winston's discussion of this section in Chap. 2.

a re-presentation of classical memory and images of revenge as female but also demonstrates a performative act of justice exemplified in the Furies' punitive spirits. Characters like Gismond, Guenevora, and Videna consequently employ a kind of double haunting of classical conventions and past wrongs in each play.

Such characters represent and complicate gendered perceptions of revenge and speak to larger issues in the performance of law. Women who take on avenging roles in these inns plays reconsider views of the ancient *lex talionis* as retributive justice and illustrate some of the larger ethics of legal performance. As scholars like Tassi have argued, female avengers often challenge legal authority, show failures of civic justice, and reveal corruptions of a male-dominated political system (2011: 22). This larger pattern of gender and revenge pulls together iconographic history and textual genealogies of inns of court plays. In *Gismond of Salerne*, Megaera in particular points to the increasing interrelationship between fortune, justice, and revenge so that the play can be read as a form of history that is re-presenting legal memory during a critical time at the inns and the development of the English legal system.

Performing Authority and Legal Violence

The supernatural embodiment and classical representations of performing vengeance are also specifically tied to socio-political elements of legal performance in *Gismond* and similar plays. Woodbridge, for example, synthesises ideas of fortune, justice, and revenge in political readings of revenge literature by examining Senecan influences and resistance theory (2010). Applying political readings of *Gismond* to the performance of law demonstrates how gender dynamics inherent in Boccaccio's tale and its afterlife explore the authority of legal performances such as the legal power of the monarch, as well as the ethics of legal performative violence. Boccaccio is clearly invested in the interrelated topics of ethics, poetics, and politics through Ghismonda's story and the tale echoes ethical concepts from his introduction to day four (Kriesel 2016: 427). Yet, in a detailed study of the adaptations and afterlives of this particular tale, Peter Stallybrass uncovers a larger shift in later versions, and especially *Gismond of Salerne*, that focus on the staging of power and sovereignty (1991–1992: 317–18). Examining the play's gendered representation of legal-political power, especially in the monarch's lethal legal performance, adds another layer to the intricate connections between gender and revenge at the inns of court.

Scholars have analysed the political environment of the inns and their aims in performing plays for Queen Elizabeth. For example, Jessica Winston's *Lawyers At Play* expertly details how the inns used literary texts to establish their own networks, strengthen their authority, and provide advice to the monarch. In political interpretations of *Gismond*, scholars such as Marie Axton, Jane Kingsley-Smith, and Curtis Perry have argued that the play comments specifically on issues surrounding Elizabeth's marriage and succession (see, for example, Perry 2014: 282). Such studies point to parallels in the play that relate to key political debates between Elizabeth and parliament in the 1560s and discuss strong connections to the secret union between Catherine Grey and Edward Seymour, earl of Hertford.[5] This political context makes sense of the play's portrayal of desire and control as threatening, destructive, and destabilising forces. Kingsley-Smith asserts 'Elizabeth's defiance of desire makes her an obvious target for Cupid's revenge' and details how the play's casting of desire as a disease could relate to Elizabeth's recent health concerns as threats to the monarch's physical body and ability to maintain order (2008: 206–10). Perry similarly connects physical and emotional threats surrounding the succession debate to issues of stability, claiming the play illustrates how Tancred's 'efforts to control marriage and succession prove stifling and culminate in tyranny' (2014: 288). While Perry argues that the play's portrayal of tyranny might advertise the inn's ability to contribute to a more balanced style of government, this political context also brings us back to the gendered connections between fortune and revenge.

The volatility of Elizabeth's succession aligns with the portrayal of Fortuna's mutability in countless revenge narratives, and *Gismond* continually highlights gendered connotations of this sense of governmental instability. Avengers in early modern theatre often confront tyrannical characters acting as unpredictable and capricious as fortune in their performance of authority. Furthermore, inns' revenge narratives like *Gismond* build from classical portrayals of political corruption. Highlighting gendered elements—in which the play often anatomises and symbolises the lovesick, female body—locates *Gismond* within Senecan conventions representing corruption (Kingsley-Smith 2008: 200). Common themes of incestual desire and familial strife connect it to the plays mentioned in the

[5] Scholars have noted that changing Gismond's secret lover to be an earl would parallel Catherine Grey, and Perry describes how the later printed edition has an epistle and dedication that frame text as a 'Grey family artifact' (2014: 283).

previous section too, including *Misfortunes of Arthur*, *Gorboduc*, and *Jocasta*. As a particularly strong example of this connection between gender and classical views of political instability and tyranny, Perry reads the addition of Gismond's Aunt, Lucrece, to the play as a Senecan model of decline and decay of the state (2014: 288). Here, as with the other inns plays, *Gismond* echoes Seneca as an 'invaluable literary model for the representation of political imbalance and social degeneration' (289). Political readings of *Gismond* open up a larger view of gender dynamics in classically influenced representations of political authority and stability. At the same time, the play's politics and power dynamics also raise issues of performing law through a gendered lens, especially regarding the emotion and violence connected to a monarch's legal performance.

Tancred's character is unpredictable and emotional to a fault in both Boccaccio's tale and *Gismond*. Scholars have described how his behaviour fits into a larger gendered analysis of passion as unpredictable and unfitting to a ruling persona. Tancredi / Tancred's inability to rule over himself is thus perceived as effeminate as well as a reason why he should not rule over others (Sherberg 2011: 123; Winston 2016: Chap. 8). Within political interpretations of the play, both Tancred and Gismond could be mirrors for Elizabeth—either in her 'exemplary chastity', as 'the antidote to the effeminate passions elsewhere on display', or in her authoritative desire to control her succession (Perry 2014: 284). Kristine Steenbergh argues that Senecan revenge plays at the inns set up a contrast between feminine fury and masculine control as a way for the inns to establish a difference between legal order and passionate revenge (2012: 133). While this is certainly a part of the representation of gender and emotion in inns plays, the line between order and revenge is continually blurred in plays like *Gismond*. Consequently, even when such plays reinforce gendered stereotypes, they also inevitably illustrate interesting questions about emotion in legal power and processes.

This overlap of gender and emotion in the performance of authority is vital to key legal scenes from Boccaccio and *Gismond*. Ghismonda's character in the *Decameron* initially appears to be another example of widows who threaten civic stability, a conventional trope common to Italian writers like Dante and Petrarch (Wainwright 2023). However, scholars such as Guido Ruggiero have argued that Ghismonda and Guiscardo represent the cultural values of honour and *virtù*, which are particularly emphasised when reading the text within a Florentine context. In this perspective, Ghismonda's character is a direct contrast to Tancredi's lack of self-control, and the lovers' burial and ceremony creates a public approval of their love that solidifies their legacy (2014: 1181). Yet there are gendered elements crucial to this sense of *virtù* in which Ghismonda takes on the disposition of a man to be in line with the gendered associations of tragedy (Kriesel 2016: 433). Comparing the actions of Ghismonda's character to legal performances in *Gismond* allows for further exploration of emotion and gendered perceptions of performing authority. Boccaccio includes a lengthy, logical defence from Ghismonda when she is confronted by her father, and this is a moment that scholars have argued mirrors a court scene. This legal debate between Ghismonda and Tancredi is absent in the inns play and instead, *Gismond* focuses on the intense emotions and grisly violence of Guishard's execution. A comparison of the different focal points of legal performance in these two versions highlights critical questions on the ethics of performing legal authority.

Ghismonda's sense of *virtù* stems in large part from this pivotal defence scene. Once Tancredi has spied on the lovers, he confronts Ghismonda and she offers a detailed defence of her actions and finds fault in Tancredi's lack of reason. In his book on law and gender in the *Decameron*, Michael Sherberg describes this scene as operating like a trial in which Ghismonda replies with 'juridical argumentation' and 'peppers her discourse with references to law and sin, presenting a careful theory of both' (2011: 122). As a part of this defence, Ghismonda offers critical views of Tancredi's authority and incorporates religious ideas relating to equity in the body politic (Kriesel 2016: 434). Ghismonda's legal-political discourse acts as a stark contrast to Tancredi's emotional rule and contributes to the complicated synthesis of emotion, *virtù*, and authority in Boccaccio's novella. While Ghismonda's performance in this scene offers insights into gendered portrayals of emotion and legal-political authority, the authors of *Gismond of Salerne* sharpen these same questions within emotion and the performance of legal power.

Gismond does not share this same defence in the play because Tancred claims he has already decided on his course of action for the 'vile traitor' Guishard (4.3.26). When asked to defend her life, Gismond defiantly refuses, stating she would if there were any possibility of Tancred changing his mind (4.3). Instead, the play focuses on the lethal performance of the monarch in Guishard's execution scene, transferring the legal performance of Ghismonda's defence to an illustration of state performative violence. In the *Decameron*, Tancredi commands those guarding Guiscardo to strangle him without any noise in the night and take his heart, which they 'performed according to their charge' (Kingsley-Smith 2008: 211). However, the play heightens the violence and emotion of this scene through the character Renunchio, who acts as a Senecan messenger describing the execution's extreme violence which occurred offstage:

> After his breath was gone
> Bereft thus from his brest by cruell force
> Streight they despoiled him, and, not alone
> Contented wth his death, on the dead corps,
> Whom savage beastes do spare, ginne they to showe
> New crueltie, and wth a swerd they pearce
> His naked belly, and unrippe it soe
> That out the bowelles gush. Whoe can rehearse
> The dolefull sight, wherewth my hart even bledde?
> The warme entrailes were toren out of his brest
> Wthin their handes trembling not fully dead:
> His veines smoked: his bowelles all to strest
> Ruthelesse were rent, and throwen amidde the place:
> All clottered lay the blood in lompes of gore,
> Sprent on his corps, and on his paled face.
> His hart panting out from his brest they tore,
> And cruelly upon a swordes point
> They fixe the same, and in this woful wise
> Unto the King this hart do they present,
> A sight longed for to fede his irefull eyes. (5.1.173–92)

The violence in this description amplifies the Senecan aspects of the play and resembles public executions for Elizabethan traitors. Articles on *Gismond* by Stallybrass, Perry, and Kingsley-Smith all discuss this moment as a legal performance of the monarch's power over a subject's life, displaying Tancred's political authority over a rebellious criminal body. However, as with public executions, such violence can also be a disruptive force to this display of power. As the execution is conducted in a dark, hidden, and private space, there is a subversive emotional effect on those performing the execution and in its retelling.

The audience hears about Guishard's execution from a conversation between the Chorus and Renuncio, who goes into dramatic detail similar to a lawyer's presentation of a past crime. In his retelling, Renuncio's character incorporates circumstantial and forensic detail in a rhetorical mode common to training at the inns (Hutson 2007, 2015). Renuncio discusses at length how the hidden away place where the execution occurred is sinister, describing the location as an 'uggly', dark, horrible cave. He then claims servants had been sent 'to *perform*' (emphasis mine) 'the horror' and rage of King Tancred's 'furious brest' (5.1.63–72). Renuncio's description of the shock and revulsion of the officials in charge of performing Tancred's fury is in stark contrast to his account of Guishard: 'whome neither grefe ne fere could taint' (5.1.91). When analysing gendered elements of the play, Perry argues Tancred's unruly emotion 'is complemented by the depiction of Guishard's death, an account which emphasises his stoic, masculine self-control in the face of terror' (2014: 285). Yet this same effeminate passion extends to the location of the execution, the legal authorities performing legal violence, and Renuncio's own performance retelling the act to the Chorus. Renuncio is the voice of lament in this play, beginning Act 5 with the lines: 'O cruel fate! O dolefull destinie! / O heauy hap! O woe can not be told!' (5.1.1–2). The emotional performance of lament, particularly in *lex talionis* systems of justice, has a long history of gendered connotations similar to the role of classical furies dramatising the memory of past wrongs. Yet Renuncio's continual lament, as well as the heightened depictions of emotion in violent legal performance, demonstrates a more complicated view of the way emotion is tied to legal processes.

Renuncio's passionate lament is also skeptical of Tancred's authority. His character asks: 'Is this Salerne I see? / What? Doeth king Tancred gouern here, and guide? / Is this the place where ciuile people be?' (5.1.21–23). Here, lamenting questions tie political readings of the play to a critical view of performing power and legal authority. This stark contrast with the death of Guiscardo in Boccaccio's tale, as well as the contrast with Ghismonda's perceived trial scene, demonstrates how the play utilises Senecan elements to probe questions of emotion, violence, and authority that become so central to revenge tragedy. *Gismond*'s depiction of gender dynamics connected to legal power and political corruption not only contributes to a larger pattern of gender and revenge narratives at the inns but also anticipates later politically charged revenge plays by writers like Marston, Ford, and Webster.

Performing Legal Vengeance

While Guiscardo's execution provokes a critical view of authority and lethal legal performance in Boccaccio and the play, Ghismonda's death in retaliation further highlights a conflation of law and revenge. This creates a logic in which Tancred is operating as revenge and Gismond as justice, despite the gendered and political identities associated with their characters. In each version of the story, Ghismonda creates a public, ritualised spectacle, utilising the heart of her executed lover that has been brought to her in a cup. Both versions similarly call attention to the bitter turns of fortune, with Gismond saying to the heart of Guiscard that it has been dispatched 'fro snares / of fortunes venomed bayt' (5.2.34–35). In both versions, Ghismonda / Gismond emphasises her death is to ensure justice for Guiscardo. While Ghismonda's actions in Boccaccio exemplify honour and vendetta contexts crucial to Italian conceptions of justice, at the inns of court her death is further stressed as an act of both revenge and justice. This act of legal vengeance, especially read through the lens of gender, challenges patriarchal legal authority and characterises legal performance as a performance of revenge.

Ghismonda's death in Boccaccio is a ritualised performance, with Kriesel noting the religious parody of Guiscardo's heart in a cup and the significance of her surrounding ladies presenting as a chorus (2016: 435). This ritualistic death is also, as Stallybrass describes, 'staged for public consumption' in front of her ladies-in-waiting and her father' (1991–1992: 306–07). While Ghismonda's actions in the story have often been in secretive settings, her death as a public performance also fits within the logic of Italian vendettas. Legal historians like Edward Muir have detailed the cultural importance of vendettas when preserving honour and *virtù*, in which the logic of getting even requires one to match 'anger with anger, insult with insult, injury with injury, death with death' (Woodbridge 2010: 41). Ghismonda's death calls attention to this important value in her vendetta for Guisciardo's murder.

At the same time as Ghismonda's death signifies the logic of Italian vendettas, her character's lasting legacy in the community of Boccaccio's story stems from her actions fulfilling this vengeance. The tale ends by explaining how this was the lamentable end of the lovers and that Tancredi repented his cruelty too late. And, most importantly, Boccaccio details the communal mourning of everyone in Salerno, in which the lovers were honourably placed together in the same tomb. Ruggiero states that the ending of the tale displays both 'the noble and enobling' anguish of these lovers and their deaths—where the conclusion focuses on the 'public mourning that invariably evaluates both the life and love of the couples positively' (2014: 1170). In this same line of thinking, Stallybrass focuses on how Ghismonda's character transforms the perceived 'infamy' of an unchaste woman into a memorialised fame for herself and her lover, specifically relating this to the Italian legal concept of *fama* (or reputation) when claiming Ghismonda appropriates 'the masculine definition of *fama* as honour and glory while attributing to Tancredi the feminized definition of *fama* as infamy' (1991–1992: 306). Ghismonda consequently subverts legal-political power and authority and this continues through the long trajectory of this popular tale as well. Ghismonda's challenge to legal power and order is perhaps part of the reason her story has such a lasting legacy through multiple translations and adaptations, leading to the version performed at the inns of court.

The play calls further attention to Gismond's performative revenge as legal vengeance. When Gismond is made aware of Guiscard's death, she states: 'Shall I not work some iust reuenge on him / That thus hath slayen my loue?' (5.2.65–66). The sentiment of 'just revenge' is repeated multiple times in this scene and represents Guiscard's execution as a wrong that requires retribution. Similarly to Boccaccio, Gismond creates a ritual that counteracts her lover's execution and, in this process, inverts the lethal patriarchal power of Tancred. The political aspects of legal legitimacy questioned in Gismond's actions are further explained in Stallybrass: 'It is Gismund who turns her death into a public display which recasts Tancred's power as the dark and secretive workings of tyranny. Staging the heart of her lover, Gismund eclipses the head of family and state alike'. Stallybrass thus concludes that Gismond's death collapses 'the violent hierarchy of the body politic' (1991–1992: 321–22). Gismond's vengeance, operating as justice, cuts at the core legitimacy and political power of law embodied in Tancred. Her death as a public legal performance unites classical understandings of performing revenge with a clear alternative to the political power of a monarch. This legal vengeance consequently stems from both the long history of gender and revenge ingrained in the play's Senecan and Italian influences, as well as the gendered legal-political questions at the forefront of inns plays in this period.

While Gismond's death is a performative moment conflating revenge and justice, her requested epitaph further exemplifies the sense of law as a performance of memory.

> "Loe here within one to[m]be whear harbor twaine,
> Gismonda Quene, and Counte Palurine:
> She loued him, he for her loue was slayen,
> For whose reuenge eke lyes she here in shrine." (5.3.45–48)

Gismond frames the collective memory of her death as vengeance for the murder of Guischard, memorialising these actions as 'just revenge'. Woodbridge makes this connection in her study of how revenge narratives in England were tied to a sense of Italian bookkeeping or *ricordanza*—in which revenge 'balances the books' in the same way justice rights a wrong. Gismond's death, as a legal performance, balances the past wrong of her lover's death and this is then captured as a collective memory in the epitaph. By adding this crucial epitaph, the authors of *Gismond of Salerne* dramatise the way law is performance as well as the memory or record (*ricordanza*) of that performance.

The conflation of performing law and revenge in these versions of the Ghismonda tale is especially relevant to an inns' context. Members of the inns of court were constantly practising and contemplating the performative aspects of the profession, as detailed in Julie Stone Peters' recent book *Law as Performance* (2022). Authors in this collection, such as Jackie Watson and Jessica Winston, have similarly addressed the different legal performances occurring within the inns, including moots and revels. This performance of *Gismond* even relates to the way inns capture legal memory and precedent at this crucial time in English law. As demonstrated in this case study of *Gismond*, gender is an important lens through which to view these performances. Steenbergh discusses inns of court plays as employing gender to reinforce patriarchal legal power, claiming they 'seek to discredit private revenge as passionate and excessive, and mark it as feminine to counter aristocratic discourses in which revenge is regarded as a masculine duty' (2012: 129). While there are certainly moments in inns plays reinforcing stereotypes of feminine passion and fury, they are challenged in a play like *Gismond* where Tancred's actions as the legal monarch are perceived as 'private' and 'passionate' and Gismond's death a public duty to regain the *virtù* or honour of the couple. *Gismond* thus speaks to innsmen's concerns about the difference between performing revenge and performing justice.

Recent scholarship on gender and revenge has demonstrated how women's vengeance can act as a counternarrative to legal power, question ethical and moral elements of legal performance, and critique patriarchal systems of governance and law (Tassi 2011: 12). Interestingly, this also extends to the common conception of legal authorities operating as ministers of God's moral vengeance. Justice as a performance of God's vengeance directed through a given magistrate is an extremely common argument in popular pamphlets describing executions and other forms of legal violence (Kesselring 2019: Chap. 5). Such sources illustrate the messy distinctions between vengeance and justice in the early modern period that also continue in courtrooms today. Woodbridge points to this understanding of lethal punishments as God's divine vengeance as one of the reasons revenge tragedy becomes so popular on stage, suggesting that such plays 'finely calibrated retaliations mimic justice, claiming a rival legitimacy' (2010: 18). With the overlapping and critical views of fortune and justice as 'blind' described earlier, revenge narratives complicate our understanding of what kind of action, violent or otherwise, should occur to achieve justice in a community.

Gismond of Salerne is just one example of a larger group of plays at the inns of court focused on revenge, gender, and legal performance. *Misfortunes of Arthur*, *Gorboduc*, *Jocasta*, and others exhibit how gender is linked to revenge narratives at the inns of court. These plays' obsession with tyranny and courtly environments, in part stemming from classical and Italian sources, created a template for popular revenge stories and foregrounded important questions regarding the legitimacy, violence, and emotion of legal performance. With the popularity of revenge tragedy, such questions quickly moved beyond the inns of court in plays by Kyd, Shakespeare, Webster, and Marston, all continuing this pattern of gendered revenge as a place to interrogate issues of legal performance. Metatheatrical moments so common to revenge tragedy, as well as the intertextuality at the genre's core, contribute to the sense that these stories of gendered revenge are performing the past: holding both legal and historical memory.

Works Cited

Bacon, Francis. 1619. *The Wisdome of the Ancients*. London.

Brown, Felicity. 2021. "Sourcing *Misfortunes*: Translation and Tragedy." *Early Theatre* 24, no. 2: 157–70.

Cunliffe, J. W., ed. 1912. *Early English Classical Tragedies*. Oxford: Clarendon Press.

Dawson, Lesel, and Fiona McHardy, eds. 2018. *Revenge and Gender in Classical, Medieval, and Renaissance Literature*. Edinburgh: Edinburgh University Press.

Domenichelli, Mario. 2019. "Senecan Tragedy in the English Renaissance." In *The Routledge Research Companion to Anglo-Italian Renaissance Literature and Culture*, edited by Michele Marrapodi, 129–44. New York: Routledge.

Dunne, Derek. 2016. *Shakespeare, Revenge Tragedy, and Early Modern Law*. Basingstoke: Palgrave.

Hutson, Lorna. 2007. *The Invention of Suspicion: Law and Mimesis in Shakespeare and Renaissance Drama*. Oxford: Oxford University Press.

———. 2015. *Circumstantial Shakespeare*. Oxford: Oxford University Press.

Irish, Bradley J. 2009. "Vengeance, Variously: Revenge Before Kyd in Early Elizabethan Drama." *Early Theatre* 12, no. 2: 117–34.

Kesselring, K. J. 2019. *Making Murder Public*. Oxford: Oxford University Press.

Kiefer, Frederick. 1977. "Love and Fortune in Boccaccio's Tancredi and Ghismonda Story and in Wilmot's 'Gismond of Salerne'". *Renaissance and Reformation* 1, no. 1: 36–46.

Kingsley-Smith, Jane. 2008. "'Gismond of Salerne:' An Elizabethan and Cupidean Tragedy." *The Yearbook of English Studies*. 38, no. 1/2: 199–215.

Kriesel, James. 2016. "Boccaccio and the Early Modern Reception of Tragedy." *Renaissance Quarterly* 69, no. 2: 415–48.

Perry, Curtis. 2014. "*Gismond of Salern* and the Elizabethan Politics of Senecan Drama." In *Gender Matters: Discourses of Violence in Early Modern Literature and the Arts*, edited by Mara R. Wade, 279–95. New York: Rodopi.

Peters, Julie Stone. 2022. *Law as Performance: Theatricality, Spectatorship, and the Making of Law in Ancient, Medieval, and Early Modern Europe*. Oxford: Oxford University Press.

Ruggiero, Guido. 2014. "Getting a Head in the Renaissance: Mementos of Lost Love in Boccaccio and Beyond." *Renaissance Quarterly* 67, no. 4: 1165–90.

Sherberg, Michael. 2011. *The Governance of Friendship: Law and Gender in the Decameron*. Columbus: The Ohio State University Press.

Stallybrass, Peter. 1991–1992. "Dismemberments and Re-memberments: Rewriting the Decameron, 4.1, in the English Renaissance." *Studi sul Boccaccio* 20: 299–324.

Steenbergh, Kristine. 2012. "Emotions and Gender: The Case of Anger in Early Modern English Revenge Tragedies." In *A History of Emotions, 1200–1800*, edited by Jonas Liliequist, 119–34. London: Routledge.

Tassi, Marguerite. 2011. *Women and Revenge in Shakespeare: Gender, Genre and Ethics*. Selinsgrove, PA: Susquehanna University Press.

Wainwright, Anna. 2023. "Widows, Lament, and Ottoman Anxieties in Renaissance Florence." In *Gendering the Renaissance: Text and Context in Early Modern Italy*, edited by Meredith K. Ray, 23–43. Newark: University of Delaware Press.

Winston, Jessica. 2006. "Seneca in Early Elizabethan England." *Renaissance Quarterly* 59, no 1: 29–58.

———. 2016. *Lawyers at Play: Literature, Law, and Politics at the Early Modern Inns of Court, 1558–1581*. Oxford: Oxford University Press.

Woodbridge, Linda. 2010. *English Revenge Drama: Money, Resistance, Equality*. Cambridge: Cambridge University Press.

CHAPTER 12

Robert Ashley's Translations and Paratexts (1589–1639)

Renae Satterley

Introduction

Robert Ashley (1565–1641) was admitted to Middle Temple from New Inn in 1588 and called to the bar on 24 October 1595, residing at the inn until his death in 1641 (Kelser *et al.* 2021). He bequeathed over 6000 books to re-establish a library at the inn; all of the original books had been stolen by the time of Henry VIII (BL Cotton MS Vitellius C. IX, fol. 323^r). Ashley's library encompassed history, languages, natural philosophy, religious disputations, and travel, concentrating on printed books in Latin and European vernacular languages. In this chapter, I will discuss an adjunct to Ashley as a bibliophile and barrister: his work as the translator of seven works from French, Italian, Latin, and Spanish. Ashley used his translations to present himself as a learned individual, one with a demonstrable interest in foreign affairs, who was able to use his books and learning to address those in power and advertise his own usefulness to the commonweal. This message is evidenced by the books themselves, their

R. Satterley (✉)
Librarian, Middle Temple, London, UK
e-mail: r.satterley@middletemple.org.uk

E. Rhatigan, J. Watson (eds.), *Mapping the Early Modern Inns of Court*, Early Modern Literature in History,
https://doi.org/10.1007/978-3-031-77445-4_12

subject matter, and their paratexts: dedications, addresses to the reader, commendatory verses. Some of the original texts for his translations were in his library, and for those I examine the interaction between his marginal annotations, and the translated text, to shed light on how he read and his processes of translation.

The inns of court were societies where members felt confident enough in their status to directly address men and women of state. This was often achieved through translations, which:

> fostered a political culture at the Inns, one that expressed and developed members' interest in and care for the rule of the state, even as it implied that the Inns were an alternative political unit, a province, within an angular relationship to the political nation, both separate from and dependent upon the political hierarchy. (Winston 2016: 123)

Translations were an integral part of the literary culture at the inns of court: a culture that promoted a vision of innsmen as 'informed, authorized, and crucial participants in governance', and allowed them to 'respond to important personal experiences and public events, and to demonstrate their sophistication and wit' (Marotti 2017: 220). Wilfrid Prest has stated that 'translations from the classics and modern languages' were 'virtually monopolised' by members of the inns of court in the sixteenth century, but that there was a shift from the production of translations to their consumption by the seventeenth century, due to an increased focus on legal professionalism amongst inn members; the only inn residents to publish translations between 1603 and 1640 were Ashley and William Style (Inner Temple) (Prest 2023: 199–200).

Many illustrious innsmen, and those affiliated with the inns, translated in their 'spare time', such as Francis Bacon (Gray's Inn) and John Sparrow (Inner Temple). Other contributors to this volume, such as Jessica Winston and Jessica Apolloni, have looked at the interaction between translations at the inns and drama. Translations were an integral part of the thriving book trade between England and Europe, making continental books more accessible to the English market and culturally mediating between English readers and an 'increasingly accessible European marketplace of ideas'.[1] Innsmen used their translations to publicise their 'intellectual preparedness

[1] 'Travel, transculturality, and identity in England, *c.* 1550–1700'. www.tideproject.uk. Accessed 17 January 2024.

for services of all kinds', contributing to an unofficial early modern humanist programme of applied learning in a wide variety of subjects, including linguistic skills (Coldiron 2015: 169; Boutcher 2006). Ashley's translations, like those of his inns of court peers, were the product of a humanist educational background augmented by further self-education, and they enabled him to promote himself as one who could carry out the state service that this education had prepared him to perform (Winston 2016: 112). Innsmen carefully chose content to translate that would appeal to patrons and which illustrated this ability to perform useful state service.

It was through their paratexts that translators demonstrated their erudition and learning, and articulated their reasons for producing the work, focusing on the book's importance, novelty, and usefulness. Reasons for producing the translation often included encouragement from friends and illustrious contacts to translate a text that they themselves did not have the language skills to read (or at least not fluently). Some of these friends were prospective or current patrons, and translators made the most of their paratexts to gain and confirm patronage. Ashley's translations, including the only one not printed, 'Of Honour', but excluding the final one, *David persecuted*, were dedicated to influential men, including Charles I; three of these men were innsmen.

Ashley's translations are firmly divided between the two centuries of his lifetime. His first four translations were produced when he was a student and a young barrister residing at Middle Temple, between 1589 and approximately 1596, and the second three after gaining some success as a barrister, between 1627 and 1637. As there is no definitive explanation for the very long gap of 31 years between them, I have presented my discussion of them in chronological order.

Ashley's Sixteenth-Century Translations

Political Advice: *A Comparison of the English and Spanish Nation*

Ashley's first translation, *A comparison of the English and Spanish nation*, was published in April 1589 by John Wolfe and dedicated to Sir William Hatton. In the paratext to this anti-Spanish polemic, Ashley artfully explained that it was produced at the behest of his friends, but as he finalised it, a competing version appeared (*A politike discourse most excellent for this time present*).[2] Ashley decided to continue with his translation, explaining that the competing Italian translator did not have the means to produce a finessed English version. Wolfe had published the original French version in 1588 as *Discours politique, tres-excellent pour le temps present.*[3] The authorship of *Discours politique* is unclear: according to Denis Woodfield (based on third-hand information), it was Philippe de Mornay, seigneur du Plessis-Marley (1973: 130, 133 fn. 52).[4] But John Wolfe seems a more likely author: he produced anti-Spanish propaganda like this one in the 1580s and 1590s at the behest of William Cecil (Massai 2005: 117). He used false imprints and published fraudulent letters and news items to carry out Cecil's instructions (Donaldson 1988: 103). *A comparison* and its source work, *Discours politique*, were part of the flow of late sixteenth-century anti-Spanish works that encouraged English readers 'not to fear but to scorn the "braveries" of a nation so inferior to the English' (Jorgensen 1970: 340). Although not a well-known statesman like his uncle, Sir Christopher Hatton, the younger William Hatton was a member of parliament and on a committee that conferred with the Lords about proposing war against Spain.[5] Published a year after the Spanish Armada, Ashley's dedication to Hatton exemplifies innsmen translators' ability to address those in power, providing political advice through its encouragement to the state to actively resist Spain: Ashley writes that he hopes the work 'may stirre up that courage which ought still to remaine in our English harts' (Gentil-homme 1589: A2[v]).

[2] This was also published in 1589 by Wolfe, and the translator was Francesco Marquino, one of Wolfe's translators of French news. Centre for the Study of the Renaissance. *Renaissance Cultural Crossroads*. https://www.dhi.ac.uk/rcc/index.php?page=full_record&id=1376&result_set=0&logic=and&search_type=kw&lkw=ashley. Accessed 17 January 2024.

[3] There are two copies at the British Library. Denis Woodfield claimed British Museum shelfmark 114.k.4 as the original edition, but there is nothing to distinguish between 114.k.4 and 1195.g.32 (both *English Short Title Catalogue* S118994); the watermarks and chainlines are the same (Woodfield 1973: 30).

[4] *English Short Title Catalogue* does not corroborate the authorship, nor did *Catalogue collectif de France* or the *Universal Short Title Catalogue*.

[5] https://historyofparliamentonline.org/volume/1558-1603/member/hatton-%28formerly-newport%29-sir-william-1565-97.

Addressing Statesmen: *Urania*

In 1589, Ashley presented Sir Henry Unton with a copy of *A comparison*. Unton was not only a fellow Middle Templar but an important diplomat connected to Robert Dudley and Sir Christopher Hatton (Greengrass 2008). This presentation is outlined in the dedication to Unton in Ashley's 1589 Latin translation of Guillaume de Salluste Du Bartas's *L'Uranie ou muse celeste, Urania sive musa colestis*. The publication has the original French text with the translation on the facing page.[6] According to Peter Auger, *Urania* was translated from the 1579 edition of *Les oeuvres de G. de Saluste Seigneur du Bartas* (various editions published between 1579 and 1583) (Auger 2021). In the Latin paratext, Ashley explains that he completed the translation while still a boy at Oxford, that is, between 1580 and 1582, and that Unton had requested it after being presented with a copy of *A comparison* (Du Bartas 1589: A2^{v}, A3^{v}). *A comparison* was an apt gift for Unton, an emissary to Milan, sent to pay a ransom for his brother Edward Unton, who fell foul of the Spanish Inquisition. *Urania's* paratext includes an ode to Ashley written by Josias Mercier, editor of Phrygius Dares and Tacitus. Ashley may have met Mercier when the latter was exiled to England in the late sixteenth century or during the 1591 siege of Rouen against the Catholic League, at which Ashley also fought (D'Arcier 2006: 193; Kelser *et al.* 2021: 22).

Du Bartas was a popular writer, whose works were routinely translated into English. Both James VI and I and Ashley's school classmate Joshua Sylvester produced translations of the French Protestant divine's works.[7] In the paratext to *A comparison*, Ashley described *Urania* as of 'some greater importance' than *A comparison*, despite the latter being arguably more politically significant (A4^{r} and D3^{v}).[8] The paratext advertises his erudition and scholarly aptitude through its strategic use of quotations from Callimachus, Horace, and Juvenal to praise Unton (D3^{r} [mis-signed D3]). A Latin translation of Du Bartas, combined with Ashley's judicious use of classical quotations, speaks to the high literary and diplomatic culture of the kind with which Unton and other innsmen were associated.

[6] Entered at the Stationers on 10 May 1589. The entry states that the book will be printed in Latin, French and English, but it was only issued in Latin and French.

[7] For example, James VI and I. 1585. *The essayes of a prentise, in the diuine art of poesie*. Edinburgh: Joshua Sylvester. 1590. *A canticle of the victorie obteined by the French king, Henrie the fourth. at Yvry*. London.

[8] With thanks to George Brocklehurst for his translations of the Latin and Greek quotations.

From the Middle Temple: *Of the Interchangeable Course*

In 1594, Ashley published his translation of Louis Le Roy's *De la vicissitude ou variete des choses en l'univers,* dedicating it to Sir John Puckering (Lincoln's Inn), to whom he was secretary. Ashley humbly avers to Puckering that, while translations are of lesser importance than original writings (of which he is incapable), *his* translation is nonetheless important, and worthy of recognition: by making this work available to an English-speaking audience, he was a 'welwisher to all good Inuention' (Le Roy 1594: A2r–A2v). Ashley also respectfully disagrees with Théodore de Bèze's assertion that translations fall 'short of the good grace of the Original' (A2r). As with the references to Horace and Juvenal in *Urania,* Ashley's reference to Bèze is deliberate, made to demonstrate his erudition, breadth of reading, and scholarly ability to challenge a respected author's interpretation.

The paratext also reveals some details about life at an inn of court. In the dedication, Ashley explains that his service to Puckering forced him to command an 'intermission' of his common law studies and exercises (A2v). As we know, it was common for men to join an inn of court and live there without dedicating themselves to the study or practice of the law, and such men routinely took up lucrative secretary posts. The book's publication at the 'house' of Charles Yetsweirt, in 'Fleetstreete neere the Middle Temple gate', further reveals the close relationship between barristers and booksellers, printers, publishers, stationers, and authors based at the inns of court: a nexus touched on in this volume by Joshua Eckhardt and Julian Neuhauser in Chap. 8 and Sharon Harris in Chap. 7. This close relationship made it easy for innsmen like Ashley to acquire books for their work and study, and printers and booksellers like Yetsweirt responded by dealing in books that would be of interest to innsmen, such as plays, poetry, histories, and even law books (see, for example, Young 2017).

Although we do not know how many of his 6000 books Ashley acquired during his first years at the inn, we can determine from his marginalia that he owned the third edition of *De la vicissitude* (Paris, 1579), and likely used it for his translation.[9] In it, Ashley underlined various sections, highlighted others using side brackets, and noted contradictions and errors in the text. At F2r for example, he underlined: 'il est certain que les perpetuelles, comme le ciel, le soleil, la lune, & autres astres, demourent

[9] Now Middle Temple Library shelfmark BAY L (FOLIOS).

constamment en mesme estat', noting: 'v. contr. le 2 in principio', and contra-indicated the text at A2^{v}. Ashley did not make any corrections in his translation, however, instead translating directly 'It is certaine that those which are perpetuall, as the heauen, the sunne, the moone, and the other starres, remain, constantly alwaies in one selfe same estate' (Z3^{v}) (Fig. 12.1).

Another, more complicated, marginal note appears at A4^{r}. Using the insert symbol ^, Ashley indicated that additional text should be placed between 'iusques au' and 'trentieme': '[?]iesme quand elle est aux basses eaux et au 22ieme le semblable et au 23iesme quasi y est: puis le 24ieme [?] est poincte d'eau quelle com[m]ence un peu a croistre et de la en avant elle va croissant par chacun jour jusque au'.[10] Ashley's motives with this marginal insertion are unclear. Le Roy's wording is an exact copy from *L'art de naviguer* by Pedro Medina but is missing the following, which should appear where Ashley placed his insert symbol: 'vingt-deuxieme, qu'elle est du tout amoindrie. Au vingt-troisieme, il est poincte d'eau, & croist de iour en iour, iusques au'.[11] Does Ashley's marginalia indicate his knowledge that this was copied text, despite the lack of attribution to Medina? There is no evidence that Ashley had a copy of Medina's work, but it seems an oddly coincidental note to make if not.

Ashley omitted all of this from the translation, which may indicate that, as a (soon-to-be) lawyer, not an astronomer, he observed a contradiction in Le Roy's work. This contradiction mirrored those prevalent at the time between the teachings of Copernicus versus the established doctrine of Ptolemy. Ashley may have decided not to correct or highlight the discrepancy, as he lacked the technical knowledge to do so authoritatively, and did not want to engage in the scientific veracity of the text. He may also have wanted to remain 'true' to the original text, despite its obvious errors, or been unwilling to highlight Le Roy's potential plagiarism. It is also entirely possible that the annotations postdate the translation: while the handwriting is clear and precise, suggesting they were written when he was younger, there is nothing to indicate when they were written. It is nevertheless a

[10] Translated as: '21st the same when it is at low water and at the 22nd the similar and at the 23rd almost there: then the 24th [it] is at a point of water which begins to rise a little and from there forward it increases by each day until' B5^{r}.

[11] Medina's work went through many editions, from 1553 until at least 1633. Ashley's annotation is slightly different from Medina's, using 'quand elle' instead of 'car alors, elle' and 'quasi y est' instead of 'quasi y compris'. Compare, for example to C3^{r} in the Lyon, 1569 edition (*Universal Short Title Catalogue*, 24447).

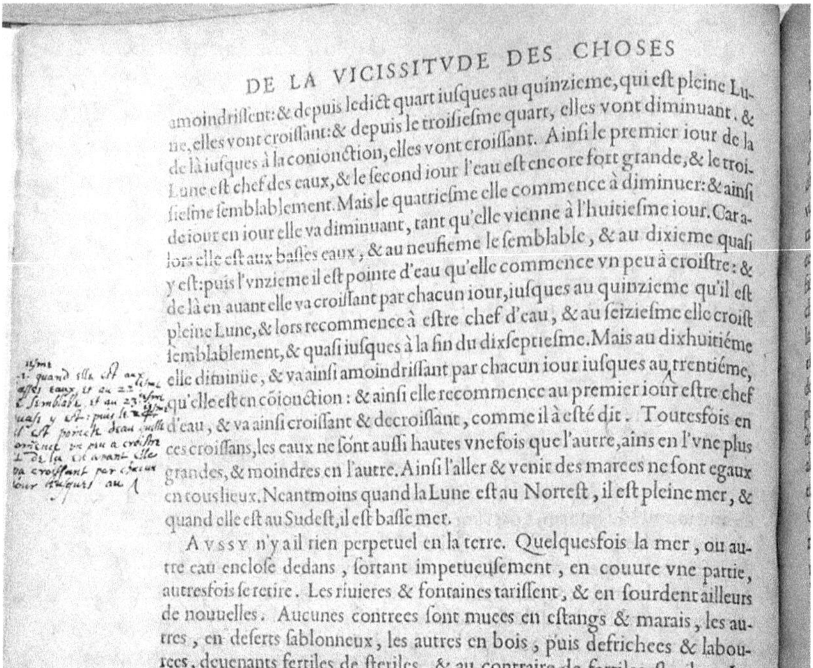

Fig. 12.1 *De la vicissitude des choses* (1579), A4r, showing Ashley's marginal addition. By kind permission of Middle Temple Library

good example of how Ashley read Le Roy and transformed (or not) those signs of reading into his translation.

This transformation is additionally apparent in Ashley's suppression of two sections about syphilis (including Girolamo Fracastoro's poem on the subject) and a 'unique reference to Lutherans as a seditious religious sect', and his amendment of Le Roy's extolment of France to neutral declarations of praise for one's country (Gundersheimer 1966: 134). While Ashley's editing of patriotic sentiments and criticism of Protestantism is unsurprising, his reasons for omitting mention of syphilis are less clear. He had seven books on the subject, including Fracastoro's *Syphilis* (Lyon, 1547), and it was a common ailment at the time. Ashley's transformations continued with his creation of new English words, such as mackle (the spoiling of a sheet of paper); august (worthy of respect); recision (repealing a law/decision); and gymnast, amongst others.[12] Le Roy's book was already a highly useful one, but Ashley's editorial changes rendered it into something even more suitable for English readers, including his dedicatee, Puckering (Boutcher 2006).

A fellow innsman, Francis Bacon, used Le Roy's work (either the translation or original language version) as inspiration for his *Novum organum*. Bacon copied Le Roy's term *vicissitudes*, applied his overall analysis, including its idea of 'eternal progress linked to eternal change' (Koller 1938: 236), and adopted Le Roy's theory that three inventions (printing, gunpowder, and the compass) had a significant impact on the workings of the modern world (Lux 2015: 193). Ashley's translation and Bacon's application of Le Roy's ideas meant that the Frenchman's work became a seminal one 'in the tradition of British philosophical and scientific empiricism' (Gundersheimer 1966: 134). Bacon, with *Novum organum*, and Ashley, with his translation, addressed their peers and the state, promulgating their own ideas about cultural comparators and technological innovations to (English) 'men of much businesse and employment' (A2^{v}).

[12] See *Oxford English Dictionary*, s.v. "mackle (v.1)," July 2023, https://doi.org/10.1093/OED/6337513718; *Oxford English Dictionary*, s.v. "august (adj.)," July 2023, https://doi.org/10.1093/OED/1194566522; *Oxford English Dictionary*, s.v. "recision (n.)," July 2023, https://doi.org/10.1093/OED/2745838130; *Oxford English Dictionary*, s.v. "gymnast (n.)," July 2023, https://doi.org/10.1093/OED/4621865360.

Literary Culture: 'Of Honour'

Ashley's manuscript, 'Of Honour', has long been thought to be an original work, but in 2016 Antonio Espigares Pinilla identified it as a translation of Sebastián Fox Morcillo's *De honore* (Basel, 1556) (Pinilla 2016). As evidenced by Pinilla's analysis of the marginalia, Ashley used his own copy for the translation.[13] Contemporary to Pinilla's findings, I determined that there were two additional copies of the manuscript: Trinity College Cambridge, MS R.14.20, and Bodleian Library, Ashmole MS 1148.[14] All three are undated and written by different scribes, and all have inns of court connections. The first copy (Trinity MS R.14.20) was dedicated to Sir John Puckering, dating it prior to 1596.[15] The second (MS Ellesmere 1117) was dedicated to Sir Thomas Egerton (Lincoln's Inn), who succeeded Puckering as lord keeper of the great seal in 1596. Dedicating the same work to two different patrons was common practice at the time (Carlson 1993: 45). The third copy has no dedication or preliminary material, and forms part of a collected volume of manuscripts that belonged to Elias Ashmole (Middle Temple).[16] Although Ashmole MS 1148 is not in Ashley's hand, it contains many corrections, scored through segments of text, and some added text. Pinilla has determined that the corrected edits are all found in the Trinity MS (fols. 9ᵛ–10ʳ) and Ellesmere MS (fol. 10ʳ), suggesting that it was a draft used by Ashley to produce the first presentation copy (Pinilla and Satterley 2022: 36).

'Of Honour' was not published. Ashley may have been unable to get Puckering's approval to do so prior to his death, and after that, Egerton presumably decided not to give Ashley patronage, thus impeding any

[13] Middle Temple Library Shelfmark BAY L530. There is an inscription on the last blank leaf of the final part: 'Anthony Crompton Animus cælestia cogitate'. The volume shows two hands in the marginalia, with Ashley's hand distinctively recognisable. The second hand is not identified, but could be that of Crompton.

[14] Prior to this, only the Huntington Library, MS Ellesmere 1117 was attributed to Ashley. The Trinity College copy is digitised and available to view online at: https://mss-cat.trin.cam.ac.uk/Manuscript/R.14.20.

[15] In the dedication, Ashley mentions his 'late absence from [his] attendance' on Puckering (fol. 2ʳ) which, as he left his employ by 1595, suggests that the manuscript could have been written around this time.

[16] It is bound as item V and paginated (not foliated) as 131–170. I was not able to verify any watermarks, which could date the manuscript. Heltzel described the watermark in Ellesmere as like one used in London in 1584: 'two columns, intertwined, surmounted by a crown, with 'I.RICHAR' below, similar to Briquet 4444 and 4445, the former used in London in 1584' (Ashley 1947: 17).

further attempts to publish it. But Virgil Heltzel's assessment that Ashley's punctuation in the manuscript was 'inconsistent, as if he regarded such a mechanical matter as something the printer was expected to take care of' does indicate some intention to have it published (Ashley 1947: 19). His inability to have the work published may also stem from the fact that Puckering or Egerton knew it was a translation of a Spanish work on the topic of honour, and were unwilling to sponsor such a work in a febrile anti-Spanish climate. There was a deluge of 'Hispanophobic' propaganda published at this time (Griffin 2009), and Ashley's own dedication to Hatton in *A comparison* exemplified this 'Hispanophobia', encouraging its readers to 'learne to despise those magnificent Dom Diegos and Spanish Caualieros, whose doughtiest deedes are bragges and boastinges, and themselues (for the most part) shadowes without substaunce' ($A2^v$–$A3^r$). But the many Spanish translations published in the sixteenth century, including two works translated by Francis Meres and dedicated to Egerton, Luis de Granada's Guía *De peccadores* (Salamanca, 1568) and *The sinners guyde* (London, 1598), make this hypothesis unlikely, and we can only speculate regarding Ashley's intentions to publish 'Of Honour'.

As Pinilla has determined, the dedication to Egerton (which is significantly longer than that to Puckering) was semi-plagiarised, and includes many elements from Fox Morcillo's dedication to Ruy Gómez de Silva, first prince of Éboli (2022: 44). This was not unusual, however. Sussana de Schepper has shown how the paratexts to English translations of navigational works in this period were often direct copies from their original source material (2013: 189–91), and Sidney Lee that sixteenth-century English lyricists and poets regularly plagiarised foreign authors (1910: 249). Ashley's re-use of dedicatory material, and concealment of 'Of Honour' as a translation, tallies with his own assertion, in the 1589 dedication to Sir William Hatton in *A comparison of the English and Spanish nation*, that he was incapable of creating original works (see Pym 1998 and Marin-Lacarta 2017 on indirect translations).

Despite not being printed during Ashley's lifetime, 'Of Honour' remains an important example of the concept of honour in early modern English literature. Ashley's dedication of the work to Puckering, and then Egerton, demonstrates his ability to speak to men in power and provide them with advice, in the form of literature. As Marotti discusses in Chap. 9, manuscript circulation was a vibrant part of early modern culture, particularly at the inns of court. Consequently, despite not being printed,

Ashley's work would have had a wider audience than his two dedicatees, as indicated by Ashmole's ownership of a copy.

Ashley's Seventeenth-Century Translations

Advice to Princes: *Almansor*

Although all of his early attempts at gaining patronage ended in failure, it was presumably obtaining success in his legal practice that allowed Ashley the free time to recommence translating in the seventeenth century (*Almansor*, long S4ʳ).[17] As Prest has attested, 'most of the creative non-legal work of early modern common lawyers seems to have been produced either before the age of 30 or after they had given up legal practice altogether' (1986: 207). Ashley's paratext in *Almansor* reflects his move away from seeking patronage, as reflected in his earlier translations, instead concentrating on how he can use his work to speak to those in power, offering them advice and advancing the commonweal.

Almansor is a translation of the first section of the second part of Miguel de Luna's *Verdadera historia del rey Don Rodrigo*, published in Saragoza in 1603. According to the paratext, the original dedicatee was James VI and I, but he died before it was published (publication had been delayed due to the death of some of the printers and outbreaks of plague), and Ashley subsequently decided to dedicate it to Charles I (Long S2ʳ). Ashley based his translation on a copy at the Bodleian Library, which he visited in December 1622/January 1623, coming across an 'Arabian Historie concerning the losse of Spaine by Roderigo King of the Gothes … translated into Spanish out of' Arabic (Long S4ᵛ and A4ʳ).[18]

As Ashley himself noted, De Luna's *Verdadera historia del rey Don Rodrigo* was ostensibly based on a Spanish translation of an Arabian manuscript originally found in El Escorial Library, which Ashley visited in 1618

[17] Registered at the Stationers on 4 November 1626. There is the possibility that he did translate other works during these thirty years and that they remained unattributed in manuscript or print.

[18] I have examined the copy at the Bodleian Library that Ashley used for his translation (shelfmark 4to A 32 Art. (1)), but it does not show any trace of his marginalia. Ashley donated a copy of Almansor to the Bodleian, shelfmark 4to. H.4.Art. The (badly trimmed) dedicatory inscription reads: 'Bibliothecae Bodleianae Acad. Oxon. celeberrimae li[brorum] ac linguarum locupletissimae Anglicanam hanc ex [Hispanico?] ibidem exemplari decerptam editionem Robert[us] Ashley eiusd[em] olim Acad. indignus alumnus, dicat et [dedicat]'.

(de Luna 1627: A1^{r}). In the original, De Luna presented himself as the saviour of a lost work and an authoritative figure who mastered the ancient language of Arabic to translate the text into Spanish. It was in fact one of the many pseudo-works that proliferated in late sixteenth-century Spain, an 'alternate version of the official story and foundational myth of King Rodrigo, the last Visigoth king in the Peninsula' (Mendez-Oliver 2017: 735, 749). Ashley left it to his readers to 'dispute the truth of [this] historie; or whether it bee not a patterne of perfection described: as many have supposed the like of *Cyrus*, described by *Xenophon*' (Long S3^{r}). Rather than dwell on the veracity of the text, Ashley uses the paratext to emphasise the value of his translation, which will make the work of 'better use … then to be buried in silence' (Long S3^{r}).

The paratext additionally demonstrates how innsmen like Ashley drew on international frames of reference in their writings and translations, reaching beyond Britain's borders. Ashley presents the translation as one that can teach its readers (and the dedicatee, Charles I) the validity of learning from non-Christian countries and rulers: he argues that 'by comparing our selves with Heathens, with Infidels, with Mahometans, and other Misbeleevers; we attaine the better and cleerer knowledge of our advantages and defects', insisting 'hee that knoweth no countrey but his own, knoweth not the worth or wants of his owne' and 'no one Climate or Region affordeth all kind of knowledge in full measure' (Long S3^{r}, S4^{r}). The paratext extols Almansor's qualities as a strong leader, despite his status as a 'heathen', and the virtues of past leaders whom Almansor resembled: the 'magnamitie' of Alexander the Great; the 'clemencie' of Julius Caesar; the 'integritie' of Aristides; the 'constancie' of Cato; and the 'justice and goodnesse' of Trajan (Long S2^{v}). These comparisons are directed to Charles I, providing the new monarch examples to emulate. At the time of *Almansor's* publication, Charles I was engaged in an unpopular war in France, with taxes levied without parliamentary consent (the 'Forced Loan' of 1626–1627) to fund it; Ashley's advice here is for Charles to learn from the sage role model of Almansor, and his 'wisdome of gouernment' (A1^{r}).

Ashley's paratext also reveals that it was through 'trauaile [travel], bookes, and conference' that he obtained the requisite knowledge to translate the book. 'Conference', the exchange of information through conversation and discourse, was readily practised at the inns of court. Francis Bacon wrote that 'reading maketh a full man, conference a readye man, and writing an exacte man' (1597: B1^{v}). The work's place amid such conference is reinforced by Ashley's artful mention that he decided to translate it in order to 'giue satisfaction' to those who 'longed to have [the book] communicated vnto them, in a tongue which they better understood', a reason that was also mirrored in *A comparison* ($A1^v$). The men for whom Ashley made his translations—the named, such as Unton, and unnamed others—were part of social, literary, and linguistic networks positioned, like him, at the inns of court.

Reading and the Commonweal: *Cochin-China*

Ashley's next translation, *Cochin-China,* continues to reveal his participation in these linguistically engaged social networks, and his use of translations to address and advise those in power. *Cochin-China* is a partial translation of Cristoforo Borri's *Relation de la novvelle mission des Peres de la Compagnie de Iesus, au royaume de la Cochinchine* (Rennes, 1631), which itself was a French translation of *Relatione della nuova missione delli PP. della Compagnia di Giesu, al regno della Cocincina* (Rome, 1631). Ashley dedicated it to Sir Maurice Abbot (1565–1642), governor of the East India Company.[19] Seventeenth-century English merchants like Abbot increasingly relied on translations of travel and exploration books to provide them with useful information that enabled them to expand their territories and colonial investments, particularly into countries of which they had little prior knowledge (Das *et al.* 2021: 265). Ashley's address to Abbott underlines his intentions to make Borri's text useful to English merchants, to promote trade into Cochin-China (i.e. Vietnam), and to clarify readers' misconceptions of this unknown and strange land. He states that there will be two sorts who will be unhappy with the publication: those who think that China and Cochin-China are too far distant, lack established trade links with England, and that their riches are exhausted, and thus not worth the effort of investment; and those who 'censure all strange reports of things which they have not seene at home' (Borri 1633: $A3^r$). The latter sort are ignorant, they dare to condemn learned men, such as Herodotus, Sir John Mandeville, Pliny, Solinus, Strabo, and Paulus Venetus, and if they had their way, the 'discoveries' of explorers like Columbus would not have succeeded. Ashley avers that the

[19] Registered at the Stationers on 3 October 1633. Ashley's is a partial translation, as he omitted the second part of Borri's account, which detailed local religious beliefs and Jesuit missionary attempts in Vietnam.

way to truth (and riches) is by suspending 'iudgment in things not yet thoroughly discovered', and prefaces this with a maxim from Horace: 'stulti dum vitant vitia, in contraria currunt' [when fools try to avoid errors, they run into the opposite errors] ($A3^v$).[20]

As with his translation of De Luna's *Almansor*, Ashley was interested in Borri's account of Vietnam because of the importance he placed on learning about foreign cultures. Emily Stevenson and Lauren Woking describe in Chap. 13 innsmen's interests in 'travel knowledge' and colonialist endeavours, and Julian T. S. Neuhauser and Joshua Eckhardt discuss John Selden's ownership of Thomas Coryate's travel book, *Coryats Crudities* in Chap. 8 (Ashley also had a copy of Coryate's book). Selden, as we know, invested heavily in accounts of Asia for his library; the Bodleian has dedicated a webpage to his map of China.[21] Ashley's investment in this knowledge is evidenced by the large number of travel books he collected, including at least 32 Jesuit missionary accounts. His copy of *Relatione de la novvelle mission des Peres de la Compagnie de Iesus, au royaume de la Cochinchine* is annotated with his marginal notes, underlining, and a Senecan quotation on the title page: 'Cum hac persuasione vivendum est: non sum uni angulo natus, patria mea totus hic mundus est', which was reproduced on the title page of *Cochin-China*. The maxim reinforces Ashley's commitment to learning from other nations: 'One should live by this motto: I was not born to one little corner; this whole world is my country.'

The evidence of Ashley's investment in learning about other cultures through books is further underlined in the paratext's statement that he had addicted himself 'to a more curious search and inquisition *of this glorious and wondrous workemanship of the World, (whereof the one moity is in a maner vnknowne to the other)* endeauouring to giue my selfe some satisfaction, by all such Relations and Discoueries as I could procure, of those Conntreys least knowne unto us; whether described by our Countreymen or by other forraine Trauellers' ($A1^r$: original italics) (Fig. 12.2).

He bolsters this argument by name-checking Giovanni Battista Ramusio, Richard Hakluyt, and Samuel Purchas, and points out that the latter two not only recorded the exploits of England but also collected and published 'what they find worth the regarding amongst forreigners, that may any way be serviceable for the instruction of ours' ($A2^v$). Ashley is

[20] The maxim is unattributed, but is from Horace's *Satires*, book one, satire two.

[21] https://seldenmap.bodleian.ox.ac.uk/.

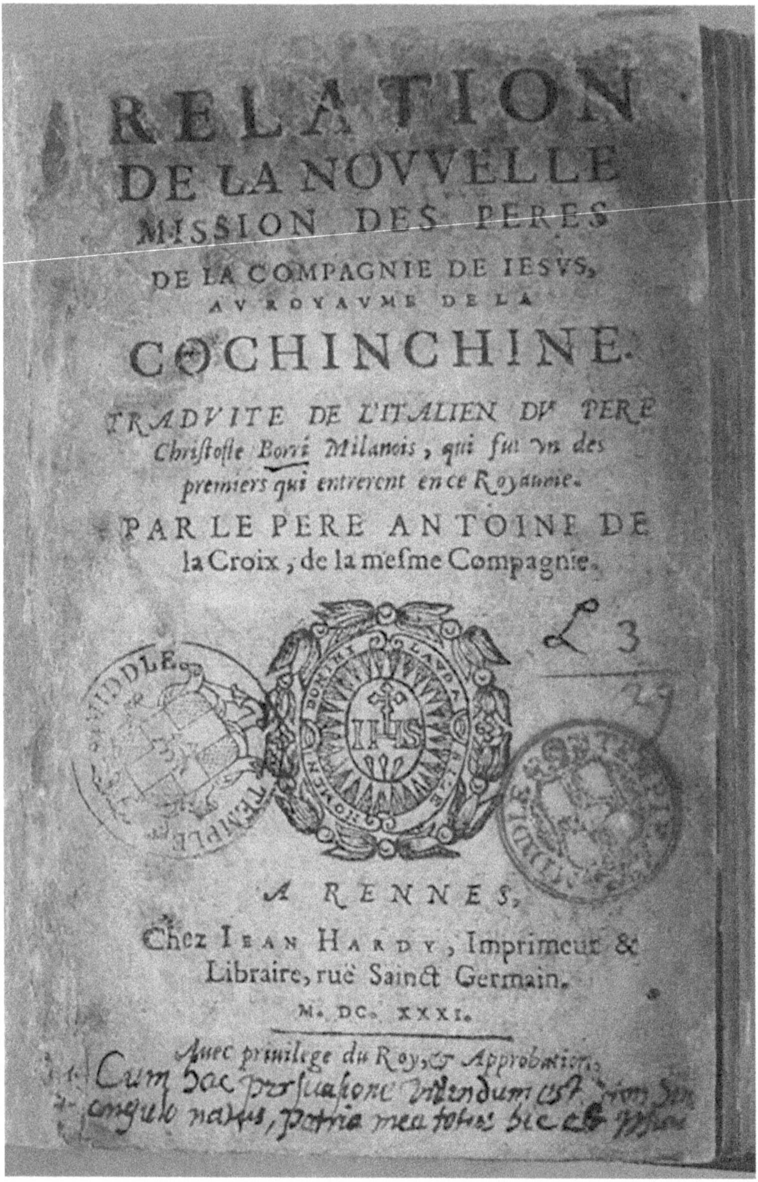

RELATION
DE LA NOVVELLE
MISSION DES PERES
DE LA COMPAGNIE DE IESVS,
AV ROYAVME DE LA
COCHINCHINE.
TRADVITE DE L'ITALIEN DV PERE
Christofle Borri Milanois, qui fut vn des
premiers qui entrerent en ce Royaume.
PAR LE PERE ANTOINE DE
la Croix, de la mesme Compagnie.

A RENNES,
Chez IEAN HARDY, Imprimeur &
Libraire, ruë Sainct Germain.
M. DC. XXXI.
Auec priuilege du Roy, & Approbation.

Fig. 12.2 Title page to *Relatione de la novvelle mission des Peres de la Compagnie de Iesus, au royaume de la Cochinchine* (1631), showing Ashley's addition of a quotation from Seneca. By kind permission of Middle Temple Library

saying that it is through such accounts that Englishmen will learn how to penetrate seemingly impenetrable countries and exploit their riches.

In order to present the region as accessible to English trade, Ashley points out in the paratext that Cochin-China is actively open to trade for *all* foreigners in 'cleane contrary' to China (A3ᵛ). But, odd as it may seem, it is Ashley's omission of a key portion of text that enables him to present Vietnam as accessible to English traders. His translation condenses some text from chapter eight which described a Portuguese victory over the Dutch (England's allies), at which English and/or Dutch merchants and sailors were massacred, and cargo with a value of £708 was lost.[22] While Ashley's paratext does allude to 'some late disastrous events and accidents', his omission of these key facts risked putting potential trade missions in danger, since Borri's text clarified the Portuguese trade monopoly in the region (A1ᵛ).

Ashley's copy of *Relation de la novvelle mission* shows his signs of reading at chapter eight (F7ʳ): he underlined the words 'Faifo', 'Holla[n]dois', 'Portugais', and the name of the Italian missionary in Vietnam, 'Ferdinand de Costa'. Further along, at F8ʳ, he used a bracket in the left-hand margin to highlight the section on Dutch and Portuguese attempts to establish trading posts in the region, underlining the words 'Portugais' and 'de Turon' (the port of Da Nang). Ashley may have omitted this text from his translation because he knew that it was English (not Dutch) merchants who had been massacred. If so, it would indicate he had access to information about English trading ventures in South Asia, as details of the massacre were not published. This theory is bolstered by notes he made in his copy of Dudley Digges' *The defence of trade* (London, 1615). In this pro-East India Company treatise, Ashley copied out a list of goods (cotton, diamonds, pepper, silk, etc.) returned from India on May 1619 on the ships the *Dragon* and *Expedition*. This expedition was the one that had brought Sir Thomas Roe (Middle Temple) to India as ambassador in 1615 (Strachan 2011). Ashley's censorship of some key facts in *Cochin-China* may have been because the massacre was a state or trade secret, or because including this unpleasant news would negatively impact his attempts to encourage English trade to the region.

[22] For details on this massacre, and whether Borri mistook Dutch traders for English ones, see Baron (2006: 65); Bonifacy (1931: 335–36 fn.); Maybon (1920: 65); Cocks (1883).

Silently Speaking to Those in Power: *David persecuted*

Ashley's final translation continued his attempts to address those in power. In 1637, he published *David persecuted*, a translation of Virgilio Malvezzi's *Il Davide perseguitato* (Venice, 1634).[23] Like *Almansor*, this was a moralised and political biography and an 'advice to princes' handbook. Malvezzi's book presented Old Testament stories 'embedded in digressions on morality and politics' (Kattenberg 2023: 134). But *David persecuted* differs significantly from Ashley's other translations in lacking any paratextual material, so his reasons for translating it, and its intended audience, remain conjectural.

Although originally from Italy, Malvezzi was a diplomat, court historian, and advisor to the Madrid court; it was from there that he was sent as a Spanish ambassador to England in 1640. While ambassador Malvezzi met some of his translators, but there is no evidence that he met Ashley. Malvezzi's books were commonly read by innsmen. In his commonplace books, Sir William Drake (Middle Temple) made notes from Malvezzi's edition of Tacitus, his Aristotlean quotations, and his *Successi principali della monarchia di Spagna nell' anno M.DC.XXXIX* (Clark 1977: 69, 56, 61, 64). The royalist political author Dudley Digges (Gray's Inn) had a copy of Malvezzi's *Discorsi sopra Cornelio Tacito* (Venice, 1635), and Sir Thomas Roe a copy of 'Il Romulo. Il Tarquinio superbo'.[24] In addition to owning a copy of *Il Davide perseguitato*, Ashley owned two other works by Malvezzi, both concerning the politics and nobility of Spain: *Il ritratto del privato politico Christiano* (Bologna, 1635), and *Sucesos principales de la monarquia de España en el año de mil i seis cientos i treinta i nueve* (Madrid, 1640).

Ashley made only one small sign of his reading in his copy of *Il Davide perseguitato*: 'Goliath gigante era bastardo pag 40', written on the final endleaf. His interest in Goliath may have been due to the giant's status as a 'bastard', one who was the product of an 'amorous' match, 'begot … in a desperate manner', and thus not in a stately one like a legitimate king such as David (there is no further marginalia in the book, including underlining) (Malvezzi 1637: C2^{v}). Posthumous editions of *David persecuted* were published in 1648 and 1650, and the publication's political stance reinforced ideas of regal legitimacy by containing a frontispiece depicting Charles I as

[23] Registered at the Stationers on 9 March 1637.

[24] All Souls College Library, Oxford, shelfmark Gallery f.4.13, and PLRE.Folger 274.436.

Fig. 12.3 *Il Davide perseguitato* (1634), showing Ashley's note that Goliath the giant was a bastard. By kind permission of Middle Temple Library

King David. There is no evidence as to Ashley's affiliation, royalist or parliamentarian, but his translation of this book in particular reveals his continued interest, so late in life, in transforming continental literature for English audiences, and his assuredness in publishing 'mirrors for princes' texts (Fig. 12.3).

Conclusion

Ashley's translations served him a variety of purposes. In the sixteenth century, he used them in his attempts at gaining and confirming patronage, and in the seventeenth century, he used them to advertise his usefulness to the commonweal. Throughout his lifetime of translating, his ability to address those in power is made possible by his privileged position at an inn of court, and through his erudition and scholastic abilities, which he advertises through the paratexts. Not everyone was capable of translating (and translating *well*) authors such as Du Bartas and Le Roy, nor of quoting relevant modern and classical writers such as Hakluyt, Horace, Seneca, and Xenophon. These abilities complemented Ashley's motives to serve the state through his translations: from his first works to his last, he translated important texts that encouraged and profited the English commonweal.

Although Ashley expressed misgivings about not being able to write anything original, his translations nonetheless enabled him to achieve cultural status by benefiting others, many of whom were associated with the inns of court or were statesmen. His translations reached a wider audience than the original language versions and introduced continental works to a new, English audience. Even his only unpublished translation, 'Of Honour', reflects this, as we now know that it exists in three copies, one of which belonged to Elias Ashmole.

At the early modern inns of court, translations were the product of innsmen's education and practical knowledge. They were complex works whose authors fashioned an authoritative textual identity, vindicated by their humanist educations, placement at the inns, knowledge of continental languages, and travel experiences (armchair and actual). This chapter has shown how Ashley used his translations to seek patronage and to impart information that would be useful to the commonweal and the nation's cultural heritage. By transmitting this valuable and rare material, he in turn ensured his status as a learned individual. His paratexts reflect how he applied his learning, reading, erudition, and broad-minded views to present himself as such.

Works Cited

Ashley, Robert. 1947. *Of Honour*. Edited by Virgil B. Heltzel. San Marino, CA: Huntington Library.

Auger, Peter. 2021. "Astrological Description in Spenser and Du Bartas." *Spenser Review* 51, no. 1. Accessed 17 January 2024. http://www.english.cam.ac.uk/spenseronline/review/item/51.1.5.

Bacon, Francis. 1597. *Essayes*. London.

Baron, Samuel. 2006. *Views of Seventeenth-century Vietnam*. Ithaca, NY: Cornell University Southeast Asia Program Publications.

Bodleian. Ashmole Manuscript 1148.

Bonifacy, A., trans. 1931. "Relation de la nouvelle mission au royaume de Cochinchine." *Bulletin des Amis du Vieux Hué* 18, nos 3–4: 279–402.

Borri, Christophoro. 1633. *Cochin-China: containing many admirable rarities and singularities of that countrey*. Translated by Robert Ashley. London.

Boutcher, Warren. 2006. "The Renaissance." In *The Oxford Guide to Literature in English Translation*, edited by Peter France. Oxford: Oxford University Press. Accessed 17 January 2024. https://www.oxfordreference.com/view/10.1093/acref/9780198183594.001.0001/acref-9780198183594-e-152.

British Library. Cotton Manuscript Vitellius C. IX.

Carlson, David R. 1993. *English Humanist Books: Writers and Patrons, Manuscript and Print, 1475–1525*. Toronto: University of Toronto Press.

Clark, Stuart. 1977. "Wisdom Literature of the Seventeenth Century: A Guide to the Contents of the 'Bacon-Tottel' Commonplace books. Part II." *Transactions of the Cambridge Bibliographical Society* 7, no. 1: 46–73.

Cocks, Richard. 1883. *Diary of Richard Cocks, Cape-Merchant in the English Factory in Japan, 1615–1622: with Correspondence*. Edited by Edward Maunde Thompson. London: Hakluyt Society.

Coldiron, A. E. B. 2015. *Printers Without Borders: Translation and Textuality in the Renaissance*. Cambridge: Cambridge University Press.

D'Arcier, Louis Faivre. 2006. *Jean (c. 1525–1570) et Josias (c. 1560–1626) Mercier: l'amour de la philologie à la Renaissance et au début de l'âge classique*. Paris: Champion.

Das, Nandini, Joao Melo, Haig Smith, and Lauren Working. 2021. *Keywords of Identity, Race, and Human Mobility in Early Modern England*. Amsterdam: Amsterdam University Press.

Donaldson, Peter S. 1988. *Machiavelli and Mystery of State*. Cambridge: Cambridge University Press.

Du Bartas, Guillaume de Salluste. 1589. *L'uranie ou muse celeste de G. de Saluste Seigneur du Bartas = Vrania sive mvsa cœlestis Roberti Ashelei de Gallica G. Salustij Bartasij delibata*. Translated by Robert Ashley. London.

Gentil-homme, François. 1589. *A comparison of the English and Spanish nation: composed by a French gentleman against those of the League in Fraunce, which went about to perswade the King to breake his alliance with England, and to confirme it with Spaine. By occasion whereof, the nature of both nations is liuely decyphered*. Translated by Robert Ashley. London.

Greengrass, M. 2008. "Unton [Umpton], Sir Henry (*c.* 1558–1596), 'diplomat and solder.'" *Oxford Dictionary of National Biography*. Accessed 10 May 2024. https://www.oxforddnb.com/view/10.1093/ref:odnb/9780198614128.001.0001/odnb-9780198614128-e-28001

Griffin, Eric. 2009. "Nationalism, the Black Legend, and the Revised *Spanish Tragedy*." *English Literary Renaissance* 39, no. 2: 336–70.

Gundersheimer, Werner L. 1966. *The life and works of Louis Le Roy*. In *Travaux c'humanisme et renaissance*, Vol. 82. Geneva: Droz Viator.

Huntington. Manuscript Ellesmere 1117.

Jorgensen, Paul. A. 1970. "Sources for Elizabethan Notion of the Spaniard." *Viator*, 1: 337–44.

Kattenberg, Lisa. 2023. *The Power of Necessity: Reason of State in the Spanish Monarchy, c. 1590–1650*. Cambridge: Cambridge University Press.

Kelser, Astrid, Jennifer Nelson, and Renae Satterley. 2021. "A Transcription and Translation of Sloane MS. 2131, Robert Ashley's (1565–1641) Vita: with Additional Biographical Details." *Electronic British Library Journal* 10. https://www.bl.uk/eblj/2021articles/article10.html.

Koller, Katherine. 1938. "Two Elizabethan Expressions of the Idea of Mutability." *Studies in Philology* 35: 228–37.

Lee, Sidney. 1910. *The French Renaissance in England: an Account of the Literary Relations of England and France in the Sixteenth Century*. Oxford: The Clarendon Press.

Le Roy, Louis. 1594. *Of the interchangeable course, or variety of things in the whole world … Written in French by Loys Le Roy Called Regius*. Translated by Robert Ashley. London.

de Luna, Miguel. 1627. *Almansor the learned and victoriovs king that conquered Spaine. His life and death*. Translated by Robert Ashley. London.

Lux, Jonathan E. 2015. "Characters Reall." *Renaissance Studies* 29, no. 2: 184–203.

Malvezzi, Virgilio. 1637. *Il Davide perseguitato = David persecuted*. Translated by Robert Ashley. London.

Marin-Lacarta, Maialen. 2017. "Indirectness in Literary Translation: Methodological Possibilities." *Translation Studies* 10, no. 2: 133–49.

Marotti, Arthur F. 2017. "The Verse Nobody Knows: Rare or Unique Poems in Early Modern English Manuscripts." *The Huntington Library Quarterly* 80, no. 2: 201–21.

Massai, Sonia. 2005. "John Wolfe and the Impact of Exemplary Go-Betweens on Early Modern Print Culture." In *Renaissance Go-Betweens: Cultural Exchange in Early Modern Europe*, edited by Andreas Höfele and Werner von Koppenfels, 104–18. Boston: De Gruyter.

Maybon, Charles B. 1920. *Histoire Moderne du Pays d'Annam (1592–1820)*. Paris: Plon-Nourrit et Cie.

Mendez-Oliver, Ana. 2017. "'Translating' the Origins of the Spanish Nation in Miguel de Luna's Verdadera historia del Rey don Rodrigo. Pseudo-translation and cultural identity." *Canadian Review of Comparative Literature* 44, no. 4: 735–54.

Pinilla, Antonio Espigares. 2016. *Sebastián Fox Morcillo. De honore. Estudio y traducción*. Madrid: Ediciones Complutense.

Pinilla, Antonio Espigares, and Renae Satterley. 2022. "The three manuscript copies of Robert Ashley's Of Honour and Sebastián Fox Morcillo's *De honore*. Study of a Translation Plagiarism." *Sederi* 32: 31–65.

Prest, Wilfrid R. 1986. *The Rise of the Barristers*. London: Longman.

———. 2023. *The Inns of Court Under Elizabeth I and the Early Stuarts, 1590–1640*. 2nd ed. Cambridge: Cambridge University Press.

Pym, Anthony. 1998. *Method in Translation History*. Manchester: St Jerome.

Schepper, Sussana de. 2013. "'For the Common Good and for the National Interest': Paratexts in English Translation of Navigational Works." In *Renaissance Cultural Crossroads: Translation, Print and Culture in Britain*, edited by S. K. Barker and Brenda M. Hosington, 185–208. Leiden: Brill.

Strachan, Michael. 2011. "Roe, Sir Thomas (1581–1644), diplomat." *Oxford Dictionary of National Biography*. Accessed 10 May 2024. https://www.oxforddnb.com/view/10.1093/ref:odnb/9780198614128.001.0001/odnb-9780198614128-e-23943.

Trinity College Cambridge. Manuscript R.14.20.

Winston, Jessica. 2016. *Lawyers at Play: Literature, Law, and Politics at the Early Modern Inns of Court, 1558–1581*. Oxford: Oxford University Press.

Woodfield, Denis B. 1973. *Surreptitious Printing in England, 1550–1640*. New York: Bibliographical Society of America.

Young, Jennifer M. 2017. "Minding their F's and Q's: Shakespeare and the Fleet Street Syndicate 1630–32." In *Historical Networks in the Book Trade*, edited by Catherine Feely and John Hinks, 83–100. London: Routledge.

CHAPTER 13

Between Ship and Library: Global Knowledge and Spaces of Exchange at the Middle Temple, 1586–1636

Lauren Working and Emily Stevenson

Research for this chapter began when its authors, then on the TIDE project at the University of Oxford, curated an exhibition at Middle Temple Library that ran from September 2021 to January 2022. 'Middle Temple to Manoa: Global Networks at the Inns of Court' combined manuscripts and rare books from Middle Temple Library with new artworks by the globemaker and ceramicist Loraine Rutt. The authors would like to thank Loraine, and Renae Satterley and Barnaby Bryan at the Middle Temple, for encouraging their research and bringing new questions and insights to the material; and Sarah Knight and Michelle O'Callaghan for their generous comments on an earlier draft.

L. Working (✉)
Department of English and Related Literature, University of York, York, UK
e-mail: lauren.working@york.ac.uk

E. Stevenson
School of English Literature, Language and Linguistics, Newcastle University, Newcastle, United Kingdom
e-mail: emily.stevenson@newcastle.ac.uk

E. Rhatigan, J. Watson (eds.), *Mapping the Early Modern Inns of Court*, Early Modern Literature in History,
https://doi.org/10.1007/978-3-031-77445-4_13

Introduction

From the wooden chambers where they read the latest news to the ship cabins that carried them across the world, Elizabethan and Jacobean innsmen frequently engaged with real and imaginary travel, fuelled by the growing availability of travel literature, trade reports, and colonial letters. The buildings of the Middle Temple were located on the edge of the Thames, filling lawyers' rooms and gardens with the sounds of the river. These liquid highways connected the inns to other districts within the metropolis, and to other ports and cities, bringing in knowledge and objects from places ranging from Paris to Mexico. In August 1586, recently returned from a voyage to the West Indies, Francis Drake entered Middle Temple hall and was applauded with 'great joy' by the benchers who had gathered there (Hopwood 1904: 285–86). In the months before his return, news circulated that Drake had conducted a series of raids against Spanish settlements in the Caribbean and Florida, freeing a large number of captive 'Turks' from Cartagena and stopping by the struggling English settlement in Roanoke to bring its colonists back home (Bigges 1589) (Fig. 13.1).

The enthusiasm with which Middle Temple gentlemen greeted Drake generates a series of questions. What kind of knowledge did those who rose to cheer him possess about exploration and conquest? How did such Atlantic voyaging enter into the literary culture of the inns? What role did the inns play in helping gentlemen foster their global interests on a day-to-day level? Although the multivalent language of 'empire' was widely discussed in late sixteenth- and seventeenth-century England, the practical administration of territorial expansion was only just beginning (Dimmock 2022; MacMillan 2001; Das *et al.* 2021). In their positions as lawyers, secretaries, and clerks, innsmen directly contributed to this practical administration in a variety of ways, from legal debate to drafting charters.[1] At the same time, professional responsibility or hopes for advancement existed alongside the real desire, even compulsion, to travel beyond the bounds of Europe and endorse projects in the Americas.

In her exploration of the intellectual topography of the early modern inns of court, Jessica Winston draws on the work of Pierre Bourdieu to

[1] On the emerging role of lawyers in legal imperial administration, particularly from the reign of Charles I, see Brewer (2021) and Tomlins (2010).

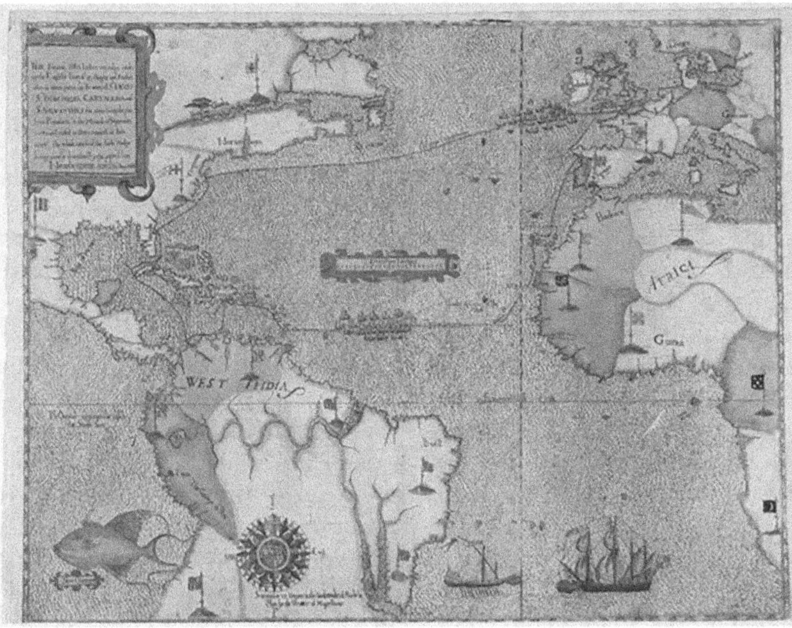

Fig. 13.1 Map by Baptista Boazio of 'The famouse West Indian voyadge made by the Englishe fleete' captained by Francis Drake in 1585–1586, showing the outward and return journey, including stops in Cartagena, Santo Domingo, Florida, and Roanoke (London, 1589?). Yale Center for British Art/Public domain [CC0 1.0]

examine communality at the inns through the idea of 'habitus', where a 'collective set of styles, habits, and tastes' helped create 'a "system of dispositions"' acquired through shared experiences and 'schemes of perception, thought and action' (2016: 32). Literary play was central to this habitus, and, by extension, to the identities of gentlemen who came to learn about the legal profession and to partake in the literary culture these institutions had to offer (as Blessin Adams discusses in Chap. 5). This chapter examines how travel knowledge impacted the literary and material sociability of the Elizabethan and Jacobean inns, focusing on the Middle Temple and its members' growing investment in colonialism. Members of other inns exhibited interests in global travel and expansion, but each institution, though overlapping and closely connected, has a distinct culture that requires sustained research into its place within, and expression of, these networks (Working 2018: 29–51). Given the variety of textual, material, and performative expressions that this interest took at the Middle Temple, it serves here as a primary case study. Its members had personal links to various members of the Virginia Company and the fast-growing merchant communities of London, and, through members such as Richard Hakluyt the Elder, William Crashaw, and Robert Ashley, access to a vast number of manuscripts and printed texts engaging with the latest travel knowledge. The terrestrial and celestial globes made by Emery Molyneux in the early 1590s were some of the first to be created in England and remain on display in Middle Temple Library today. Extant supper bills catalogue the sugar, spices, and tobacco consumed by benchers in the hall.

When they were admitted to the inns of court, where did gentlemen spend their time, and how did these settings generate forms of encounter with the wider world? In a volume on mapping the inns of court, this chapter looks at the macrocosm of the world as it was experienced in the microcosm of several key spaces. The interpersonal spaces of the Middle Temple—here discussed through private chambers and libraries, the hall, and Temple Church—and the intellectual and social pursuits they encouraged can be viewed as 'small spaces' in London where ideas about colonialism, refinement, and status developed in relation to each other. The architectural historian Swati Chattopadhyay's study of the 'small spaces of empire' focused on micro-spaces such as bookshelves, staircases, and medicine cabinets, but the questions she poses can be applied to places within the inns: how did such small spaces furnish the imagination, and how do they 'sit in relation to empire?' (Chattopadhyay 2023: 6). Focusing on space also emphasises 'the materiality of social exchange', demonstrating how inns gentlemen, through their 'possessions, backgrounds, networks, and imaginations', could share 'overlapping yet idiosyncratically constituted worlds of their own' (Kümin and Usborne 2013: 317; Gordon and Klein 2001). The way these spaces fostered various forms of knowledge-sharing, conversation, and performance offers additional perspectives on the habitus of the inns while presenting a multi-layered understanding of how transoceanic commercial and colonial projects shaped a generation of gentlemen and their literature.

Chambers and Libraries: The World on a Table

When Francis Drake made his entrance into Middle Temple hall in 1586, the inn's only library to speak of was a room containing a small collection of legal books that were regularly being stolen (O'Callaghan 2023: 479). This changed in 1641 when Robert Ashley bequeathed his books to the society, leading to the official founding of the library. Part of this collection is discussed by Renae Satterley in Chap. 12 and the significance of libraries is also explored in Joshua Eckhart and Julian Neuhauser's analysis of John Selden's book collection in Chap. 8.

Admitted to the Middle Temple in 1588 and called to the bar in 1595, Ashley's large collection of some 6000 books was gradually collected during his long residence at the inn (Satterley 2021: 272). In his will, he reflected on this life spent largely within this habitus, where 'I have addicted myselfe to the general studdy of the great booke of the world' (Heltzel 1947: 354). His study had been punctured by 'short excursions to acquaint myself with our neighbouring nations', including travels to Madrid in 1618 (354). Ashley's book collection included language manuals, romances, cosmographies, and treatises about travel and trade. He was captivated by how 'no one soyle or territory, yeeldeth all fruits alike, so no one Climate or Region affordeth all kind of Knowledge in full measure', and expressed a belief in the value of Richard Hakluyt and Samuel Purchas' immense volumes on English traffic and colonialism (356, 359). More than a collection of books, Ashley's collection and the shelves on which they were kept become part of 'a larger geography of social relations that it supports and mediates' (Chattopadhyay 2023: 254).

Other members' studies and chambers served as miniature libraries in their own right, demonstrating their owners' status, taste, and access to knowledge. Building them involved buying and collecting books, many of which could be purchased from the booksellers within the precincts of the Temple. Innsmen also showed interest in other objects commonly found in studies, such as maps and globes (Finkelpearl 1969: 26; Satterley 2008: 208–19; O'Callaghan 2023: 479). The importance of these spaces to the developing imperial culture of the Middle Temple in the 1560s and 1570s can be seen in an anecdote recounted by the travel writer Richard Hakluyt in the first edition of his seminal work, *The Principal Navigations, Voyages and Discoveries of the English Nation* (1589). Hakluyt spent his childhood in London as one of the queen's scholars at Westminster School and appears to have regularly visited his cousin, Hakluyt the Elder, in his rooms at the Middle Temple. On one of these visits, he happened to notice 'lying open upon his boord certain books of Cosmographie, with an universal Mappe' which his cousin, seeing him 'somewhat curious in the view thereof, began to instruct my ignorance', pointing to 'all the knowen Seas Gulfs, Bayes, Straits, Capes, Rivers, Empires, Kingdoms, Dukedomes, and Territories of ech part, with declaration also of their speciall commodities, & particular wants, which by the benefit of traffike, & entercourse of merchants, are plentifully supplied' (2).

This map had been produced by the Antwerp mapmaker Abraham Ortelius to precise specifications. In a letter written between 1567 and 1568, Hakluyt the Elder requested Ortelius make him a map with a 'length of twelve feet, and a height of three or at most four feet', and included sketches for how it would be rolled and unrolled with a set of rods' (Hakluyt 1935: 1.81–82). By doing so, he wrote that Ortelius would be performing 'a most acceptable service to a number of English lawyers, to the students of both Oxford and Cambridge Universities, and to the citizens of London' (82). The Middle Temple chamber where this considerable map was housed appears to have been a focal point for educational visitors interested in travelling.

As well as these physical visits, the chamber was a place of work, serving as an important node within a densely linked epistolary network. Hakluyt's letter to Ortelius was one of many shared between the two men, with his link to the map-maker in turn connecting him to an even wider community. Within England, Ortelius's connections included the mathematician and astronomer John Dee, the antiquarian William Camden, and his cousin Emanuel van Meteren, the consul for the Dutch merchants in London, who played a vital role within the republic of letters as the Dutch postmaster (Harkness 2007: 25). Anything sent from Ortelius to London or from London to Antwerp made its way through van Meteren and his network of merchants, travellers, and sailors. The presence of Ortelius' map in Hakluyt the Elder's chambers, then, did not demonstrate an abstract or purely intellectual interest in geography but rather represented its place within the wider transnational networks that linked London to European exploration.

Gentlemen's lodgings in the Middle Temple also appeared in networks of print, connecting inns coteries to courts and territories elsewhere. Writing from 'the Court of the great Mogul' Jahangir 'in the Towne of asmere [Azmir]' in India, the traveller Thomas Coryate prefaced his text by naming a range of gentlemen associated with the 'Sirenicall Fraternietie' of wits, many of them innsmen, who met at the Mermaid Tavern on the first Friday of every month. In his dedication to the Middle Templar Edward Phelips, Coryate sent greetings to 'M. Martin' and 'M. Christopher Brooke', along with 'M. *Equinoctiall Pasticrust* of the middle Temple, M. *William Hackwell*, and the rest of the worthy gentlemen frequenting your Honourable table' (1616). Coryate's earlier travels and his connections to the 'sireniacs' had also inspired a range of poems published in 1611 by over 50 contributors, including Ben Jonson, Richard Martin, Christopher Brooke, Michael Drayton, and John Donne, which humorously likened Coryate to 'Columbus, Magellan, and Drake' (Coryate 1611: D^{r}; and see O'Callaghan 2007).

As they consulted maps and books, many gentlemen consumed a plantation-sourced good that tangibly connected them to Atlantic spaces. By the Jacobean period, tobacco—an Indigenous plant that had been central to Native social relations, diplomacy, and spiritual practices for thousands of years—entered into the pipes and pockets of Londoners from both the Spanish Americas and the fledgling English plantations in North America (Working 2022). Satirising the follies of tobacco smoking in 1613, Samuel Rowlands conjured the smoky spaces where friends met to discuss travel: 'When *Thraso* meetes his friend, he sweares by God / Unto his Chamber he shall welcome bee', where 'heele present most kind, exceeding franke, / The best *Tobacco* that he ever dranke' (Rowlands 1613: A5^{r}). The gentleman in Rowlands' epigram sought to enhance his connections to the plant by placing himself within the narrative of exploration: 'Such as himself did make a voyage for, / And with his owne hands gatherd fro[m] the ground'. In Chap. 3, Rhatigan discusses the close communities innsmen formed: their chambers were now smoky dens full of that 'rare compound' of 'English Fire, and of India Smoke', encouraging that sociability (Fig. 13.2).

Even before the development of plantation economies in English America, these networks of taste, supply, and demand were entangled in practices of slavery. Until James VI and I granted English colonies a monopoly on tobacco in 1624, Londoners mostly smoked tobacco sourced from the Spanish-occupied West Indies, grown and picked by enslaved African and Indigenous people. A pamphlet from 1615 complained of the corrupted commodity that Spanish and Portuguese merchants sold in London, where the 'blacke colour which it hath, and for

Fig. 13.2 Johann Neander, *Tabacologia* (Leiden, 1622). By kind permission of Middle Temple Library/Image © Lauren Working

which our Shoppe-keepers praise it, is Artificiall', dyed with 'tawnie Berries, with which the Indians paint their bodies, and their beds'. Berries that Native people in the Caribbean had long used for a variety of practical purposes were deployed to mask the 'rotten, withered, & ground-leaves' of the tobacco Londoners ingested, and that enslaved people thousands of miles away had tended (Norton 2008). Several engravings from Johann Neander's *Tabacologia* (1622), a book in Robert Ashley's collection, reflect the sanitised, pastoral world that Protestant gentlemen evoked when they sought to distinguish their plantation projects from Spain's *encomienda* system of enslavement and tribute. Like the tobacco in Rowlands' epigram, 'such as himself did make a voyage for', the engravings of tobacco cultivation in the Middle Temple's collection erased the mass system of exploitation and enslavement that made tobacco accessible to gentlemen.

The Hall: 'To *Quivera* by the West'

The inns' halls were vital places for dining, sociability, and also performance. Modelled on practices at the royal court, the inns appointed an annual master of the revels. Plays and masques were performed, and stages were erected to turn halls into theatrical spaces, establishing these spaces as ones of spectatorship and display (Burkhart 1991). These late sixteenth- and early seventeenth-century performances indicate how an attention to global mobility began entering into performances at the inns. The first recorded performance of Shakespeare's *Twelfth Night* took place in Middle Temple hall in February 1602 (Gras 1989; see Watson, Chap. 4 for further discussion). The comedy begins with the drama of a shipwreck that separates the twins Sebastian and Viola, while the character of Sir Toby Belch delights in causing havoc through his revelling and drinking. Drawing on popular metaphors in late Elizabethan love lyric, he greets the gentlewoman Maria by calling her 'my metal of India', comparing her to the glittering bounty of South American wealth (Shakespeare 2008: 2.5.13).

Transoceanic travel and imperial expansion also informed the *Prince d'Amour* Middle Temple revels of 1597/98, from the presence of travellers in the audience to the source material the performance drew on. When the 'Sirenicall gentleman' and wit Richard Martin played the Prince of Love, his movements in the performance signalled a kind of *translatio imperii*, a traversing from eastern lands to Atlantic conquests. The prince was 'Chief General of all *Venus* forces from *Japan* to *Quivera* by the West ... *Japan* is an Island in the furthest part of the Longitude of the earth by the East, where his Excellency first began his exploited, and so marched up continually till he came to the uttermost point Westward, where he ended in *Quivera*' (Arlidge 2000: 127). Quivira was part of the south-eastern region of North America that fell under the designation of 'Florida', mentioned in numerous cosmographies and continental texts, including Richard Hakluyt's translation of the Huguenot René de Laudonnière's travels to Florida (1587).

The mock knighting ceremony in the performance was interrupted by an *ex-tempore* 'Fustian speech' by John Hoskins that included a short defence of tobacco (Arlidge 2000: 143–44). This may have been inserted into the performance in part because Raleigh himself seems to have been at the revels, and pressured Hoskins, along with Martin, to deliver the oration (O'Callaghan 2007: 32). Raleigh, a Middle Templar, had recently returned from his first voyage to Guiana, bringing several Tupi interpreters and samples of gold ore back with him (Vaughan 2002). As a whole, and not unlike Raleigh's recently published *The discoverie of the large, rich, and beautiful empire of Guiana* (1596), the revels blended chivalry and masculine bravado, where the language of sexual desire and lover-knights melded with 'exotic' geographical coordinates. Just as Raleigh recounted how, with the help of 'my Indian interpreter' in the tropical forests of Greater Amazonia, he 'made [the Arawaks] understand that I was a servant of a Queene, who was a great *Casique* of the north', the Middle Temple's chivalric codes elevated the sovereignty of 'my Lady and Mistris [who] is the true Princess *d'Amours* ... civilizing her subjects, whom time past accounted barbarous' (Raleigh 1596: 7).

Raleigh's presence in the hall points to an underexplored area of inns' members' global interests: silver and gold mining in the Americas. Travel news and exchanges between friends melded lucrative possibilities with the thrill of 'discovery'. 'Last year I wrote to you about one Frobisher who, rivalling Magellan, has investigated the strait which, he thinks, washes the Northern part of America', a youthful Philip Sidney, enrolled at Gray's Inn, wrote to the French reformer Hubert Languet in 1577 (Kuin 1998: 562). Sidney followed with the story of 'a certain youth' in Frobisher's crew who had picked up a glittering rock, bringing it to London to test it and finding 'that it consisted of exceedingly pure gold'. Languet wrote back to Sidney in a grave tone, advising him to consider instead whether those regions might be suitable for agricultural settlement, and warning him that 'those golden islands have possessed your mind too deeply'. Sidney, however, retained ambitions for more dazzling feats of exploration. In the mid-1580s, he attempted to join the West Indies expedition that ended with Drake's triumphant visit to Middle Temple hall (576).

The feverish excitement for golden mines became a focal part of *The memorable masque of the Middle Temple and Lincoln's Inn*, performed on the night of 15 February 1613. It began with a torchlit procession of 50 'Virginians' parading in a riot of rich fabric embroidered with gold and silver thread and in feather ruffs through Chancery Lane and down the Strand. The staging of *The memorable masque* in Whitehall Palace's great hall was equally flamboyant. It centred around 'an Artificiall Rock, whose top was neere as high as the hall it selfe', with a set of winding stairs around it for the actors to climb up and down. The rock was 'run quite through with veines of golde' and topped on one side with 'a silver

Temple' surrounded by silver statues. After the god of riches, Plutus, delivered his first speech, the rock broke into pieces and 'vanisht', with the upper part turned into a cloud, 'discovering a rich and refulgent mine of golde' where the masquers were seated. There was so much gold, in fact, that even when hidden by the rock's structure and lit only by torch bearers, 'the least spangle or spark of [their] rich habites might with ease and cleerenesse be discerned' (Chapman 1613: A6^{r}). The character of Capriccio then entered, carrying a pair of bellows, and while admiring the mines, he conflated the various geographic spaces within the masque, referring to the 'isle' adjacent to Virginia and 'this Ile' which is 'divided from the world ... [and] stands fixt on her owne feete, and defies the Worlds mutability' (B3^{r}). The wealth of the mine, 'this rare accident of the arrivall of Riches, in one of his furthest-off-scituate dominions', proved England's providential blessedness and the spread of its global power.

The mines in *The memorable masque* connected disparate elements—feathered garments, silver statues, lumps of golden ore—into one overwhelming display. This link between South American mines and the Chesapeake had been made by Hakluyt the Younger in his dedication in *Virginia richly valued* (1609), where he wrote of the 'rich mines of gold reported to be in the province of Yupaha' and the 'rich and famous golden mines of Chisca', as well as copper and gold mines and 'red mettall just west of the former colonie of Roanoke' (A2^{v}). Reports of these mines appeared in Brereton's *A briefe and true relation*, which included 'testimonies touching sundry rich mines of Gold, Silver, and Copper, in part found and in part constantly heard of, in North Florida, and the Inland of the Maine of Virginia' (1602: 47). In citing 'Hakluyt the elder, sometime student of the Middle Temple', Brereton acknowledged the role of the Middle Temple as a centre of information about these mines. It was already clear by 1613 that Virginia was not a gold-rich location to rival the mines of South America or Raleigh's fantasies of El Dorado (Hollis 2015: 133–34). Staging the mine and linking it to Virginia regardless allowed gentlemen to promote the inns as a centre of colonial pursuit, bound by 'Eunomia', or 'the law', while creating a dazzling vision of English sovereignty that celebrated knightly adventure and access to colonial wealth.

While revels and masques might licence more extravagant celebrations, everyday interactions in the hall equally involved social performance. Drake's entrance, including the applause sparked by his arrival, combined elements of the theatrical and social performances which were conducted there on a regular basis. Even today, the Middle Temple holds two items linked to his voyage. New barristers enter their names in the inn's books on 'Drake's cupboard', a table reputedly made from a fore-hatch cover taken from his ship, when called to the bar.[2] 'Drake's lantern', hanging over the entrance to the hall, is reportedly taken from the deck of the ship. The original was destroyed in bombing raids during World War II but has since been replaced by a replica, showing the item's almost totemic importance.

Meals at the Middle Temple were an opportunity to display the conspicuous consumption of expensive goods. A supper bill from 1613 lists regular expenditure on 'hard sugar', 'allmonds', 'reasones' [raisins], and 'tobacco' alongside more extravagant items such as 'blewe figges' and 'orringes', and quotidian expenditure on 'butter', 'flouer', and 'mutton' (MT.7/SUB/1). These goods were sourced from across the globe: the raisins likely part of the 'great store of corrwants [currants]' which came from Tripolis to England, the focal point of many trading agreements; the oranges brought with lemons and 'great ynnions [onions]' from Portugal; almonds and sugar from the Levant (Read 1914: 519, 523). These could be fraught with political concerns alongside the practical: the licence for the trade of raisins had originally been given by Elizabeth I to the northern Italian merchant Acerbo Velutelli in 1575. As more merchants joined the Levant trade, they put pressure on the queen to recall the licence, which she did in 1583. The trade was then fought over by two trading companies, the Venice Company and the Turkey Company, before they were combined into the Levant Company in 1592 (Stevenson 2022: 353). Even something as simple as a raisin was part of complex histories and negotiations.

The consumption of these goods was the result of long processes of growth, production, and transport which relied on the exploited labour of people across the globe. In his tale of the fallen gallant seduced by the pleasures of the inns of court, Francis Lenton wrote of 'bowles of Nectar, fill'd up to the brim' and 'Oysters, Lobstars, Caviare, and Crabs, / With which he feasted his contagious drabs; / Oringoes, Hartichoakes, Potatoe pies, / Provocatives unto their luxuries' (1629: 19). Aphrodisiacs pile up at 'Bacchus shrine', including '[p]otatoe pies', a sweet dish flavoured with East Indies spices such as nutmeg, and relying on access to colonially sourced potatoes (Folger MS V.a.8: 16–17).

[2] 'Elizabethan & Jacobean Times | Middle Temple' <https://www.middletemple.org.uk/about-us/history/elizabethan-and-jacobean-times> [accessed 31 August 2023].

Fig. 13.3 Silver spice box made in London by 'W.R.', 1602. Met Museum/Public domain [CC0 1.0]

The objects that displayed or encased these goods added further networks of global trafficking to the table. The owner of the scallop-shaped box pictured in Fig. 13.3 is unknown, but such boxes would have been used by gentlemen to carry those spices, or even sugar, that inns' members catalogued in lists of ships' cargoes, while the silver may have come from Potosí.[3] A list compiled in the mid-1630s of the Middle Temple's silver plate indicates its large collection of silver, much of it consisting of gifted or donated display objects or tableware that might be used in ceremonial occasions such as banquets (MT.2/TAS/1). The presence of silver objects, brought out at mealtimes or for special events, might have made reading about silver mines, or penning masques about the Americas, seem all the more tangible, where 'both Indias of spice and mine' brought together in love poems equally appeared in objects on the table (Donne 2010: 'The Sun Rising', l. 17).

[3]'Spice box' by W.R., 1602/3, Met Museum, accession number 68.141.277; see Bigleow (2020).

Temple Church: 'This Sermon, Spoken and Published for Incouragement of Planters'

Temple Church became a space for fostering pro-imperial expansion at the Middle Temple, in large part through the activities of the preacher William Crashaw. Crashaw's position as preacher of Temple Church gave him access to one of 'the most prestigious pulpits in early modern London', but in a space with 'less political oversight than [those at] court or Paul's Cross' (Rhatigan 2011: 109). As a result, those studying the law for the sake of profession, and those frequenting the inns as 'a convenient base from which to launch themselves into the social and administrative life of the City and royal court', were exposed to Crashaw's strongly anti-Catholic, pro-colonial stance (109).

The church was the spiritual heart of the Middle Temple, and its history as a space for intersecting points of faith, travel, and legal history makes it a key site within the inns for the ongoing conceptualisation and theorisation of colonialism. Jointly owned by the Middle Temple and Inner Temple, the Knights Templar built Temple Church in the twelfth century as their English headquarters. Its design was derived from the Church of the Holy Sepulcher in Jerusalem, notably in the context of the crusades to 'reclaim' the Holy Land from Muslim rulers (Morel 2019: 309). From its beginnings, the Church played a multifaceted role within the inns as a spiritual institution and a commercial and legal centre. Its history was important to contemporary framings of the Church, which was celebrated in a 1637 petition as having been 'a church of eminency … exempt from episcopal jurisdiction, and first subject to the Knights Templars, then after to the Hospitallers, and now immediately to your Majesty' (SP 16/355: fol. 262).

Crashaw was appointed preacher to the Inner and Middle Temple in 1605, at a time when Temple Church was widely known as a place of financial and social exchange as well as spiritual contemplation. Pamphlets and plays described secret meetings by civil servants who met outside the church to conduct their affairs. But for Crashaw, the post offered 'the most comfortable and delightfull company for a scholler that . . . this kingdome yields', placing him at an important confluence between political and religious projects (1606: 3). In this post, he invested in and worked closely with the Virginia Company, delivering a sermon in 1610 for Thomas West, Lord de la Warr, the newly appointed governor of Jamestown. Crashaw used this sermon as an opportunity to promote colonisation in Virginia, calling for the 'Church of God [to be] established in Virginea, even there where Satans throne is', and asking his audience to 'judge what joy is amongst that blessed fellowship [in heaven], when this newes comes to heaven that England hath enterprized the conversion of Virginia: whereby so many thousand soules shall be brought to heaven' (1610: K4^{r}, L4^{r}).

The sermon conveys a sense of the intensity with which Crashaw urged his congregation to take part in the Virginia venture. The project to extend English society and religion to America depended on personal, highly individualised relationships. Crashaw wrote that his patron's 'peculiar knowledge' of 'Master *Whitaker*', the Cambridge-born minister preparing to travel to Virginia, rendered him 'an honorable witness with me, and an evidence beyond all exception' of the good work happening in the colony (Whitaker 1613: D^{r}). Members of the audience, Crashaw maintained, could be assured of the honour of this venture because of the many 'friends and assistants which this busines hath: which are such and so great' (1610: I^{v}). He emphasised the importance of those in his congregation taking action, whether by contributing funds, travelling, or finding other means of advancing and 'encouraging' the project. 'By inclining the hearts of our mighty King & noble Prince [Henry]', Crashaw said, 'to make themselves *fathers and founders* of this plantation and protectors of this royall enterprize', colonial promoters were actively involved in the fate of the nation by urging the Stuart royal family to become 'new Constantines or Charles the great', combining Protestantism with imperial glory (1610: I2^{r}).

More so than his other printed endorsements of colonialism, Crashaw's sermon combined religious fervour with a subtle attention to the law. Appealing to his specific audience, he praised the role of the law in upholding good governance. Just as a '[s]tate of *long continuance,* which is ripe and rotten for want of reformation, will easily be brought into order in a new government', so 'there is and will be better government, and better execution of lawes in a *little territorie*, then in a great and populous kingdome, and in a new begun rather then an old and setled State' (F^{v}). In professing that 'I be not worthy to be thine Apostle, yet doe vow and devote my selfe to be in England thy faithfull factor and solicitor', Crashaw used the language of business and transaction—both the work of the 'factor' or merchant, and the 'solicitor', interceding on behalf of another—to place himself as an agent who might use his position in the church as a node through which to effect the imperial project (L2^{r}). In a strategy reminiscent of the entertainments performed in the hall, the sermon ended with a dialogue between God, Virginia, and England, conducted through biblical quotations. It is unclear whether Crashaw delivered this dialogue himself or whether it was an addendum to the printed text, but as the tone is decidedly in keeping with the sermon and the text was printed without his leave, it seems likely that it was part of his original delivery.

Although Crashaw viewed himself as a 'solicitor' or mediator between the Church and colonial planters, his enthusiasm was not only theoretical. A 'William Crashawe, Clerke, Bachelor of Divinity' was listed as one of the people incorporated into the Virginia Company's 1609 charter, and he appears to have contributed £37 10s to the additional subscription of 1610/11 (Fisher 1974: 108). In 1613, Crashaw edited an account of Bermuda, adding a dedicatory epistle which praised God's 'all-governing providence', and in 1614 he published an exhortatory letter from Alexander Whitaker in Jamestown in an attempt to combat criticisms against the colony (108). As with those chaplains employed by trading companies to advance Protestant evangelism abroad, Crashaw's commitment to the colonial project viewed the spiritual mission of plantation as intrinsically linked to its governance (Smith 2022: 39).

A large part of Crashaw's income also went into the expansion of his personal library. Crashaw is notable for owning what he referred to as 'one of the most complete libraryes in Europe', including around 4000 printed books and at least 200 manuscripts (Fisher 1974: 105). After being appointed Temple preacher, he spent over £240 on stairs, rails, and a new upper story to the chambers adjoining the church to house his library and compose his lectures. This extensive 'private' library was 'not private in any restrictive sense', but interacted with 'other sites of exchange within a wider urban terrain', including the antiquarian Robert Cotton's library, nearby printing houses, and parliament (O'Callaghan 2023: 481–82). This library (a substantial part of which is now at St. John's College, Cambridge) contained works on theology and law alongside colonial interests, in addition to what Crashaw described as 'one of the fairest paire of globes in England' (Fisher 1974: 106).

These globes, one each for the terrestrial and celestial worlds, were possibly those created by Emery Molyneux, measuring over two feet in diameter and constructed out of flour paste to keep them safe from humidity while at sea. Molyneux was a well-known instrument maker, linked to Hakluyt, Drake, Raleigh, and Thomas Cavendish. The terrestrial globe depicts the extent of English cartographic knowledge in the sixteenth century, updated in 1603 to include recent developments. The celestial globe was based on Gerardus Mercator's 1551 globes, updated with the latest astronomical observations. These globes were intended to represent Elizabethan mastery over the spheres, with the world mapped and displayed for future discovery. Along with books and maps, globes brought the world into the Middle Temple, condensing centuries of geographic knowledge into single orbs, but they also represent the inns' place within a wider global network. Like the ship passing through the pillars on the frontispiece of Francis Bacon's *The Great Instauration* (1620), their position in the library brings the viewer through the known frontiers of ancient and classical knowledge, and into new realms of possibility for human learning and discovery. Their setting within an inns library turns the room into a site for the creation, dissemination, and enforcement of English law within the country and across the world.

Crashaw's zealous endorsement of English colonialism in Temple Church was a distinct feature of the Jacobean Middle Temple. Reactions to his sermon do not survive, but the competing groups within the Virginia Company—many of them associated with the inns, parliament, other trading companies, and church reform—likely divided opinion and impelled conversation in halls and chambers afterwards. Crashaw promised his audience that they would 'eternize your owne names both heere at home & amongst the *Virgineans*', going so far as to assure those present that they would be 'happy men whether you live or die: if you live, by effecting so glorious a worke: if you die, by dying as Martyrs or Confessors of Gods religion' (1610: K4^{r}). Drawing on the language of friendship, honour, 'business', and moral standing, Crashaw framed colonisation as a suitable project for the gentlemen of the inns and their various social and political concerns.

Afterlives: The Prince of Love Reprised

When the poet William Davenant was commissioned to write an entertainment in honour of Charles I's nephews, to be staged at the Middle Temple during the princes' visit to London, he resurrected the Prince d'Amour. *The Triumphs of the Prince d'Amour* was performed in February 1636, attended by princes Rupert and Charles Louis, as well as Queen Henrietta Maria and some of her ladies (Lewcock 2008: 52). Rupert had already begun to establish a reputation as a militant Protestant prince, and many in London at the time of his visit, including Davenant, encouraged the brothers to advance English interests in the Indian and Atlantic oceans (Davenant 1628; Working 2023).

The figure of the Prince of Love not only drew on the Middle Temple's own performance history but aptly reflected the tastes of the Caroline court. The fashionable neoplatonism and motifs of 'Platonick Love' instigated by Henrietta Maria regularly featured in masques, plays, and poems in the 1630s, setting 'the Wits of the Town on Work' (Dawson 2008: 138). Just as the chivalric codes of Elizabeth I's court had directed the way the Prince d'Amour expressed his power in the 1597/98 revels, the neoplatonism of Henrietta Maria's circle dictated Davenant's tale in which raucous figures of war were banished by the gentle prince and his refined followers. Like the spices and sugar that flavoured the banquet accompanying the revels, the geopolitics of global travel were present on the stage erected in Middle Temple hall for the occasion. The scene 'at the upper end of the hall' included 'a Village consisting of *Alehouses* and *Tobacco* shops', fronted by blocks 'on which blacke Indian Boyes sate bestriding Roles of Tobacco, and in the place of Signes, Globes hung up, stuck up full of broken Pipes' (Davenant 1635: 103). Plantation industry and labour melded with the pastoral landscape of domestic villages and alehouses.

The inns' role as foundational legal institutions with strong ties to court and parliament, and as spaces of global knowledge exchange, continued to develop in tandem as the seventeenth century progressed. Dedicating himself to restoring Virginia's reputation against slanders and 'false reports', the colonial promoter William Bullock offered his readers 'full satisfaction in the truths that any way concerns this Place': any who sought news from the colony could be 'directed to my Chamber in the Middle-Temple' (1649: 66). Not far from his lodgings, women and men flocked to the collector William Courten's chambers to view coconuts, West Indian moss, a 'cup from Surinam', wampum, coral, and 'a habit of an Indian woman made of beads' (Kusukawa 2017: 10). Courten turned his lodgings into a fantastical place of curiosities, containing at least six cabinets, and displaying goods sold or donated by sailors, merchants, botanists, and collectors, including several women. Though much had changed between the fledgling colonial projects of the Jacobean era and the systems of trade, colonialism, and enslavement that marked Courten's time, his decision to take chambers at the inn does not seem incidental. Among Courten's surviving papers are a range of documents relating to colonialism, some of them drawing on the vast amount of travel information gathered in the late sixteenth and early seventeenth centuries. Courten copied information about a 'Project for keeping New England dependent on England', and transcribed notes that referred to Drake and Purchas' geography (Sloane MS 3962, fols. 54ʳ, 85ʳ, 179ʳ).

By the time Middle Temple hosted *The Triumphs of the Prince d'Amour* in 1636, many gentlemen had embraced and directly contributed to colonial expansion. Though the Elizabethan and Jacobean fascination with global travel was not exclusive to the inns of court, this chapter has sought to draw out some of the ways these environments facilitated conversation and modes of sociability that fuelled these interests in concrete, though by no means uniform, ways (Ramachandran 2015; Gillies 1994: 58). The ideas about travel and colonialism encountered in these spaces of spirited debate and exchange informed a highly stylised sense of play and literary innovation that its members viewed as important to their civil self-fashioning. The gentility gentlemen conferred upon commercial and colonial projects was partly what Drake had so valued in the prospect of having Sidney join his West Indies voyage. 'Sir Francis found that Sir Philip's friends', Fulke Greville recounted, 'with the influence of his excellent inward powers, would add both weight and fashion to his ambitions . . . [and yield] honour to him in this voyage' (Greville 1986: 43). Material culture, from the rare and expensive Molyneux globes to the staged gold mine in *The memorable masque*, helps shed light on a further dimension of how gentlemen drew on their studies to create 'works of the imagination', though more work remains to be done on their contentions and varying attitudes towards colonialism (Hutson 2017: 16).

Over a decade after playing the Prince of Love, Richard Martin wrote from his chambers at the Middle Temple to William Strachey, then in Jamestown, that his commitment to the Virginia plantation burned 'like a fire that flames out to the view of every one'. All those who became 'partakers of this promise', he wrote, would 'shine as the stars in the firmament' (Folger MS V.a.321, fol. 62ʳ). Between hall and chapel, the spaces of the inns and the associations forged within them had helped shape Martin's trajectory from Prince of Love to impassioned advocate of Atlantic plantation. Martin's belief that Strachey was a fit '*Achates* for such an *Aeneas*, as is our Noble & worthie Generall the lord *Delawarre*', was perhaps cemented some months before, on hearing or reading Crashaw's sermon at De La Warr's sending off. If so, Martin would have been reassured by Crashaw that plantation is 'a most lawful, an *honourable* and a *holy* action' (1610: H4^{v}). Further, even in the midst of the wide variety of global projects explored at the inns—'of all voiages ever attempted in this Nation'—the '*Virginean voiage* is the most honourable . . . therefore every wise man and *morall* man may be allured', and called to act (I$^{r–v}$).

Works Cited

Arlidge, Anthony. 2000. *Shakespeare and the Prince of Love: The Feast of Misrule*. London: Giles de la Mare.

Bigges, Walter. 1589. *A summarie and true discourse of Sir Frances Drakes West Indian voyage*. London.

Bigleow, Allison Margaret. 2020. *Mining Language: Racial Thinking, Indigenous Knowledge, and Colonial Metallurgy in the Early Modern Iberian World*. Durham: University of North Carolina Press.

British Library. Sloane Manuscript 3962.

Brereton, John. 1602. *A briefe and true relation of the discoverie of the north part of Virginia*. London.

Brewer, Holly. 2021. "Creating a Common Law of Slavery for England and its New World Empire." *Law and History Review* 39: 765–834.

Bullock, William. 1649. *Virginia impartially examined*. London.

Burkhart, Robert E. 1991. "The Playing Space in the Halls of the Inns of Court." *South Atlantic Review* 56: 1–5.

Chapman, George. 1613. *The memorable masque*. London?

Chattopadhyay, Swati. 2023. *Small Spaces: Recasting the Architecture of Empire*. London: Bloomsbury.

Coryate, Thomas. 1611. *Coryats crudities*. London.

———. 1616. *Thomas Coriate traveller for the English wits: greeting from the court of the Great Mogul*. London.

Crashaw, William. 1606. *Romish forgeries and falsifications*. London.

———. 1610. *A sermon preached in London before the right honorable the Lord Lawarre*. London.

Das, Nandini, Joao Melo, Haig Smith, and Lauren Working. 2021. *Keywords of Identity, Race, and Human Mobility in Early Modern England*. Amsterdam: Amsterdam University Press.

Davenant, William. 1628. *Madagascar*. London.

———. 1635. *The Triumphs of the Prince d'Amour*. London.

Dawson, Lesel. 2008. *Lovesickness and Gender in Early Modern English Literature*. Oxford: Oxford University Press.

De Laudonnière, René. 1587. *A notable historie containing foure voyages made by certayne French captaynes unto Florida*. Translated by Richard Hakluyt. London.

Dimmock, Matthew, 2022. *Writing Tudor Exploration: Richard Eden and West Africa*. Cambridge: Cambridge University Press.

Donne, John. 2010. *The Complete Poems of John Donne*. Edited by Robin Robbins. Harlow: Pearson.

Finkelpearl Philip J. 1969. *John Marston of the Middle Temple: An Elizabethan Dramatist in His Social Setting*. Cambridge, MA: Harvard University Press.

Fisher, R. M. 1974. "William Crashawe and the Middle Temple Globes, 1605–1615." *The Geographical Journal* 140: 105–112.

Folger. Manuscript V.a.8.

Folger. Manuscript V.a.321.

Gillies, John. 1994. *Shakespeare and the Geography of Difference*. Cambridge: Cambridge University Press.

Gordon, Andrew, and Bernhard Klein, eds. 2001. *Literature, Mapping, and the Politics of Space in Early Modern Britain*. Cambridge: Cambridge University Press.

Gras, Henk. 1989. "*Twelfth Night, Every Man Out of His Humour*, and the Middle Temple Revels of 1597/1598." *The Modern Language Review* 84: 545–64.

Greville, Fulke. 1986. "The Life of the Renowned Philip Sidney." In *The Prose Works of Fulke Greville*, edited by John Gouws. Oxford: Clarendon Press.

Hakluyt, Richard. 1589. *The Principal Navigations, Voyages and Discoveries of the English Nation*. London.

———. 1609. *Virginia richly valued*. London.

Hakluyt, Richard, and Richard Hakluyt. 1935. *The Original Writings and Correspondence of the Two Richard Hakluyts*. Edited by Eva Germaine Rimington Taylor. 2 vols. London: The Hakluyt Society.

Harkness, Deborah 2007. *The Jewel House: Elizabethan London and the Scientific Revolution*. New Haven, CT: Yale University Press.

Heltzel, Virgil B. 1947. "Robert Ashley Elizabethan Man of Letters." *Huntington Library Quarterly* 10: 349–63.

Hollis, Gavin. 2015. *The Absence of America: The London Stage, 1572–1642*. Oxford: Oxford University Press.

Hopwood, Charles Henry, ed. 1904. *The Middle Temple Records, Vol. 1: 1501–1603*. London: Butterworth & Company.

Hutson, Lorna. 2017. "Introduction." In *The Oxford Handbook of English Law and Literature, 1500–1700,* edited by Lorna Hutson, 1–19. Oxford: Oxford University Press.

Kuin, Roger. 1998. "Querre-Muhau: Sir Philip Sidney and the New World." *Renaissance Quarterly* 51: 549–85.

Kümin, Beat, and Cornelie Usborne, 2013. "At Home and in the Workplace: A Historical Introduction to the 'Spatial Turn'." *History and Theory* 52: 305–18.

Kusukawa, Sachiko. 2017. "William Courten's Lists of 'Things Bought' from the Late Seventeenth Century." *Journal of the History of Collections* 29: 1–17.

Lenton, Francis. 1629. *The young gallants whirligig*. London.

Lewcock, Dawn. 2008. *Sir William Davenant, the Court Masque, and the English Seventeenth-Century Scenic Stage, 1605–1700*. Amherst, NY: Cambria Press.

MacMillan, Ken. 2001. "Discourse on History, Geography, and Law: John Dee and the Limits of the British Empire, 1576–1580." *Canadian Journal of History* 36: 1–25.

Middle Temple Library. MT.2/TAS/1.

Middle Temple Library. MT.7/SUB/1.

Morel, Anne-Françoise. 2019. *Glorious Temples or Babylonic Whores: The Culture of Church Building in Stuart England through the Lens of Consecration Sermons*. Leiden: Brill.

Norton, Marcy. 2008. *Sacred Gifts, Profane Pleasures: A History of Tobacco and Chocolate in the Atlantic World*. New York: Cornell University Press.

O'Callaghan, Michelle. 2007. *The English Wits: Literature and Sociability in Early Modern England*. Cambridge: Cambridge University Press.

———. 2023. "Contexts for Circulation: Universities, Inns of Court, Households and Professional Circles." In *The Oxford Handbook of the History of the Book in Early Modern England*, edited by Adam Smyth, 474–92. Oxford: Oxford University Press.

Raleigh, Walter. 1596. *The discoverie of the large, rich, and bewtifull empire of Guiana*. London.

Ramachandran, Ayesha. 2015. *The Worldmakers: Global Imagining in Early Modern Europe*. Chicago, IL: The University of Chicago Press.

Read, Conyers. 1914. "English Foreign Trade under Elizabeth." *The English Historical Review* 29: 515–24.

Rhatigan, Emma. 2011. "Preaching Venues: Architecture and Auditories." In *The Oxford Handbook of the Early Modern Sermon*, edited by Hugh Adlington, Peter McCullough, and Emma Rhatigan, 99–119. Oxford: Oxford University Press.

Rowlands, Samuel. 1613. *The letting of humors blood in the head-vaine*. London.

Satterley, Renae. 2008. "The Libraries of the Inns of Court: An Examination of their Historical Influence." *Library History* 24: 208–19.

———. 2021. "Robert Ashley and the Authorship of Newberry MS 5017, *The Book of Magical Charms*." *Manuscript Studies* 6: 268–99.

Shakespeare, William. 2008. *Twelfth Night*. Edited by Kier Elam. London: Bloomsbury.

Smith, Haig Z. 2022. *Religion and Governance in England's Emerging Colonial Empire, 1601–1698*. London: Springer.

National Archive, UK. SP 16/355, fol. 262^{r}.

Stevenson, Emily. 2022. "Mapping *Principal Navigations* in the Levant." *Cultural and Social History* 19, no. 4: 353–70.

Tomlins, Christopher L. 2010. *Freedom Bound: Law, Labour, and Civic Identity in Colonizing English America, 1580–1865.* Cambridge: Cambridge University Press.

Vaughan, Alden T. 2002. "Sir Walter Ralegh's Indian Interpreters, 1584–1618." *The William & Mary Quarterly* 59: 341–76.

Whitaker, Alexander. 1613. *Good newes From Virginia.* London.

Winston, Jessica. 2016. *Lawyers at Play: Literature, Law, and Politics at the Early Modern Inns of Court, 1558–1581.* Oxford: Oxford University Press.

Working, Lauren. 2018. "Locating Colonization at the Early Modern Inns of Court." *Historical Journal* 61: 29–51.

———. 2022. "Tobacco and the Social Life of Conquest in London, 1580–1625." *The Historical Journal* 65: 30–48.

———. 2023. "'Not as a poet, but a pioner': Fancy and the Colonial Gaze in William Davenant's *Madagascar* (1638)." *Renaissance Studies* 37: 319–44.

Index[1]

[1] Note: Page numbers followed by 'n' refer to notes.

E. Rhatigan, J. Watson (eds.), *Mapping the Early Modern Inns of Court*, Early Modern Literature in History,
https://doi.org/10.1007/978-3-031-77445-4

O

P

R

www.ingramcontent.com/pod-product-compliance
Lightning Source LLC
Chambersburg PA
CBHW071555290626
47387CB00006B/872
9783031774447